Direito da Saúde
ESTUDOS EM HOMENAGEM AO
PROF. DOUTOR GUILHERME DE OLIVEIRA

Direito da Saúde

ESTUDOS EM HOMENAGEM AO
PROF. DOUTOR GUILHERME DE OLIVEIRA

VOLUME III
SEGURANÇA DO PACIENTE E CONSENTIMENTO INFORMADO

2016

Coordenadores
João Loureiro
André Dias Pereira
Carla Barbosa

DIREITO DA SAÚDE
ESTUDOS EM HOMENAGEM AO
PROF. DOUTOR GUILHERME DE OLIVEIRA
VOLUME III – SEGURANÇA DO PACIENTE E CONSENTIMENTO INFORMADO

COORDENADORES
João Loureiro
André Dias Pereira
Carla Barbosa

EDITOR
EDIÇÕES ALMEDINA, S.A.
Rua Fernandes Tomás, nºs 76-80
3000-167 Coimbra
Tel.: 239 851 904 · Fax: 239 851 901
www.almedina.net · editora@almedina.net

DESIGN DE CAPA
FBA.

PRÉ-IMPRESSÃO
EDIÇÕES ALMEDINA, SA

IMPRESSÃO E ACABAMENTO
Pentaedro, Lda.
Agosto, 2016

DEPÓSITO LEGAL
414174/16

Apesar do cuidado e rigor colocados na elaboração da presente obra, devem os diplomas legais dela constantes ser sempre objeto de confirmação com as publicações oficiais.
Toda a reprodução desta obra, por fotocópia ou outro qualquer processo, sem prévia autorização escrita do Editor, é ilícita e passível de procedimento judicial contra o infrator.

BIBLIOTECA NACIONAL DE PORTUGAL – CATALOGAÇÃO NA PUBLICAÇÃO
DIREITO DA SAÚDE
Direito da saúde : estudos em homenagem
ao Prof. Doutor Guilherme de Oliveira / coord.
João Loureiro, André Dias Pereira, Carla
Barbosa. – v.
3º v.: Segurança do paciente e consentimento
informado. – p. – ISBN 978-972-40-6566-3
I – LOUREIRO, João
II – PEREIRA, André Dias
III – BARBOSA, Carla
CDU   34

VOLUME III
SEGURANÇA DO PACIENTE
E CONSENTIMENTO INFORMADO

Patients' rights relating to patient safety

JOHAN LEGEMAATE[*]

1. Introduction[1]

During the past decade the attention given in health care to patient safety had increased considerably. Patient safety relates to the reduction of risk and is defined as "freedom from accidental injury due to medical care, or medical errors".[2] Patient safety is about managing this risk, using a wide variety of policies and instruments, including –but not limited to– building a safety culture, the development of clinical guidelines, reporting and analyzing adverse events, training doctors and other health professionals in the management of quality and safety and, last but not least, patient empowerment. Patient safety is a global issue. Both at the national and the international level numerous initiatives have been taken to develop sound patient safety infrastructures, which are aimed at reducing the number of patients who are unintentionally harmed when undergoing medical care.[3] On the basis of data gathered from studies performed in

---

[*] PhD, Professor of health law, Academic Medical Center/University of Amsterdam. E-mail: j.legemaate@amc.uva.nl

[1] This paper is an updated and expanded version of: J. Legemaate. Patients' rights and patient safety, in: D Delnoij, V Hafner (eds), Exploring patient participation on reducing health-care-related safety risks. Copenhagen: WHO/Regional Office for Europe, 2013, p. 11-32.

[2] LT Kohn, JM Corrigan, LS Donaldson. To err is human – Building a safer health system. Institute of Medicine, 2000.

[3] See http://www.euro.who.int/__data/assets/pdf_file/0015/111507/E93833.pdf.

the United States, Australia and a number of Western European Countries it is estimated that between 8 % and 12 % of patients admitted to hospital suffer from adverse events whilst receiving healthcare.[4] In actual practice this number may even be higher, due to the significant and widespread under-reporting of adverse events.

This paper describes and analyses the regulatory aspects of patient safety and more specifically the relationship between patient safety developments and patients' rights. The aim of this paper is to explore the legal context of patient safety, with a focus on obligations and possibilities to increase patient involvement and patient participation in the area of safety and quality of care. Patients' rights applicable in this area should not only try to achieve the intrinsic goal of protecting patients against unwarranted interventions (the traditional legal role) but should also try to promote the patient's well-being as well as the realization of equal access of all citizens to patient-centered care that is safe and of good quality. The key issue is to empower and inform citizens and patients: involving patient organizations in policy making, informing patients about standards, safety measures, remaining risks and complaints procedures, and developing core competencies in patient safety for patients.[5]

2. Normative guidelines from international bodies
In recent years international bodies and organizations like the Council of Europe, the OECD, European Union and WHO/WHA (World Health Organization/World Health Assembly) have undertaken many activities in the area of patient safety, ranging from defining principles and standards to developing down-to-earth approaches and tools regarding specific and concrete areas of patient safety. This paper is not the place to present a complete overview of all these activities.[6] However, it is important to assess the normative view of these organizations on the key-aspects of patient safety in relation to patients' rights. These key-

---

[4] Technical report 'Improving Patient Safety in the EU' prepared for the European Commission, published 2008 by the RAND Cooperation.

[5] Recommendation of the Council of the European Union of 9 June 2009 on patient safety EU website http://ec.europa.eu/health/patient_safety/docs/council_2009_en.pdf.

[6] See for a more extensive overview: http://www.euro.who.int/__data/assets/pdf_file/0015/111507/E93833.pdf.

-aspects can be deduced from a number of leading documents, the most important of which, in this context, are:

- WHA55.18 Resolution 'Quality of care: patient safety' of 2002, in connection with the Draft guidelines for adverse event reporting and learning systems, as published by the World Health Organization in 2005;
- The Luxemburg Declaration on Patient Safety of April 2005 (under the auspices of the European Union);
- Recommendation 2006/7 of the Council of Europe on the management of patient safety and prevention of adverse events in health care;[7]
- The Recommendation of the Council of the European Union of 9 June 2009 on patient safety, including the prevention and control of healthcare associated infections;
- The Directive of the European Union on the application of patients' rights in cross-border healthcare of 9 March 2011;
- The case law of the European Court of Human Rights.

2.1. The World Health Organization

The WHO document most relevant to the legal aspects of patient safety and patient participation is the draft guideline on adverse event reporting and learning systems. This document was published in 2005 by the World Alliance for Patient Safety and can be seen as a one of the means to implement WHA55.18 Resolution 'Quality of care: patient safety' of 2002.[8] The 2005 document focuses specifically on the role of reporting adverse events in enhancing patient safety: "In seeking to improve safety, one of the most frustrating aspects for patients and professionals alike is the apparent failure of health-care systems to learn from their mistakes. Too often neither health-care providers nor health-care organizations advise others when a mishap occurs, nor do they share what they have learned when an investigation has been carried out. As a consequence, the same mistakes occur repeatedly in many settings and patients continue to be harmed by preventable errors. One solution to this problem is reporting: by the doctor, nurse, or other provider

---

[7] https://wcd.coe.int/wcd/ViewDoc.jsp?id=1005439&Site=CM.
[8] See http://apps.who.int/gb/archive/pdf_files/WHA55/ewha5518.pdf.

within the hospital or health-care organization, and by the organization to a broader audience through a system-wide, regional, or national reporting system. Some believe that an effective reporting system is the cornerstone of safe practice and, within a hospital or other health-care organization, a measure of progress towards achieving a safety culture. At a minimum, reporting can help identify hazards and risks, and provide information as to where the system is breaking down. This can help target improvement efforts and systems changes to reduce the likelihood of injury to future patients".[9] It is important to note that reporting incidents is not a panacea. Different reporting systems exist, and the effectiveness and efficiency of these reporting system may vary, depending upon the structure, the scope and level (institutional, regional, national) of the reporting system. However, there are strong indications that well-considered reporting systems may have great value.

The draft guidelines of WHO do not explicitly deal with the issues of patients' rights, but the underlying message is clear: patient safety reporting systems play such a fundamental role that if such systems are not in place it will be difficult if not impossible to realize the patient's right to good care.

2.2. The European Union

EU policies are aimed at providing citizens with a high level of health protection. Seen from this perspective it is not surprising that the Luxemburg Declaration on Patient Safety of 2005, created under the auspices of the European Commission, recommends that "Patient Safety" needs to have a significant place high on the political agenda of the EU, nationally in the EU Member States and locally in the health care sector.[10] The European Union is engaging with a range of areas that can facilitate the improvement of patient safety.[11] Over the years the EU has been regulating the safety of blood, tissues and cells. More recently the

---

[9] http://www.who.int/patientsafety/events/05/Reporting_Guidelines.pdf.
[10] HDC Roscam Abbing. Patients' right to quality of healthcare: how satisfactory are the European Union's regulatory policies? European Journal of Health Law 2012; 19: 415-422.
[11] JV McHale. Regulating patient safety in the European Union: realistic aspiration or unattainable goal? In: J Tingle, P. Bark (eds), Patient safety, law policy and practice. London: Routledge, 2011, 150-164.

right to free movement of patient and health professionals has generated patient safety concerns at the EU level. In its 2009 Recommendation on patient safety (including the prevention and control of healthcare associated infections) the Council of the European Union expresses a more general view on patient safety in the EU context.[12] The EU Recommendation focuses on empowering and informing citizens and patients by:

(a) involving patient organizations and representatives in the development of policies and programmes on patient safety at all appropriate levels;

(b) disseminating information to patients on: (i) patient safety standards which are in place; (ii) safety measures which are in place to reduce or prevent errors and harm, including best practices, and the right to informed consent to treatment, to facilitate patient choice and decision-making; (iii) complaints procedures and available remedies and redress and the terms and conditions applicable;

(c) considering the possibilities of development of core competencies in patient safety namely, the core knowledge, attitudes and skills required to achieve safer care, for patients.

In addition, the European Union Directive on patients' rights in cross border healthcare of 2011 underlines the importance of helping patients to make an informed choice when they seek to receive healthcare in another Member State. Healthcare providers should provide relevant information to help individual patients to make an informed choice on the availability, quality and safety of the available healthcare services. In general, the Directive clearly stipulates the right of access to safe and high-quality cross-border healthcare.[13] It is one of the examples of the increasing expansion of EU power in the area of health law and policy.[14]

---

[12] See http://ec.europa.eu/health/patient_safety/docs/council_2009_en.pdf.

[13] See the various contributions in the special issue of the European Journal of Health Law on the EU Cross-border Care Directive (EJHL 2014; 21: 1-96).

[14] A de Ruijter. A Silent revolution: the expansion of EU power in the field of human health – A rights-based analysis of the UE health law and policy. Amsterdam: University of Amsterdam, 2015 (PhD thesis).

2.3. The Council of Europe

Recommendation 2006/7 of the Council of Europe outlines a comprehensive policy to improve patient safety[15] and departs from the viewpoint that access to safe health care is the basic right of every citizen in all member states of the Council. Furthermore the Recommendation considers that patients should participate in decisions about their health care, and recognizes that those working in health-care systems should provide patients with adequate and clear information about potential risks and their consequences, in order to obtain their informed consent to treatment. The Recommendation is accompanied by an extensive Appendix which provides a full technical and scientific background and justification of the Recommendation. The Recommendation of the Council of Europe strongly emphasizes the importance of protecting patients' rights. The Recommendation promotes a comprehensive approach, including not only an adverse event reporting system but, in addition, a fair and open complaints system, a just and adequate compensation system and an efficient and reliable supervisory system.

2.4. The case law of the European Court on Human Rights

Patient safety is an issue at the level of the European Court on Human Rights as well. In the 2004 case of Selisto versus Finland the Court stated that patient safety was an important aspect of health care and raised serious issues affecting the public interest. In the 2009 case of Codarcea v. Romania the Court pointed out that under the European Convention of Human Rights States have an obligation to introduce regulations compelling both public and private hospitals to adopt appropriate measures for the physical integrity of their patients.[16] It also stressed that any patient should be informed of the consequences of a medical operation and be able to give or withhold their consent in full knowledge thereof. In more recent cases the Court emphasized that the Convention also requires an effective independent judicial system to be set up so that the harm caused to patients in the care of the medical profession, whether in

---

[15] Th Perneger. The Council of Europe recommendation Rec(2006)7 on management of patient safety and prevention of adverse events in health care. International Journal for Quality in Health Care 2008; 20: 305–307.

[16] European Court of Human Rights (ECHR) 2 June 2009, nr. 31675/05 (Codarcea v. Romania).

the public or the private sector, can be determined and those responsible held accountable. According to the Court this can for instance be done by granting patients full access to civil proceedings or to disciplinary proceedings which may lead to liability for medical negligence. Furthermore, the Court emphasized that in case of harm done to patients claims for compensation should be dealt with speedily.[17]

3. Patients' rights in the area of patient safety

In general terms, the relationship between legal rights and patient safety was clearly summarized in a draft report on 'Human rights, the right to health and patient rights', prepared by WHO Europe in 2009: "The fulfillment of the right to health (a human and patient right) involves all health care actors: patients/consumers, governments and health care providers/stakeholders in rendering it concrete. All binding and non--binding international documents revised emphasize that international frameworks and policy instruments should be used to protect the fundamental human rights including patients' rights. In the quest towards strengthening political commitment of member states, the WHO Declaration on the promotion of patients' rights in Europe and the European Charter of patients' rights, seek to render the right to health concrete, applicable and appropriate to the current transitory situation in health services across the region. Work towards a common European framework for action and international instruments for realizing national policies in the field of patients' rights recorded substantial progress according to reported data. Most of the European member states have national dedicated policies and charters addressing patient rights. The implementation of local instruments as juridical legislation or extra juridical organisms (e.g. national or regional ombudsman) have to be encouraged and promoted to render effective the patient/ consumer protection. The right to safety is a key point in the implementation of the right to health. Promoting patient safety is strictly connected with the development of consumer empowerment, and involvement in the process of health promotion and care, including participation in the policy making process. It is expec-

---

[17] See ECHR 23 March 2010, nr. 4864/05 (Oyal v. Turkey), ECHR 25 September 2012, nr. 19764/07 (Spyra & Kranczkowksi v. Poland), ECHR 13 November 2012, nr. 41108/10 (Bajic v. Croatia) and ECHR 15 January 2013, nr. 8759/05 (Csoma v. Romania).

ted to support the active partnership needed in the process of improving safety, quality and efficiency of health service delivery".[18]

In this paragraph the focus will be on the specific rights of patients in the area of patient safety. In the past decades the rights of patients have been identified and elaborated in international documents and guidelines, national legislation, case law, deontological codes and so on. A number of these rights are relevant in the area of patient safety.

3.1. The right to health care which is safe and of good quality

Every citizen's right to health care can be found in many international treaties and guidelines as well as in national legislation (either at the level of a Constitution or Charter or 'translated' in to the specific national legislation on health care insurance). Already in 1946, the WHO Constitution stated that "the enjoyment of the highest attainable standard of health is one of the fundamental rights of every human being". The right to health care has both collective and individual dimensions. At the collective level this right stipulates that national authorities should strive to realize a health care system that is comprehensive (prevention, cure, care), accessible (both geographically and financially) and of good quality (safe, state of the art). At the individual level the right to health care is embodied in the entitlements of citizen regarding health care as defined in the national legislation. These entitlements may vary from country to country as well as over time, dependent on various factors, including the availability of resources.

The WHO Declaration on the Promotion of Patients' Rights in Europe of 1994, the socalled Amsterdam Declaration, stipulated that patients have the right to a quality of care marked by high technical standards and a humane relationship between the patient and health care providers.[19] The European Charter of Patients' Rights of 2000 mentions that "each individual has the right to be free from harm caused by the poor functioning of health care services, medical malpractice and errors, and the right of access to health services and treatments that meet high standards".

[18] WHO Europe. Human rights, the right to health and patient rights in the WHO European region. Copenhagen, 2009, p. 39 (draft, internal report).
[19] HDC Roscam Abbing. Twenty years WHO principles of patients' rights in Europe, a common framework: looking back to the future. European Journal of Health Law 2014; 21: 323-337.

The Luxemburg Declaration on Patient Safety of 2005 values the access to high quality care as a key human right. The international recommendations I described earlier in this paper are based on the same assumption. In national legislation several examples can be found of provisions concerning the safety and quality of care that has to be provided. A clear example is Article 2 of the Dutch Quality of Care in Institutions Act of 1996: "The care providers offers appropriate care. Appropriate care implies care of a good level, that is effective, efficient, patient centered and adjusted to the needs of the patient". It is not always common to make an explicit distinction between the quality and safety of health services, but it is important to do so, because quality levels may vary, while safety is a baseline that has to be maintained in all circumstances.

3.2. The right to participate in policymaking

It is broadly acknowledged that patients or their organizations or representatives should take part in the development of health policies, at all levels (national, regional, local). Patient centered care can only be achieved if the views and experiences of patients are used as input for policymaking, next to other relevant sources of information. Recommendation 2 of the European Union Recommendation on Patient Safety of 9 June 2009 stipulates that patient organizations and representatives should be involved "in the development of policies and programmes on patient safety at all appropriate levels".[20] There are many ways to realize this, varying from consulting national patient organizations on policy issues to creating a legislative basis for clients' councils in health care institutions. See in more detail Recommendation No. R (2000)5 of the Committee of Ministers of the Council of Europe on the development of structures for citizen and patient participation in the decision-making process affecting health care.[21]

This right implies that governments and health authorities stimulate and facilitate the establishment of patient groups and organizations and that these groups and organizations are well-informed. At the level of individual patients it is important that they are free to participate in representative bodies and organizations and that they are supported if

---

[20] See http://ec.europa.eu/health/patient_safety/docs/council_2009_en.pdf.
[21] See https://wcd.coe.int/wcd/ViewDoc.jsp?id=340437&Site=CM.

necessary to develop the relevant skills and competencies. It should be normal to include patients' views and experiences when developing standards regarding the quality and safety of health care.

3.3. The right to information about the safety and quality of health services

If circumstances allow citizens to make a choice between providers of health services it is important that information is available about the safety and quality of the services rendered by these providers. This has resulted in the emergence of a right to information about the safety and quality of health services. This information allows to patient to choose for the service provider that meets that patient's wishes and desires, which is especially relevant in health care systems with a market orientation.

The right to information about the safety and quality of health services can be seen as an individual right, but collecting the relevant information (on the basis of performance indicators etc.) can best be realized at a collective level. This requires a definition of the data that have to be offered by health service providers. These data should be valid and comparable. These data may be accessible through websites, annual reports or other sources. The right to information about the safety and quality of health services has a clear connection with the earlier mentioned right to health care which is safe and of good quality. The latter right cannot be fully exercised if information about the safety and quality of health services is not available. This implies that health services providers are transparent and accountable with regard to the safety and the quality of their services. The right to information about the safety and quality of health services is not only relevant at the national level, but at the international level as well, due to the increasing patient mobility and cross border health care. Section 20 of the 2011 European Union Directive on cross-border healthcare stipulates: "In order to help patients to make an informed choice when they seek to receive healthcare in another Member State, Member States of treatment should ensure that patients from other Member States receive on request the relevant information on safety and quality standards enforced on its territory as well as on which healthcare providers are subject to these standards. Furthermore, healthcare providers should provide patients on request with information on specific aspects of the healthcare services they offer and on the treatment options".[22]

3.4. The right to information with regard to the proposed treatment (informed consent)

One of the most crucial individual rights of patients is the right to be informed about the proposed treatment.[23] [24] A patient can only give valid consent if this is based on clear and adequate information. The information has to focus on the nature of the patient's condition, the (possible) effects and side-effects of the proposed treatment, the possible alternatives and the likely impact of not treating the patient. The importance of the right to information with regard to the proposed treatment goes way beyond legitimizing consent. Without this information the patient cannot fully exercise other important rights (such as the right to refuse treatment, the right to privacy, the right to access his medical records etc.). Furthermore, the provision of clear and adequate information may strengthen the relation between the patient and the health professional and thereby stimulate patient compliance. Information with regard to the proposed treatment is also relevant in a more social context: the information may enable the patient to communicate with his family members and, if necessary, to take care of work– or business-related issues. Without clear and adequate information with regard to the proposed treatment the patient cannot exercise self-determination or personal autonomy. Finally, good information plays an important role in the management of expectations with regard to the possible outcome and risks of health interventions. The patient who is well-informed knows what he can expect, and will be able to deal better with unexpected events. From a patient safety point of view this may be very important.

The relevant information has to be provided to the individual patient in the specific context of his or her health situation. The health professional responsible for conveying the information may be assisted by

---

[22] See http://eur-lex.europa.eu/LexUriServ/LexUriServ.do?uri=OJ:L:2011:088:0045:0065: EN:PDF.

[23] See for instance R Faden, T. Beauchamp. A history and theory of informed consent. New York: Oxford University Press, 1986.

[24] J Legemaate. The development and implementation of patients' rights: Dutch experience of the right to information. Medicine & Law 2002; 21: 723-734.

other persons and may use additional agents (such as brochures, dvd's, websites etc.), but he retains full responsibility for both the process and the content of the information given to the patient.

3.5. The right to be informed about adverse events and medical errors

The delivery of health care is aimed at stabilizing or improving the patient's health situation with a minimum of damage. Damage cannot always be avoided. Some forms of damage are unavoidable (wounding the patient in order to perform an operation), other forms may occur unintended, depending upon the circumstances (adverse events, complications). Unintended adverse events and complications are inherent to the delivery of health care and do not automatically constitute a medical error that justifies a compensation of damages. In a number of cases, however, the legal requirements for compensation are met and a financial arrangement should be realized. In all cases of an adverse event with noticeable effects the patient should be informed about the nature, the cause and the consequences of the adverse event.[25] This requires a clear 'open disclosure' policy.[26]

The right to be informed about adverse events and medical errors is sometimes seen as a integral part of the aforementioned right to information with regard to the proposed treatment: if there is a legal duty to inform the patient about prognostic aspects concerning a treatment decision, it is logical that the patient has to be informed about an unintended or undesirable outcome of the treatment (regardless of whether this outcome is the result of a medical error). However, the right to be informed about adverse events and medical errors can also be seen as a legal right with its own, separate legal foundation. The information pro-

---

[25] It is commonly assumed that this right does not extend to so-called 'near misses'. These 'near misses' should be reported in the context of the health provider's quality assurance scheme, but need not to be reported to the patient.

[26] SP Fein a.o. The many faces of error disclosure. Journal of General Internal Medicine 2007; 22: 755-761; TH Gallagher, D Studdert, W Levinson. Disclosing harmful Medical errors to patients. N Engl J Med 2007; 356: 2713-2719; RA Iedema a.o. Practising open disclosure: clinical incident communication and systems improvement. Sociol Health Illn 2009; 31: 262-277; W Levinson. Disclosing medical errors to patients: a challenge for health care professionals and institutions. Patient Educ Couns 2009; 76: 296-299.

vided under this right enables the patient to understand his actual situation and to decide whether of not he wants to make use of his right to complain or to take further (legal) action.

3.6. The right to participate in quality assurance schemes

The responsibility to deliver health care which is safe and of good quality has to be fulfilled in the first place by the providers of health care. This responsibility cannot be transferred to the patient. However, fulfilling this responsibility implies that patient views and experiences are collected in a systematic manner and that these views and experiences are taken seriously. Article 3(c) of the 2009 European Union Recommendation on patient safety stipulates that patients, their relatives and informal caregivers should be given opportunities to report their experiences. There are many well-developed and well-researched ways to collect the views and experiences of patients in health care. This may range from interviewing patients, using methods like the CQ-Index (Consumer Quality Index), analyzing messages in the social media, to allowing patients to report incidents and adverse events to the health provider's incident reporting system. If it is a legal obligation to deliver health care which is patient centered and adjusted to the needs of the patient (see § 3.1 above), it is unavoidable to develop a systematic way to collect and analyze the views and experiences of individual patients and/or patient organizations.

The right to participate in quality assurance schemes aims at using the views and experiences from individual patients to improve the safety and quality of health care in general. These views and experiences can be derived at an individual and at a group level. As far as the individual level is concerned it is important to prevent the transfer of inappropriate (legal or medical) responsibilities to the patient. This right has to be distinguished from educating patients to improve their health condition and/or to be aware of factors that may threaten the safety or effectiveness of the health care they receive.

3.7. The right to complain

The legal position of patients in health care should be based on three elements: substantive rights (access to health care, informed consent, privacy etc), procedural rights (right to complain, other mechanism to enforce patients' rights) and adequate information about the existence and the content of the applicable substantive and the procedural rights. In this context the right to complain is of vital importance, not only as a tool to enforce the compliance with existing rights but also to have a forum to debate rights and entitlements that have not yet been laid down in legislation or case law. Seen from the perspective of the health care provider, complaints lodged by patients or their family can be used as indicators to evaluate and, if necessary, to improve the safety and quality of care. Each complaint is a free advice. Some health professionals tend to view a complaint as a burden or even as a lack of trust from the side of the patient. This is not the right attitude. It is inherent to the delivery of health care, as to any service, that patients may be dissatisfied with regard to the services offered. It is only natural that they are given possibilities to voice dissatisfaction or to file a complaint. Health services providers have to respond to this in a serious and constructive manner and should avoid defensive or legalistic responses. For that reason the Council of Europe Recommendation 2006/7 requires "the existence of a fair and open complaints system".

The right of patients to complain can be shaped and implemented in various ways, ranging from the services of informal, easily accessible patient advocates or complaint officials to a independent ombudsman and legal proceedings before a court.[27] [28] [29] One way or the other a balanced complaint system should incorporate all these elements. European jurisdictions show a rather wide variation in complaint systems, depending on variables as the structure and organization of health care and the legal culture or tradition. Research has shown that patients strongly favor informal and swift procedures to deal with dissatisfaction or complaints. Only if a complaint cannot be solved at this level, a formal and/or independent authority, committee or court may be required.[30]

---

[27] J Legemaate. The patient's right of complaint: opinions and developments in the Netherlands. European Journal of Health Law 1996; 3: 255-271.

[28] L Fallberg, S Mackenney. Patient Ombudsmen in seven European countries: an effective way to implement patients' rights? European Journal of Health Law 2003; 10: 343-57.

[29] RD Friele, EM Sluijs. Patient expectations of fair complaint handling in hospitals: empirical data. BMC Health Serv Res 2006: 106.

[30] FY Alhafaji, BJM Frederiks, J Legemaate. The Dutch system of handling complaints in health care. Medicine & Law 2009; 28: 241-255.

In the context of a patient safety management system it is important to combine information from different sources: incidents reported by health professionals or patients, complaints filed by patients with a complaints official or a complaint committee, claims for the compensation of damage due to an alleged medical error etc. An integrated analysis of these data may identify trends and developments in the area of safety and quality of care that would otherwise have been missed.

3.8. The right to be compensated in case of damage

In case of damage that can be attributed to the delivery of health care "a just and adequate compensation system" (Council of Europe Recommendation 2006/7) should be in place. The traditional legal view is that patients are entitled to compensation in the case of culpable damage. In popular terms: damage that is the result of a medical error. In some European jurisdictions (Nordic countries, France, Belgium) the traditional legal system of civil liability has been supplemented with possibilities to compensate patient for damage that has not been caused by a medical error, if certain conditions are met (no fault compensation systems). In general, patients should have easy access to procedures for handling complaints and/or claims. Futhermore, claims of patients to compensate damage should be dealt with as speedily as possible. Legal battles should be avoided. Traditional mechanisms in the area of liability law may not be sufficient to deal adequately with cases in the area of medical negligence. This calls for proposals and ideas to simplify existing procedures and to increase the possibility that patients with a true claim for compensation actually receive compensation[31]. It is important to emphasize the responsibilities of health care providers and the health care system in general. The resolvement of any case in which a patient suffers damage that could have been avoided should start with a quick response by the responsible health care provider, including open disclosure, aftercare as well as putting pressure on all parties concerned, such as lawyers and insurance companies, to handle the patient's claim within a reasonable period of

---

[31] In the US various strategies have been developed as an alternative to the existing, inefficient medical liability system. See SK Bell a.o. Disclosure, apology, and offer programs: stakeholders' views of barriers to and strategies for broad implementation. Millbank Quarterly 2012; 90: 682-705; MM Mello, TH Gallagher. Malpractice reform -opportunities for leadership by health care institutions and liability insurers. N Engl J Med, 2010; 362 : 1353.

DIREITO DA SAÚDE

time. In most countries there is a large gap between the number of patient suffering from avoidable damage and the number of patient being compensated. We should do all we can to bridge that gap.

3.9. The right to be supported

The right to be supported finds its ratio in the factual circumstances of health care. Due to a wide variety of circumstances patients may not always be in the position to claim or exercise the rights mentioned earlier. These circumstances may include: inequalities in the relationship between patient and health professional, lack of knowledge or competencies (health literacy) at the side of the patient, fear for disadvantages, vulnerability or inability as a result of the patient's health condition etc. It is not realistic to expect that all patients are the autonomous agents the legislation often presupposes. Some of the rights mentioned above are intended to 'compensate' or prevent difficulties a patient may experience in exercising his rights (e.g. the right to information) and thereby substantiate the patient's right to be supported. However, this right also requires specific measures and activities, examples of which are:

- the availability of services to empower individual patients through education (not only to guarantee that the rights of patients are met but also to broaden the knowledge about health problems, promote healthy living, disease prevention and ways of taking responsibility for their own health);
- the availability of services to physically support patients who otherwise will not be able to exercise their rights;
- the availability of patient representatives in cases in which a patient, as a result of (partial) incompetency or other reasons, is not (fully) capable of voicing his wishes of exercising his rights;
- the availability of the services of a patient advocate as part of a comprehensive complaint system.

3.10. The right to privacy

Like informed consent the patient's right to privacy is a key feature of the patients' rights catalogue. In an era in which information technology is rapidly expanding, in health case as well as in other branches of society, it is crucial to protect the privacy rights of patients. Traditionally, privacy in health care is realized through the legal and professional norms of medical confidentiality. As a general rule, health care professionals are supposed not to disclose patient information to others persons or parties, except when legitimized by patient consent, legal obligations or emergency circumstances.[32]

The rules regarding medical confidentiality may create problems in the context of quality improvement, for instance when quality improvement schemes require coded or even identifiable patient information and regulations in the area of medical confidentiality and/or privacy do not allow that. The same problem may rise in the context of national or international medical research in the area of patient safety and quality of care. It is obvious that privacy protection is an important part of the legal position of individual patients. However, these patients, as well as future patients, may benefit from the result of quality assurance schemes and medical research in the area of patient safety. It is important to balance the privacy interests of individual patients with the societal interest in improving the safety and quality of health care, if necessary by allowing exceptions to the general rules regarding privacy and medical confidentiality. For instance: adverse event reporting procedures may underperform if, at least in the first phase of the reporting process, it is not allowed to use identifiable patient data to check whether the reported information is complete or to ask more information from the health professional who reported the event.

It can be assumed that in general patients do not object to using their identifiable data for quality and safety improvement purposes. Important preconditions are that patients receive general information about the possibility that their data may be used, that they are given to possibility to object, that identifiable data are only used when less intrusive options are not possible and that adequate safeguards are put in place. However, in some cases it may be necessary to change existing legislation, in order to increase effectiveness of patient safety schemes. This requires a careful analysis of various interests involved and to balance the privacy interests of individual patients with the societal interest of improving the safety and quality of health care.

---

[32] HDC Roscam Abbing. Medical confidentiality and patient safety: reporting procedures. European Journal of Health Law 2014; 21: 245-259.

4. Conclusions and recommendations

A draft report on human rights and patient safety prepared by WHO Europe in 2009 mentioned the following 'key statements': "Patient safety is an issue of increasing concern in healthcare systems all over the world. It involves in the same time various actors, with the patient/ consumer at its core. Only an informed and empowered consumer can actively contribute to improve communication as well as health care outcomes. The right to safety is one of the fundamental patients' rights, as the right to informed consent, the right to participate in safety promotion, and the right to fair procedure. It is necessary to introduce an integrated approach, with patient safety at the core of high performing healthcare systems, by bringing together all factors which can potentially impact the quality and safety of processes. Promoting patient empowerment and involvement in the process of health promotion and care will support the active partnership needed in the process of improving safety, quality and efficiency of health service delivery".[33]

The rights of patients described and analyzed in this paper clearly underpin and fuel these 'key statements'. The goal of this paper was to describe and analyze the regulatory aspects of patient safety and more specifically the relationship between patient safety developments and patients' rights. In the previous section the legal context of patient safety has been explored, with a focus on obligations and possibilities to increase patient involvement and patient participation in the area of safety and quality of care. Legal rights and developments cannot be isolated from 'surrounding' aspects and influence. One has to be aware of issues that may strongly influence (in a positive or a negative direction) the effectiveness of legal interventions in the area of patients' rights and patient safety.

It is important to acknowledge the rights of patients relating to patient safety and to regulate them in the national legislation in such a way that patients are able to use and enforce them. Patients have a right to health care which is safe and of good quality. This right underpins the responsibility of health care providers to develop and take part in quality and safety improvement systems.

---

[33] WHO Europe. Human rights, the right to health and patient rights in the WHO European region. Copenhagen, 2009, p. 38 (draft, internal report).

Patient participation starts with the availability of valid, clear and relevant information at various levels:

a. information on the basis of which patients can differentiate between (the quality and safety of) health care providers;
b. information with regard to the patient's health situation, the available treatment options and the potential risks for the patient's safety;
c. information about how to get involved in patient safety activities.

It is important that health care providers invite, encourage and empower patients to take part in patient safety activities and that they try to eliminate barriers in that respect. By doing so patients can contribute to their own safety and to the safety of future patients and situations.[34] Adverse event reporting systems should include the possibility of adverse events being reported by a patient or his family. Patients should be clearly informed about the possibility to report to this system. Patients and their organizations should also be allowed to participate in policy development, at various levels. Policy makers at all levels should actively seek the involvement of patients and their organizations.

Apart from the substantive rights of patients, their procedural rights should be recognized and implemented. Patients should be given opportunities to file a complaint, ranging from informal proceedings (discussing the complaint with the health provider concerned; if necessary supported by a patient advocate or a patient advice and liaison service) to the possibility to obtain the decision of an independent authority (a formal complaint committee, a judge or a ombudsman). It is important that the available complaint options meet the expectations of patients. Many patients are dissatisfied with the way in which their complaints are handled, a phenomenon that exists in a number of countries and is not well understood. If patients' expectations are not met or not met in full, they may feel disappointed or even frustrated. Fair complaints handling

---

[34] Research has shown that an important motive for patients to file a complaint is to prevent that other patients experience the same situation. See C Vincent, M Young, A Phillips. Why do people sue their doctors? A study of patients and relatives taking legal action. The Lancet 1994; 343: 1609–1613 and M Bismark a.o. Accountability sought by patients following adverse events from medical care: the New Zealand experience. CMAJ 2006; 175: 889–894. This finding indicates that the possibility to improve quality and safety in general may be an important motivator for patients to participate in patient safety activities.

is highly significant in restoring patients' trust in health care and in renewing patients' commitment to the health care provider or organisation.[35] Furthermore, the complaint procedures should function in such a way that the outcome of complaint proceedings is integrated in the health provider's quality and safety improvement system.

Each of the rights of patients analyzed in section 3 this paper should be given sufficient attention in practice, policy and legislation. It may be worthwhile to develop programs and strategies that facilitate several of these rights at the same time. Many of these rights are closely connected. This is the case, for instance, with regard to the right to be informed about adverse events and medical errors, the right to complain, the right to be compensated in case of damage and the right to be supported. In that area so-called *disclosure and offer programs* may be very effective.[36] A comprehensive solution to patients' rights problems in the area of patient safety is also provided by the report published in 2006 by the Harvard Hospitals.[37]

Across Europe, many activities aimed at improving patient safety have been undertaken. However, the evaluation, published in 2012, of the 2009 Recommendation of European Union on patient safety makes it clear that there is still a lot to be done to realize the active involvement of patients in patient safety.[38] Patient safety contributes to reducing unnecessary harm to patients and to an increase in quality of life. Good patient safety policies include a wide range of measures and activities. The policies cannot be successful without a change of culture amongst health care providers and institutions. Creating a regulatory framework with regard to patient safety and patients' rights along the lines set out in this paper may be instrumental in improving the legal position of patients with regard to patient safety.

---

[35] RD Friele, EM Sluijs, J Legemaate. Complaints handling in hospitals: an empirical study of discrepancies between patients' expectations and their experiences. BMC Health Services Research 2008; 8: 199.

[36] See Bell a.o. (footnote 28 above) as well as MM Mello, A Kachalia. Evaluation of options for medical malpractice system reform – A study conducted by staff from the Harvard School of Public Health and the Harvard Medical School for the Medicare Payment Advisory Commission. Boston, 2010.

[37] Harvard Hospitals. When things go wrong: responding to adverse events: a consensus statement of the Harvard Hospitals. Boston: Massachusetts Coalition for the Prevention of Medical Errors, 2006.

[38] See http://ec.europa.eu/health/patient_safety/docs/council_2009_report_en.pdf.

A natureza de complexidade dos sistemas de saúde
– Implicações para a segurança dos doentes e para a responsabilidade médica

PROFESSOR DOUTOR JOSÉ I G FRAGATA*

Introdução

A prestação de cuidados de saúde é uma actividade de enorme complexidade. Essa complexidade reside no perfil dos doentes tratados, no modelo da prática, seja em consultórios, clínicas ou hospitais, no modelo da organização e, é também o resultado da diversidade de interesses dos *stakeholders* envolvidos na Saúde. Sejam eles financiadores, pagadores, organizações governamentais ou não governamentais.

Uma das características dos sistemas de saúde é a produção de *outcomes,* tipicamente incertos. Seja pela variação inesperada – muitas vezes devida a erros e a complicações de diagnóstico ou do tratamento, que arrastam elevados custos de eficiência e crescentes graus de insatisfação por parte dos doentes, da sociedade, dos pagadores e dos próprios prestadores. Não deixa de ser curioso o facto de, as medidas tomadas ao longo da última década para reduzir os erros nos sistemas de saúde, ou

---

* FETCS, FESC
Cirurgião Cardiotorácico
Professor Catedrático de Cirurgia

o uso de *guidelines* de vinculação terapêutica e tantas outras iniciativas, aparentemente boas, não terem conseguido fazer com que a prestação de cuidados de saúde seja mais previsível nos resultados, constituindo uma actividade segura, eficiente e uniformemente geradora de valor, e também de satisfação.

É que, os sistemas de saúde têm sido tomados como sistemas "mecânicos", dos quais que se espera reprodutibilidade. Mas são, na sua essência, sistemas "complexos", governados por teorias de complexidade, devendo, por isso, ser tratados como tal. Este artigo aborda, precisamente, a "complexidade" na Saúde e o modo como, se olharmos a Saúde dessa perspectiva, poderemos melhorar a sua segurança e olhar de modo diferente o tema da responsabilidade médica.

Serão os Cuidados de Saúde uma Actividade Segura?

Andar de avião, em companhias aéreas comerciais, é hoje tido como muito seguro. Calcula-se que possa morrer um passageiro por cada 10 milhões de descolagens – aterragens (10^7), um nível de segurança que se designa industrialmente por "*sigma*^{7}". Actividades reguladas, como o tráfego rodoviário, são bem menos seguras, com níveis de risco de "*sigma*^{4}", enquanto actividades como o alpinismo apresentam riscos da ordem de 1 por mil!. Nos hospitais, entre nós, como à escala global, o risco de morte por erro evitável, ocorrido durante o internamento, é de 1 para 300 doentes internados e o risco de eventos adversos, de qualquer tipo, atinge cerca de onze em cada ceminternamentos ... Imaginemo-nos na porta de embarque para um voo intercontinental em que a hospedeira, após as boas vindas e a informação sobre os dados da viagem, nos avisasse com honestidade, que o risco de morte no voo seria de 1 em 300. Pergunto-me quem embarcaria?. No entanto, nos hospitais, todos os dias são admitidos milhões de doentes, que irão, sem saberem, incorrer num nível de risco equivalente!.

Com efeito, a prestação de cuidados de saúde acha-se a nível de "*sigma*^{3}", excepção feita para a Anestesiologia que, sendo muito mais segura, atingiu hoje níveis de "*sigma*^{5}". Esta insegurança confunde-se com a imprevisibilidade nos resultados, ou seja, com uma excessiva variação aleatória, que caracteriza transversalmente a prática dos cuidados de Saúde. As razões profundas para esta excessiva variação de *outputs* e de *outcomes* residem na incerteza extrema do fenómeno biológico e pelos desvios da performance diagnóstica e terapêutica. Na aviação civil, talvez a variação associada à meteorologia e às aeronaves, seja muito menor, mas com toda a certeza, o nível de performance humana e do Sistema antecipa e controla muita da variação operacional que porventura exista, tornando a actividade dominantemente previsível e muito, muito mais segura que a da Saúde.

Determinantes do Resultado em Saúde

Os resultados em Saúde, como para qualquer outra actividade de base humana, são determinados por factores da **dificuldade da actividade** (gravidade da doença ou complexidade do procedimento), factores **ambienciais condicionantes** (condições locais de momento, pressões, dotação de *staff*), factores de **performance** (individual, de equipa e da organização) e factores **aleatórios** (variação não explicável). A dificuldade técnica representa um potencial conhecido para morte, e para gerar complicações, estas levando sempre ao agravamento marcado dos custos (estes serão considerados *outputs* negativos). Esta complexidade e dificuldade técnica, poderá, dentro de certos limites, ser compensada pelo acréscimo de performance. Entende-se assim que, qualquer resultado em Saúde deva ser indexado e adaptado para o nível da complexidade tratada. Isto é hoje feito pela estratificação do risco, possibilitando a apresentação de resultados segundo o modelo de índices **resultado obtido/ /resultado esperado (O/E)**. Percebe-se assim que uma correcta gestão de risco clínico, possa ajudar a obter melhorias de performance e, logo, melhores *outputs*. A complexidade de um caso é constante, é transportada por cada doente; contudo, o risco que lhe estará associado varia em função da performance e poderá ser modelado. Mesmo assim, nunca poderão ser evitados, em absoluto, erros e eventos adversos (complicações), resultantes de acção humana directa e de defeitos organizacionais a múltiplos níveis. Obrigam-se os prestadores – indivíduos e organizações – a uma total correcção de processos, mas não se poderão vincular, nunca, à obtenção de um dado resultado que, na esmagadora maioria dos casos, os utentes dos cuidados de saúde esperam bom.

Variação Aleatória em Saúde

Desde muito cedo se soube que os resultados em Medicina estavam associados a uma variação incerta. Sir William Osler, reputado médico canadiano do século XIX, afirmava ser a Medicina a *"arte do incerto e a ciência da probabilidade"* e, apesar de todos os avanços tecnológicos, sociológicos e organizacionais verificados nos últimos anos, esta citação nunca nos pareceu tão actual ! Mas de onde provem a variação excessiva em Medicina?. Em campos de grande exigência tecnológica e ainda maior dependência interdisciplinar e organizacional, como a cirurgia das cardiopatias congénitas, a variação de resultados de mortalidade e complicações para os defeitos cardíacos mais graves e exigentes, como, por exemplo, a cirurgia de *Norwood* para a síndrome do coração esquerdo hipoplásico (*), chega a variar 20 vezes conforme os centros, o seu nível de experiência, o volume de casos e... a sua localização geográfica!. Diremos que a variação excessiva tem um impacto e um resultado indesejáveis na Saúde, factos que a tornam ainda mais imprevisível. Há, portanto, uma variação expectável de distribuição (biológica e *gaussiana*) normal, e uma variação indesejável, que a estatística define como ultrapassando dois ou três desvios padrão em torno da média, consoante os níveis de exigência. A variação em Medicina pode, assim, ser de dois tipos – a esperada e a inexplicável (também chamada por *Wennberg*, de variação indesejada). Esta variação inexplicável é cada vez mais conotada com má performance clínica, sendo hoje um indicador de má qualidade nos Cuidados de Saúde. Com efeito, para actividades médicas muito complexas, interdisciplinares e com grande dependência organizacional, os resultados melhores parecem inequivocamente associados ao maior volume de casos, facto que coloca a responsabilidade da variação indesejada ao lado da má performance. Na Medicina decidimos num quadro muito variável de concordância e de certeza e raramente estamos cem por cento concordantes e certos (na área da chamada Medicina Baseada na Evidência), a maior parte das vezes estamos no que Stacey 2003 apelidou de *margem do caos*. Este "caos decisional" resulta do facto da actividade de prestação dos cuidados de saúde ser exercida não no seio de **sistemas mecânicos** deterministas (Newtonianos) em que as mesmas causas, repetidas, condicionam os mesmos resultados, mas sim no seio de **sistemas de complexidade**, cuja variação dinâmica é a regra. Estes sistemas que tentam explicar, à escala cósmica, as interacções verificadas no espaço, no sistema imune, na meteorologia ou na variação financeira dos mercados, entre outras realidades cósmicas, também explicam a aludida variabilidade excessiva no campo da Saúde.

Sistemas Complexos e os Cuidados de Saúde

Tomemos, por exemplo, um automóvel. Para o melhorarmos poderemos decompô-lo em partes ou sistemas (motor, suspensão, sistema eléctrico...), melhorando cada parte e montando de novo; Este processo de decomposição hierárquica funciona bem para sistemas mecânicos, mas não para sistemas de complexidade dinâmica, porque estes sistemas, sendo não lineares, não têm pontos conhecidos de equilíbrio, parecendo antes aleatórios e caóticos. São constituídos por muitos agentes (médicos, enfermeiros, doentes, pagadores, gestores...) que tendem a actuar, dentro de redes profissionais, mas independentemente, levados por interesses próprios e, certamente, diferentes, não raro, mesmo, conflituantes. Mais, estes agentes são inteligentes, ganham cultura – experiência, que muda em função do tempo, adaptando-se, num processo de imparável auto-organização e, talvez o mais importante, não apresentam pontos únicos de controlo, ou seja, ninguém está verdadeiramente em controlo. Assim sendo, serão sempre mais facilmente auto-influenciáveis no seu comportamento do que, movíveis por um qualquer controlo externo e directo. Um sistema como este, o Sistema de Saúde, não pode ser decomposto hierarquicamente, sob pena de vermos perder-se a informação relacional mais relevante. Entende-se assim, que a complexidade do Sistema de Saúde o tornará mais vulnerável a erros e mais resistente às mudança e melhorias. Quais as medidas que, actuando neste tipo de sistemas, mais efeito teriam na redução da variação aleatória excessiva e na qualidade global dos serviços de saúde?

- À medida que a complexidade da Medicina aumenta, a simplificação de processos, quer para doentes, quer para prestadores (médicos, técnicos e enfermeiros) deverá também aumentar. Uma forma de o fazer é recorrendo a *"workflows" e "clinical pathways"*, suportados tecnologicamente, modalidades que agilizam a prática, enquanto concorrem para a segurança. Esta mesma tendência tem sido protagonizada pelas empresas de telecomunicações e informática, como foi feito pela Apple®. Assim, quanto maior a complexidade da tarefa, maior deverá ser a simplificação dos sistemas e dos processos em que a tarefa se desenrola.
- Um outro aspecto prende-se com o desenho de toda a actividade, a montante, que deve primar pela integração. Assim, desde os fluxos de tratamento dos doentes, que não devem ser parcelares mas

contínuos, ao funcionamento dos cuidados em rede (primários, secundários e terciários) até à concepção do modelo de saúde global, o desenho deverá privilegiar a integração e a flexibilidade, enquanto monitoriza e influencia padrões de actuação, numa base de, cada vez maior, responsabilidade e menor utilização do tradicional controlo profissional directo.

- Finalmente, o modo como estes sistemas serão geridos deverá evoluir, dado que estas organizações tendem a aprender, a adaptar-se e a auto-organizar-se por si próprias, num processo de mudança constante. Ao invés das organizações tradicionais, geridas para minimizar custos, as organizações de saúde devem ser geridas para maximizar o Valor.

Organização Tradicional e Sistema Adaptativo – quadro comparativo

Sistema Tradicional	Sistema Dinâmico
Gestão	Liderança
Comando e Controlo	Incentivos e Inibições
Actividades	Resultados Finais
(actos médicos isolados)	(doente "final" tratado)
Foco na Eficiência	Foco na Agilidade
Relação Contractual	Envolvimento Pessoal
Forte base de Hierarquia	Hetrarquia (ordem consensual)
Desenho Organizacional Rígido	Predomínio de Auto-Organização

O modelo que melhor responde às necessidades de modulação de um sistema complexo, como o da prestação de cuidados de saúde, será o que contempla a **informação** e a **incentivação**. A informação deve fluir livremente a todos os níveis, por exemplo, o reporte de eventos adversos ocorridos, que levará à ulterior aprendizagem e ao redesenho do sistema, reporte este feito sem culpabilização, votado para o sistema e não para o individuo, e servindo sempre a aprendizagem, que leva ao conhecimento, este feito ferramenta de segurança adaptativa. Em sentido lato, a informação abrange *workflows, checklists, clinical pathways...*que tanto limitam os erros e melhoram a eficiência; abrange ainda a comunicação e a dinâmica da equipa, aspectos a que a *Joint Comission for Accreditation of Hospital Organizations* atribuiu responsabilidade de 70 % sobre a génese dos eventos adversos em Saúde! Esta dinâmica de equipa será, porventura, o meio mais eficaz de servir o modelo de *microssistema* clínico de prestação de cuidados, que tanto parece limitar erros e desperdícios na prestação de cuidados. A incentivação é uma dimensão lata, que tanto pode significar a remuneração adicional, pelo que se produz efectivamente (valor criado ou *outcome* de tratamento final conseguido) ou, o mero conhecimento inclusivo desse resultado. É curioso pensarmos que um dos meios mais poderosos de incentivar o reporte de eventos é o do *feed-back* dos resultados da análise, das medidas e o seu impacto no terreno, para quem reportou os eventos. A segurança na saúde requere uma atitude verdadeiramente inclusiva de todos, a par com uma resiliência muito própria. Mas todos estes valores que descrevi fazem parte de uma dimensão muito mais elevada – a **Cultura de Segurança** de que trataremos a seguir.

Cultura de Segurança – impacto na prestação de cuidados de saúde

"Complexity Science encourages healthcare leaders to work with, rather than against, overwhelming complexity by focusing on relationship building, organizational values and culture, and widespread participation, rather than tight integration, formalization and centralized decision-making. The leader serves the organization by making sense of a complex world, rather than providing neat answers that promise success" – JIM BEGUN

O conceito de "Cultura de Segurança" emergiu do desastre da central nuclear de Chernobyl, que a não tinha, e vem ganhando relevo para os cuidados de saúde, na linha do que sucedeu com a aviação civil, onde se mostra, hoje, exemplar. A Cultura de Segurança aplicada à Saúde tem uma componente de percepção e outra, associada, de comportamentos de segurança, componentes que devem estar interiorizadas nos indivíduos, residir nas equipas, e fazer parte integrante do ADN das organizações. Assim se entende que existam camadas ou ambientes distintos de cultura sectorial, mas cujos valores serão comuns e baseados numa atitude permanente de **reporte sem culpa**, de **focagem no sistema,** de **aprendizagem e redesenho** e de geração de conhecimento aplicável**, de proactividade** em relação **aos eventos possíveis** e **sentido de vulnerabilidade** e, ainda, de **resiliência.** Estas dimensões devem ser exercidas em equipa com uma forte componente de auto-organização e perfeita comunicação, envolvendo todos os seus membros, a cada nível, de modo inclusivo, incorporando as normas e as preocupações com a segurança nos "genes" da organização, que assim, se tornará verdadeiramente segura.

DIREITO DA SAÚDE

Esta cultura de segurança deverá ser uma cultura "just" – ou seja, responsabilizando sem culpabilizar, deixando a culpabilização exclusivamente para os casos em que exista a violação de normas de segurança.

Responsabilidade Médica na Prática dos Cuidados de Saúde

Como referimos, a prestação de cuidados de saúde é uma actividade de resultado incerto, de que podem resultar danos não esperados, estes, por vezes, com enorme impacto para os doentes e suas famílias. Os profissionais de saúde e as instituições onde trabalham vêm sendo chamados, cada vez mais, a "responder", no âmbito da responsabilidade civil, da responsabilidade disciplinar / deontológica e, mesmo, penal. Respondem porquê ?. Respondem perante a sociedade e os Tribunais pela "coisa confiada", que é a saúde dos cidadãos; claro está, isto independentemente do "julgamento da alma" e do impacto sobre a sua própria reputação.

A Lei portuguesa, como tantas outras, nomeadamente a dos Estados Unidos da América do norte, trata a Saúde e no que respeita à responsabilidade civil, sob o modelo de "responsabilidade subjectiva", orientada mais para o encontrar de um culpado directo e não tanto para a consideração da Saúde como uma actividade que é de risco. É sempre difícil fazer aplicar um sistema em que a culpa é proporcional ao dano apurado e, logo, linear dessa perspectiva – o sistema jurídico, a um sistema, como o da Saúde, em que a variação se acha, tão frequentemente, fora de qualquer culpa por comissão ou omissão directas, mas antes o resultado da variação excessiva. Saúde e Direito "casam", assim, mal, pela natureza intrínseca da prática dos cuidados de Saúde.

A responsabilidade médica, cuja elaboração jurídica, na sua componente de responsabilidade civil ao Professor Doutor Guilherme de Oliveira, tanto deve entre nós, assenta no apurar de um dano induzido (para a responsabilidade criminal será simplesmente necessário e independentemente do dano, a colocação em risco da vida de outrem). Em qualquer caso, exige-se, necessariamente e para além do facto culposo, estabelecer um nexo de causalidade. Mas, não só o apuramento da culpa se revela complexo, como se torna ainda muito difícil a verificação do nexo causal, dada a natureza intrincada e interdependente da prática. Direito, Ética e Medicina encontram aqui uma plataforma de difícil convergência. Se, para o Direito, o apuramento de um culpado é pré-requisito de condenação, não será, no campo ético da ciência da moral e dos valores, justo não indemnizar os lesados, estes também sem culpa própria. Sendo o objectivo principal da Justiça promover a defesa dos cidadãos, que é um direito da sua própria cidadania, parecerá incoerente não poder, pela Justiça, compensar um utente lesado, sem culpa própria deste, e também sem culpa apurável por parte de outrem.

Relativamente à Medicina, a necessidade de apuramento de um culpado, perverte a necessidade de auto-revelação e de "disclosure", uniformemente aceites como imprescindíveis à gestão de risco e à Segurança dos Doentes -Culpa e Erro nunca se ligaram bem no âmbito da Medicina. Como poderíamos, assim, compatibilizar a necessidade imperiosa de promover a Segurança dos Doentes e a gestão do risco clínico, com a necessidade de indemnizar justamente os doentes lesados e salvaguardar os direitos da cidadania e a obrigação dos profissionais e das instituições de responderem isolada ou solidariamente, perante um dano produzido?.

Se dispuséssemos para a Medicina, pela especificidade e delicadeza da sua matéria, de um sistema de "no fault", ou seja, compensação fundada na socialização do risco em Saúde, como se dispõe nalguns países do Norte da Europa, na Nova Zelândia e na Austrália, poderíamos compatibilizar todos esses desidrata, indemnizando automaticamente e com base num seguro social. Um sistema deste tipo indemniza de imediato qualquer dano ocorrido, numa base de seguro, deixando para um segundo momento, a análise de uma eventual responsabilidade do profissional de saúde, e sem negar à família e ao doente o direito de acionamento da via jurídica (embora em alguns dos modelos existentes os lesados estejam impedidos de usar, ulteriormente, a via judicial) para fins de apuramento de responsabilidades e eventual indemnização acrescidas. Este modelo parecerá o mais adequado para lidar com a extrema complexidade do sistema de Saúde, no qual, mesmo em presença de uma total adequação de processos e do cumprimento da "arte", se obtém, por vezes, resultados indesejáveis, que requerem reparação. Como dizia William Osler, a *"Medicina é a Ciência do Incerto e a Arte da Probabilidade"* ora, para lidar com esta realidade precisar-se-ia de um sistema que substituísse uma cultura de "accountability" por uma cultura "just" – que punisse severamente a negligência mas desculpabilizasse o "erro honesto", responsabilizando--o, sim, numa perspetiva de aprendizagem e melhoria da segurança e, sobretudo, deixando o mecanismo de indemnização não dependente de um apuramento de culpas eventuais. Culpas que, na maior parte dos casos não chegam ou podem vir a ser imputadas. O sistema actual é moroso, dispendioso e, sobretudo, raramente indemniza o lesado, enquanto prejudica as estratégias de segurança na Saúde, para já não falar nas flagrantes discrepâncias na atribuição de ónus de culpa e determinação de responsabilidade médica, que se verificam nos diversos sectores da Saúde – privado e público, em regimes contractual e extra – contractual de prestação de cuidados. Com toda a modéstia, julgamos que este sistema deveria ser alterado, o mais rapidamente possível, também para bem da segurança dos doentes. Não sendo o modelo "no fault" isento de críticas, parecerá bem mais ajustado à realidade da Saúde, por não tornar dependente a indemnização de um doente lesado, do apuramento da culpa dos profissionais que o trataram.

Conclusões

A prestação de cuidados de saúde é exercida em sistemas de muita complexidade real – a natureza da doença e do doente, as falhas humanas e organizacionais, a par com graves defeitos de enfoque organizacional, contribuem para uma excessiva variabilidade de resultados, sinónimo de consequente má qualidade na prestação. Estes resultados, estão em flagrante contraste com outras áreas de actividade, como a aviação civil, onde a segurança é extrema.

A melhoria da segurança na Saúde só pode ser obtida imediatamente, mediante uma abordagem sistémica que privilegie o **sistema** e só será obtida de forma sustentada mediante o desenvolvimento de uma **cultura de segurança**. Ora os cuidados de Saúde são o exemplo de um sistema não tradicional, antes gerido em **complexidade,** que requer respostas modeladoras adequadas. Estas passam muito pela informação, pela dinâmica das equipas, no treino e na comunicação, e ainda pelo desenvolvimento de uma cultura própria, tal como a definimos acima.

Se é certo que o fenómeno da complexidade permite explicar, pelo menos em parte, a variação nos resultados em Saúde – variação expectada e variação indesejada, sendo esta cada vez mais atribuída à deficiente performance, também é certo que a complexidade poderá ser modelada, se o sistema for desenhado e gerido da forma adequada. Estes modelos, que pouco vemos ainda em uso no sistema, tal como o conhecemos hoje, mas que têm sido usadas com enorme eficácia nas organizações ditas fiáveis (aviação, industria química e militar....), devem agora passar a ser

A NATUREZA DE COMPLEXIDADE DOS SISTEMAS DE SAÚDE

aplicadas, também à Saúde, onde se espera venham a ter impacto igualmente favorável. Trata-se de tratar de forma diferente o que é diferente, e o sistema de Saúde é, na verdade, muito diferente dos tradicionais sistemas lineares. Este facto talvez explique tantas barreiras à mudança e tão pouco avanço efectivo, após tantas e tantas medidas tomadas desde a publicação, pelo IOM nos EUA, do livro "To Err is Human".

Uma vez que se aceite a Saúde como uma prática complexa e de risco, só virá como natural a introdução de um sistema de "no-fault", que permita indemnizar os lesados, mesmo na ausência de culpa, deixando mais espaço à investigação sobre a segurança na saúde, de forma a aprender e a melhorá-la, mantendo mesmo assim intactas todas as garantias de cidadania, por eventual recurso aos tribunais.

Agradecimento – Agradeço à Profª Doutora Vera Lúcia Raposo a revisão final do texto.

Bibliografia

FRAGATA J.-Segurança dos Doentes–Uma abordagem prática, LIDEL 2011

FRAGATA J. – Risco Complexidade e Performance. Edições Almedina 2006

ROUSE B. W. – Health Care as a Complex Adaptive System: Implications for Design and Management – The Bridge, Sring 2008

LIPSITZ L. A. Understanding Health Care as a Complexity System – JAMA, 2012; 308-3:243

STACEY R.D. Strategic Management and Organizational Dynamics: the challange of complexity – 4th ed. Harlow: Pearson Education Ltd 2003

ANDRÉ G. DIAS PEREIRA "Responsabilidade civil dos médicos: danos hospitalares – alguns casos da jurisprudência", Lex Medicinae – Revista Portuguesa de Direito da Saúde, Nº 7, 2007, 53-67

KUNZLE B et al – Ensuring Patient Safety through effective leadership behaviour: a literature review. Safety Science 2011; 48-1:1 – 17

To Err is Human, 1999 – Institute of Medicine

Patients' right to access to quality of healthcare throughout the european union: the role of eu legislation

PROF. DR. HENRIETTE ROSCAM ABBING[*]

I. Introduction

As a source of human capital, health has a value of its own. Good health is an essential condition for social cohesion. National health systems should guarantee quality and equity and be sensitive to the different needs of the population.[1] Patients' rights, patient centeredness and patient safety are important elements of quality of healthcare.

In geographically increasing the possibilities to receive good quality healthcare, the EU Directive on the application of patients' rights in cross-border healthcare[2] provides opportunities for improving health of the individual and of the population of a country. This includes possibilities for cross border e–and m– health, and also for outsourcing of health services (eg. laboratory services).

---

[*] Professor emerita of Health Law

[1] Conference report 'Health in Europe making it fairer', European Union, 18 March 2014, p. 11.

[2] Directive 2011/24/EU of 9 March 2011

DIREITO DA SAÚDE

Patients may unexpectedly require medical care during their stay in another Member State. They may also actively seek forms of healthcare in another country. For instance because the nearest possibility for an appropriate healthcare service is across the border, because they need highly specialised care not available in the country of affiliation, because they want to have a different method of treatment than that provided in the Member State of affiliation, or because they believe that they will receive better quality healthcare in another Member State. (whereas para. 39 Cross Health Care Border Directive). Possible impediments for patients to have timely access to cross border healthcare services should be removed.[3]

Not only patients, but also health professionals, medical diagnostic services, medical devices, medicaments and human bodily material increasingly cross European borders. This is supported by technological (ICT) developments.

The Cross Border Health Care Directive acknowledges the Member States' responsibility for providing safe, high quality, efficient and quantitatively adequate healthcare in accordance with Member States and Union legislation on safety standards.[4]

The European Union has an overall obligation to ensure a high level of human health protection in the definition and implementation of all Union policies, notably in the context of the functioning of the internal market and of the free movement of persons, goods and services (article 35 Charter of Fundamental Rights of the EU, article 168 TFEU).

As an effect of the Cross Border Directive, the legal duties and responsibilities of the European Union for safe health products and services have increased. Thus, the Commission has gradually broadened its activities in the field of patient safety to the field of quality of care.[5]

---

[3] Refund of expenses could for instance be guaranteed through special agreements in border regions. Régine Kiasuwa and Rita Baeten, Strategic positioning and creative solutions: French patient flows to hospitals and polyclinics in the Belgian Ardennes (Belgium–France), In: Hospitals and borders, seven case studies on cross border collaboration and health system interactions, edited by Irene A. Glinos, Matthias Wismar. Observatories studies series 31, World Health Organization 2013, Ch. 4, pp 91-73.

[4] Whereas para. 4, article 4.

[5] H. Vollaard et al. The emerging EU quality of care policy: From sharing information to enforcement. Health Policy (2013), http: //dx.doi.org/10.1016/j.healthpol.2013.05.004, p. 4.

Faulty quality of healthcare caused by for instance a medical error, an inefficient healthcare service, deficient medical devices, unsafe medication, human organs and tissues, and also disrespect for patients' individual rights (eg. informed consent, protection of private life) are serious threats to patient safety.

The Luxemburg Declaration on Patient Safety of April 2005[6] highlights the fact that access to high quality healthcare is a key human right to be valued by the EU. In Council Conclusions on Patient Safety (1-12--2014), the Commission is called upon to finalise by December 2016 a framework for a sustainable EU collaboration on patient safety and quality of care. According to the Council, activities in this field on the basis of art. 168, para. 3 Treaty of Lisbon must remain non-binding (soft law).

To attain safe, high quality, efficient, cost-effective and patient centered healthcare in the context of the EU, good quality, effective EU health legislation[7] is an essential condition. This particularly also where competitiveness of the European health industry, smooth functioning of the internal market and strengthening of the link between technological innovation and commercialisation are major drivers of revisions of health related EU legislation,[8] next to the re-establishment of the integrity of health systems and independent control bodies.[9, 10]

This contribution to Guilherme de Olieveira's Festchrift addresses the quality of EU health related legislative frameworks. It focuses on recent and current reforms of various legislative sectors. Of necessity, choices had to be made. In the following Chapters the EU regulatory agenda of healthcare quality (coordination or standardisation), legislative reforms relating to medical doctors, medicaments and medical devices will pass the review.

---

[6] The Declaration was the outcome of a conference held in Luxemburg, 4-5April 2005, under the auspices of the Luxemburg EU Presidency and the European Commission.

[7] Legislation in a 'broad sense': formal law (legally binding) as well as 'soft law' (not legally binding).

[8] See for instance the '*Health for Growth Programme, 2014 – 2020*'.

[9] European Commission, Study on corruption in the healthcare sector, Executive summary, HOME/2011/ISEC/PR/047 –A2, October 2013.

[10] Henriette D.C. Roscam Abbing, "Patients' Right to quality of healthcare: how satisfactory are the European Union's regulatory policies", *European Journal of Health Law* 19 (5) (2012) 415-422.

II. EU regulatory agenda of healthcare quality: coordination or standardisation?

II.1. General

Common values shared by EU Member States are necessary to ensure patients' trust in cross border healthcare. They must guarantee a high level of health protection, without which patient mobility within the EU would not be achieved. Each individual Member State is responsible for the practical ways in which the common values and principles are implemented.[11]

It follows from the Patient's Rights Cross Border Directive that it is for reference networks[12] to develop quality and safety benchmarks and to help develop and spread best practices within and outside the network.[13]An earlier draft of the Patients' Rights Cross Border Directive would have allowed the Commission further legislative interference, through the development of guidelines in cooperation with Member States.[14] But as was stated by the Standing Committee of European Doctors (Comite Permanent des Medecins Europeens (CPME)), an 'EU healthcare quality board' for the coordination of all EU initiatives in health care quality', a 'Health System Performance Analysis Framework' at EU level, and a leading role for the EU in the drafting of recommenda-

---

[11] Whereas para. 5 of the Patients' Rights in Cross Border Directive.

[12] 'Reference networks' refers to European reference networks between healthcare providers and centres of expertise in the Member States. (Article 12 of the Cross Border Directive) They are in particular focused on rare diseases. Their development is supported by the European Commission who adopts a set of criteria and conditions to be fulfilled by the networks and their participants (article 12, 2 under g Cross Border Directive). See Commission Delegated Decision, setting out criteria and conditions that European Reference Networks and healthcare providers wishing to join a European Reference Network must fulfil (2014/286/EU of 10 March 2014) and Commission Implementing Decision, setting out criteria for establishing and evaluating European Reference Networks and their members and for facilitating the exchange of information and expertise on establishing and evaluating such Networks (2014/287/EU).

[13] Standing Committee of European Doctors, CPME: response to the European Commission consultation on the preliminary opinion of the EXPH– Future EU Agenda on Quality of Care with special emphasis on Patient Safety, 009/108.

[14] H. Vollaard et al. The emerging EU quality of care policy: From sharing information to enforcement. Health Policy (2013), http://dx.doi.org/10.1016/j.healthpol.2013.05.004, p.5.

tions on health care quality, another suggestion by the EXPH,[15] would be contrary to the Treaty of Lisbon. *'European standards for technical qualifications, ethical requirements and professional regulations as well as for professional duties would infringe on the rights of Member States to independently organise and deliver health services and medical care as guaranteed by TFEU article 168.'*[16]

Instead, the CPME recommends the establishment of a European Reference Centre, a network for exchanging best practices regarding quality of care to facilitate comparison across health policies and their impact. Such a network could be used by Member States as a tool to support work at national level similar to the Health Technology Network (HTA). HTA is one of the fields where the Cross Border Directive foresees co-operation among Member States.[17] Moreover, for HTA to be useful, it should not comprise solely economic and financial factors, as suggested by the EXPH, but also ethical, legal, social and organizational aspects, as is rightly pointed out by the CPME[18]. It is important to realise that HTA is not only about costs involved with medical devices, medicaments and health technology per se. Health technology should be looked at in the context of healthcare interventions overall.[19]

II.2. Standardisation of health services

Because of the specificity of the sector, healthcare and pharmaceutical services provided by qualified professionals are excluded from the Directive 2006/123EC on services in the internal market.[20] Healthcare servi-

---

[15] Expert Panel on effective ways of investing in Health (EXPH), Preliminary report on the future EU agenda on quality of health care with a special emphasis on patient safety, Approved for public consultation, July 2014.
The EXPH was set up by Commission Decision 2012, C198/06. Health law is not included into the fields of expertise to be covered by the Panel.

[16] CPME Answer to the European Commission consultation on the preliminary opinion of the EXPH – Future EU Agenda on Quality of Care with special emphasis on Patient Safety, CPME/AD/EC/11.09.2014/076_Final.

[17] Article 15 of the Directive.

[18] Standing Committee of European Doctors, reply nr 078. Available on the EC Public Health website under Patient Safety.

[19] Miro Palat, Is HTA going to save healthcare budgets or are its premises inherently flawed, Eurohealth Vol 16 no 4, 2011, pp 8-17.

[20] Healthcare services provided by health professionals to patients to assess, maintain or restore their state of health where those activities are reserved to a regulated health profession.

ces cannot be equated to services that are purely commercial in nature. Nor is the demand and supply of healthcare services subject to conventional market forces or competitiveness, the purported drivers of standardisation. This also extends to the self-regulatory competence for the profession which may be established at national level.

In cross-border regions, healthcare co-operation is stimulated. But according to the before mentioned 2006 Council Conclusions on Common Values and Principles in European Union Health Systems, it is not appropriate to try to standardise health systems. Yet, currently attempts are noticeable to introduce standards in clinical medical care, developed by non-medical standardisation bodies "which neither have the necessary professional ethical and technical competencies, nor a public mandate".[21] The annual European Union programme of work on European Standardisation published in July 2013 includes a feasibility study for standardisation of healthcare services. Until now, the CEN (the European Standardisation body) has developed standards or technical specifications on a request of national standardisation bodies. Though its application remains voluntary, conflicting standards of national standardisation bodies have to be withdrawn. The purpose of the standards is to regulate the service provided, before, during and after an intervention, but not the clinical procedures.[22]

The Patient Cross Border Health Care Directive EU/2011/24 requires that Member States provide healthcare in accordance with standards and guidelines on quality and safety, inform patients about standards and guidelines in place, and work together on quality and safety standards and guidelines. But it does not specify what is meant by a standard.[23]

---

[21] World Medical Association, Council Resolution on Standardisation in Medical Practice and Patient Safety, 64th World Medical Association General Assembly, Brazil, October 2013.

[22] Information to patients, patient management/safety, good and best practices, education and training, competences, code of conducts and ethical framework, marketing and advertising. Source: CEN/CENELEC, Healthcare Services, European Standardization Activities, Cinzia Missiroli & Maitane Olabarria, CEN-CENELEC Management Centre, power point presentation, meeting of the Patient Safety & Quality of Care Working Group, Brussels, 14 February 2014.

[23] A standard is a technical specification adopted by a recognised standardisation body for repeated or continuous application with which compliance is not compulsory. Art. 2 Regulation 1025/2012.

Hence concerns for overlap with clinical standards and insufficient consultation with appropriate stakeholders.[24] On the other hand, it is questionable whether the Cross Border Directive can be considered as a legal basis to justify standardisation of healthcare services, as it is for Member States to ensure that healthcare services are provided in accordance with the standards and guidelines of quality and security in the Member State of treatment.[25]

Despite this, for instance the CPME remarks that standardisation by standardisation institutes has become increasingly present in healthcare systems. *"Traditionally, technical standardisation provided specifications ensuring the safety and universal applicability of products used in healthcare. It ensured that healthcare settings fulfilled physical requirements which constituted an appropriate framework for the delivery of healthcare. In contrast to these activities, recent initiatives in standardisation, also at EU level, have focussed not on the products and facilities supporting healthcare, but on the services delivered by healthcare professionals in patient care. This development can be seen in Regulation EU 1025/2012 on European Standardisation, which applies both to products and services.*

"While the practice of the medical profession is shaped by evidence-based guidelines and recommendations, an essential characteristic is the ability to divert from these guidelines when a doctor believes it to be in the best interest for a patient's individual care. Such professional autonomy is fundamental to ensure both quality of treatment and patients' rights. To ensure the quality of decision-making, professional autonomy is counterbalanced by professional liability. This balance is embedded in the regulatory framework of the profession, including monitoring and sanction mechanisms. Standards, such as those developed with the involvement of standardisation institutes, created outside of these structures cannot rely

---

[24] Katja Neubauer, Feasibility study on standardisation in the area of health services, Presentation at the meeting of the Patient Safety and Quality of Care Working group, Brussels, 14 February 2014. European Commission Public Health website, Patient Safety. See also European Commission, DG Enterprise and Industry, Sustainable Growth and EU 2020, Preliminary draft of the Annual Union Work Programme on European Standardisation, doc 04/2013 (Committee on Standards) .

[25] Article 4.1. under b of the Directive. This view was voiced by the French representative after the meeting of the Patient Safety and Quality of Care Working Group, 14 February 2014. See minutes of 13 March 2014, p. 5, point 5. Concerns were also voiced about possible conflicts of interest.

on these mechanisms, thus creating ambiguity as to their enforcement."[26] Hence CPME's insistence to exclude a feasibility study of healthcare services from the scope of the annual Union Programme on Standardisation.[27] On the other hand, such a study could be useful to draw a clear line between areas to be covered and not to be covered by CEN standards.[28] To ensure patient safety and high quality health care, the EU should '*continue to reflect local needs as well as unique characteristics on national (regional) health systems and respect the relevant national laws, professional self-regulation and ethical codes.*'[29, 30]

The insurance industry fears a strong negative effect on professional liability and hospital insurance as a consequence of standardisation of healthcare services. Medical treatment is not appropriately assessable by standardisation, a simple and general standardisation of healthcare services jeopardises the quality of healthcare, as it would jeopardize proper treatment and patients' safety.[31]

To avoid a potential hurdle of 'standardisation' of health services, the European Commission recently introduced the term "configuration" in relation to health services in border regions.[32]

---

[26] CPME, Standardisation of Healthcare Services, 2014, 021Final. Healthcare services cannot be equated with services in a purely economic context. See for instance CPME answer to the health services consultation SEC (2006) 1195/4, 26 January 2007.

[27] RA Birgit Beger, CPME Secretary General, Standards and HealthCare a norm for future medicine? Power Point presentation, EFMA Forum 2014, Belgrade, 14-3-2014. Ima.org.il

[28] Minutes meeting of the Patient Safety & Quality of Care Working Group, Brussels, 14 February 2014, adopted 13 March 2014, p. 4.

[29] Council of European Dentists, CED, General Meeting, Press Release, 25 November 2015.

[30] This situation is considered to be different for aesthetic services involving surgery and for other supplementary health-related services in particular important for the elderly. ANEC: The European consumer voice in standardisation; services, para 2,: health, care and support services. Brussels, 2015. www.anec.eu.

[31] German Insurance Association on Standardisation of medical treatment and (other) healthcare services at EU level, December 2014.

[32] European Commission, Expert Panel of Health on Effective Ways of Investing in Health, EXPH, Request for an opinion: Cross border cooperation. European Health Care news, no 33, March 2015.

III. EU regulatory agenda of healthcare quality: legislative reforms

III.1. health professionals

"In an environment where health professionals and patients are encouraged to move across Member States, a risk to patient safety in one Member State is potentially a patient safety risk in another Member State."[33]

The EU open market has the potential to contribute to the increase of equity in access to healthcare of good quality for European citizens.[34] One of the conditions to achieve this objective is that EU legislation adequately protects the patient against poorly performing health professionals.

Directive 2013/55/EC on the recognition of professional qualifications addresses a number of the weak spots in relation to patient safety in the former legislation.[35] Among the novelties introduced in the 2013 legislation are:

- a new 'fitness to practice' alert mechanism in the case of loss or restriction of a licence to practice (art. 56a),
- an EU wide recognition regime through the issuing of an European Professional Card,
- a requirement of necessary language knowledge when a health professional is seeking to practice in another Member State,
- a 'fast track' registration based on mutual recognition of professional qualifications,
- minimum education and training requirements for mutual recognition of professional qualifications,
- the requirement to share expertise on continuing professional development,
- the possibility of partial access.

It is left to the host Member States when implementing the Directive whether they will accept such a mechanism, or will exclude the

---

[33] General Medical Council response to the European Commission Consultation on Patient Safety and Quality of Healthcare, 28 February 2014, www.gmc-uk.org.

[34] Professional mobility can diminish this effect. This aspect is not dealt with.

[35] Effective 18 January 2016. The Directive allows for automatic recognition of qualifications of e.g. doctors, dentists, nurses and midwives. This article concentrates on medical doctors.

DIREITO DA SAÚDE

possibility.[36]The acceptance of partial accessibility entails special information duties towards the patient.[37]

Compatible (continued) education and training requirements are indispensable in the context of both patients' and doctors' mobility within the EU. Competence assurance must be based upon 'content' comparability rather than upon the length of training. [38],[39] It is for the European Commission to undertake a thorough audit of basic and specialist medical qualifications in Europe as a means of identifying and confirming 'content comparability'. "The findings should be used as a basis from which to periodically revise the recognition of professional qualifications legislation and to develop policies that reduce the risk that practitioners appear more qualified for certain posts than they are in practice, with the consequential risk to patient safety."[40]

The 'fitness to practice requirement' is another important, albeit most difficult to implement improvement of the new Directive. EU legislation in this field must guarantee patients that medical professionals who make use of their right of free movement within the EU are known to be appropriately qualified and fit to practice. The effectiveness of the requirement depends on the quality of the implementing acts.

For the sake of patient safety, the European Professional Card (EPC), foreseen in the new legislation, must include the specificity of the medical profession; robust document verification and fraud prevention procedures must be embedded in the secondary legislation introducing the EPC.[41] The EPC may increase collaboration between Competent

---

[36] CPME Newsletter issue 8, June 2013, p. 3.

[37] Medical migration within Europe: opportunities and challenges, Kate Ling, Paul Belcher, Clinical medicine 2014, vol. 14, no. 6, pp 630-632.

[38] General Medical Council (GMC) response to the European Commission consultation on patient safety and quality of healthcare, 28 February 2014, www.gmc-uk.org.

[39] European Union of Medical Specialists (UEMS) provides for standard setting and accreditation of CME/CPD.

[40] General Medical Council Response to the European Commission consultation on patient safety and quality of healthcare, 28 February 2014, www.gmc-uk.org.

[41] The European Network of Medical Competent Authorities (ENMCA) advises to have home competent authorities certify documents they have themselves issued (reducing workload for the host CA). See also ENMCA response to the implementing act on the European Professional Card and alert Mechanism, 9 February 2015.

Authorities (CA's). But the card also brings the challenge of finding the right balance between flexibility of the requirements for processing an application on the one hand and guarantees of the quality of the assessment on the other. The volume of alerts to be managed should in any case not play a role in the choice of the EPC system.[42]

Patients can only have justified trust in the EPC with a careful process of both recognition (of which the card is proof) on the one hand, and of granting access to the profession on the basis of essential patient safety checks on the other.[43]

Any envisaged system requires thorough testing prior to its entry into force.[44] This the more so, where as such the Qualification Directive is not destined for health professionals only, but has a much broader scope, designed from the perspective of increased competition and economic growth, strengthening the internal market. From the perspective of the patient, categorical legislation for health professionals would have been preferable.

Another tedious task under the new legislation is to establish an effective and efficient alert system through the Internal Market Information System (IMI) in case sanctions of a disciplinary or criminal nature or other kinds of lawful decisions impose constraints on the entitlement to practice the medical profession in the Member State of origin. The dysfunction of the alert system for medical doctors was one of the major shortcomings of the former Directive.[45] A related problem is that Member States' rules regarding revocation of licenses to practice and regarding warnings, differ.[46] Erasure or suspension from the medical register in Member States are not necessarily based on the same or comparable

---

[42] A concern expressed by ENMCA. See ENMCA analysis of responses to ENMCA questionnaire on the alert mechanism, July 2014.

[43] Several Member States grant recognition and access simultaneously. For that reason, in order to avoid confusion, third party accessibility should not be implemented for the medical profession. ENMCA response to the EC Professional card consultation, May 2014.

[44] CPME Response to the consultation on introducing the European Professional Card (EPC), 5 June 2014,, CPME/AD/Brd/05062014/057_Final/EN.

[45] Council Directive 93/16/ EC of 5 April 1993.

[46] H.D.C. Roscam Abbing, Quality of medical practice and professional conduct in the European Union, Molengraaff Intitute for Private law, Utrecht university, 1997. H.D.C. Roscam Abbing, the right of the patient to quality of medical practices and the position of migrant doctors within the EU, European Journal of Health Law, 1997, 347-360.

criteria. Differences exist in any case where ethical questions (like euthanasia and abortion) are in play.

The effectiveness of the alert system not only depends on the criteria for the type of sanctions to be included (eg. suspension, deprivation of licence, limitation of scope of professional activities), but also on the reasons for sanctioning a health professional. Host countries' must have the latitude to take into account in their admittance decisions possible ethical and moral reasons of the country of origin for barring a health professional from the legal exercise of his/her profession.

III.2. Medicaments

– General

"Regulators have a legal mandate to evaluate medicines. In doing so, they should only focus on the science and the best interests of patients. The decision-making process should be protected against external pressures from whatever direction. Once a decision has been reached, this consideration no longer applies."[47]

In the year 2015, the EU pharmaceutical legislation was 50 years in existence, the European Medicine Agency (EMA) 20 years.[48] The European system offers several routes for the authorisation of pharmaceutical products.[49] The centralised procedure is the task of the European

---

[47] EMA, European Medicines Agency policy on publication of clinical data for medicinal products for human use, 2-10-214, effective 1-1-2015, Policy/ 0070.

[48] The EU agency in charge of monitoring the safety of medicines.

[49] * The *centralised* procedure, which is compulsory for products derived from biotechnology, for orphan medicinal products and for medicinal products for human use which contain an active substance authorised in the Community after 20 May 2004 (date of entry into force of Regulation (EC) No 726/2004) and which are intended for the treatment of AIDS, cancer, neurodegenerative disorders or diabetes. The centralised procedure is also mandatory for veterinary medicinal products intended primarily for use as performance enhancers in order to promote growth or to increase yields from treated animals. Applications for the centralised procedure are made directly to the European Medicines Agency (EMA) and lead to the granting of a European marketing authorisation by the Commission which is binding in all Member States.

*. The *mutual recognition* procedure, applicable to the majority of conventional medicinal products, is based on the principle of recognition of an already existing national marketing authorisation by one or more Member States.

*. The *decentralised* procedure, which was introduced with the legislative review of 2004, is also applicable to the majority of conventional medicinal products. Through this procedure

Medicines Agency (EMA). The official standards published in the context of the European Pharmacopeia[50] provide a legal and scientific basis for quality control during the development, production and marketing processes.[51]

The EMA and the European Directorate for the Quality of Medicines (EDQM, Council of Europe) cooperate closely on matters aimed at ensuring the quality of medicines and protection of public health.[52] Compliance with Good Manufacturing Practices for medicinal products is granted with a certificate, ensuing inspections, and through control programmes.

an application for the marketing authorisation of a medicinal product is submitted simultaneously in several Member States, one of them being chosen as the "Reference Member State". At the end of the procedure national marketing authorisations are granted in the reference Member State and in the other concerned Member States. Purely national authorisations are still available for medicinal products to be marketed in one Member State only.

Companies can apply for the simultaneous authorisation of a medicine in more than one EU country if it has not yet been authorised in any EU country and it does not fall within the mandatory scope of the centralised procedure. Special rules exist for the authorisation of medicinal products for paediatric use, orphan drugs, traditional herbal medicinal products, vaccines and clinical trials.

[50] The European Pharmacopeia ensures the quality of pharmaceutical raw materials for the production of medicaments. The Pharmacopeia is based on an international binding Convention of the Council of Europe, destined for regulatory authorities, those engaged in quality control and manufacturers. The Pharmacopeia is elaborated since 1964 by the European Directorate for the Quality of Medicines and Health Care (EDQM) of the Council of Europe. EU pharmaceutical legislation makes direct reference to the European Pharmacopoeia and other activities under EDQM responsibility.

[51] Since 1994, the control programmes for the quality of raw materials used to manufacture medicines cover raw materials from all over the world. All producers of medicines and substances for pharmaceutical use must apply these quality standards in order to be able to market their products in the Signatory States of the Convention. This means that companies must follow these standards when applying to the EMA for admittance of a medicament in the central procedure, and include reference to the monographs in the quality part of their applications.

[52] In 2010, the first international treaty against counterfeit medical products involving threats to public health, including the marketing of medical devices that do not comply with conformity requirements, was drawn up by the Council of Europe.

DIREITO DA SAÚDE

Lack of transparency and insufficient independency of EMA as well as fraud and embezzlement in the sector of medicaments [53] were at the basis of a major revision of EU legislation for the pharmaceutical sector and of adaptation of EMA's policies.[54] The most important ones include

– Internet sales: cross border access to medicines
Internet is not only a forum for distribution of falsified medicines. [55] Medicaments that are legally on the market are also sold via internet. To allow the patient to identify legally operating online pharmacies/retailers of medicines, the EU legislator introduced an obligatory logo.[56] The logo provides patients with a mechanism to ensure that they are buying from a legally operating pharmacy or retailer; it also ensures the safety of the products being purchased. Each Member States has the right to impose certain conditions and limitations to the distribution of medicaments via internet, e.g. by not allowing online sale of prescription only medicines.[57]

[53] And also the medical devices sector. European Commission, "Study on corruption in the healthcare sector", Executive Summary, HOME/2011/ISEC7PR/047-A2, October 2013. See also H.D.C. Roscam Abbing, Patients' Right to Quality of Health Care: How satisfactory are the European Union's Regulatory Policies, European Journal of Health Law 19 (2012), pp. 415-422.
[54] The monitoring of medicines has been strengthened. The competent authorities must be informed of reasons for stopping the marketing of a product and an urgent Union procedure must be initiated in the case of serious safety risks with regard to a medicinal product. More medicinal products then before are automatically put on a special monitoring list (publicly available), since 2013 recognisable by a black inverted triangle as symbol.
[55] Manufacturers and distributors are obliged to report any suspicion of falsified medicines. The first international treaty against counterfeit medicinal products and similar crimes involving threats to public health, the so called Medicrime Convention, was drawn up by the Council of Europe (2010). The Convention covers the supply and trafficking in counterfeit medical products, the falsification of documents, the unauthorised manufacturing or supplying of medical products as well as the marketing of medical devices that do not comply with conformity requirements. The follow up of the Convention is ensured by a special committee.The Convention also lays down a framework for national and international co-operation between the competent health, police and customs authorities on both the national and international levels, measures for crime prevention by also involving the private sector, and the effective prosecution of crime and the protection of victims and witnesses.
[56] Directive 2011/62/EU on falsified medicines and its implementing Regulation 669/2014.
[57] Article 30 EC Treaty cannot be relied upon to justify an absolute prohibition on the sale by mail order of medicinal products which are not subject to prescription in the Member State Concerned. Case C-322/1, Deutscher Apothekerverband eV v 0800Doc Morris NV and Jacques Waterval, 2003.See also Nicolas de Sadeleer, Restrictions of the sale of

The diversity of national systems and approaches towards the disposability of medicaments allow patients to have cross border access (via internet) to medicines without prescription, in a situation where the product in question is a prescription only medicine in the country of affiliation.[58] But under those circumstances refund is not guaranteed. The considerable variety in availability of non-prescription medicines within the EU Member States is an indication of a different appraisal of the safe and appropriate use of a medicine without medical supervision. EU legislation has not (yet) aligned the national policies in this respect. This issue deserves to be looked into form the perspective of patient safety.

– 'Off label' use of medicines
Another issue of concern is the use of 'off label' medicines. In times of financial shortages, 'off label' use of medicines[59] is considered one of the possibilities to ensure patients (equal) access to medicines. Though it falls outside the formal EU regulatory system, 'off label' use is not against the law. But it leaves the responsibility and hence the burden of proof with the physician.[60] Medicines used 'off-label' are not systematically tested to the same stringent standards for the off-label indication as is required for authorized medicines. Therefore, 'off-label' use is likely to be financially advantageous for Member States. Pharma is of the opinion that Member States' promotion of 'off-label' use purely for economic reasons would put patients at unnecessary risk as it challenges the European regulatory standards.[61]But an extensive use of an 'off label' pratice may also be a sign of an overly rigid regulatory system.[62]

pharmaceuticals and medical devices such as contact lenses over the internet and the free movement of goods, EJHL, 19, no. 1, March 2012, pp 3-28.

[58] Report of the Working Group on promoting good governance of non-prescription drugs in Europe, Final, adopted by the Steering Group on 17-4-2013.

[59] Off label use of medicines is the use of medicines for an indication for which they do not have marketing authorisation.

[60] Christian Lenk, Gumar Duttge, o.c. footnote 55, p. 540.

[61] French law approved in 2014 broadens the use of off – label medicines, under a temporary authorisation for use, RTU, even if a therapeutic alternative is available, provided that this alternative does not have the same active substance, dosage and pharmaceutical form. Article L5121-12-1 PHC specifies that only therapeutic considerations should guide the prescription of a medicinal product under RTU. The new law further requires that prescription of a medicinal product under RTU be made after a thorough examination of the

DIREITO DA SAÚDE

– Transparency and accountability, pricing and reimbursement policies vs timely market access

According to a 2014 study by the Dutch National Institute for Public Health and Environment (RIVM) on sustainability of the EU regulatory system for pharmaceuticals, "the dual objectives of the system of protection of public health and safeguarding the interests of the European pharmaceutical industry, is the cause of permanent tension. Transparency and accountability not only by the regulators (including EMA), but also by the pharmaceutical industry are indispensable."

Safety and efficacy, innovation, costs and availability of (new) medicinal products are strongly interdependent themes. Interventions in one theme will have an effect on another one. "The lack of transparency and accountability both in the pharmaceutical industry and among regulatory authorities leads to public distrust in the system. It also hinders innovation, raises costs and restricts the availability of necessary pharmaceuticals."

According to the RIVM report, the European regulatory system has been built on the pillars of 'public health' and 'economic interests'. It guarantees on the one hand the safety of medicines available on the market. It safeguards at the same time, the interests of the European pharmaceutical industry. This dual nature of the regulatory regime causes tension between economic interests and public health, which is a constant factor in the policymaking process surrounding pharmaceuticals. Legislation should keep pace with (fast) changes in society and adopt societal dynamics.

Establishing a robust baseline of transparency and accountability is a prerequisite for success. There ought to be a balance between ensuring medicine safety on the one hand, the need to promote innovation, to ensure availability and contain costs on the other.[63]

---

patient and based on the patient's specific medical needs.When Italy followed this example in 2015, Pharma filed a complaint to the European Commission against an Italian law promoting the use of medicines for an indication for which they do not have a marketing authorisation, purely for economic reasons. EUCOPE press releases 11 July 2014 and 26 February 2015.

[62] Christian Lenk, Gunnar Duttge, Ethical and legal framework and regulation for off-label use: European Perspective, Therapeutics and Clinical risk Management, 2014, nr 10, 537.

[63] RIVM study-report 'Minds open: sustainability of the European Regulatory System for Medicinal Products', 2014, nr. 0033, summary p. 8 -10.

This brings me to decisions on pricing and reimbursement of medicinal products.[64] Marketing authorisation decisions being more or less uniform in the EU, the same does not hold for the national pricing and reimbursement decisions for pharmaceuticals.[65] Different pricing regimes may stimulate cross border "shopping". 'Off label' use of medicaments under the title of 'compassionate use'[66] does not take away the primary causes for 'off label' use: current pricing systems of pharmaceutical industry, coupled with refund systems in times of economic austerity and absence of transparency. When looked upon from that perspective, it is rather unfortunate that in 2014, the Commission dropped its 2012 proposal for a Directive relating to transparency of measures regulating the prices of medicinal products for human use,[67] as being too controversial for Member States. The Directive's purpose was to further foster both the functioning of the Internal Market (preventing pricing and reimbursement discrimination against imported medicinal products and ensuring objective and verifiable criteria) and faster access for patients to drugs. Timely access to medicines is often delayed by lengthy, sometimes complex procedures of pricing and reimbursement decisions. As a result, Member States unnecessarily exceed the mandatory time limits for pricing and reimbursement decisions.[68] Moreover, in some countries, pricing restrictions are based on HTA procedures which aim at determining the benefit for patients, where in other countries the restrictions are based on reference pricing schemes. The system of pricing for innovative products in Europe should not be based on the assumption

[64] Likewise, the system of pricing and reimbursement for medical devices is the exclusive competence of the EU Member States. Similar questions of pricing and refund of pharmaceuticals rise in relation to medical devices.

[65] These decisions are of national competence. Commission Staff Working Document, Pharmaceutical Industry: a strategic sector for the European economy, Brussels, SWD (2014) 216, final 2 of ! August 2014.

[66] Article 83, subsection 2 EU Regulation 726/2004: Humanitarian reasons to a group of patients suffering from a debilitating and chronic or serious illness or whose disease is considered to be life-threatening.

[67] The proposal was an update of the 1989 Directive "relating to the transparency of measures regulating the pricing of medicinal products for human use and their inclusion in the scope of national health insurance system." MEMO/12/148,Brussels,1 March 2012.

[68] Impact Assessment Proposal Transparency Directive for Medicinal Products, 1-3-2012, SWD (2012) 30 Final, Part I, prices and refund, p. 11.

that innovation is a mere cost factor, but rather on the fact that – next to improving patients' health – innovation is a driver of competitiveness and economic growth. Improving patients access to innovative medicines will not occur unless a balance is struck between the objectives of rewarding innovation, improving patients access to innovative medicines and controlling healthcare reimbursement on the basis of comparative effectiveness.[69] The contribution of a new drug to patients' health is a factor of consideration. Without a transparency directive budgetary constraints still have to be met, while patients at the same time must have access to therapeutically necessary medicines. Therefore, in an attempt to somehow align pricing strategies at the occasion of the launch of a new product, the Pharmaceutical Forum Working Group on Pricing and Reimbursement made public in 2014 their 2012 'Guiding Principles for good practices implementing a pricing and reimbursement policy'. A relevant quote from the document: "Member States are not interested in fixing prices of products that are only transiting through their territory to be utilised within other Member States. They should, therefore, abstain from fixing prices for products that will not be used within their territory and that will not impact on their national budgets." [70]

– Clinical trials (medicines) and transparency

Next to fostering innovation through simplification of the clinical trial process, the increase of transparency and availability of information on clinical trials and their results are among the major objectives of the recent EU Clinical Trials Regulation 536/2014. [71, 72, 73]

---

[69] Thomas B. Cueni, Can Europe afford innovation? Eurohealth 2008, vol.4, no 2, pp 8-10.

[70] Guiding principles for good practices implementing a pricing and reimbursement policy, document date 2-9– 2008, published 19-11-2014. ,

[71] At the earliest applicable as of 28th May 2016.

[72] Important instruments for transparency are a clinical trial portal, a database of clinical trial applications and authorisations within the EU.

[73] The Regulation gives the European Commission the power to adopt a variety of delegated and implementing acts as well as guidelines: a Delegated Act to specify the principles and guidelines of Good Manufacturing Practice (GMP) and detailed arrangements for inspections of investigational medicinal products (Article 63 of the Regulation); an Implementing Act on detailed arrangements for inspections procedures on Good Clinical Practice (GCP), including qualifications and training requirements for inspectors (Article 78 of the Regulation); guidelines on voluntary sharing of raw data (Article 37(4) of the

EMA's transparency policy on pharmaceutical data that entered into force the first of January 2015[74] relates to clinical data, composed of clinical reports and individual patient data (IPD), submitted under the centralised marketing authorisation procedure. This is distinct from EMA's policy on access to documents related to medicinal products for human and veterinary use.[75]

EMA's international cooperation in the regulation of clinical trials must also prevent situations where drugs have to be suspended. As was the case with drugs marketed by one of the largest Indian generic drug companies after findings of drugs having been manipulated by an Indian biosciences contract research organisation acting on behalf of marketing authorisation holders.[76] Marketing authorisation applications for medicines from outside the EU/EEA submitted to the EU regulatory authorities are only accepted for medicinal products for human use on the condition of proof that the products are based on clinical trials submitted to an ethics committee that operates within an established regulatory framework with ethical standards equivalent to those applying in the EU. In relation herewith, reference is made not only to e.g. the Declaration of Helsinki (2008), but also to the Convention on Human Rights and Biomedicine (1977) and the Protocol to it on Biomedical Research (2005).[77] In my opinion, such an approach should also be followed in the Transatlantic Trade and Investment partnership (TTIP) negotiations between the EU and the USA. To be in compliance with the Treaty of Lisbon,

---

Regulation). The Regulation also empowers the Commission to adopt an Implementing Act on cooperation between Member States in the assessment of the information on safety reporting (Article 44 of the Regulation). The adoption of this act is at the Commission's discretion.

[74] 2 October 2014, EMA 24810/2013

[75] Policy 0043, effective since 1 December 2010.

[76] C&EN web date 28 January 2015, Europe seeks drug suspensions of pharmaceuticals tested by GVKL biosciences, drugs: Jean-Francois Tremblay. As data– manipulation had been found during an inspection, the Committee for medicinal products for human use (GHMP) recommended suspension, unless the drugs were critical for patients (decision left to national authorities). There was no evidence of harm or lack of efficiency linked to the studies. Following the CHMP's January 2015 recommendation, some marketing authorisation holders have requested a re-examination.

[77] European Medicines Agency, Reflection Paper on ethical and GCP aspects of clinical trials of medicinal products for human use conducted outside of the EU/EEA and submitted in marketing authorisation applications to the EU Regulatory Authorities.

the pre-cautionary principle should be the main guiding principle in the regulatory cooperation.[78]

The EU Clinical Trial Regulation[79] applies to interventional studies with medicaments, including medicinal products incorporated into medical devices, but not to the device itself.

The Regulation seeks to strike the right balance between transparency and public access, the need to protect the economic interests of companies and research organisations, so that they are not placed at a competitive disadvantage. It also addresses the need to protect patient privacy.[80]

As to the sharing of patient-level data, the EMA favors a prudent approach. "There are ways and means to anonymise data and protect patients from retroactive identification. Yet, the Agency is primarily concerned that emerging technologies for data mining and database linkage will increase the potential for unlawful retro-active patient identification. The Agency, therefore, takes a guarded approach to the sharing of patient-level data, which is done to enable legitimate learning from sharing patient-level data while preventing rare but potentially damaging instances of patient identification. Furthermore, patients' informed consent should be respected. Secondary analysis of personal data will have to be fully compatible with the individual privacy of clinical trial participants and data protection.[81]

The European Federation of Pharmaceutical Industries and Organisations (EFPIA) welcomed the legislative approach to transparency, which respects the need to protect personal patient data as well as commercially confidential information (CCI). CPME on the other hand insists that all results of clinical trials, whether they are positive, negative or inconclusive should be made publicly available. Clinical trial data should

---

[78] Members of EU Parliament (ENVI) vote of 15 April 2015

[79] Regulation 536/2014 (applicable 28 May 2016).

[80] All information in the EU database submitted in the clinical trials application and during the assessment procedure shall be in principle publically accessible unless the confidentiality of the information can be justified on the basis of any of the following grounds: protection of commercially confidential information; protection of personal data; protection of confidential communication between the MS in relation to the preparation of the assessment report; ensuring effective supervision of the conduct of clinical trial by Member States.

[81] European Medicines Agency Policy on publication of clinical data for medicinal products for human use, 2-10-2014, EMA/240810/2013, p. 4.

not be considered commercially confidential once a marketing authorization has been obtained. "The legitimate economic interest of the sponsor should be defined in a restrictive way, the overriding public interest in a broad manner."[82] Once a clinical trial has led to marketing authorization, data generated during the clinical trial should be fully accessible. EMA has to provide for transparency of all documents, exceptional cases excepted.[83]

It is a balancing act between commercially confidential information and the general public's right to access documents. Pharmaceutical enterprises have interests that are not necessarily in line with those in need of safe medication of good quality. Transparency of clinical trial data on medicines is of prime importance for protecting health of the individual; transparency reinforces evidence-based medicine.[84]

III.3. Medical devices

The term 'medical device' covers a vast range of products from scalpels and sticking plasters to spinal implants and heart valves. Also included are drug delivery devices such as infusion pumps and tubing sets. Hence the division of medical devices into risk classes. Implants, invasive devices and other devices that pose a risk for safety are so-called class III devices.

The Regulatory approach of medical devices is different from the one on medicines. This is apparent already by the fact that medicaments fall under the DG health, while medical devices are placed under the DG internal market. The governance structure for medical devices itself is

---

[82] CPME response to the EMA public consultation 'draft proposal for an addendum on transparency to the functional specifications for the EU portal and EU database to be audited – EAMA/42176/2014, CPME 2015/008 FINAL, 12 February 2015.

[83] See for instance EMA's letter to the European Ombudsman of 30 January 2015 (EMA554447/2015). Clinical reports are not considered commercially confidential, apart from some very limited clinical information when the Agency does some redaction. This is a dynamic process. The Agency also publishes each month an overview listing all safety signals discussed in the Pharmacovigilance Risk Assessment Committee (PRAC) meeting and the recommendations given to them (centrally and nationally authorised medicines). Since January 2015, recommendations for updates of product information are translated into all official European Union (EU) languages.

[84] HAI Europe, protecting citizens' health: transparency of clinical trial data on medicines in the EU, Policy Paper, October 2013.

rather different from the one for pharmaceuticals. The latter being a combination of a decentralised marketing authorisation and a centralised structure, based on the nature of the medicament, the system for medical devices under legislative regime of Directives a decentralised one.[85]Assessment of medical devices takes place in the Member States either by the manufacturer or by a 'Notified Body', and by evaluation of the clinical data by the 'Competent Body' (CE-Marking).[86] As a consequence, national systems lack heterogeneity. This negatively affects the quality of data in the European databank, Eudamed.

Another difference when compared to the pharmaceutical sector is that medical devices do not have a ten-year exclusivity and market protection. For both systems intellectual property, data protection issues and clinical investigations are relevant.

The 2012 reform proposal of the European Commission for the medical devices legislative regime was triggered by the failure of the legislative system to ensure patient safety. Another reason was the necessity to anticipate on new technological developments that bring safety and data security risks, eg. networked devices and other mobile health technologies (mHealth). Innovation brings the need for improved device scru-

---

[85] Directive 90/385 Active Implantable Devices, Directive 93/42 Medical Devices, Directive 98/79, IVD medical devices. The Directives will be replaced by Regulations (a process started since 2012). The new regime is planned to be effective as of 2016. At the moment of writing this contribution (early 2015), decisions on a partially centralised system still have to be taken.

[86] A Competent Authority is a body with authority to act on behalf of the Member State to ensure that Member States transposes requirements of the medical devices Directives into their national law and apply them. The Competent Authority reports to the Minister of Health of its Member State.

A Notified Body is a public or private organisation that has been accredited by a European's Member State Competent Authority, to validate the compliance of the device to the European Directive, i.e. to determine if a product or system meets applicable requirements for CE marking. To be able to make this decision, a consultation process takes place, such as that defined in Annex II section 4.3 of the Medical Device Directive 93/42/EEC. The involvement of a Competent Authority to verify the quality, safety and usefulness of the medicinal substance when this is an integral part of the medical device, is necessary. The opinion given by the Competent Authority should be taken into account in the overall assessment made by the Notified Body.

Medical devices that pertain to class I (on condition they do not require sterilization or do not measure a function) can be marketed by self-certification.

tiny and health information protection, so as to better protect patients' health.[87] In this new context, the legislative framework for medical devices technology requires a heterogeneous approach by Member States. This explains the Commission's move towards the Regulation as legislative instrument.

Under the new legislative regime, the scope of the medical devices legislation is extended to implants for aesthetic purposes, and – in the case of in vitro diagnostic medical devices – to tests providing information about the predisposition to a disease (e.g. genetic tests). Mobile health apps also may fall under the medical devices regulatory system (as a means necessary for the proper functioning of the device or as an accessory to the device).[88] The new legislative regime includes rules for increased control of the supply chain, traceability of medical devices back to the suppliers (unique device identification), a comprehensible and interoperable European databank, accessible for the public and health professionals.[89] The system must meet the expectations about a European databank in terms of completeness, data quality, interlinkage and transparency.

Next to this, the Regulation foresees new accreditation requirements and stronger supervision of independent conformity assessment bodies (Notified Bodies) by national authorities, additional powers for Notified Bodies vis-à-vis the manufacturers, including unannounced inspections in factories, safety and clinical performance reports of all class III + implantable devices, and liability insurance of the manufacturer.

The Medical Devices legislation ought to be sufficiently waterproof to cover safety concerns arising from reprocessing single-use medical

---

[87] Public concerns were raised by the scandal of a French manufacturer using industrial silicone for breast implants in France.

[88] The EU Article 29 Working Party ("WP29") has clarified the scope of Health Data processed by lifestyle and well-being apps in a letter to the European Commission of 5 February 2015. The Annex to the letter contains criteria to determine when personal data qualify as 'health data'.

[89] The European Databank on Medical Devices (EUDAMED), Commission Decision 9 April 2010, (2010/2363), operative since 2011, is a tool for transparency and market surveillance enhancement in the Member States. Commission Decision 9 April 2010, (2010/2363). According to the internal evaluation of EUDAMED of 11 October 2012, undertaken in the context of the new legislative framework for medical devices, EUDAMED should become a more comprehensive and transparent information system on medical devices.

devices through conformity assessments and controls. Not all devices are apt for re-use.

The pre– and post-marketing systems for higher risk medical devices under the new regime should be efficient and effective. The main instruments in this respect are Special Notified Bodies (fulfilling special requirements) designated by the European Medicines Agency to assess conformity of all high risk and implantable devices, improved post-market clinical evaluation class IIII devices through pooling of expertise, as well as – most contested during the legislative process –an independent central scrutiny of potentially high risk devices.[90]

Where the approval process of medical devices lays with the Notified Bodies, the responsibility for the post-marketing surveillance is incumbent upon the Competent Authorities. They are the ones who have to follow legally binding requirements for the clinical follow-up studies.[91]

A newly created Medical Device Coordination Group (MDCG) should facilitate a harmonised interpretation of the rules. Arguments held by the medical devices industry against an opinion by a central committee of specialists for all high risk medical devices on the basis of a systematic assessment of clinical data, especially when binding for the notified bodies, are mostly the delays for patients' treatment, extra costs and administrative burdens it would involve. [92] This preference for only a post-market mechanism for medical devices is understandable as financial gains are in principle faster made with post marketing assessments than with pre-market approvals. However, more often than not, this effect is annulled by delays in reimbursement decisions, as in the case of pharmaceuticals mainly caused by an increased demand for health

---

[90] With a role for the MDCG coordination Group. Progress report prepared by the Presidency with a view to the meeting of the Council (EPSCO) on 1 December 2014, 25 November 2014, 15881/14. A suggested way forward towards systematic guarantees of a high quality and independent clinical review could be the creation of a new EU level Register of Clinical Experts, controlled by the MDC and the Commission, and vetted by authorities, who will independently evaluate the manufacturer's clinical evidence as part of the conformity assessment process.

[91] Separate Annex (XIII -B) to the Medical Device Regulation.

[92] Dagmar Roth-Behrendt, Regulating Medical Devices: a Harsh Fight for more Patient Safety, The European Files, December 2013/January 22015, pp. 23-25.

technology assessments of products already admitted to the market, thereby delaying commercial benefits.[93]

To guarantee patients a high level of health protection, a centralised admittance system[94] for high risk devices, including high risk in vitro diagnostic devices (genetic testing) as in the USA,[95] would be the safest way forward, consistent with the pre-cautionary principle. For the sake of patient safety, a centralised admittance system for high risk medical devices, combination products and high risk IVD's is preferable to a system whereby the Notified Bodies – even if they must comply with specific requirements – would be the only ones responsible for the assessment. Binding, impartial expert opinions prior to a marketing authorisation are indicated for all high risk class III medical devices/IVD's and not only for implantable high risk class III devices, as voted for by the European Parliament.[96]

The greater the risk posed by a medical technology, the more stringent the rules should be. The legislation should take the nature of the risk into account (eg. clinical evidence and post marketing follow-up (safety risk assessments)). There is no reason not to align the legislative approach for high risk medical devices and high risk IVD's (such as genetic tests) to the legislative approach for pharmaceuticals (e.g. regarding a central admittance system, internet sales and especially for high risk IVD's a prescription only requirement, a prohibition of direct to consumer advertising, provision of scientific based product information). With a condition of prescription only, requirements such as in the case of genetic tests IVD's genetic counselling and informed consent, can be appropriately met.

---

[93] Australian Government, Department of Health and Ageing, Therapeutic Goods Administration, Changes to pre-market assessment requirements for medical devices, Regulation impact statement, 26 June 2013.

[94] Evaluation of the clinical dossier by a special independent group of experts, with a flexible composition, depending on the required expertise. The outcome of the evaluation should have binding effect.

[95] The EU's lower approval standard and private party review implies that high risk devices come earlier on the market than in the USA.

[96] See for instance European Patient Forum, EPF Recommendations for Council Common Position on Medical devices, 2014, www.eu.patient.eu.

As with pharmaceuticals, the outcomes of clinical investigations are the primary basis for the scrutiny of medical devices/IVD's. Here also, for the sake of legal clarity and patient safety, clinical trials with high risk (implantable) devices and high risk IVD's should as far as possible follow the same legislative approach as for medicaments. As in the case of medicaments, public availability of the outcome of the scrutiny through the EUDAMED system is an essential condition. [97,98] Eventually, a periodic re-examination of clinical tests performed on high risk devices (post-marketing studies with a focus on safety and vigilance) could make the system more flexible and adaptable to the fast moving field of medical device technology.[99]

The admittance system must be efficient (avoiding bureaucracy) and adequate to respond to new (expected) developments, in particular those in the field of networked devices and other (m) health technologies. As with pharmaceuticals, EU level decision making for high risk medical devices/IVD's is the best guarantee for patient safety; it also has a simplification effect and is economic advantageous, where central decisions avoid undertakers a patchwork of national laws.[100]

IV. Final remark

"To face up to the challenges ahead of us, policies, laws and regulations need to adapt to the fast pace of technological change, to foster innovation, to protect the welfare and safety of Europeans. This is the standard

---

[97] EUDAMED is an information system for exchanging legal information related to the application of European Union legislation on medical devices between the European Commission's Enterprise and Industry Directorate General and the Competent Authorities in the European Union Member States. The Regulation adapts the EUDAMED system.

[98] Device specific approach, setting clear, attainable and scientifically valid requirements for devices as suggested by Eucomed. Eucomed, The revision of the EU Medical Devices Directives, 1 April 2014, p.4-6.

[99] Nora Berra, Should we set up a premarket authorizations for high risk medical devices? The European Files, December 2013/January 2014, p. 37.

[100] IVD's are a special category of devices. Unlike for other medical devices or pharmaceuticals, it is the nature of the information which is being collected that determines the risk posed by the IVD medical device, not the direct effect of the intervention on the patient. While IVDs do not provide any treatment, they are essential for managing healthcare decisions. This calls for a focus on quality of information provided to patients, also in the case of self-testing.

which the European Commission has set itself, and this is why we have made Better Regulation one of our core priorities."[101]

Where health has become a lucrative market, and healthcare and health research increasingly become commercialised, only good quality EU health – legislation can guarantee patients equity in a access, patient safety and quality of care. EU health legislation must be regularly assessed for its effectiveness in that respect.

[101] European Commission, Better Regulation – simply explained, 2006.

The information rights of the patient in the European Patients' Rights Directive

HERMAN NYS*

I. Introduction

On 9 March 2011 the European Parliament and the Council adopted Directive 2001/24/EU on the application of patients' rights in cross-border healthcare (hereinafter: Patients' Rights Directive – PRD).[1] It entered into force on 24 April 2011[2] and had to be implemented by the Member States by 25 October 2013.[3] The PRD contains five chapters dealing with or containing (I) (general) provisions on its scope, relationship with other provisions of EU law and definitions, (II) responsibilities of Member States with regard to cross-border healthcare, (III) reimbursement of the costs of cross-border healthcare, (IV) cross-border cooperation and (V) implementing and final provisions. This contribution mainly deals with chapter II, the responsibilities of the Member States with regard to cross-border healthcare. 'Taking account of the principles of universali-

---

* Professor of Health Law, University of Leuven, Belgium
Member, European Group on Ethics, EU

[1] *OJ L* 2011, 88/45. Other abbreviations are, depending on the perspective 'Patient Mobility Directive' and 'Patient Directive'.

[2] Article 22 PRD.

[3] Article 21.1 PRD.

DIREITO DA SAÚDE

ty, access to good quality care, equity and solidarity' (article 4.1 PRD) the PRD imposes on the Member States of Treatment (MST) duties to ensure that there are available transparent complaint procedures to patients suffering harm arising from healthcare received and systems of professional liability insurance. In addition, there must be available systems of professional liability, the fundamental right to privacy with respect to the processing of personal data must be respected and, to ensure continuity of care, patients will have to be given a written or electronic medical record of treatment received. Moreover both the Member State of Affiliation (MSA) and the MST and the healthcare providers established in a MST have informational responsibilities. From the point of view of patients, these responsibilities may be considered as patients' rights.

This contribution deals in particular with the informational responsibilities of the Member States or the informational rights of patients. In the next paragraph I will shortly present efforts in the past to protect and stimulate patients' rights in the European Union. Next follows a paragraph on the legal basis of the Directive followed by a paragraph on whether these patients' rights only profit to mobile patients or also to domestic patients. Then I will move on to the informational rights followed by concluding remarks.

II. European Charters on Patients' Rights

On 19 January 1984 the European Parliament approved a resolution on a European Charter on the Rights of Patients.[4] This resolution invited the Commission to submit as soon as possible a proposal for a European Charter on the Rights of Patients. The Resolution also stressed that this Charter must incorporate different rights, including 'the right to information concerning diagnosis, therapy and prognosis, the patient's right of access to his own medical data, and the patient's right to give his consent to or refuse the treatment proposed'. However, the Commission did not respond to this invitation. In the following years the Parliament approved other resolutions for special categories such as hospitalized children (1986), women who recently gave birth to a child (1988) and disabled persons (1995). These Charters had only a declaratory and no legally binding value. The *Active Citizenship Network* established in 2002

---

[4] *OJ C* 1984, 46, 103-105.

the 'European Charter on Patients' Rights'. Article 3 determines that 'Every individual has the right to access to all kind of information regarding their state of health, the health services and how to use them, and all that scientific research and technological innovation makes available'.[5] This version of the Charter has been 'welcomed' and 'acknowledged' by the European Economic and Social Committee in its Opinion on 'Patients' rights'.[6] The European Commission motivated the *Active Citizenship Network* to approve a final version of the Charter which happened on 18 April 2008.[7] Because of its lack of competence (see below) the Commission used an innovative method: instead of adopting a legally binding act it stimulated a citizens' organization to adopt a Charter.[8] Although not legally binding, the Charter has the merit that it clarifies what European citizens may expect regarding patient's rights in all Member States of the Union.

III. The legal basis of the Directive

The Directive has a dual legal basis, namely articles 114 and 186 TFEU.[9] Article 114 is the appropriate legal basis since the majority of the provisions of this Directive aim to improve the functioning of the internal market and the free movement of goods, persons and services (recital 2). This is justified by the fact that although the *Kohll and Decker* jurisprudence of the European Court of Justice on cross-border care, clarified patients' rights, they have not proven sufficient in and of themselves to enable patients to avail themselves of these rights widely or in an effec-

---

[5] Active Citizens' Network, European Charter of Patients' rights, Rome, 15 November 2002 www.activecitizenship.net.

[6] *OJ C* 2008, 10/68.

[7] As requested by the European Economic and Social Committee in its Opinion on Patients' Rights, 18 April has been established as yearly 'European Patients' Rights Day'.

[8] Based on E.RIAL-SEBBAG, G.CHASSANG en F. TABOULET, « Quelle gouvernance pour les droits de patients en Europe? », *Revue des affaires européennes* 2011, afl. 3, 559; see also X.BIOY, « Le droit fondamental à l'accès aux soins en Europe. Vers un standard de conciliation entre libertés économiques et droits du patient? », *Revue des affaires européennes* 2011, afl.3, 501.

[9] S. DE LA ROSA, "The Directive on cross-border healthcare or the art of codifying complex case law", *Common Market Law Review* 2012, 27; otherwise, M.PEETERS, "Free movement of patients: Directive 2011/24 on the application of patients' rights in cross-border healthcare", *European Journal of Health Law* 2012, 33: 'The legal base remains only the internal market (Article 114 TFEU) despite political pressure to install a dual basis by adding public health as legal base (Article 168 TFEU)'.

tive manner.[10] The reference to article 114 would arguably have sufficed. The reference to article 168 TFEU, added by the Council on first reading, does not by itself justify the inclusion of binding rules in the Directive inasmuch as the normative competence that this provision grants to the Union does not cover the movement of patients. The reference to article 168 TFEU, which provides the legal basis for supporting competences, is essentially designed to preserve the competence of States in public health and to justify cooperation instruments under the Directive.[11] Thus, a balance was found between the application of internal market law to healthcare services and the competences of the Member States for the organization and provision of health care services.[12] All by all, it remains remarkable that the EU legislator succeeded in establishing a healthcare specific directive although article 167.7 prohibits harmonization in this domain explicitly.[13]

IV. Rights for mobile and domestic patients.

An important point of discussion is whether the patients' rights in the directive only apply to patients making use of cross-border care (the so called mobile patients) or whether these rights also profit to patients that receive healthcare in the Member State where they reside (the so called domestic or static patients). Of course, the right to reimbursement of costs incurred by an insured person who receives cross-border healthcare only applies to mobile patients. The question is however relevant for the individual patients' rights in the directive, especially the rights to information. Taken literally, the title of the directive seems to suggest that these rights only apply to mobile patients. Also, most individual patients' rights are part of article 4 which is included in Chapter II of the directive,

---

[10] W.SAUTER, *Harmonisation in healthcare: the EU patients' rights Directive*, Research Paper Tilec, 2011/06, 9.

[11] S. DE LA ROSA, "The Directive on cross-border healthcare or the art of codifying complex case law", *Common Market Law Review* 2012,27-28 who adds: 'This dual legal basis also explains the rather shaky final text, which recognizes rights benefiting patients, yet preserves the competence of States as much as possible';

[12] T.HERVEY, "Cooperation between health care authorities in the proposed directive on patients' rights in cross-border healthcare", in J.W. VAN DE GRONDEN, e.a. (eds), *Health Care and EU Law*, The Hague, Asser Press, 2011,166.

[13] S.A. DE VRIES, "De Europese patiëntenrichtlijn: van privileges naar rechten voor alle patiënten in Europa?", *Nederlands Tijdschrift voor Europees Recht* 2011, 224.

entitled: 'Responsibilities of Member States with regard to cross-border healthcare'. And article 4.1 explicitly refers to 'cross-border healthcare'. It is therefore no surprise that some authors argue that the patients' rights only profit to mobile patients.[14] However, the definition of 'patient' given in article 3 h) is broad and not limited to mobile patients.[15] Also the definition of healthcare[16] in article 3 a) is not limited to cross-border healthcare. Several authors come to the conclusion that for these reasons the Directive is also applicable to domestic patients.[17] Others refer to article 4.3 of the directive that opens the possibility for the MST where it is justified by overriding reasons of general interest, such as planning requirements relating to the aim of ensuring sufficient and permanent access to a balanced range of high-quality treatment in the Member State concerned or to the wish to control costs and avoid, as far as possible, any waste of financial, technical and human resources, to adopt measures regarding access to treatment aimed at fulfilling its fundamental responsibility to ensure sufficient and permanent access to healthcare within its territory. In other words, MST may under strict conditions refuse access to treatment to mobile patients. In this way the directive increased the rights of domestic patients.[18] Also article 5 c) points in the same direction. According to this provision the MSA shall ensure that where a patient has received cross-border healthcare and where medical follow-up proves necessary, the same medical follow-up is available as would have been if that healthcare had been provided on its territory. It is difficult to imagine that this follow-up treatment would not be available to the

---

[14] N. De Grove-Valdeyron, « La directive sur les droits des patients en matière de soins de santé transfrontaliers. Véritable statut juridique européen du patient ou simple clarification d'un régime de mobilité? », *RTD eur.* 2011, 326.

[15] 'patient means any natural person who seeks to receive or receives healthcare in a Member State'.

[16] 'healthcare means health services provided by health professionals to patients to assess, maintain or restore their state of health, including the prescription, dispensation and provision of medicinal products and medical devices'. Moreover, article 3 e) contains a separate definition of cross-border healthcare.

[17] W.Palm and R.Baeten, 'The quality and safety paradox in the patients' rights directive', *European Journal Public Health* 2011, 273; W.Sauter, *Harmonisation in healthcare: the EU patients' rights Directive*, Research Paper Tilec, 2011, afl. 6, 20.

[18] E.Szyszczak, 'Patients' rights: a lost cause or missed opportunity?', in J.W. van de Gronden, e.a. (eds), *Health Care and EU Law*, The Hague, Asser Press, 2011, 111.

domestic patients in this Member State. Therefore, we conclude that the individual patients' rights are universal rights that apply to all patients. Below I will come back to this matter whenever relevant.

V. The patients' rights to information in the Directive

The Directive imposes informational responsibilities upon both the MSA and the MST. Of course, these responsibilities differ. The MSA shall ensure that there are mechanisms in place to provide patients on request with information on their rights and entitlements in that Member State relating to receiving cross-border healthcare, in particular as regards the terms and conditions for reimbursement of costs in accordance with article 7.6 and procedures for accessing and determining those entitlements and for appeal and redress if patients consider that their rights have not been respected (article 5 b). This right to information underpins the right to receive cross-border healthcare.

The informational responsibilities imposed upon the MST and the healthcare providers in this state clarify the healthcare provided and the circumstances in which it is provided. They may be distinguished in two categories: information to be made available upon a request by a patient to the national contact point for cross-border healthcare of the MST on the one hand, and information to be provided by healthcare providers of the MST on the other hand.

1. Information by the national contact point for cross-border care upon request of the patient

Each Member State has to designate one or more national contact points (NCP) for cross-border healthcare and communicate their names and contact details to the Commission (article 6.1).

a) *Relevant information on standards on quality and safety of healthcare*

The MST has to ensure that patients receive from the NCP, upon request, relevant information on the standards and guidelines on quality and safety laid down by that Member State, including information on which healthcare providers are subject to these standards and guidelines (article 4.2 a). The Commission initially intended to oblige Member States to define standards for care provided on their territory and to set in place mechanisms aimed at ensuring that providers meet such standards. However, since this would come close to a minimum harmonization, most Member States favored introducing duties to provide patients information enabling them to make an informed choice.[19] However, giving this kind of information requires that effective mechanisms for quality of care exist in each Member State.[20] At least Member States might feel pressure to install such standards and guidelines and/or to adjust or evaluate them through mutual comparison.[21]

b) Relevant information on supervision and assessment of healthcare providers

The MST has to ensure that patients receive from the NCP, upon request, relevant information on provisions on supervision and assessment of healthcare providers (article 4.2 a).

c) Information on the accessibility of hospitals for persons with disabilities

The MST has to ensure that patients receive from the NCP, upon request, information on the accessibility of hospitals for persons with disabilities (article 4.2 a).

d) Information on a specific provider's right to provide services

In order to enable patients to make use of their rights in relation to cross-border healthcare, NCP of the MST shall provide them with information concerning healthcare providers, including, on request, information on a specific provider's right to provide services or any restrictions on its practice (article 6.3).

e) Information on patients' rights, complaints procedures, mechanisms for seeking remedies and options available to settle disputes

The NCP of the MST shall also provide patients upon request with information on patients' rights, complaints procedures and mechanisms

---

[19] A.P.VAN DER MEI, "The new directive on patients' rights in cross-border healthcare", *Maastricht Journal of Comparative and European Law* 2011,389-340.

[20] H. Legido-Quigley a.o. "Cross-border healthcare in Europe: clarifying patients' rights", *British Medical Journal*, 2011, vol.342, 365.

[21] M.PEETERS, "Free movement of patients: Directive 2011/24 on the application of patients' rights in cross-border healthcare", *European Journal of Health Law* 2012, 55.

for seeking remedies, according to the legislation of that Member State as well as the legal and administrative options available to settle disputes, including in the event of harm arising from cross-border care (article 6.3).

The obligation to inform mobile patients of mechanisms for their protection and for seeking remedies in the event of harm for healthcare provided on their territory has to be understood against the background of article 4.2 c and d). According to these provisions the MST shall ensure that 'there are transparent complaints procedures and mechanisms in place for patients, in order for them to seek remedies in accordance with the legislation of the MST if they suffer harm arising from the healthcare they receive' and 'systems of professional liability insurance, or a guarantee or similar arrangement that is equivalent or essentially comparable as regards its purpose and which is appropriate to the nature and the extent of the risk, are in place for treatment provided on its territory'. It is unthinkable that only mobile patients in a given MST could profit from these mechanisms. Once again it is clear that the directive has also important consequences for domestic patients and not only on the informational level. This is also illustrated by recital (23): 'Systems for addressing harm in the MST should be without prejudice to the possibility for Member States to extend the coverage of their domestic systems to patients from their country seeking healthcare abroad, where this is more appropriate for the patient'.

f) Information on NCP in other Member States
NCP shall provide patients on request with contact of NCP in other Member States (article 6.2)

2. The right to receive information from healthcare providers to make an informed choice.
The MST shall ensure that healthcare providers provide relevant information to help individual patients to make an informed choice (article 4,2 b). This article does not refer to the request of the patient which means that such information has to be given spontaneously.[22]

---

[22] However, recital (20) states: 'Furthermore, healthcare providers should provide patients on request with information on specific aspects of the healthcare services they offer and the treatment options'. Also Dubouis supposes that the information has to be requested

It contains a non-comprehensive enumeration of the subjects of this information: (a) treatment options; (b) the availability, quality and safety of the healthcare they provide[23]; (c) clear invoices and clear information on prices; (d) their authorisation or registration status and,(e) their insurance cover or other means of personal or collective protection with regard to professional liability.

Article 4,2 b) further disposes: 'To the extent that healthcare providers already provide patients resident in the Member State of treatment with relevant information on these subjects, this Directive does not oblige healthcare providers to provide more extensive information to patients from other Member States'. This apparent restriction of the right to information of mobile patients instead implies a major expansion: it extends the right to information needed to informed choice to all citizens of the different Member States even when they are not exercising their rights to consume cross-border healthcare. 'The interaction between the two halves of article 4.2 b) is not just that they are corresponding vessels – in that if limited information is available nationally more must be provided for border crossings patients and vice versa, if ample information is provided nationally less is required for patients from abroad – but that a level of comparable information must presumably be provided to both kind of patients. In other words, this Directive may eventually have much more impact on national policies than on cross-border consumption of care. It will trigger national governments to initiate the measurement and publication of quality of care indicators, if they have not done so already. More importantly, these quality indicators have to be relevant for consumer choice'.[24] To put the potential of the directive in perspec-

---

by the patient as he writes: 'Combien de patients s'autorisent-ils à questioner de la sorte le specialiste auquel ils vont s'en remettre dans l'espoir d' améliorer leur état de santé?' L.DuBOUIS, « La directive n° 2011/24 relative à l'application des droits des patients en matère de soins de santé », *RDSS* 2011, 1068.However, this is not in accordance with the text of the directive that takes precedence.

[23] The references to information concerning 'outcomes of the healthcare provided' have been purged from the Directive, see W.SAUTER, *Harmonisation in healthcare: the EU patients' rights Directive*, Research Paper Tilec, 2011, afl. 6, 20.

[24] D.DELNOIJ and W.SAUTER, "Patient information under the EU patients' rights Directive", *European Journal of Public Health* 2011, 271. See also W.PALM and R.BAETEN, "The quality and safety paradox in the patients' rights directive", *European Journal Public Health* 2011, 273: 'the

tive, it is worth noting that the relevant information to enable patients to make an informed choice is hardly available at national level at the moment, let alone information relevant to patient choice that is comparable to information derived from other Member States.

Especially the 'relevant' information on treatment options and the availability, quality and safety of the care provided, raises questions. Should the relevant information concerned facilitate making choices between treatments in different Member States or just between treatment options? At least the latter appears probable, according to Sauter.[25] According to this author, as regards relevant information, the main issue would appear to be whether quality (as well as availability and safety) information will have to be made available by the individual health-care providers in a format that will make it comparable between Member States. To do so would be something like reaching for the holy grail of consumer choice for health care in the European Union. If this view is taken, a number of issues are unresolved: presumably, the information would at a minimum have to be comparable but not actually presented as part of a comparison with other providers in the MST or elsewhere. This raises the question of what kind of standards would be needed to make information enabling choice comparable and who would set these standards? Or could there be competing standards allowing some degree of comparison either nationally or between (sets of) Member States? The directive provides no mechanism for this.[26] Does the information should be presented in a comparative format assessing provider's performance in terms of quality and safety? The directive does not seem to suggest this in any way.[27] A major challenge for policymakers and for the research community lies in defining what is relevant and what constitutes useful information. Consumers define quality of care differently than profes-

---

information obligation towards healthcare providers in article 4 §2 b) may indeed help to increase transparency, including for domestic patients'.

[25] W.SAUTER, *Harmonisation in healthcare: the EU patients' rights Directive,* Research Paper Tilec, 2011, afl. 6, 20.

[26] D.DELNOIJ and W.SAUTER, "Patient information under the EU patients' rights Directive", *European Journal of Public Health* 2011, 271

[27] W.PALM and R.BAETEN, "The quality and safety paradox in the patients' rights directive", *European Journal Public Health* 2011, 273.

sionals define it. Consumers view quality in terms of access, costs, having a choice of doctors, having doctors who spend enough time with them and doctor qualifications. Professionals present quality information based on performance indicators and on provider's characteristics and services.[28]

Some authors understand the obligation to provide information to help individual patients to make an informed choice in a different way. According to Davies, making an informed choice is something that can only be achieved if the patient understands their prognosis, the possible treatments and their risks and side-effects. This provision can therefore only be sensibly read as requiring states to ensure their doctors *fully* inform patients about all these things. It is hard to object to this idea in abstract according to Davies, but translated to concrete rules it may well conflict with well-established medical traditions. The idea that doctors should fully inform patients about risks, side-effects or prognoses may well be accepted in some States, but will not be the practice in others. Legislating for a patient's right to information is also an intervention in the autonomy and freedom of the doctor. In this sensitive context an EU demand for national implementing legislation addressing such matters may be expected to provoke some resistance, perhaps intermittently outrage.[29]

In our opinion, the obligation to inform patients in order to make an informed choice in article 4.2. b) does not coincide with the obligation to inform patients about their health status and the risks and side-effects of possible treatments with a view to give informed consent. There are no indications at all in the preamble of the Directive that article 4.2. b) has to be understood in this sense. The right to receive information to

---

[28] D.DELNOIJ and W.SAUTER, "Patient information under the EU patients' rights Directive", *European Journal of Public Health* 2011, 272.

[29] G.DAVIES, "Legislating for patients' rights", in J.W. VAN DE GRONDEN, e.a. (eds), *Health Care and EU Law*, The Hague, Asser Press, 2011, 206 (discussing article 5. 1 c) of the proposed directive which had the some contents as article 4, 2, b) of the directive); see also M.PEETERS, "Free movement of patients: Directive 2011/24 on the application of patients' rights in cross-border healthcare", *European Journal of Health Law* 2012, 43 and 54 referring to 'the right to receive information and to provide informed consent' in the context of article 4.2.

make an informed choice is not the same as the 'classic' right to information about one's health status or the 'classic' right to give an informed consent although one cannot deny that there is some overlap between them. The 'classic' rights to information and consent are well established in the European Union and its Member States. According to article 3.1 of the Charter of Fundamental Rights of the European Union everyone has the right to respect for his or her physical and mental integrity. Article 3.2 adds that in the fields of medicine and biology, the free and informed consent of the person concerned, according to the procedures laid down by law, must be respected. By referring to 'procedures laid down by law' this provision on informed consent leaves a considerable degree of discretion to the Member States and thus implicitly recognizes the prospect for a wide range of different approaches as to what informed consent means and who can give that consent.[30] In this context, it is not a surprise that the directive does not harmonise the right to informed consent. In this respect the assessment of the directive made by the Active Citizenship Network offers an interesting perspective. It looked at the reception of the European Charter of Patients' Rights by the directive and came to the following conclusion: 'Of the 14 rights of the European Charter of Patients' Rights, those most greatly absorbed by the Directive are 6 in number: the right to access; the right to information; the right to free choice; the right to innovation; the right to complain and to compensation and the right to privacy'.[31] The Active Citizenship Network admits that the right to informed consent, which is mentioned in the Charter is not among the rights of the Charter that have been incorporated in the Directive, although the Network 'fought to get the contents of the Charter of Patients' Rights included in the Directive'.[32]

To my knowledge, the right to receive information for an informed choice is not yet widely recognized by the Member States. For instance, the Dutch law on patients' rights actually does not contain such a right. There is a bill pending in the Dutch parliament in order to replace the existing patient's rights law by a law on clients' rights in the care sec-

---

[30] J. Mc Hale, "Fundamental rights and health care", in E. Mossalios (ed.), *Health Systems Governance in Europe: the role of EU law and policy*, Cambridge University Press, 2010, 300.

[31] Active Citizenship Network, *The EU Charter of patients' rights, a civic assessment*, 2011,77 available on www.activecitizenship.net.

[32] Active Citizenship Network, *The EU Charter of patients' rights, a civic assessment*, 2011,73 .

tor. One of these rights is the right to receive information to make an informed choice. This brings me to another important question. Is the right to receive information for an informed choice an individual patients' right such as the right to informed consent or is it of a different nature? The right to informed consent is an individual, enforceable right that has to be respected by an individual healthcare provider. Some authors seem to consider this right to information also as an individual right. Peeters states that 'Information about the quality and the safety of the healthcare must also be provided in the relationship patient vs. healthcare provider, in order to help him to make an informed choice'.[33] This is not a surprise as she regards this right as synonymous to informed consent. The directive itself is not clear in this respect. The wording of article 4.2 b) gives the impression that it is more an individual than a collective (social) right: 'the MST has to ensure that healthcare providers provide relevant information to help *individual* patients to make an informed choice including (.....) the quality and safety of the healthcare *they* provide'. The provision does not state literally that the information has to be *given* to the individual patient. The information has to *help* individual patients to make an informed choice and this leaves room for a more collective form of informing them[34] (see also below). As the first addressee of this provision is the individual patient seeking cross-border care who needs the information in order to make an informed choice regarding the healthcare provider who will treat him of her, it is almost self evident that he or she has to be informed individually. Looking at it from this perspective this right to information is closely related to the right of a patient to freely choose a healthcare provider. This is also a 'classic' patients' right recognized in a number of patients' rights charters[35] and

---

[33] M.PEETERS, "Free movement of patients: Directive 2011/24 on the application of patients' rights in cross-border healthcare", *European Journal of Health Law* 2012,55.

[34] This may be the reason why De Grove is classifying this provision under the title : 'droit à l'information collective' ; see N. DE GROVE-VALDEYRON, « La directive sur les droits des patients en matière de soins de santé transfrontaliers. Véritable statut juridique européen du patient ou simple clarification d'un régime de mobilité? », *Revue trimestrielle de droit européen*, 2011, 318.

[35] See for instance article 3 (d) of the European Charter on the Rights of Patients, approved by the European Parliament in 1984: 'the right to free choice of medical practitioner and healthcare establishment' and right n°5 (right to free choice) of the European Charter of patients rights approved by the Active Citizenship Network: 'Each individual has the right

DIREITO DA SAÚDE

national patients' rights laws, such as in article 6 of the Belgian law on patients' rights. The 'classic' right to free choice is often considered as a 'negative' right or freedom: a patient should not be compelled to be treated by a healthcare provider not freely chosen, except when there is a legal basis to do so. In a more modern and progressive interpretation the right to free choice becomes a 'positive' right: the right to select a healthcare provider on the basis of relevant information. The different wording of the European Charters cited in footnote 35 typically illustrates this evolution in the scope of the right to free choice. The obligation to give information to patients in order to make an informed choice fits very well in this new approach. In this respect the directive is certainly innovative. However, Palm and Baeten rightly doubt if healthcare providers themselves are the best placed to provide this kind of information because the information they provide could not be objective and could present a conflict of interests.[36] Moreover, informing patients in an individual way on these aspects is a time consuming and costly procedure. This pleads for a more collective approach. Interestingly, recital (20) of the directive leaves room for such an approach, be it without neglecting the individual approach: 'Nothing should prevent the MST from also obliging other actors than the healthcare providers, such as insurance providers or public authorities, to provide the information on specific aspects of the healthcare services offered, if that would be more appropriate with regard to the organisation of its healthcare system'.

It is clear that the right to receive information to make an informed choice does not fit very well in the classic patients' rights approach with its emphasis on patients' protection. Several authors have stressed that the directive took rather a consumer protection approach emphasizing the need to ensure quality and safety and enabling informed consumer choice.[37] By stressing the freedom of choice patients are transformed into (circumspect) consumers or even European citizens when exercis-

---

to freely choose from among different treatment procedures and providers on the basis of adequate information'.

[36] W.PALM and R.BAETEN, "The quality and safety paradox in the patients' rights directive", *European Journal Public Health* 2011, 273.

[37] W.PALM and R.BAETEN, "The quality and safety paradox in the patients' rights directive", *European Journal Public Health* 2011, 273.

ing their free movement rights.[38] However, the Directive does not seem to fully achieve this. It does not oblige healthcare providers to provide information in other languages than those that are official languages in the Member State concerned, although they may choose to deliver information in other languages (article 4.5). [39] This may be true, but the strength of this provision lies in its application to domestic patients as well. Therefore, I agree with Davies that this provision 'is somewhat more impactful than may be initially apparent'.[40]

VI. Concluding remarks

In this contribution the informational rights in the patients' rights directive have been analyzed. For more than one reason the directive will have important consequences for the protection of patients' rights. First of all, because it has introduced a new right, the right to make an informed choice that is not formally recognized in many Member States. Second, because this right and other (informational) rights are not limited to mobile patients but also, and in the first place, will profit to domestic patients. And third, because it will start a process of (creeping) harmonization of patients' rights in Europe.

---

[38] J.W. VAN DE GRONDEN AND E. SZYCZCZAK, "Conclusions: constructing a "solid" multi-layered health care edifice", in J.W. VAN DE GRONDEN, e.a. (eds), *Health Care and EU Law*, The Hague, Asser Press, 2011, 488; also E.SZYSZCZAK, 'Patients' rights: a lost cause or missed opportunity?', in J.W. VAN DE GRONDEN, e.a. (eds), *Health Care and EU Law*, The Hague, Asser Press, 2011, 106: ' in the context of health care, Europeans have a new relationship with the welfare state: a consumer-citizen who needs ancillary rights to exercise her choice of health care provision'; W.SAUTER, *Harmonisation in healthcare: the EU patients' rights Directive*, Research Paper Tilec, 2011, nr. 6, 24: 'the Directive fits well in a consumer (and/or citizen) oriented approach to European integration'.

[39] A.P.VAN DER MEI, "The new directive on patients' rights in cross-border healthcare", *Maastricht Journal of Comparative and European Law* 2011,390.

[40] G.DAVIES, "Legislating for patients' rights", in J.W. VAN DE GRONDEN, e.a. (eds), *Health Care and EU Law*, The Hague, Asser Press, 2011, 206.

Notificação de incidentes e eventos adversos: o peso da "culpa" e a não regulamentação em Portugal

PAULA BRUNO*

I. Da Segurança dos Doentes

O acesso a cuidados de saúde de qualidade e em segurança é um direito fundamental do cidadão, exigível nos diferentes níveis de prestação de cuidados de saúde. Ao doente (utente/paciente) é-lhe reconhecida legitimidade para exigir e reclamar essa qualidade e segurança em todas as unidades onde lhe são prestados cuidados, e tem o direito a ser ressarcido pelos danos sofridos resultantes da prestação de cuidados. São inúmeros os diplomas legais que consagram o direito à saúde, à integridade física e moral, à inviolabilidade da vida humana, à proteção da saúde e a consequente responsabilidade jurídica adveniente da violação dos aludidos direitos, incluindo os ilícitos penais que também tutelam esses bens jurídicos (vida, saúde, corpo).[1]

---

*Advogada
(paula.bruno.martins@gmail.pt)
[1] Art. 24º, 25º, 64º Constituição a Republica Portuguesa; Art. 70º, 483º, 798º, Código Civil; Base XIV da Lei de Bases da Saúde (Lei 89/90 de 24/08); Art. 3º, 4º, 24º Convenção Direitos do Homem e a Biomedicina; art. 7º, 8º, da Lei 67/2007 de 31/12; art. 137º, 148º do Código Penal.

DIREITO DA SAÚDE

A prestação de cuidados de saúde é reconhecida como uma atividade perigosa, que comporta riscos e danos resultantes do tratamento. Muitos estudos internacionais revelam que os erros médicos assumem uma dimensão elevada.[2] A Organização Mundial de Saúde (OMS) considera a insuficiente segurança dos doentes um grave problema de saúde pública e desde 2004 lançou a *World Aliance for Patient Safety*, que investiga e promove a segurança dos doentes, sendo uma das suas principais áreas de atuação a notificação de incidentes e eventos adversos e sua aprendizagem.[3]

A União Europeia (EU), desde 2005, também vem trilhando caminho no *Patient Safety*; destacamos a Recomendação do Conselho da União Europeia (2009/C 151/01), criada para reforçar a cooperação entre os Estados-Membros (EM), e a aproximação dos Sistemas de Segurança do Doente na União Europeia.[4,5].

As taxas de Eventos Adversos (EA) e Infeções Associadas aos Cuidados de Saúde (IACS), evidenciam que todos os anos milhões de doentes na UE são sujeitos a EA decorrentes dos tratamentos a que são submetidos, e não da doença.

Segundo um relatório elaborado pela *Rand Corporation* [6] e o Centro Europeu de Prevenção e Controlo das Doenças, nos Estados-Membros 8% a 12% dos doentes internados em hospitais são afetados por EA e, em média, as IACS afetam 1 em cada 18 doentes hospitalizados; ou seja, 3,2 milhões de doentes por ano na UE, o que significa que 80 mil doentes são infetados todos os dias[7].

Em Portugal, estima-se que, pelo menos, 5 em cada 100 doentes internados nos hospitais portugueses poderão ter adquirido uma infeção

---

[2] Kohn, T. Linda; Corrigan, M. Janet; Molla, S. Donaldson – To err is human: building a safer health system. Institute of Medicine. Washington, DC : National Academy Press, 2000.

[3] WHO. Draft guidelines for adverse event reporting and learning systems. World Health Organization, 2005

[4] RECOMENDAÇÃO 2009/C. *Jornal Oficial da União Europeia.* (Junho) 151/01-151/6 – Do Conselho da União Europeia sobre a segurança dos pacientes, incluindo a prevenção e o controlo de infecções associadas aos cuidados de saúde.

[5] Art. 168º Tratado sobre o Funcionamento da União Europeia.

[6] RAND EUROPE – Technical Report improvement patient safety in EU, 2008.

[7] European Centre for Disease Prevention and Control. Annual Epidemiological Report 2013.Reporting on 2011 surveillance data and 2012 epidemic intelligence data. Stockholm: ECDC; 2013.

NOTIFICAÇÃO DE INCIDENTES E EVENTOS ADVERSOS

resultante do seu internamento[8]. Segundo os resultados do estudo realizado em 3 hospitais portugueses, a incidência dos eventos adversos é de 11,1%, sendo que 53,2% poderiam ter sido evitados.[9]

Evento Adverso (EA) é o incidente do qual resultam danos para o doente e Incidente aquele que atinge o paciente, mas não causa danos (termos uniformizados pela taxonomia internacional da SD)[10]. Podem resultar de IACS, de erro de diagnóstico, erro de medicação, erro relacionado com cirurgia, com dispositivos médicos, e as consequências (danos) podem ser moderadas, graves, ou mesmo fatais.

O que para o doente se traduz em danos físicos/morais/patrimoniais, indemnizáveis pelo Direito, para o profissional de saúde envolvido o que está em causa é a sua dignidade profissional, e pode conduzir à sua responsabilização. E para a instituição são despesas e prejuízos (mais dias de internamento, mais recursos e indemnizações), que se traduzem em custos para o sector da saúde, que num contexto de crise económica e de escassez de recursos, é importante controlar, gerir e minimizar, ainda mais, quando grande parte dos EA poderiam ter sido ser prevenidos, como concluíram os estudos internacionais que os quantificaram.[11]

II. Da Recomendação da União Europeia

Da Recomendação do Conselho da EU, relativa a questões de Segurança do Doente, importa salientar a 4ª., onde se lê *"Apoiar a criação ou reforço dos sistemas de notificação de eventos adversos não recriminatórios"*; ou seja, a EU apela aos EM para implementarem sistemas de notificação de EA não recriminatórios.[4]

Em 2012, a Comissão Europeia COM (2012)658[12] analisou o nível de implementação da recomendação, e decidiu prolongar por mais dois anos a sua monitorização.

---

[8] PINA, E. et al. – Infecções associadas aos cuidados de saúde e Segurança do Doente. Rev Port Saúde Pública. 2010;Vol Temática (10): 27-39.

[9] Sousa P, et al. Escola Nacional de Saúde Pública, 1ª. edição. Maio de 2011.

[10] WHO. The Conceptual Framework for the International Classification for Patient Safety. 2009.

[11] Cfr. pag. 34 e 35 Bruno, Paula. Registo de Incidentes e Eventos Adversos: Implicações Jurídicas da Implementação em Portugal (20), Wolters Kluwer/Coimbra Editora, 2010.

[12] COMISSÃO EUROPEIA – Relatório da Comissão ao Conselho relativo á aplicação da recomendação 2009/C 151/01 COM(2012)65, Bruxelas 13.11.2012.

Em 2014 (COM (2014) 371)[13], a UE emitiu um segundo relatório ao Conselho, relativo à aplicação da Recomendação sobre a Segurança do Doente, tendo concluído que, em face dos progressos desiguais na EU, seria necessário um acompanhamento e monitorização da aplicação da recomendação por mais dois anos. Mais concluiu que apenas seis países respondem plenamente à recomendação no que respeita aos sistemas de notificação, ou seja, que fornecem informação sobre os eventos adversos, distintos dos procedimentos disciplinares, e que o complementam com os outros sistemas de notificação (i.e. farmacovigilância/dispositivos médicos).

III. Portugal

Volvidos 5 anos, será que Portugal responde positivamente à Recomendação da EU[4], ao nível da notificação de incidentes e eventos adversos? Os profissionais de saúde e os doentes notificam? O sistema de notificação nacional serve o propósito para que foi criado?

Deveríamos estar na posse de elementos consistentes que nos permitissem responder as estas questões e retirar conclusões, mas infelizmente não estamos e ainda não dispomos de divulgação pública suficiente. No entanto, vejamos os dados existentes.

Sistema Nacional de Incidentes – NOTIFIC@

A Direção-Geral da Saúde (DGS), em Maio de 2013, disponibilizou aos profissionais de saúde e aos cidadãos o Sistema Nacional de Notificação de Incidentes (SNNIEA)[14], que em 2014 passou a designar-se de Sistema Nacional de Incidentes – NOTIFIC@[15]. É uma plataforma informática[16], apresentada como *anónima, e não punitiva de melhoria contínua da qualidade e segurança do doente que, ao ser implementada, promove, progressivamente uma cultura de segurança do doente em todos os prestadores de cuidados de saúde.* Para o seu funcionamento é necessário que as unidades criem uma estrutura responsável pela gestão e análise interna dos incidentes e eventos adversos, e um gestor local obrigado a validar as notificações, a identificar os

---

[13] COMISSÃO EUROPEIA – Relatório da Comissão ao Conselho relativo á aplicação da recomendação 2009/C 151/01 COM(2012)65, Bruxelas 19.6.2014.

[14] Norma nº 008/2013 de 15 de Maio da Direção-Geral de Saúde.

[15] Norma nº. 015/2014 de 25 Setembro da Direção-Geral de Saúde.

[16] www.dgs.pt no microsite do NOTIFICA.

fatores contributivos e as medidas correctivas, entre outras tarefas, tudo conforme resulta da citada norma. Através do NOTIFIC@ é estabelecida ligação ao gestor local da instituição onde ocorreu o incidente, para que internamente (na instituição) sejam identificados, analisados, e corrigidos os fatores causais e se previnam futuros incidentes. Curiosamente, da leitura atenta da citada norma[15] resulta que, em relação ao NOTIFIC@ e aos dados recolhidos deste sistema, apenas cabe à DGS elaborar e divulgar relatórios de progresso de monitorização. Se na posse dos dados colhidos do NOTIFIC@, o Departamento da Qualidade na Saúde (DGS) apenas elabora e divulga relatórios de progresso de monitorização, então estamos longe (para além de atrasados) em relação ao que é feito noutros países, por outras entidades congéneres, como por exemplo, o *National Patient Safety Agency* pertencente ao National Health Service (NHS) de Inglaterra.[17]

Cumpre esclarecer que os sistemas de notificação têm como objetivo principal fornecer informação sobre a natureza, o grau, o tipos de evento e as causas dos mesmos, mas evidentemente que a primeira condição é que os profissionais de saúde adiram ao sistema, e que notifiquem os eventos. Após, espera-se que as entidades competentes, na posse de todos os dados agregados, os analisem, verifiquem quais as tendências, apurem os fatores de risco, os fatores contributivos, comparem os dados entre instituições e emitam alertas e recomendações, com vista à aprendizagem com o erro e à prevenção de futuros eventos.

O Ministério da Saúde lançou o Plano Nacional para a Segurança do Doente 2015-2020 (Despacho nº 1400-A/2015 publicado no Diário da República de 10 Fevereiro de 2015), cuja coordenação ficou a cargo da DGS. Entre outros objectivos estratégicos, consta no nº 8 o objectivo de assegurar a prática sistemática de notificação, análise e prevenção de incidentes. Colhe-se deste documento que ações, tais como, promover a adesão dos profissionais à notificação, analisar as causas, implementar medidas preventivas e auditar as práticas realizadas na análise de incidentes, ficam a cargo das instituições prestadoras de cuidados de saúde do SNS. Assim sendo, mais uma vez, somos forçados a concluir que o papel da DGS parece esgotar-se na criação deste sistema. Como referimos, as entidades congéneres, que têm em funcionamento e recolhem os

---

[17] http://www.nrls.npsa.nhs.uk.

DIREITO DA SAÚDE

dados nacionais do sistema de notificação, propõem-se a muito mais, e assumem maiores responsabilidades, do que aquelas que, em nossa opinião, ficaram a cargo da DGS.

Vejamos, então, o Relatório de Progresso de Monitorização do SN-NIEA-2013[18], o único divulgado pela DGS até à presente data (Maio de 2015), do qual resulta que, no ano de 2013, apenas foram efetuadas 244 notificações por profissionais e 74 por cidadãos. Das notificações efetuadas pelos profissionais, 23% estavam relacionadas com acidentes do doente, 4% com IACS e 17% com procedimento clínico. Não temos dúvidas em afirmar que estes números estão muito longe de refletir a realidade, e revelam a fraquíssima adesão dos profissionais de saúde ao sistema de notificação; veja-se, a título de exemplo, que as taxas de IACS assumem valores tão elevados em Portugal (10,6%), acima da média europeia (6,1%), mas no SNNIEA apenas 9 profissionais de saúde notificaram este evento!

Confidencialidade e não Punibilidade

Segundo as recomendações da EU e da OMS, os sistemas de notificação devem ser confidenciais e não punitivos, sob pena de ineficácia dos mesmos, por falta de adesão dos profissionais de saúde. [3, 19]

Ora, atendendo a que não existe em Portugal legislação que garanta essa confidencialidade e não punibilidade, ou seja, proteção legal, parece-nos que estamos perante um problema de subnotificação, ou seja, de ineficácia do sistema nacional e dos sistemas locais existentes nas instituições.

Considerando o que resulta da citada Recomendação da EU, as elevadas taxas de EA, os custos que envolvem, e considerando que os sistemas de notificação são ferramentas válidas [18,20], apelamos às entidades competentes que façam mais pela promoção e eficácia destes sistemas, e não simplesmente criá-los e apresentar os números das notificações efectuadas, como vem acontecendo.

---

[18] Informação nº.002/2014 de 25/2/20214 da Direção-Geral da Saúde.
[19] WHO. Draft guidelines for adverse event reporting and learning systems. World Health Organization, 2005.
[20] National Patient Safety Agency. Seven steps to patient safety, Step 1: Build a safety culture. 2004.

Atendendo ao supra descrito, e em suma, não nos parece que Portugal, responda eficazmente ao recomendado pela UE em matéria de segurança do doente, nem que esteja a cumprir a Recomendação da UE quanto aos sistemas de notificação de incidentes e eventos adversos.

IV. Cultura de Segurança do Doente Vs. Direito

Na literatura em saúde são proclamados uma cultura de segurança do doente e um ambiente livre de culpa, que incentive os profissionais à notificação e à revelação dos erros médicos.[21] Sem prejuízo da sua enorme importância, a verdade é que, em nossa opinião, tal não é suficiente para uma mudança de cultura; a ambicionada mudança deverá ser equacionada, também, dum ponto de vista jurídico, de molde a perceber se, para alcançar um ambiente livre de culpa, não seriam necessárias mudanças ao nível do regime legal de responsabilidade jurídica e da regulamentação dos sistemas de notificação em Portugal.

Existe uma enorme discrepância entre os ditames do Direito e os da Segurança do Doente em relação à CULPA. O Direito tem como pressupostos da responsabilidade civil a verificação cumulativa do **facto voluntário** (por ação ou omissão); da **ilicitude** (contrariedade à ordem jurídica e às *legis artis*); da **CULPA** (sob a forma de dolo ou negligência), sendo que agir com culpa significa que a conduta do agente merece a reprovação/censura do direito, quando, em face das circunstâncias concretas da situação, o agente podia e devia ter agido de outro modo; do **dano** (patrimonial ou moral) e do **nexo de causalidade** entre o facto ilícito e o dano.

E no apuramento da responsabilidade criminal, são pressupostos da mesma a existência de uma ação típica, ilícita e **culposa.**

Assim sendo, o nosso regime jurídico, regra geral, está assente num dos pressupostos fundamentais – a **CULPA** do profissional de saúde.

Contrariamente, para os princípios da segurança do Doente, imputar a **culpa** ao profissional de saúde não é correto nem aceitável, porque, não resolve a questão de fundo. É consensual para a Segurança do Doente que o erro não tem apenas um fator causal, e que os danos causados por falhas individuais representam uma pequena percentagem. Se culpabilizarmos o indivíduo, não será possível desenhar uma estra-

---

[21] Wachter and Pronovost, Balancing "No Blame" with Accountability in Patient Safety, New engl j med 361;14 (2009).

DIREITO DA SAÚDE

tégia correta e efectiva, que garanta a melhoria da segurança. Em vez de questionar "quem", deveremos antes questionar "como". Só nesta perspetiva, e em prol da segurança do doente, será possível motivar todos os envolvidos no processo de cuidar, para a compreensão da problemática do erro na prestação de cuidado. [22]

Se é assim para a segurança do doente, não o é para o Direito, pois os princípios da Segurança do Doente e as regras do Direito não se compatibilizam. Todas as recomendações internacionais, publicações, formações, palestras mundiais e nacionais sobre o tema proclamam *a não culpabilização dos profissionais, a não perseguição do culpado* e, por conseguinte, não acolhem os princípios do Direito que, neste particular, **procura o culpado para apurar responsabilidades**.

Mais, quando ocorre um dano na prestação de cuidados, regra geral cabe ao doente o ónus da prova, ou seja, para além do dano, da ilicitude e do nexo de causalidade entre o fato e o dano, aquele tem que provar em tribunal ainda a culpa do autor do dano (ressalvadas as poucas situações de responsabilidade objectiva e previsões legais de presunção de culpa). É indiscutivelmente, e na maior parte dos casos, uma tarefa muito difícil, onerosa, morosa, incerta e prejudicial para a relação de confiança entre o profissional de saúde e o doente. Não é recomendável para nenhuma das partes envolvidas, pois, como refere a literatura, o profissional de saúde é a segunda vítima do erro médico. [23]

Consideramos que o nosso regime civil de responsabilidade jurídica, aplicável à responsabilidade médica (e de outros profissionais de saúde), está obsoleto, pois não responde eficazmente às necessidades, nem de prevenção de danos, nem de compensação aos lesados. Não está preparado para a massificação da procura de cuidados e para a evolução tecnológica dos meios complementares de diagnósticos e farmacologia, com toda a enorme complexidade e perigosidade que lhe é inerente, nem para o facto de o doente estar agora mais informado dos seus direitos e, consequentemente, mais exigente na responsabilização. Acresce um outro fenómeno negativo muito relevante – a prática da medicina defensiva – decorrente da insegurança dos profissionais de saúde, relacionada com

[22] James Reason, Human error: models and management, BMJ 2000; 320:768–70.
[23] Wu et al., Disclosure of adverse events in the United States and Canada: an update, and a proposed framework for improvement, Journal of Public Health Research 2013; volume 2: e 32.

NOTIFICAÇÃO DE INCIDENTES E EVENTOS ADVERSOS

a complexidade e os riscos da prática médica e o receio de litígios, que se repercutem em mais despesas para o sector da saúde e potenciam mais incidentes e EA.

Nesta reflexão teremos igualmente que considerar a dimensão da jurisprudência portuguesa nesta área; não é abundante, contudo cresceu e revela mudanças na responsabilização dos tais eventos adversos, revelando principalmente as dificuldades e a ineficácia do regime jurídico em vigor. Vejam-se as conclusões retiradas dos estudos de jurisprudência[24,25], para as quais se remete. Também advogamos a ineficácia do modelo ressarcitório, pelo diminuto número de sentenças favoráveis ao lesado, e porque o nosso regime jurídico português está a prestar um mau serviço à segurança dos cidadãos e aos profissionais de saúde.

Todas estas realidades alertam-nos para necessidades legislativas. Se espreitarmos além-fronteiras, percebemos que este problema não é pátrio e que também já levou a mudanças legislativas noutros países. Um dos exemplos é a criação de resoluções alternativas de litígios, designadamente sistemas extrajudiciais de ressarcimento dos danos, na Noruega, Suécia, Finlândia, Dinamarca, Islândia, Nova Zelândia e França, onde o enfoque não é a culpa, nem o culpado, nem o recurso aos tribunais.[26]

Curioso é que, já em 1995, o visionário do Direito da Medicina em Portugal, Professor Guilherme de Oliveira, nos prevenia para o fim da "arte silenciosa"[27], e das "vestes do sagrado" que, secularmente, garantiram a impunidade jurídica; como referiu, a responsabilidade médica está aí, e nós (que laboramos nos tribunais) testemunhamos a sua presença e o seu crescimento na sociedade portuguesa.

Para além das arduidades do regime jurídico de responsabilidade civil, também este cria um enorme entrave à notificação dos incidentes e eventos adversos. Os sentimentos de medo das repercussões legais, de culpa

---

[24] Castanheira Neves, Mafalda. A Jurisprudência portuguesa em matéria de responsabilidade civil medica; o estado da arte, cadernos de direito privado, 35º, Abril/Junho 2012.

[25] Cfr. André Gonçalo Dias Pereira, "Responsabilidade civil dos médicos: danos hospitalares – alguns casos da jurisprudência", Lex Medicinae – Revista Portuguesa de Direito da Saúde, Nº 7, 2007, 53-67; ID.

[26] Cfr. pag. 840 a 858 Dias Pereira, André. Direitos dos Pacientes e Responsabilidade Médica (22), Coimbra Editora. 2015.

[27] Oliveira, Guilherme. Revista de legislação e de Jurisprudência, ano 128º (1995).

DIREITO DA SAÚDE

e vergonha dos profissionais de saúde são, para a literatura internacional, as principais causas da subnotificação.[28,29].

Guilherme de Oliveira alertou, ainda, para a necessidade do reconhecimento de que as condições legais existentes em Portugal – que permitem a identificação dos profissionais responsáveis e a utilização de todos os dados em tribunal – torna difícil a adesão dos profissionais de saúde.[30]

Cotejada esta factualidade incontornável, com os imperativos da segurança do doente e com as recomendações da UE e da OMS, afigura-se-nos que uma iniciativa legislativa influenciaria positivamente a cultura da notificação, de aprendizagem com os erros e, consequentemente, a melhoria da segurança do doente em Portugal.

Sabemos que actualmente, em Portugal, coexistem já sistemas locais de notificação nos Hospitais do Serviço Nacional de Saúde (SNS), com o sistema nacional da DGS. Ora, considerando o regime legal em vigor, só a criação de proteção legal garantirá as características recomendadas (confidencialidade e não punibilidade) aos sistemas de notificação; por conseguinte, presentemente os profissionais de saúde apenas contam com as promessas de confidencialidade e não punibilidade, em que uma notificação não seja utilizada contra o profissional notificante.

Além do mais, a regulamentação dos sistemas de notificação de incidentes e eventos adversos é essencial também para garantir a respectiva aplicabilidade e cumprimento em todo o território português. A implementação do sistema de notificação só fará sentido se for aplicável a nível nacional, quer ao sistema de saúde, quer a todo o sector privado da prestação de cuidados de saúde, e não apenas ao SNS. Caso contrário, o Estado, através do seu órgão competente (DGS), estaria a promover a proteção da saúde e a segurança dos cuidados apenas para os cidadãos que recorrem ao SNS.

Em nossa opinião, todas estas razões conduzem à defesa de uma legislação dos sistemas de notificação, essencial para definir o objeto, o

---

[28] Bruno, Paula. Registo de Incidentes e Eventos Adversos: Implicações Jurídicas da Implementação em Portugal (20), Wolters Kluwer/Coimbra Editora, 2010.

[29] Bruno, Paula. Sistema Nacional de notificação de incidentes e Eventos Adversos: legislar ou não legislar. Lex Medixinae. Ano 10. Nº 19 (2013).

[30] Oliveira, Guilherme. Sistema Nacional de Notificação de Incidentes e de Eventos Adversos (SNNIEA). «Lex Medicinae» Revista Portuguesa de Direito da Saúde, ano 2012, nº 18, Coimbra, Centro de Direito Biomédico/Coimbra Editora, 2013, p. 5-11.

âmbito de aplicação, as suas caraterísticas, as questões da confidencialidade dos dados e da identidade do notificante, e o não poder ser utilizado para punir quem notificou, à semelhança da legislação criada noutros países.[31] Tal será essencial para criar uma maior e tão ansiada transparência, confiança e segurança jurídica de todos os envolvidos e, assim, contribuir para promover a tão desejada cultura de segurança em todas as unidades prestadoras de cuidados de saúde em Portugal.

Uma última referencia à Lei nº 52/2014, de 25 de Agosto, que procedeu à transposição da Diretiva 2011/24/UE relativa ao acesso a cuidados transfronteiriços, e que veio facilitar o acesso e a mobilidade de doentes, permitindo a livre circulação de doentes a cuidados de saúde transfronteiriços seguros e de elevada qualidade dentro dos países membros da EU. Os direitos advenientes desta Lei, afiguram-se-nos mais uma forte razão para se investir na segurança do doente em Portugal. Pese embora, por ora, os portugueses ainda desconheçam os direitos consagrados nesta Diretiva[32], a verdade é que, a manter-se a falta de confiança na prestação de cuidados de saúde e a insuficiente segurança dos cuidados de saúde de saúde em Portugal, tal conduzirá à transferência e procura de cuidados noutros países da EU, com o correspondente reembolso em Portugal, sem esquecer que o nosso país não será atrativo para cidadãos de outros estados membros.

A propósito da qualidade dos cuidados de saúde, os resultados do Eurobarómetro revelaram que os portugueses consideram que a qualidade dos cuidados em Portugal é pior do que nos outros Estados-Membros; consideram provável vir a ser lesados nos cuidados hospitalares no nosso país (75% considera provável e 21% considera improvável); os resultados são muito semelhantes quanto às lesões provenientes de cuidados não hospitalares, diagnósticos, tratamentos ou medicamentos.[33].

Por fim, diremos tão só que a afirmação do Professor Guilherme de Oliveira [34] é absolutamente verdadeira, e mais uma vez antecipada,

---

[31] Cfr. Análise de direito comparado, pag. 97 a 116 do livro Bruno, Paula. Registo de Incidentes e Eventos Adversos: Implicações Jurídicas da Implementação em Portugal (20), Wolters Kluwer/Coimbra Editora, 2010.

[32] COMISSÃO EUROPEIA – Eurobarómetro 82.2. Resultados para Portugal. 2014.

[33] COMISSÃO EUROPEIA – Eurobarómetro 80.2. Resultados para Portugal. 2014.

[34] Sistema Nacional de Notificação de Incidentes e de Eventos Adversos (SNNIEA). «Lex Medicinae» Revista Portuguesa de Direito da Saúde, ano 2012, nº 18, Coimbra, Centro de

DIREITO DA SAÚDE

quando refere que os sistemas de saúde vão distinguir-se pelas competências em segurança do doente, em que os países mais evoluídos conseguirão libertar os sistemas de saúde de muitos "erros evitáveis" e pouparão danos e vidas, e são esses que os cidadãos mais capacitados procurarão, agora incentivados pela Lei do acesso a cuidados transfronteiriços.

Direito Biomédico/Coimbra Editora, 2013, p. 5-11.

Fines de la pena e inhabilitación profesional: su relevancia para la inhabilitación profesional médica*

PROF. DR. JAVIER DE VICENTE REMESAL**

SUMARIO: I. La inhabilitación profesional como pena y como medida de seguridad en el CP español. II. La discusión acerca de la naturaleza jurídica de las privaciones de derechos. La inhabilitación profesional sólo como medida de seguridad: el StGB alemán y el CP portugués. III. Los fines de la pena de inhabilitación profesional. 1. Prevención general y límites del *ius puniendi* impuestos a la misma. 2. Prevención especial. a) Inhabilitación profesional e intimidación especial, aseguramiento o inocuización. b) Inhabilitación profesional y reeducación y reinserción social. IV. La relación del delito con la profesión y su correspondencia con la relación de la pena con la profesión: su relevancia para la determinación del alcance de la inhabilitación profesional médica. Bibliografía

---

* Trabajo realizado en el marco del Proyecto de Investigación *"Responsabilidad de personas físicas y jurídicas en el ámbito médico-sanitario: estrategias para la prevención de errores médicos y eventos adversos"*, DER2011-22934, del Ministerio de Ciencia e Innovación (España). IP: Javier de Vicente Remesal.
** Catedrático de Derecho Penal
Universidad de Vigo

I. La inhabilitación profesional como pena y como medida de seguridad en el CP español.

La base del sistema de penas del CP español está constituida por las penas privativas de libertad, la multa y las penas privativas de derechos.

Entre las penas privativas de derechos previstas en el CP (art. 39), la de inhabilitación especial puede tener cuatro contenidos distintos: inhabilitación para empleo o cargo público[2], inhabilitación para el derecho de sufragio pasivo[3], inhabilitación para el ejercicio de patria potestad, tutela, guarda o curatela[4] y, finalmente, (art. 45) inhabilitación para profesión u oficio, industria o comercio o cualquier otro derecho, que priva al penado de la facultad de ejercerlos durante el tiempo de la condena y ha de concretarse expresa y motivadamente en la sentencia. Será únicamente a esta última a la que me referiré cuando utilice la expresión "inhabilitación profesional" sin otra especificación complementaria (aunque la inhabilitación especial para cargo público también sea en realidad una inhabilitación profesional que incide sobre un funcionario)[5]. Dicha pena puede ser, por otra parte, principal o accesoria, radicando la diferencia entre ambas en su autonomía o técnica legislativa empleada para su previsión y en el tiempo de duración[6].

Como pena principal –esto es, cuando se prevé expresamente en el artículo correspondiente de la parte especial del CP, lo que sucede en muchos tipos penales y con frecuencia de forma conjunta con la pena de prisión– tendrá, según dispone el art. 40 CP, una duración de tres meses a veinte años[7] y, según sea superior o inferior a cinco años,

---

[2] Art. 42: produce la privación definitiva del empleo o cargo sobre el que recayere, aunque sea electivo, y de los honores que le sean anejos; asimismo la incapacidad para obtener el mismo u otros análogos, durante el tiempo de la condena. En la sentencia habrán de especificarse los empleos, cargos y honores sobre los que recae la inhabilitación.

[3] Art. 44: priva al penado, durante el tiempo de la condena, del derecho a ser elegido para cargos públicos.

[4] Art. 46: priva al penado de los derechos inherentes a la primera, y supone la extinción de las demás, así como la incapacidad para obtener nombramiento para dichos cargos durante el tiempo de la condena.

[5] Así lo advierte también –citando en el mismo sentido a Quintano Ripollés, A. (1966)– Manzanares Samaniego, J. L. (1975), 193.

[6] Cfr. Cardenal Montraveta, S. (2011), 138; Domínguez Izquierdo, E. M. (2014), 143.

[7] Art. 40.

puede ser pena grave o menos grave[8]. No se prevé, sin embargo, como pena leve: ni en general, en el art. 33.4 (donde se relacionan las penas leves)[9], ni tampoco, en particular, en los hechos cometidos por imprudencia menos grave[10].

La pena de inhabilitación profesional puede tener también carácter de pena accesoria, cuando acompaña a las correspondientes penas principales. Esto es, cuando no imponiéndolas especialmente, la Ley declare que otras penas las llevan consigo[11]. En tal caso tendrá la duración que respectivamente tenga la pena principal, excepto lo que dispongan expresamente otros preceptos de este Código[12]. Según el art. 56.1, en las penas de prisión inferiores a diez años, los jueces o tribunales impondrán, atendiendo a la gravedad del delito, como penas accesorias, alguna o algunas las previstas en él; entre ellas (art. 56.1.3ª) la de inhabilitación especial para empleo o cargo público, profesión, oficio, si estos derechos

---

[8] Art. 33.

[9] El art. 33.4 únicamente contempla, en su letra c) la inhabilitación especial para el ejercicio de profesión, oficio o comercio que tenga relación con los animales y para la tenencia de animales de tres meses a un año.

[10] El PREÁMBULO a Ley Orgánica 1/2015, de 30 de marzo, por la que se modifica la Ley Orgánica 10/1995, de 23 de noviembre, del Código Penal (BOE de31 de marzo de 2015) manifiesta al respecto: ".En cuanto al homicidio y lesiones imprudentes, se estima oportuno reconducir las actuales faltas de homicidio y lesiones por imprudencia leve hacia la vía jurisdiccional civil, de modo que sólo serán constitutivos de delito el homicidio y las lesiones graves por imprudencia grave (apartado 1 del artículo 142 y apartado 1 del artículo 152), así como el delito de homicidio y lesiones graves por imprudencia menos grave, que entrarán a formar parte del catálogo de delitos leves (apartado 2 del artículo 142 y apartado 2 del artículo 152 del Código Penal). Se recoge así una modulación de la imprudencia delictiva entre grave y menos grave, lo que dará lugar a una mejor graduación de la responsabilidad penal en función de la conducta merecedora de reproche, pero al mismo tiempo permitirá reconocer supuestos de imprudencia leve que deben quedar fuera del Código Penal. No toda actuación culposa de la que se deriva un resultado dañoso debe dar lugar a responsabilidad penal, sino que el principio de intervención mínima y la consideración del sistema punitivo como última ratio, determinan que en la esfera penal deban incardinarse exclusivamente los supuestos graves de imprudencia, reconduciendo otro tipo de conductas culposas a la vía civil, en su modalidad de responsabilidad extracontractual o aquiliana de los artículos 1902 y siguientes del Código Civil, a la que habrá de acudir quien pretenda exigir responsabilidad por culpa de tal entidad."

[11] Art. 54.

[12] Art. 33. 6.

DIREITO DA SAÚDE

hubieran tenido relación directa con el delito cometido, debiendo determinarse expresamente en la sentencia esta vinculación[13].

Pero la inhabilitación profesional no sólo aparece contemplada como pena en el CP español, sino también (art. 96.3.1ª) como medida de seguridad bajo determinadas condiciones y previa concurrencia de ciertos requisitos. Aparte de los establecidos por el art. 95 para la aplicación de las medidas de seguridad en general (comisión de un hecho previsto como delito y pronóstico de comportamiento futuro que revele la probabilidad de comisión de nuevos delitos), dispone el art. 107 que el juez o tribunal podrá decretar razonadamente la medida de inhabilitación para el ejercicio de determinado derecho, profesión, oficio, industria o comercio, cargo o empleo, por un tiempo de uno a cinco años, cuando el sujeto haya cometido con abuso de dicho ejercicio, o en relación con él, un hecho delictivo, y cuando de la valoración de las circunstancias concurrentes pueda deducirse el peligro de que vuelva a cometer el mismo delito u otros semejantes, siempre que no sea posible imponerle la pena por encontrarse en alguna de las situaciones previstas en los números 1º, 2º y 3º del artículo 20. Esto es, en situaciones de exención de responsabilidad criminal por enajenación mental o trastorno mental transitorio, intoxicación y alteraciones en la percepción; circunstancias éstas que no suelen concurrir en el ejercicio de la profesión médica.

Asimismo, la imposición de la medida de seguridad de inhabilitación profesional está sujeta –como es lógico– a otros límites y presupuestos generales tanto para las penas como para las medidas de seguridad. Para que sea constitucionalmente legítima debe cumplir lo dispuesto en el art. 25.2 CE, según el cual, las medidas de seguridad (al igual que las penas privativas de libertad) estarán orientadas hacia la reeducación y reinserción social y no podrán consistir en trabajos forzados. Igualmente debe respetar el principio de legalidad, implícito en el art. 53.1 CE y, en cuanto a los presupuestos, en el art. 1.2 CP. Debe ajustarse también a los principios de garantía jurisdiccional y de ejecución (art. 3.1 y 2 CP). En lo que

---

[13] Art. 56.1.3º: "Inhabilitación especial para empleo o cargo público, profesión, oficio, industria, comercio, ejercicio de la patria potestad, tutela, curatela, guarda o acogimiento o cualquier otro derecho, la privación de la patria potestad, si estos derechos hubieran tenido relación directa con el delito cometido, debiendo determinarse expresamente en la sentencia esta vinculación, sin perjuicio de la aplicación de lo previsto en el artículo 579 de este Código."

se refiere a su ejecución, como acertadamente advierte SANZ MORÁN[14], se echa en falta en nuestra normativa un derecho de ejecución de medidas paralelo al de penas, más completo que el contemplado actualmente en los artículos 97 y 98 CP.

En atención a la peligrosidad del sujeto, durante la ejecución de la medida de inhabilitación profesional el juez o tribunal podrá decidir, a tenor de lo dispuesto en el art. 97, el mantenimiento de la ejecución de la medida, su cese (en cuanto desaparezca la peligrosidad criminal), o su sustitución por otra medida que estime más adecuada. Asimismo –a diferencia de la problemática que se plantea en relación con las penas privativas de derechos– en las medidas de seguridad se prevé expresamente la suspensión de la ejecución de la medida. En virtud de ello, el juez puede dejar en suspenso la ejecución de la medida de inhabilitación profesional en atención al resultado ya obtenido con su aplicación, por un plazo no superior al que reste hasta el máximo señalado en la sentencia que la impuso. Dicha suspensión queda, sin embargo, condicionada a que el sujeto no delinca durante el plazo fijado, y podrá dejarse sin efecto si nuevamente resultara acreditada cualquiera de las circunstancias previstas en el artículo 95 de este Código (es decir, que haya cometido un hecho constitutivo de delito y que del mismo y de las circunstancias personales del sujeto pueda deducirse un comportamiento futuro que revele la probabilidad de comisión de nuevos delitos).

II. La discusión acerca de la naturaleza jurídica de las privaciones de derechos. La inhabilitación profesional sólo como medida de seguridad: el StGB alemán y el CP portugués.

La consideración de la inhabilitación profesional conjuntamente como pena y como medida de seguridad no es ni mucho menos unánime en el Derecho comparado. La permanente discusión acerca de la naturaleza

---

[14] SANZ MORÁN, A. (2010), refiriéndose a la modificación del art. 98 por Reforma de 2010, observa que del nuevo art. 98.3 "lo primero que salta a la vista es su formulación en términos demasiado generales: sigue faltando, sin embargo, un verdadero *Massnahmenvollstreckungsrecht* (o derecho de ejecución de medidas, paralelo al de penas), como el existente en otros ordenamientos jurídicos. ...Y resulta, finalmente, discutible el trámite de audiencia a la víctima esbozado en el inciso final del precepto..., dado que las medidas se fundamentan en la peligrosidad del autor y tienen una orientación exclusivamente preventivo especial, lo que las desvincula, en principio –y aunque no suceda así en el derecho español– del delito cometido (y, por tanto, de su víctima)" 141-142.

DIREITO DA SAÚDE

jurídica de las privaciones de derechos, tanto en la doctrina extranjera como en la española[15], ha llevado en unos casos a esa doble consideración; y en otros[16], sin embargo, como en Alemania –§§ 70, 70 a) y 70 b) StGB– o en Portugal, arts. 100-103 CP–, a su previsión únicamente como medida de seguridad.

Esta configuración de la inhabilitación profesional como medida de seguridad, no en sentido propio como instrumento de reacción frente a la peligrosidad criminal del sujeto inimputable, sino como consecuencia que se dirige también a sujetos con capacidad de culpabilidad para prevenir la continuidad en la acción delictiva, ha contribuido a reforzar y a revivir la opinión de un sector de nuestra doctrina que desde hace tiempo se pronunciaba en el mismo sentido[17].

Concretamente, MANZANARES SAMANIEGO proponía trasplantar los criterios alemanes, considerando la inhabilitación como medida de seguridad[18]. Y recientemente, en esta misma línea de reflexión, opina SANZ MORÁN que "habría que reconsiderar la verdadera naturaleza de la inhabilitaciones y suspensiones y la posibilidad de evitar la doble previsión (como penas y como medidas) de las inhabilitaciones profesionales".[19]

En cualquier caso, la naturaleza punitiva de las penas privativas de derechos –frente a su consideración como medidas de seguridad o consecuencias accesorias –a modo de *Nebenfolgen* del Derecho penal alemán–

---

[15] La actualidad de dicha discusión se pone asimismo de manifiesto en el marco de la reforma de la inhabilitación profesional en la Unión Europea. Cfr. en la doctrina española VILLACAMPA ESTIARTE, C. (2007), 111 ss.; VILLACAMPA ESTIARTE, C. (2009), ss.; GUTIÉRREZ CASTAÑEDA, A. (2012), 246 ss.: en la doctrina alemana, WEDEKIND, V. E. (2006), 183 ss.

[16] Por ejemplo, en Francia, se prevé como pena principal (art. 43.2 CP).

[17] QUINTANO RIPOLLÉS, A. (1966), 329 ss.; CHOCLÁN MONTALVO, J. A. (1997), 163 ss.

[18] MANZANARES SAMANIEGO, J. L. (1981), 33 ss. Observaba MANZANARES SAMANIEGO que las inhabilitaciones y suspensiones del Proyecto, como las del Código vigente, constituyen penas. Pero, advertía, "cuando se quiere utilizar como pena lo que se prestaría mejor a ser medida de seguridad o consecuencia jurídica de la pena (*Nebenfolgen*), la construcción chirria... La prohibición del ejercicio profesional sólo tiene sentido como medida de seguridad, o sea, como medio de combatir la peligrosidad del reo." Añadía que "lo cierto es que la mayor parte de la doctrina moderna niega a las inhabilitaciones y suspensiones la naturaleza intrínseca de penas (o su idoneidad para serlo)". Y concluía, insistiendo, "en que una cosa es la mayor o menor idoneidad que una sanción ofrezca para ser utilizada como pena o medida de seguridad y otra muy distinta el uso que cada legislador haga de ella, sometiéndola a los principios reguladores de una u otra especial de sanción".

[19] SANZ MORÁN, A. (2010), 140.

FINES DE LA PENA E INHABILITACIÓN PROFESIONAL

es incuestionable en el Derecho penal español a partir del CP 1995[20]. Por una parte porque es una evidencia que se contemplan en el CP vigente (además de como penas accesorias) como penas principales. Y por otra parte –en relación con las consecuencias accesorias– porque éstas, aunque consistan también en privaciones de derechos, tienen un contenido que no se identifica con el de las penas privativas de derechos previstas en el art. 39. Esta consideración, de carácter general, alcanza también, en particular, a la pena de inhabilitación profesional.

La situación es distinta –como acabo de indicar– en el Derecho penal alemán y en el portugués.

En el Derecho penal alemán[21], la inhabilitación profesional (*Berufsverbot*) se regula como medida de seguridad en los §§ 70 (imposición de la inhabilitación profesional), 70a (suspensión de la inhabilitación profesional) y 70b (revocación de la suspensión y terminación o conclusión de la inhabilitación profesional).

Los presupuestos esenciales para la imposición de la inhabilitación profesional se contemplan del siguiente modo en el § 70 (1) StGB: si alguien ha sido condenado por un hecho antijurídico cometido con abuso de su profesión u oficio, o infringiendo gravemente los deberes relativos a los mismos[22], o si no lo ha sido porque fue probada o no puede excluirse su inimputabilidad, entonces el tribunal puede prohibirle el ejercicio de la profesión, de la especialidad, del oficio o de la rama industrial por un

---

[20] En el mismo sentido, Tamarit Sumalla, J. M. (2011), 422.

[21] El StGB no contempla penas principales privativas de derechos. Como penas accesorias sólo prevé la de privación del patrimonio (§ 43 a) y la de privación del derecho de conducir (§ 44). Entre lo que se denominan "consecuencias accesorias" (Nebenfolgen, esto es, sanciones de naturaleza propia y peculiar que en virtud de ley o por decisión judicial se unen o pueden unirse a una condena penal, sin que tenga carácter de pena accesoria ni de medida) están la inhabilitación para cargos públicos y la inhabilitación para el derecho de sufragio activo y pasivo (§§ 45 ss.) y la publicación de la sentencia (§ 103 II, 165 y 200).

[22] Es preciso, como expondré más adelante, que el sujeto se aproveche o se sirva de la actividad profesional para cometer el delito, bien con abuso del mismo –más propio de los hechos dolosos– o bien infringiendo gravemente los deberes relativos a los mismos – más propio de los hechos imprudentes. El hecho antijurídico puede cometerse tanto con dolo como por imprudencia. Cfr. Jescheck, H. H. (1978), 1147; asimismo Jescheck, H. H. (1993), 755; Sinn, A. (1996), § 70, nm. 3; Bockemühl, J. (2005), § 70, nm. 6 y 9. Las mismas observaciones son aplicables a la regulación del CP portugués, que expondré a continuación.

DIREITO DA SAÚDE

tiempo de uno a cinco años[23], cuando la valoración conjunta del autor y del hecho permita reconocer que el autor cometerá hechos punibles relevantes de la clase de los señalados en caso de un ulterior ejercicio de la profesión, especialidad, oficio o rama industrial[24]. La inhabilitación profesional puede ordenarse para siempre cuando se cuenta con que el plazo máximo legal no sea suficiente para la defensa del peligro que emane del autor. A tenor del § 70 (3), mientras la prohibición sea efectiva, el autor tampoco puede ejercer la profesión, la especialidad, el oficio o la rama industrial, para otra persona distinta de aquella para la que la había ejercido, así como tampoco a través de una persona dependiente de sus instrucciones.

En el § 70a StGB se regula la suspensión de la inhabilitación profesional. Si tras la imposición de la inhabilitación profesional hay razones suficientes para aceptar que ya no existe el peligro de que el autor cometa hechos antijurídicos relevantes de los señalados en el § 70 inciso primero, entonces el tribunal puede suspender la prohibición por libertad condicional[25]. Para ello es preciso -§ 70a (2)– que la prohibición haya durado como mínimo un año, teniéndose en cuenta a estos efectos, en su caso, el tiempo de prohibición provisional del ejercicio de la profesión[26].

Finalmente, el § 70b regula la revocación de la suspensión y la terminación o conclusión de la inhabilitación profesional. El tribunal revocará la suspensión de la inhabilitación profesional en los siguientes supuestos: cuando el condenado cometa un hecho antijurídico durante el periodo de libertad condicional, abusando de su profesión o de su oficio o infringiendo gravemente los deberes relativos a los mismos; cuando incumpla gravemente o de forma constante una orden; y cuando se sustraiga reiteradamente a la vigilancia y dirección del asistente de libertad condicional

---

[23] Según el § 70 (2) StGB el tiempo de la inhabilitación profesional provisional reducirá el mínimo del periodo de por el que se impone la inhabilitación profesional definitiva, pero no se permite que sea inferior a tres meses.

[24] Muy clara y acertadamente se manifiesta aquí –como también veremos más adelante– la correspondencia que debe existir entre la relación del delito con la profesión y la relación de la pena con la profesión. E igualmente, y con mayor concreción incluso, en el art. 100 CP portugúes, que restringe la inhabilitación a la respective "actividad".

[25] Entendida aquí, por tanto, la recuperación de libertad, no referida a la libertad de movimientos, sino al ejercicio profesional.

[26] § 70a (2) StGB. Pero no se tendrá en cuenta el tiempo que el autor ha estado custodiado por una orden oficial en un establecimiento.

y de ello resulte que el fin de la inhabilitación profesional requiera una aplicación posterior[27]. Asimismo, el tribunal también revocará la suspensión de la inhabilitación profesional cuando circunstancias del autor, que sólo han llegado a conocerse durante el periodo de libertad condicional y que habrían conducido a la negación de la suspensión, muestren que el fin de la medida requiere una continuación de la prohibición de ejercer la profesión[28]. Concluido el periodo de libertad condicional el tribunal declarará cumplida la inhabilitación profesional[29].

En el Derecho penal portugués la regulación es semejante a la alemana. El art. 100 CP, relativo a la "interdicción de actividades", dispone que quien fuere condenado por un delito cometido con grave abuso de la profesión, comercio o industria que ejerza, o con grosera violación de los deberes inherentes, o fuere absuelto de dicho delito por falta de imputabilidad, será inhabilitado para el ejercicio de la respectiva actividad cuando, en atención al hecho realizado y a la personalidad del sujeto, hubiera fundado recelo de que podría cometer otros hechos de la misma clase. El periodo de inhabilitación o interdicción se fija entre 1 y 5 años, pero puede ser prorrogado por otro periodo de hasta tres años si, finalizado el plazo fijado en la sentencia, el tribunal considera que aquél no fue suficiente para remover el peligro que fundamentó la medida. El decurso del periodo de interdicción se suspende durante el tiempo en que el agente estuviese privado de libertad a consecuencia de una medida coercitiva procesal, pena o medida de seguridad. Si la suspensión dura 2 años o más, el tribunal reexamina la situación que fundamentó la aplicación de la medida, confirmándola o revocándola.

A la vista de lo expuesto, resulta evidente que la diferencia fundamental de la regulación de la inhabilitación profesional en estos ordenamientos jurídicos frente a la prevista en el español radica en que mientras en el CP español la imposición de la inhabilitación profesional como medida de seguridad (art. 107 CP) requiere que no sea posible imponer la pena al sujeto por encontrarse en alguna de las situaciones previstas

---

[27] § 70b (1) StGB.

[28] § 70b (2) StGB.

[29] § 70b (5) StGB. Por otra parte, dispone el § 70b (3) que el periodo de suspensión de la inhabilitación profesional no se tendrá en cuenta en el plazo de prohibición. Y el § 70b (4), que los servicios prestados por el condenado para el cumplimiento de las ordénes o compromisos no se restituirán.

DIREITO DA SAÚDE

en los tres primeros números del art. 20 –y por ello, como se ha indicado, es de aplicación excepcional en el marco del ejercicio profesional médico–, en aquéllos se prevé la posibilidad de aplicar la inhabilitación profesional, como medida de seguridad (y, por tanto también, sin aquellas restricciones, en dicho marco del ejercicio profesional médico), no sólo en esos casos de falta de imputabilidad, sino también cuando se afirma la culpabilidad del sujeto. Ambos son –como destacan HANACK y BOCKEMÜHL– presupuestos esenciales para la imposición de la medida de inhabilitación profesional[30].

Así las cosas –en el Derecho alemán– en la finalidad de la inhabilitación profesional (proteger a la sociedad frente a aquellas personas que en el ejercicio de su actividad profesional cometen hechos antijurídicos que representan un abuso de su profesión u oficio o una grave infracción de los deberes profesionales que le son inherentes), el factor decisivo para la determinación de su duración, que incluso puede ser perpetua, es únicamente (con independencia por tanto del punto de vista de la culpabilidad) la prognosis criminal del sujeto, esto es – como observa JESCHECK[31]– el grado de probabilidad de comisión de nuevos delitos y la gravedad de la puesta en peligro de la comunidad. Advirtiendo, eso sí, que por suponer dicha medida una grave ingerencia en el derecho fundamental de libre ejercicio de la profesión –constitucionalmente reconocido en el art. 12 I 2 GG– la imposición de la inhabilitación debe estar justificada por su necesidad, esto es, requiriendo la probabilidad, y no la mera posibilidad, de que el sujeto cometa delitos en el futuro, y acudiendo a ella, como *ultima ratio*, cuando no sea suficiente la adopción de otras medidas o precauciones menos drásticas, a veces propuestas incluso por el que cometió en hecho delictivo; por ejemplo, la renuncia voluntaria a ejercer la profesión. Lo que determina la duración de la inhabilitación profesional –destaca HANACK[32]– es sólo la prognosis, es decir, la pregunta de cuánto tiempo es previsible que perdurará la específica peligrosidad profesional del sujeto. La inhabilitación profesional es una pura medida de seguridad y por eso sólo se orienta a fines de prevención especial, excluyéndose por tanto –como advierte, entre otros, BOCKEMÜHL[33]– la

[30] HANACK, E. W. (1996), § 70, nm. 10 y BOCKEMÜHL, J. (2005), § 70, nm. 8.
[31] JESCHECK, H. H. (1978), 1148; asimismo JESCHECK, H. H. (1993), 756.
[32] HANACK, E. W. (1996), § 70, nm 59.
[33] BOCKEMÜHL, J. (2005), § 70, nm. 2.

necesidad de expiación y los puntos de vista referidos a la culpabilidad y a la prevención general.

III. Los fines de la pena de inhabilitación profesional

La doctrina española ha mostrado un escaso interés por el estudio de los fines de las penas privativas de derechos y ello se ha debido en parte – sobre todo antes de 1995– al hecho de negarles o cuestionar, a pesar la decisión legal, su naturaleza intrínseca de penas o su idoneidad para serlo[34]. Sin embargo, las penas privativas de derechos en general, la de inhabilitación profesional en particular y, dentro de éstas, la determinación del ámbito concreto al que debe referirse la inhabilitación para el ejercicio de la profesión médica, a saber, a ésta en su conjunto o restringida, por ejemplo, a una especialidad o incluso a una actividad de la misma–encuentran y deben encontrar su fundamento tanto en la prevención general como en la prevención especial.

Trasladado lo anterior a un caso concreto, se trata de analizar la posibilidad de que la responsabilidad derivada de la incorrecta ejecución imprudente de una intervención quirúrgica, por ejemplo, por un médico ginecólogo –que infravalora la merma de sus capacidades físicas por la aparición de síntomas de Parkinson– no genere no sólo la inhabilitación para el ejercicio de la medicina en general, sino tampoco la exclusión total de ejercer como ginecólogo, restringiéndose dicha exclusión a la práctica de intervenciones quirúrgicas. Pues puede seguir siendo un extraordinario ginecólogo fuera de dichas prácticas y, por tanto, sólo esa restricción encontraría su fundamento en los fines de la pena.

1. Prevención general y límites del *ius puniendi* impuestos a la misma

La función primaria de las normas penales que prevén penas es la protección de bienes jurídicos mediante prevención general y especial de delitos. Dentro de esta función preventiva –única[35], o conjunta con la de impartir justicia[36]–, la prevención general constituye la finalidad esencial

---

[34] Manzanares Samaniego, J. L. (1981), 43

[35] Esta es la opinión de un amplio sector doctrinal, que sin embargo coexiste con la concepción mixta, antes claramente dominante.

[36] En este sentido, considerando como doble fundamento principal de la pena el preventivo-general y el justicial o de justicia (o retributivo en la terminología usual), Luzón Peña, D. M. (2012), 1/33. En *ob. cit.*, Introducción, observa lo siguiente: "he pasado definitivamente

DIREITO DA SAÚDE

de la pena y puede desplegar sus efectos, bien a través de la intimidación general –lo que suele conocerse como prevención general negativa–, o bien en virtud de la convicción general o social del valor simbólico de las normas y sanciones penales: lo que suele denominarse prevención general positiva, socialmente integradora o estabilizadora, pero que se comprende mejor –como observa Luzón Peña– con el nombre de "convicción general o social"[37].

Sobre la base de la necesidad de protección de bienes jurídicos y, por ello, de salvaguarda de la libertad como valor fundamental (art. 1.1 CE), la prevención general de delitos constituye la finalidad principal de las penas[38]: esto es, la prevención de que la generalidad de las personas cometan delitos. La prevención de futuros delitos por el concreto delincuente al que se impone la pena constituye también una finalidad de las penas, puesto que éstas se orientan además a la prevención especial; pero esta finalidad no es la principal y cede ante la prevención general en caso de conflicto[39]. Desde el punto de vista de la prevención general se requiere la previa comisión culpable de un delito. Sobre ello se basa la imposición de la pena; y no forzosamente en la peligrosidad criminal –en el juicio sobre la comisión futura de un delito por parte del sujeto– que solamente sería un presupuesto indispensable si la prevención especial fuera una finalidad primordial de las penas[40].

Por el contrario, como hemos visto, la finalidad de las medidas de seguridad es exclusivamente preventivo-especial, con independencia de

de una concepción fundamentalmente preventiva a una concepción mixta, donde junto a la protección de bienes jurídicos mediante prevención general y especial, que sigue siendo la función primaria, de protección de la libertad como primer valor del art. 1.1. CE, está como función secundaria la de impartir "justicia" como segundo valor constitucional de dicho art. 1.1; por tanto, en vez de retribución como se la suele denominar, función de justicia (frente a un hecho típicamente antijurídico e individualmente culpable) exactamente igual que en todos los demás campos del Derecho" (6).

[37] Propone esta denominación Luzón Peña, D. M. (2012), p. X (prólogo); más ampliamente en 1/50 s.

[38] Ello no significa que dicha función de protección corresponda únicamente a la prevención general, pues también compete a la finalidad preventiva especial de las penas y a las medidas de seguridad. A través de la función de prevención se realiza la función de protección. (Luzón Peña, D. M. (2012), 1/45).

[39] En este sentido, pero refiriéndolo también a la función de impartir justicia, Luzón Peña, D. M. (2012), 1/33.

[40] Cfr. Luzón Peña, D. M. (2012), 1/33.

que también puedan desplegar en algunos casos efectos de prevención general. No requieren –aunque no la excluyen– la previa comisión culpable de un delito, pero precisan en cualquier caso la peligrosidad de su comisión futura.

La cuestión que se plantea es, pues, analizar si la pena de inhabilitación profesional –tanto en general como la referida en particular al ejercicio de la profesión médica– cumple los fines de prevención general respetando los límites del *ius puniendi*[41]. A estos efectos será necesario distinguir entre el carácter principal o accesorio de la pena de inhabilitación profesional.

El análisis de la inhabilitación profesional (así como de las penas privativas de derechos en general) desde la perspectiva de sus efectos preventivos generales es muy escaso en nuestra doctrina[42], entre otras razones porque se ha visto ensombrecido por el mayor o exclusivo interés de su estudio desde los fines de la prevención especial: de inocuización (o neutralización) o de resocialización del delincuente. Consecuencia de ello han sido y son las ya referidas discrepancias doctrinales acerca del carácter de la inhabilitación profesional, considerada en algunos ordenamientos sólo como medida de seguridad. No obstante, actualmente estamos asistiendo a un replanteamiento de la posible relevancia de la inhabilitación profesional desde el punto de vista de la prevención general, en la medida en que –sobre todo en determinados ámbitos concretos, por ejemplo, frente a la delincuencia económica– se la considera una pena idónea y de gran eficacia a esos efectos[43].

La eficacia preventivo-general de una pena privativa de derechos –y en particular la de inhabilitación profesional– no viene determinada –ni fundamentalmente, ni mucho menos, sólo– por su mayor o menor contenido aflictivo, pues depende de otros muchos factores. Por ejemplo, de su cumplimiento efectivo, para lo cual es preciso reforzar los instrumentos

---

[41] Ampliamente sobre esta cuestión referida a la prevención general, cfr. DE VICENTE REMESAL, J. (2014 b), pp. 62-77.

[42] Históricamente, dichos efectos se esgrimían, como argumento para su imposición, fundamentalmente respecto de la pena de muerte o de las penas corporales, centrándose más tarde en las penas privativas de libertad. En cualquier caso, el carácter aflictivo de la pena siempre se ha considerado un factor esencial para la eficacia intimidatoria.

[43] Fundamentalmente por la pérdida de las fuentes de riqueza y frente a la ineficacia de las penas pecuniarias, cfr. TERRADILLOS BASOCO, J. (1995), 60; PAREDES CASTAÑÓN, J.M. (2002), 431; FERNÁNDEZ TERUELO, J. G. (2005), 351 ss.; NIETO MARTÍN, A. (2008), 299.

de control de la ejecución, sobre todo en la prohibición del ejercicio de las profesiones privadas en cuanto su posibilidad de incumplimiento es mayor que en ejercicio de la función pública[44].

Por otra parte, la eficacia de dicha pena depende también del papel que juega en la inhabilitación profesional lo que (en otro contexto, pero aplicable también aquí) he denominado prevención general selectiva frente a prevención general ordinaria: el reforzamiento de los mecanismos inhibidores con la amenaza de pena sobre los potenciales delincuentes no va dirigido de manera indiferenciada a la generalidad de los ciudadanos (como en el delito de homicidio, por ejemplo), sino de forma selectiva, a un círculo de sujetos, en virtud de la relación directa de la privación del derecho con el delito cometido. Y dicho reforzamiento es mayor respecto de estos sujetos en sus concretos ámbitos profesionales en la medida en que (a diferencia del destinatario general, indiferenciado) suele concurrir en ellos (aunque, ciertamente, no en todos los ámbitos por igual, pero sí especialmente en algunos, por ejemplo el económico-empresarial y médico-sanitario) el conocimiento de la norma penal (o la mayor posibilidad de obtenerlo), no sólo en cuanto al contenido de la acción típica, sino también en cuanto a sus consecuencias jurídicas: que la comisión del delito implica (generalmente además de la pena de prisión) la imposición de la pena de inhabilitación profesional.[45]

---

[44] La pena de inhabilitación profesional debe ejecutarse requiriendo al penado para que se abstenga de desarrollarla o ejercerla durante el tiempo de la condena, a cuyo efecto deberá practicarse la oportuna liquidación de condena y remitiendo el oportuno oficio al Colegio profesional correspondiente y al Consejo General de dicho Colegio. Cuando la profesión u oficio sea de las que no requieren habilitación oficial o colegiación obligatoria, el juez o tribunal podrá (en realidad también puede hacerlo en otros casos) requerir el auxilio de la autoridad policial o administrativa para comprobar la efectiva ejecución de la pena. Si el condenado incumple la inhabilitación incurrirá en el delito, del art. 468 CP, de quebrantamiento de condena

[45] DE VICENTE REMESAL, J. (2002), 1088-1090. En el contexto de la rectificación postdelictiva y más concretamente en relación con la diferencia de la atenuante genérica frente a los supuestos de atenuación específica, observaba que en ellas cabe diferenciar –aparte de otras cosas– entre prevención general ordinaria y prevención general selectiva. "La primera, basada en gran medida en la ignorancia o el desconocimiento por parte del afectado, sería la prevalente en la atenuante genérica. Por el contrario, en los supuestos específicos de atenuación o levantamiento de pena nos encontramos normalmente ante sujetos cualificados, conocedores de la norma, incluso en profundidad, de manera que esa selección de afectados cuenta a los efectos preventivos no sólo con la previsión típica de la conducta delictiva,

FINES DE LA PENA E INHABILITACIÓN PROFESIONAL

La idoneidad de la pena de inhabilitación profesional para que pueda surtir efectos desde la perspectiva de la prevención general cabe derivarla de la restricción que implica sobre las posibilidades de actuación del sujeto en la sociedad mediante la privación del ejercicio de su actividad profesional, de su significado (privación de un derecho) y de las consecuencias que conlleva su imposición, tanto patrimoniales –quizá fundamentalmente– como de otra naturaleza, de trascendencia personal o social.[46]

A continuación voy a referirme a algunas cuestiones fundamentales[47] al hilo del análisis de los límites al *ius puniendi*, pues la pretensión preventivo-general (aunque también la preventivo-especial de intimidación), para evitar excesos, debe respetar dichos límites, sometiéndose en cualquier caso y sobre todo a los principios de estricta necesidad, proporcionalidad y culpabilidad, que son en parte internos o inmanentes y en parte externos o constitucionales[48]. Veremos, por otra parte, que el carácter de pena accesoria o principal juega un papel más relevante (y diferenciado) en unos principios que en otros.

Uno de los principios en los que la función de accesoriedad de la pena de inhabilitación profesional conduce a consecuencias distintas de las derivadas de su consideración como pena principal es el de *subsidiariedad, intervención mínima o ultima ratio y carácter fragmentario* del Derecho penal. Si bien se puede echar en falta una mayor previsión e implementación de otras medidas preventivas extrapenales –menos graves pero no por

---

sino al mismo tiempo con la atenuación o levantamiento de pena que supone la realización del comportamiento postdelictivo reparador..." (1089). En otro contexto, pero en sentido semejante, ÁLVAREZ GARCÍA, F. J. (2000), 590 s.

[46] La gravedad de su imposición no se restringe a las consecuencias patrimoniales derivadas de la misma por no poder ejercer la profesión, sino que se extiende también a las derivadas de las dificultades para la consecución de un trabajo tras el cumplimiento de la pena. Por ejemplo, para acceder a los cargos públicos y a numerosas profesiones colegiadas es requisito indispensable carecer de antecedentes penales o tenerlos cancelados, lo cual significa que, sobre la base de lo dispuesto en el art. 136 CP, la inhabilitación se prolonga en el tiempo varios años después de extinguida la pena. Cfr. GRUPO DE ESTUDIOS DE POLÍTICA CRIMINAL (2005), 35.

[47] En relación con el respeto a los principios de legalidad, responsabilidad por el hecho, responsabilidad subjetiva y ofensividad o lesividad, cfr. DE VICENTE REMESAL, J. (2014 b), pp. 62 ss.

[48] LUZÓN PEÑA, D. M. (2012), 1/49.

DIREITO DA SAÚDE

ello necesariamente menos eficaces, por ejemplo, medidas proactivas como una mejor labor inspectora de la Administración o de la empresa[49], o incluso sancionadoras en el ámbito disciplinario[50]–, puede decirse (con salvedades, desde luego) que la inhabilitación profesional como pena principal responde en términos generales a dicho principio. Pues sirve de complemento a otras reacciones previstas en normas extrapenales, de carácter disciplinario, reservándose (por el principio de intervención mínima) la tipificación penal para hechos de gravedad media o alta y (en virtud del carácter fragmentario y de proporcionalidad) contemplando en la mayoría de los casos las penas privativas de derechos conjuntamente con penas privativas de libertad o pecuniarias, de mayor o menor entidad, según la gravedad del hecho.

Observaciones semejantes cabe hacer en relación con el *principio de efectividad, eficacia o idoneidad*. La previsión e imposición de la inhabilitación profesional como pena accesoria no responde en absoluto a su consideración como posible alternativa a la pena de prisión ni a la idea de que pudiendo ser ésta de corta duración pudiera actuar aquélla como complemento en atención a su mayor eficacia o idoneidad, pues ello resulta impedido por el hecho de que las penas accesorias tendrán la duración que respectivamente tenga la principal. Por el contrario, la pena de inhabilitación profesional, como pena principal, puede (y suele) tener una duración superior a la pena de prisión cuando concurre con ésta (aunque también en algunos casos dura igual o menos). Con independencia de que eso responda realmente a criterios de eficacia y de que los mismos sean aceptables (lo que requeriría analizar caso por caso, y en ello no puedo detenerme ahora), lo cierto es que la inhabilitación profesional como pena principal –a diferencia de como accesoria– sí puede respon-

---

[49] Sobre estas observaciones en el ámbito empresarial, Cfr. De Vicente Remesal, J. (2014 a), 170 ss. Destacando que el Derecho Penal ha de limitarse a veces constatar lo evidente –por ejemplo, el fracaso en el uso de una cierta tecnología o de una determinada forma de organización– y a poner, torpemente (a causa de las restricciones necesarias en el ejercicio del ius puniendi), algunos parches a la situación creada, cfr. Paredes Castañón, J.M. (2002), 406. Y asimismo, con argumentos semejantes, sobre la subsidiariedad de Derecho penal, Paredes Castañón, J. M. (2003), 125-128.

[50] En el sentido de que se restrinjan al ámbito disciplinario, cfr. Manzanares Samaniego, J. L. (2002), 1095 ss.

FINES DE LA PENA E INHABILITACIÓN PROFESIONAL

der al principio de efectividad, eficacia o idoneidad[51]. Y esto es mucho menos dudoso cuando se impone conjuntamente con una pena de multa. Así, en la delincuencia económica[52], la pena de multa es ineficaz en cuanto puede y suele transferirse a terceros. Con la pena de inhabilitación profesional, aparte de evitarse esa posibilidad, se separa al individuo de la estructura organizativa que ha dado lugar al delito o que incluso (y con mayor justificación en este caso) está orientada a su comisión[53].

De todas formas, cuando la pena de prisión y la de inhabilitación profesional se cumplen simultáneamente surge la duda acerca de si son ambas en conjunto las que contribuyen a la eficacia preventivo-general o si a estos efectos la única relevante y suficiente es la de prisión. Distinto es el caso, sin embargo, cuando se obtiene la suspensión condicional de la prisión o procede la concesión del tercer grado o la libertad condicional[54]. O cuando impuestas ambas como principales la de inhabilitación profesional supera en tiempo a la de prisión. Por ejemplo, en el homicidio cometido por imprudencia profesional, en el que la pena de prisión es de uno a cuatro años, mientras que la de inhabilitación profesional es de tres a seis años.

Por otra parte –trayendo aquí a colación lo expuesto anteriormente sobre la prevención general selectiva frente a la prevención general ordinaria– cabe preguntarse si en los casos de concurrencia de la pena de prisión con la de inhabilitación profesional sería suficiente con esta última para lograr la eficacia preventivo-general, prescindiendo de la primera.

---

[51] A ello responde, por ejemplo, el incremento de medidas alternativas, como penas principales, y entre ellas la propuesta (Regla 9) del GRUPO DE ESTUDIOS DE POLÍTICA CRIMINAL (2005), 35, de que la inhabilitación profesional debe tener una duración máxima similar a la prevista para las medidas de seguridad, fijada en 5 años.

[52] El GRUPO DE ESTUDIOS DE POLÍTICA CRIMINAL (2005), 34, en la regla 8, recomienda expresamente, incluir la inhabilitación profesional en este ámbito como pena principal.

[53] Cfr. DE VICENTE REMESAL, J. (2014 a), 170 ss. En sentido semejante, PAREDES CASTAÑÓN, J.M. (2002), 431, quien reconoce asimismo que con ello no se evita la dinámica propia de la organización, destacando a su vez que a estos efectos es fundamental una regulación adecuada de las consecuencias accesorias del delito y una revisión del importante papel que deben jugar los mecanismos de atribución de responsabilidad civil derivada de delito, pues éstos pueden cumplir también una importante finalidad preventiva.

[54] Destacando la escasa percepción de las penas accesorias automáticas en los casos de simultaneidad de su cumplimiento con la pena principal de prisión, cfr. GUTIÉRREZ CASTAÑEDA, A. (2012), 453.

DIREITO DA SAÚDE

En un principio podría pensarse que sí y que la pena de prisión –de preverse e imponerse, además de la de inhabilitación especial– respondería sólo a una finalidad retributiva porque la preventiva la cubriría total o fundamentalmente la de inhabilitación profesional en cuanto surtiría efectos ante los sujetos que más preocupan, esto es, no los ciudadanos en general, sino en cuanto pertenecientes a círculos profesionales determinados. No obstante, la pena de prisión también cumple una función preventiva frente a los sujetos para quienes se prevé la pena de inhabilitación profesional. Pues –aparte de que la pena de prisión no sólo impide el ejercicio de una profesión determinada, sino de todas (y en el mejor de los casos lo dificulta enormemente[55])–, la eficacia preventiva de la inhabilitación profesional puede ser muy dispar (y mucho más cuando se trata de inhabilitación para empleo o cargo público, en cuyo caso, lo que para unos puede ser muy gravoso, puede carecer para otros de efectos preventivos en absoluto).

Donde la pena de inhabilitación profesional plantea mayores objeciones es respecto del *principio de proporcionalidad*. Y también aquí algunos de dichos problemas se derivan del carácter –principal o accesorio– de la pena.

Si el principio de proporcionalidad significa –en términos muy generales– que la gravedad de la pena ha de ser proporcional a la gravedad del hecho antijurídico, esto es, a la gravedad del injusto, lo primero que llama la atención en la pena de inhabilitación profesional como pena accesoria es que dicha pena, aun siendo requisito necesario para su imposición la relación directa entre el derecho afectado por la misma y el delito cometido (art. 56.3º), haya de tener (en principio) –por imperativo legal general (art. 33.6) la misma duración que la pena de prisión. Y esto no creo que se deba a que los distintos factores de la gravedad del injusto tengan según el legislador el mismo peso y significado para determinar, por igual, la dimensión de ambas penas, sino sencillamente a que el análisis de los mismos no se toma en absoluto en consideración para el marco penal de la inhabilitación profesional como pena accesoria, sino sólo para

---

[55] Si a tenor del art. 56 CP, por no estar relacionada con el delito no se impone como accesoria la pena de inhabilitación profesional (y dando por supuesto que tampoco se impone como principal), el sujeto podría en principio, por ejemplo, aunque en casos muy particulares y con extraordinarias dificultades, seguir dirigiendo su negocio desde la prisión.

el de la pena de prisión, procediéndose después, una vez determinada ésta en concreto (por el juez), a la automática igualación de la inhabilitación profesional, sin que tampoco el juez tenga en cuenta a estos efectos la exigida relación directa entre el derecho afectado y el delito cometido. Con ello se conculca claramente el principio de proporcionalidad, con el resultado de que la inhabilitación profesional adquiere una dimensión exagerada (e incluso, en algunos supuestos, posiblemente superior a la principal) y en cualquier caso irreflexiva por su automatismo y carácter residual.

Todo ello resulta además contradictorio, cuando menos con lo siguiente. Primero: con el hecho de que cuando la pena de inhabilitación profesional se impone como principal, su marco penal y su duración generalmente nunca es la misma (sino generalmente mayor) que la de la pena de prisión[56]. Segundo: con lo previsto para otras penas incluidas sistemáticamente entre las accesorias, pero cuyo carácter de tales es sin embargo discutible[57] y que por ello suelen calificarse de "accesoriedad atípica"[58]. Tercero: con el hecho de que en los casos de accesoriedad típica, se considera (según la jurisprudencia y un sector de la doctrina)

---

[56] Con la salvedad de cuando, prevista como pena principal, se dispone que su duración sea "por el tiempo de la condena" de la de prisión; como es el caso, por ejemplo –en el delito de trata de seres humanos– del art. 177 bis nº 6 en relación con el nº 1, y –en el marco del tráfico ilegal o la inmigración clandestina de personas– del 318 bis 1, 2 y 3 en relación con el nº 4

[57] Así, en las contempladas en el art. 48, sobre las cuales establece el art. 57, entre otras cosas, que si el condenado lo fuera a pena de prisión y el juez o tribunal acordara la imposición de una o varias de dichas prohibiciones, lo hará por un tiempo superior entre uno y diez años al de la duración de la pena de prisión impuesta en la sentencia, si el delito fuera grave, y entre uno y cinco años, si fuera menos grave.

[58] Así, en relación con la denominada pena de interdicción domiciliaria, resume así DE LAMO RUBIO, J. (1999), las características de la accesoriedad atípica: "a) La llevaban aparejada tan sólo determinados delitos: homicidio, lesiones, aborto, contra la libertad, torturas y contra la integridad moral, la libertad sexual, la intimidad, el honor, el patrimonio y el orden socioeconómico. b) La única pena accesoria atípica era la prohibición de que el reo volviera al lugar en que hubiere cometido el delito, o acudiera a aquél en que residiera la víctima o su familia, si fueran distintos. c) Su duración no se supeditaba ni se relacionaba con la duración de la pena impuesta por el delito, sino que iba de seis meses a cinco años (art. 33, en relación con el 57), en atención a las circunstancias del caso, pudiendo ser, por tanto, pena grave o menos grave. d) Su imposición no era preceptiva, sino que, el órgano jurisdiccional podría imponerla o no, teniendo en cuenta la gravedad de los hechos y el peligro que el delincuente representase".

DIREITO DA SAÚDE

que la pena de inhabilitación profesional no puede beneficiarse de ninguna modificación durante su ejecución[59], al contrario de la pena principal, de prisión[60]. Y cuarto: ha de tenerse en cuenta que la obligatoriedad de la imposición de la pena de inhabilitación profesional como pena accesoria deja de ser tal (con las consecuencias que de ello se derivan, entre otras cosas en virtud del principio de proporcionalidad) cuando la inhabilitación profesional se prevé como pena principal en algún tipo penal, en cuyo caso su duración puede no ser la misma, sino incluso inferior, que la de la pena de prisión[61].

Por otra parte, la conculcación del principio de proporcionalidad resulta evidente en el hecho de que a tenor del art. 56 se prevé la imposición obligatoria de alguna o algunas de las medidas (entre ellas la inhabilitación profesional) aunque la pena de prisión prevista para el hecho tenga un límite inferior que puede descender incluso hasta los tres meses[62]. Por el contrario, en ese umbral inferior, de los tres meses de privación de libertad, se prevé –conjuntamente– la pena de inhabilitación como pena principal en los artículos 146 (de uno a tres años) 152 (de seis meses a cuatro años) 158 (de seis meses a dos años) y 463.2 (de dos a cuatro años).

---

[59] Eso significa que el variable tiempo de cumplimiento de aquélla no se debe a valoración alguna de los diferentes factores sobre la misma, sino a que sencillamente se aplica automáticamente y por inercia, aun a pesar, una vez más, de la exigencia de relación directa entre el derecho afectado y el delito cometido.

[60] En lo que se refiere a las penas privativas de libertad, la doctrina mayoritaria –cfr. DE LA CUESTA ARZAMENDI, J. L. (2009), 129– considera que el ámbito de aplicación de la suspensión de la ejecución alcanza a todas las penas privativas de libertad, incluida la responsabilidad personal subsidiaria –GARCÍA ARÁN, M. (1997), 101– que, por impago de la pena de multa se traduzca en una privación de libertad. Sin embargo, minoritariamente se mantiene que la suspensión sólo es aplicable a las penas privativas de libertad impuestas con carácter principal. Así, AYO FERNÁNDEZ, M. (1997), 182.

[61] Así sucede, por ejemplo, en el supuesto del art. 325. Si la pena de inhabilitación profesional no estuviese prevista en ese artículo para ese delito contra el medio ambiente, sino sólo la de prisión de dos a cinco años y ésta, valoradas las circunstancias (riesgo de grave perjuicio para la salud de las personas), se impusiese en concreto en cinco años, entonces, en virtud del art. 56.1.3º se podría (o habría que) imponer, como accesoria y con la misma duración de cinco años, la pena de inhabilitación profesional. Sin embargo, como ésta sí está prevista y su duración es de uno a tres años, sólo se podrá imponer en este máximo de tres años (sin poder llegar, por tanto, a cinco).

[62] Artículo 36: "1. La pena de prisión tendrá una duración mínima de tres meses y máxima de 20 años, salvo lo que excepcionalmente dispongan otros preceptos del presente Código".

Pero las mayores críticas a la pena de inhabilitación profesional son las que se refieren a su compatibilidad con el principio de resocialización, como veremos a continuación en el contexto de la prevención especial.

2. Prevención especial

La pena como reacción jurídica frente al delito tiene también como finalidad, aparte de la prevención general, la prevención especial de delitos. Mediante ésta se pretende que el delincuente concreto que ha cometido un hecho delictivo no vuelva a cometer delitos en el futuro; en principio de cualquier clase, pero con la pena de inhabilitación profesional se trata sobre todo de que el sujeto no vuelva a cometer hechos delictivos semejantes o de la misma clase a los cometidos en el contexto del ejercicio de su profesión, como expresamente requieren los antes referidos § 70 (1) StGB alemán y art. 100 CP portugués.

Tanto en la prevención general como en la especial la pena presupone inexcusablemente culpabilidad en el delito cometido, pero en cambio no la peligrosidad criminal del sujeto para el futuro. Por tanto, nunca se puede imponer una pena a un inculpable, mientras que sí se puede penar a un sujeto con independencia de su peligrosidad. En ello radica su diferencia con las medidas de seguridad. Por un lado, aunque éstas comparten con la pena el fin de prevención especial, esa es su exclusiva finalidad (con independencia de que pueda desplegar también efectos de prevención general) y por eso las medidas de seguridad requieren como presupuesto para su imposición la peligrosidad criminal del sujeto. Las medidas de seguridad son respuesta a la peligrosidad del sujeto y las penas al delito cometido[63]. Por otro lado, a diferencia de las penas, las medidas de seguridad no requieren culpabilidad: tanto en relación con el delito cometido por el sujeto como con el peligro de comisión de futuros delitos basta con que se trate de acciones típicas, penalmente antijurídicas, aunque no sean culpables. Ahora bien, que no se precise culpabilidad para la imposición de una medida de seguridad no significa, sin embargo, que la culpabilidad sea incompatible con las medidas de seguridad. Las medidas de seguridad no se reservan exclusivamente para sujetos no culpables pero peligrosos. A un sujeto culpable también se le puede aplicar una medida de seguridad si encaja en un estado peligroso[64].

[63] MIR PUIG, S. (2011), 92.
[64] LUZÓN PEÑA, D. M. (2012), 1/21 y 24.

La culpabilidad es ajena al fundamento de las medidas de seguridad y no debe desempeñar función alguna en su determinación y graduación; en la pena, por el contrario, la posible consideración de la peligrosidad debe ajustarse a la medida de la culpabilidad del sujeto, de suerte que la prevención especial nunca puede justificar la imposición de una pena que rebase la gravedad del delito; sí, sin embargo, que quede por debajo de dicha gravedad[65].

Esta diferenciación es especialmente relevante en este contexto del análisis del fin preventivo especial de la pena de inhabilitación profesional, pues precisamente la opinión de que esta pena (y en general las privativas de derechos) no debe tener tal carácter, de pena, sino de medida de seguridad, se basa fundamentalmente en la crítica a que dicha reacción jurídica, configurada como pena, pueda cumplir los fines de prevención especial, y en particular los de reeducación y resocialización. Corresponde ahora, pues, analizar si y en qué medida la pena de inhabilitación profesional −en general y en particular en el ámbito médico− puede lograr los fines de prevención especial mediante −por una parte− procedimientos asegurativos, de control, inocuizadores o neutralizadores o −por otra parte− mediante métodos de corrección del sujeto, de resocialización y reinserción social.

a) *Inhabilitación profesional e intimidación especial, aseguramiento o inocuización*

El efecto inocuizador de la pena de inhabilitación profesional no suele ponerse en tela de juicio. Antes al contrario, puede decirse que la doctrina en general considera que constituye su fin fundamental. Pretende sobre todo que el sujeto que ha cometido un delito en el ámbito de su profesión (cuando es pena accesoria se exige expresamente una relación directa con el hecho: art. 56 CP) no vuelva a cometer delitos, especialmente de la misma clase, con abuso del ejercicio de su profesión o infringiendo gravemente los deberes relativos a la misma. De hecho, la preeminencia de esta finalidad (junto con la crítica de que las privaciones de derechos,

---

[65] Cfr. BOLDOVA PASAMAR, M.A. (1996), 60. (Téngase en cuenta, no obstante, su observación −ob. cit. 383− de que para ciertos delincuentes imputables, como son los delincuentes habituales y profesionales de criminalidad grave, la pena ajustada a la medida de su culpabilidad no puede ser un instrumento adecuado y suficiente para hacer frente a su peligrosidad).

FINES DE LA PENA E INHABILITACIÓN PROFESIONAL

consideradas como penas, no pueden cumplir los fines de reeducación y de reinserción) constituye –como hemos visto– la base fundamental en la que se asientan las propuestas de la consideración de las privaciones de derechos como medidas de seguridad, por ser éstas las más idóneas para la consecución de esos fines.

Con la pena de inhabilitación profesional se trata de evitar la reincidencia, y fundamentalmente la reincidencia específica. Si la pena de inhabilitación profesional puede tener efectos de intimidación general (con las matizaciones que en su momento señalé), los de intimidación especial son obvios[66] o indudables y fundamentales[67]. Entre otras cosas, porque se circunscribe (o debe hacerlo) a la profesión, especialidad o actividad concreta en cuyo ejercicio el sujeto cometió el delito, y porque las consecuencias añadidas de dicha pena pueden y suelen extenderse más allá (aunque de forma desigual) del cumplimiento temporal de la inhabilitación[68], tanto si se impone como pena principal o como accesoria.

Ciertamente, cuando el cumplimiento de la pena de inhabilitación profesional concurre en el tiempo con la de prisión –y eso no sólo se produce cuando tiene carácter de accesoria de la de prisión no suspendida, sino también cuando se prevé como principal, lo cual es frecuente– el fundamental y prácticamente exclusivo efecto inocuizador corresponde a la pena de prisión.

Ahora bien, cuando la inhabilitación profesional se considera pena en lugar de medida de seguridad, dicho carácter introduce determinados límites a su imposición, a la vez que origina ciertas dificultades desde esta perspectiva de la intimidación especial. La imposición de dicha pena debe respetar la doble exigencia que implica el principio de culpabilidad: no hay pena sin culpabilidad, y la pena ha de ser proporcional al grado de culpabilidad, aunque la prognosis criminal del sujeto indique la necesi-

---

[66] En este sentido, refiriéndose a las penas privativas de derechos como penas principales, GIMBERNAT ORDEIG, E. (1980), 183, sobre la base de que se imponen cuando el delito cometido está en relación con la función o el empleo ejercidos.

[67] Por el contrario GUTIÉRREZ CASTAÑEDA, A. (2010), afirma, por una parte, que la neutralización del delincuente no constituye en modo alguno el fin preeminente, desempeñando un papel meramente secundario o accesorio respecto de la prevención general, que es el principal (416), a la vez que considera que con la inhabilitación profesional no se trata de evitar que el condenado cometa cualquier delito, sino tan sólo de eliminar o al menos de reducir el riesgo de comisión de delitos similares a los que ha dado lugar la condena (413).

[68] En el mismo sentido, DOMÍNGUEZ IZQUIERDO, E. M. (2014), 144.

DIREITO DA SAÚDE

dad de imposición de una pena que rebase la gravedad del delito. Las penas son –valga la insistencia– respuesta al delito cometido y las medidas de seguridad a la peligrosidad del sujeto. Pero esta restricción del papel que puede jugar la prognosis es precisamente la que puede limitar la eficacia de intimidación especial[69]. Así, cuando la aplicación judicial aconseja, sobre la base de la valoración individualizada del sujeto (que indica, por ejemplo, un grave riesgo de reincidencia), una respuesta de mayor duración que la prevista en la conminación penal abstracta, el juez sólo puede adoptar y adaptar esa respuesta si la inhabilitación se impusiese como medida de seguridad, pues si la impone como pena ha de respetar el límite máximo de ésta.

No obstante, deben recordarse aquí las observaciones anteriores referidas a la concurrencia de la pena de inhabilitación profesional con la pena de prisión. Y asimismo las relativas a que la eficacia preventivo-general de una pena privativa de derechos (aplicadas en este caso a la intimidación especial por la pena de inhabilitación profesional) no sólo depende de su conminación abstracta y de su aplicación, sino también del control de su ejecución.

b) *Inhabilitación profesional y reeducación y reinserción social*

El grado de consenso manifestado por la doctrina en favor del fin y del efecto intimidatorio especial de la pena de inhabilitación profesional es semejante al que manifiesta respecto del efecto de reeducación y reinserción social, pero, en este caso, en contra. Junto a la apreciación más habitual –que comparto– de su escaso o casi nulo efecto resocializador, se afirma también que dichas penas no cumplen en absoluto los fines de reeducación y reinserción social[70].

---

[69] En el Derecho alemán, WEDEKIND, V. E. (2006) destaca, por el contrario, que la consideración de la inhabilitación especial como pena eliminaría en gran medida los problemas que plantea la prognosis. Considera que un cambio del carácter de sanción –pasar de medida de seguridad a pena– aligeraría el requisito de la prognosis. Pues mediante la conversión de la inhabilitación profesional en una pena –en la cual el interés de la seguridad ya no estaría en primer plano– tendría como consecuencia que la determinación de la pena se orientaría exclusivamente a la culpabilidad y al injusto y con ello podría eliminarse la difícil prognosis de peligrosidad. (65-66).

[70] Así, expresamente, refiriéndose en general a las penas privativas de derechos políticos y profesionales (y por tanto también a la de inhabilitación profesional), GUTIÉRREZ CASTAÑEDA, A. (2010), 402.

Perseguir la finalidad de reinserción social no resulta impedido por el hecho de que dicha orientación no figure expresamente en el art. 25.2 CE respecto de las penas privativas de derechos (las cuales afectan a un derecho distinto de la libertad ambulatoria o el patrimonio, en principio[71]), aunque en verdad origina una situación paradójica. Por una parte, incluso la norma fundamental del Estado manifiesta que las penas privativas de libertad estarán orientadas hacia la reeducación y reinserción social, porque dichas penas corren el peligro de tener un gran efecto desocializador. Pero por otra parte, a las penas privativas de derechos –que también tienen un efecto desocializador y que se prevén como sanciones alternativas a las penas privativas de libertad para evitar o disminuir aquel peligro–, dicha norma fundamental del Estado no les reconoce tal orientación hacia la reeducación y reinserción social. Frente a esto cabe señalar que durante la vigencia de la Constitución (de 1978) existió la pena de interdicción civil (esto es, la incapacitación por sentencia penal por la comisión de determinados delitos), de claro carácter estigmatizador, suprimida por la reforma de 1983 del Código Penal. Pero también hoy existen penas privativas de derechos, de carácter más o menos infamante (como es el caso de la pena de inhabilitación absoluta) y de ahí que se cuestione su necesidad[72], junto con otras que entrañan peligro de desocialización, como es el caso de la pena de inhabilitación profesional, en cuanto priva al sujeto de la posibilidad del ejercicio del derecho al trabajo, que es sin duda un importante medio de integración o inserción social.

La posibilidad de eficacia de la pena de inhabilitación profesional a estos efectos de reeducación y reinserción social dependerá, en primer lugar y fundamentalmente, de que se eviten sus efectos desocializadores. Para ello es fundamental que la inhabilitación (tanto si es pena principal como accesoria) se circunscriba de la forma más ajustada posible al ejercicio de la profesión, de la especialidad o del oficio con cuyo abuso el sujeto cometió el delito, y tratando de impedir, en todo caso, una amplitud que suponga una condena al hambre, que puede derivar incluso en efectos criminógenos.

---

[71] Lo cual no es cierto a todas luces, sin embargo, en el caso de la pena prevista en el art. 39 g), privación del derecho a residir en determinados, y discutible en otros supuestos. Cfr. TAMARIT SUMALLA, J. M. (2011), 422.

[72] Cfr. MAPELLI CAFFARENA, B. (2012), 5 ss.

DIREITO DA SAÚDE

Pero en segundo lugar es preciso que se incluyan en su ejecución posibilidades y medidas que permitan al juez la orientación de la inhabilitación profesional en esa dirección. Por ejemplo, la previsión legal de su posibilidad de suspensión, con reglas de conducta adecuadas para ese fin, o la introducción de una dimensión positiva en la sanción, con esa misma orientación[73]. La pena de inhabilitación profesional aplicada a un cirujano por mala praxis tendrá un efecto preventivo indudable, pero también es indudable que si el cirujano se ha limitado, sin más, a cumplir el largo tiempo de inhabilitación, esto es, a cumplir la pena, las posibilidades de incurrir de nuevo en mala praxis con su reingreso será mucho mayores que antes.

Aun así debe reconocerse que las posibilidades de eficacia desde esta perspectiva de la reeducación y reinserción no será la misma en todos los casos. Será previsiblemente mayor en los supuestos en que la inhabilitación profesional se impone como consecuencia de la comisión imprudente de un hecho (por imprudencia profesional), que en los cometidos con dolo. Y dentro de éstos cabría diferenciar asimismo según el ámbito o sector de la criminalidad de que se trate.

IV. La relación del delito con la profesión y su correspondencia con la relación de la pena con la profesión: su relevancia para la determinación del alcance de la inhabilitación profesional médica.

En relación con las penas accesorias, la redacción vigente del art. 56, tras su reforma en 2003, contribuye a aclarar las discusiones, hasta entonces arduas, acerca de la necesidad de relación directa entre el delito cometido y el derecho del que se priva al sujeto[74]. En cualquier caso, tras la reforma operada en 2010 en la circunstancia 3ª del número 1 de dicho artículo, queda definitivamente claro que la imposición de la pena de inhabilitación profesional requiere relación directa con el delito cometido[75], debiendo determinarse expresamente en la sentencia esta vinculación.

---

73 Más ampliamente, sobre el problema de la posibilidad de suspensión de la ejecución de la pena de inhabilitación profesional como pena accesoria y como pena principal, cfr. DE VICENTE REMESAL, J. (2014 b), 92-104.

[74] Cfr. DOMÍNGUEZ IZQUIERDO, E. M. (2014), 149-152.

[75] Ya sobre la base de esta normativa anterior –que introducía dudas al respecto– tanto la doctrina como la jurisprudencia entendían que era precisa esa relación del hecho con la

FINES DE LA PENA E INHABILITACIÓN PROFESIONAL

El primer requisito formal para la imposición de la pena de inhabilitación profesional es la comisión de un delito. Es indiferente, sin embargo, su forma de comisión, activa u omisiva[76], el grado de ejecución –tentativa o consumación– o la forma de intervención, como autor o partícipe[77]. Pero además es necesario que el sujeto haya cometido el delito aprovechándose de la posibilidad que a tal efecto le ofrece el ejercicio profesional, bien dolosamente (abusando de su profesión u oficio[78]), o bien por imprudencia, infringiendo gravemente sus deberes profesionales. Y, finalmente, es preciso además, que entre el hecho cometido y el ejercicio de la profesión exista una relación estrecha, específica o interna[79]. Es decir, no basta con que se realice en su contexto, sino que debe entenderse como resultado de la actividad profesional misma o cuando menos como uno de los derivados generalmente de dicho ejercicio[80]. Cumpliría este requisito el daño causado por el médico al paciente por una intervención quirúrgica mal ejecutada, pero no, por ejemplo, el sustraerle la cartera que el paciente ha dejado mientras tanto en su habitación[81].

Esta relación del delito con la profesión es esencial para determinar el alcance que deba tener la pena de inhabilitación profesional, tanto en general como en particular en el ámbito médico. Sin embargo, ya las propias referencias legales a la inhabilitación profesional son dispares en cuanto a la determinación de su alcance, predominando la expresión genérica de inhabilitación especial para el ejercicio de la profesión, oficio o cargo; lo cual es hasta cierto punto necesario y comprensible, habida cuenta de que la concreción corresponde fundamentalmente al juzgador. Pero también se observa que en los pronunciamientos jurisprudenciales o bien falta asimismo dicha concreción, o bien se concreta de forma dife-

---

profesión u oficio, tanto en las penas accesorias como en las principales. Cfr. DE LA MATA AMAYA, J. (1994), 175; POZUELO PÉREZ, L. (1998), 26.

[76] Cfr. SINN, A. (1996), § 70, nm. 3.

[77] Cfr. HANACK, E. W. (1996), § 70, nm. 7; BOCKEMÜHL, J. (2005), § 70, nm. 6.

[78] En este sentido, MAPELLI CAFFARENA, B. (2002 b) observaba –cuando la imposición de dicha pena era potestativa según el art. 56–, que „la inhabilitación especial requiere para ser impuesta no sólo que esté prevista para un delito en concreto sino que, en la mayoría de los casos, es preciso además que el autor se haya aprovechado del cargo u oficio inhabilitado" 1010.

[79] Cfr. WEDEKIND, V. E. (2006), 41.

[80] Cfr. HANACK, E. W. (1996), § 70, nm. 18.

[81] O en el ejemplo semejante que pone DOMÍNGUEZ IZQUIERDO, E. M. (2014), 166, n. 91.

rente en supuestos semejantes. En consecuencia, habrá que analizar si y hasta qué punto -en virtud de lo dispuesto en la ley y en aplicación de los criterios o puntos de vista que considere aplicables, entre ellos el de los fines de la pena– , el juez puede optar por la prohibición en general de la profesión u oficio, o, por el contrario, ha de restringir la inhabilitación al servicio, especialidad o actividad concreta de la profesión en el que el sujeto cometió el delito.

El tenor literal del art. 45 CP supone una ayuda para solucionar el problema (en cuanto requiere que la inhabilitación ha de concretarse expresa y motivadamente en la sentencia y precisa que priva al penado de la facultad –no del derecho– de ejercer la profesión), pero a la vez (con la inclusión de la referencia a "para cualquier otro derecho") genera dificultades para la determinación del alcance de la pena de inhabilitación profesional[82]. Sea como fuere, el hecho de que el art. 45 CP recoja expresamente la diversidad de denominaciones de profesión, oficio, industria o comercio, demuestra claramente que lo que el legislador pretende es que quede incluida toda clase de ocupación laboral, sea cual sea ésta y requiera o no permiso, habilitación o licencia.

Este problema de la limitación, o no, de la inhabilitación profesional a las profesiones y oficios cuyo ejercicio requiere habilitación, permiso o licencia oficial, fue, sin embargo, arduo objeto de discusión en la doctrina antigua, que en general la restringía a dicho requisito[83], pero que en la actualidad se mantiene de forma muy minoritaria, por ejemplo por Mir[84]. Una de las razones fundamentales para sostener dicha opinión radica en que, de lo contrario, la efectividad de la sanción sería muy difícil. Pero esta dificultad en el control de la ejecución –aunque cierta– no es de recibo para excluir las profesiones u oficios que no precisan habilitación o permiso oficial. No puede condicionar la interpretación de la norma, sino

---

[82] La inclusión de esta referencia a "para cualquier otro derecho" es ambigua y por lo tanto criticable por lesionar la taxatividad que exige el principio de legalidad. Se mantiene de esta forma la línea del CP 1944, el cual no sólo extendía expresamente la inhabilitación especial a las ocupaciones manuales y a las profesiones liberales, sino que incluía también al final la cláusula general "y las de cualquier otra clase". En este sentido, Mapelli Caffarena, B. / Terradillos Basoco, J. (1996), 182.

[83] Con amplísimas referencias sobre dicha doctrina, cfr. Manzanares Samaniego, J. L. (1975), 194 s.

[84] Así, Mir Puig, S. (2011), 720.

que debe impulsar a la adopción de las medidas oportunas en ejecución de sentencia que permitan la efectividad de la ejecutoria.

La pena debe ser efectivamente muy restrictiva, pero tal rigor debe conducir a exigir, en la línea preconizada por el derecho alemán, la constancia de un abuso de su profesión u oficio y de un peligro de cometer otros hechos relevantes similares al que motiva su imposición, con independencia de cuál sea la profesión u oficio que desempeñe el penado[85].

Asimismo no cabe derivar la exigencia de licencia de la referencia del art. 45 a "cualquier otro derecho", interpretando que con ello se le priva al sujeto del derecho a ejercer la profesión. Esta interpretación, aparte de que sería contra reo[86], resulta imposibilitada por el propio art. 45 que, como norma especial, explicita que priva al penado sólo de la facultad de ejercer la profesión.

Esta posible extensión de la pena de inhabilitación profesional a todas las profesiones u oficios −aunque no como pena, sino como medida de seguridad− es también la que se mantiene la doctrina y jurisprudencia alemanas, si bien −como advierte WEDEKIND[87]− su aplicación en la actualidad es escasa y afecta esencialmente a dos grupos profesionales. Por una parte, a médicos, psicólogos, maestros y educadores en general y, por otra, a abogados, asesores de impuestos y personas relacionadas con el ámbito económico o comercial. No obstante, el § 45 StGB (relativo a la pérdida de la capacidad para el desempeño de cargos públicos, de ser elegido y del derecho de sufragio, es ley especial frente al § 70 StGB[88], aunque la doctrina es discrepante acerca del alcance § 45 StGB, por ejemplo, respecto de los notarios[89].

Ahora bien, la exigencia de que la sentencia debe concretar expresa y motivadamente el objeto de la inhabilitación no resuelve ni puede resolver por sí misma y con carácter general el problema del grado de concreción. Pero supone un paso fundamental para ello, pues no sólo permite, sino que obliga a analizar el problema caso por caso, tomando en consideración los fines de la pena en su conjunto (y no, como debe hacer la

---

[85] Cfr. DE LA MATA AMAYA, J. (1994), 176.

[86] En este sentido, POZUELO PÉREZ, L. (1998), 47.

[87] WEDEKIND, V. E. (2006), 37.

[88] BOCKEMÜHL, J. (2005), § 70, nm. 12.

[89] En contra de la opinión dominante, HANACK, E. W. (1996), § 70, nm. 33.

doctrina alemana, sólo los propios de las medidas de seguridad y por eso puede llegar a resultados distintos)[90].

Son múltiples y variados los supuestos que se han dado y pueden darse en la realidad. Pero me voy a centrar aquí en el más habitual, referido a si la inhabilitación debe restringirse a una dimensión, servicio o actividad concreta del ejercicio de la profesión, o tiene, por el contrario, que referirse a la profesión en sí misma, sin dichas restricciones[91].

Ciertamente, el juez no está obligado a restringir la prohibición al servicio, especialidad o campo concreto de la profesión en el que el sujeto cometió el delito. Y puede, por tanto, optar por la prohibición en general de la profesión u oficio. Pero tampoco está obligado a esto. Tanto una decisión como otra –ambas posibles– debe fundamentarse y motivarse desde el punto de vista de los fines de la pena. Lo cual implica en cualquier caso que el juez está obligado a concretar de la forma más exacta posible el alcance de la prohibición.

Este problema se plantea frecuentemente en ámbito médico. Así, en la STS 15-11-2001, habiéndose cometido el delito en la especialidad obstétrica, se discute si procede imponer la inhabilitación para la profesión médica en general o sólo para el ejercicio de la especialidad de obstetricia. El TS (siguiendo la línea jurisprudencial en el mismo sentido) defiende en este caso la primera alternativa por la finalidad de protección social que corresponde a la pena, que no se cumpliría si el sujeto puede seguir ejerciendo la medicina en otras especialidades.

Con independencia de que esto pueda ser lo correcto, también lo sería restringir la inhabilitación a la especialidad si ello –en el caso concreto y tras el obligado análisis del mismo de esta restricción– no se contrapone a los fines de la pena[92].

---

[90] Por ejemplo, en relación con el problema de si la pena de inhabilitación profesional sólo puede prohibir al sujeto la profesión en cuyo ejercicio cometió el delito, su opinión de que no es posible aplicar la prohibición a una profesión u oficio diferentes, aunque el desempeño de los mismos pueda ser peligroso para la comunidad –HANACK, E. W. (1996), § 70, nm. 53– requeriría en nuestro Derecho argumentos añadidos desde el punto de vista de los fines de la pena.

[91] DE LA MATA AMAYA, J. (1994), recogiendo en el mismo sentido que él mantiene las SSTS 22 febrero 1991 y 10 abril 1992, considera que "es la profesión y no un servicio específico dentro de la misma la que debe ser objeto de inhabilitación" (176)

[92] El art. 144, referido al aborto doloso, puede ser significativo a este respecto. Restringe la inhabilitación de la siguiente forma: "inhabilitación especial para ejercer cualquier profesión

FINES DE LA PENA E INHABILITACIÓN PROFESIONAL

Y el mismo planteamiento cabe hacer en otros casos en los que quepa la posibilidad de un ejercicio limitado de la profesión, restringiéndose a ella la prohibición. Por ejemplo, al profesor de música que abusó sexualmente de algunos de los alumnos de su grupo de menores, se le podría permitir seguir dando clases de música sólo a grupos de adultos. O que al médico que hizo lo mismo con una paciente se le restrinja la atención médica a pacientes varones[93].

A modo de conclusiones, y referidas éstas fundamentalmente al ámbito médico, cabe observar lo siguiente:

La imposición de la pena de inhabilitación profesional como pena principal suele sustentarse por la jurisprudencia en la fundamentación de la existencia de dicha clase de imprudencia (esto es, la denominada "imprudencia profesional"), como plus de gravedad de la imprudencia grave, derivando de ello y sólo por ello, en la mayoría de los casos, la aplicación de la inhabilitación profesional al ejercicio de la profesión médica en general.

Aparte de que el punto de referencia (la "imprudencia profesional") no es de recibo y que como tal expresión debería desaparecer del CP[94], las argumentaciones que fundamentan la existencia de imprudencia

---

sanitaria, o prestar servicios de toda índole en clínicas, establecimientos o consultorios ginecológicos, públicos o privados". A pesar de que el texto no es muy claro, cabe interpretar que la inhabilitación se centra únicamente en el ejercicio de la profesión relacionada con la ginecología, pues es sólo en ella donde radica el juicio de peligrosidad del sujeto. Esta misma interpretación habría que hacer del art. 146 (aborto por imprudencia profesional), a pesar de que aquí solamente se dice "inhabilitación especial para el ejercicio de la profesión, oficio o cargo". No olvidemos que siempre sigue vigente la necesidad de que haya habido una relación directa entre la imprudencia profesional y el hecho, con lo que es fácil colegir que dicha imprudencia profesional lo fue en el campo de la ginecología. Otra consecuencia importante que debe extraerse de esto es la siguiente: si el aborto imprudente fue consecuencia de una imprudencia profesional general, no vinculada al ejercicio de la ginecología, las razones de prevención general y especial permitirían ampliar el ámbito de la inhabilitación más allá de la propia especialidad, afectando al ejercicio global de la medicina. No obstante, aun así, los fines de la pena podrían justificar, por ejemplo, que dicha prohibición afectara únicamente al ejercicio autónomo de la medicina, pero no a ser colaborador de otro médico con el cual puede trabajar bajo supervisión o control.

[93] Cfr. WEDEKIND, V. E. (2006), 56, quien recoge asimismo las referencias jurisprudenciales correspondientes a los ejemplos expuestos.

[94] No puedo entrar en este momento en las argumentaciones correspondientes en este sentido.

DIREITO DA SAÚDE

profesional no tienen que derivar necesariamente en la aplicación de la inhabilitación profesional al ejercicio de la profesión médica en general. Para ello es preciso una motivación referida concreta y expresamente a la pena de inhabilitación profesional, y que fundamente si la misma debe aplicarse al ejercicio de la profesión médica en general o, por el contrario, sólo a un aspecto, especialidad o actividad de la misma. Este tipo de fundamentación se lleva a cabo en muy pocos casos, a pesar de la exigencia legal al respecto[95].

Pero la base del problema radica a su vez en que los tipos penales (centrándome ahora en los más susceptibles de comisión en el ejercicio de la profesión médica)[96]no contemplan una concreción o detalle similar a la que, como hemos visto, hacen el StGB (ejercicio de la profesión, de la especialidad, del oficio o de la rama industrial) o el CP portugués (ejercicio de la respectiva actividad), e incluso el propio CP español en otros tipos penales. Es muy probable que si aquellos tipos recogiesen dichas especificaciones serían más numerosas las sentencias que restringirían la inhabilitación profesional a la especialidad médica correspondiente.

La fundamentación del ámbito y alcance de la inhabilitación profesional ha de basarse en la correspondencia que debe existir entre la relación del delito con la profesión y la relación de la pena con la profesión en los términos expuestos, contemplando asimismo el punto de vista de los fines de la penal. Sobre esta base cabría admitir en principio (aunque ello precisa de un estudio más a fondo) que en los hechos dolosos cometidos en el ejercicio de la profesión médica (prácticamente inexistentes) la pena de inhabilitación profesional afecte al ejercicio de la profesión

---

[95] Dicha motivación no debe restringirse exclusivamente al caso en que la pena de inhabilitación se imponga como accesoria (requisito exigido expresamente en el art. 56.1.3º), sino que debe afectar también -y ciertamente así lo hacen algunas sentencias, aunque pocas-.a su imposición como pena principal: para determinar tanto lo que se refiere a la vinculación de la profesión médica con el delito, como el ámbito de aplicación de la inhabilitación a dicha profesión, bien sea en general o bien restringida a una especialidad o actividad concreta de la misma. Sobre el planteamiento general del problema, cfr., entre otras, STS 22-2-2008, s. nº 111/2008, recurso casación 10339/2007; STS 6-10-2009, s nº 973/2009, recurso casación 29/2009.

[96] Es decir, fundamentalmente los delitos con resultado de muerte o lesiones (junto a otros como, por ejemplo, manipulación genética, denegación de asistencia sanitaria o abandono de los servicios sanitarios; etc.), dejando fuera otros, como la falsedad documental, estafa, etc., no vinculados en principio al ejercicio de la profesión médica.

médica en general, tanto si se impone como pena accesoria (arts. 45, 54 y 56) como principal (como expresamente ya se prevé, por ejemplo, en el aborto doloso no consentido; art. 144; en la alteración dolosa del genotipo; art. 159.1; en la práctica de reproducción asistida en una mujer, sin su consentimiento; art. 161; o en la denegación de asistencia sanitaria o abandono de los servicios sanitarios; art. 196.), Por el contrario, en los delitos imprudentes (que constituyen la práctica totalidad de los cometidos en el ejercicio de la profesión médica), el principio general será la restricción de la pena de inhabilitación a la especialidad o incluso a una actividad concreta del autor del hecho; y la excepción, debidamente motivada, la extensión al ejercicio de la profesión médica en general.

Con este artículo quiero aportar afectuosamente mi pequeña contribución al libro homenaje al Prof. Dr. Guilherme de Oliveira en reconocimiento a su excelente labor en el ámbito jurídico y en particular en el Derecho médico y en agradecimiento a la cordial y fructífera relación científica con él mantenida en el Centro de Direito Biomédico, que de forma tan extraordinaria ha dirigido durante muchos años.

Bibliografía

Álvarez García, F. J. (2000), *Retribución y prevención general negativa como fines de la pena.* Cuadernos de Política Criminal, nº. 72 (2000), pp. 563-613.

Ayo Fernández, M. (1997), *Las penas, medidas de seguridad y consecuencias accesorias. Manual de determinación de las penas y de las demás consecuencias jurídico--penales del delito,* Ed. Aranzadi, Pamplona, 1997.

Baucells i Lladós, J. (1995), *Los delitos de insumisión y el nuevo Proyecto de Código Penal.* Cuadernos Jurídicos, nº 33 (1995), pp. 48-57.

Bockemühl, J. (2005), § 70: Anordnung des Berufsverbots; § 70 a: Aussetzung des Berufsverbots. En: Joecks, W. / Miebach, K. (edtrs.), *Münchener Kommentar zum Strafgesetxbuch.* t. 2/1, §§ 52-79b StGB. Ed. Beck. München, 2005.

Boldova Pasamar, M.A. (1996), En; Gracia Martín, L. / Alastuey Dobón, M.C. / Boldova Pasamar, M.A. *Las consecuencias jurídicas del delito en el nuevo Código penal español el sistema de penas, medidas de seguridad, consecuencias accesorias y responsabilidad civil derivada del delito.* Ed. Tirant lo Blanch. Valencia. 1996.

Cardenal Montraveta, S. (2011), En: Corcoy Bidasolo, M / Mir Puig, S. (Dirts.) (2011), *Comentarios al Código penal. Reforma LO 5/2010.* Ed. Tirant lo Blanch. Valencia, 2011, pp. 137-184 y 213-264.

CHOCLÁN MONTALVO, J. A. (1997), *Las penas privativas de derechos en la reforma penal.* Actualidad Penal nº 8, 17 a 23 de febrero de 1997. 163 ss.

CORCOY BIDASOLO, M / CARPIO BRIZ, D. (2011), En: CORCOY BIDASOLO, M / MIR PUIG, S. (Dirts.) (2011), *Comentarios al Código penal. Reforma LO 5/2010.* Ed. Tirant lo Blanch. Valencia, 2011, pp. 970-1044.

CORCOY BIDASOLO, M / MIR PUIG, S. (Dirts.) (2011), *Comentarios al Código penal. Reforma LO 5/2010.* Ed. Tirant lo Blanch. Valencia.

DE LA CUESTA ARZAMENDI, J. L. (2009), *Formas sustitutivas de las penas privativas de libertad en el Códogp penal espàñol de 1995.* En, Echano Basaldúa, J. I (coord.). Estudios jurídicos en Memoria de José María Lidón. Ed. A cargo del Área de Derecho Penal. Universidad de Deusto, pp. 125-153

DOMÍNGUEZ IZQUIERDO, E. M. (2014), *Cuando la pena accesoria de inhabilitación especial requiere relación directa con el delito cometido.* Cuadernos de Política Criminal, nº 112, Época II, mayo 2014, pp. 137-194..

FERNÁNDEZ TERUELO, J. G. (2005), *La inhabilitación profesional del delincuente económico-empresarial.* En: CARBONELL MATEU, J. C. / DEL ROSAL BLASCO, B. / MORILLAS CUEVA, L. / ORTS BERENGUER, E. / QUINTANAR DÍAZ, M. (Coords.) Estudios penales en homenaje al profesor Cobo del Rosal. Ed. Dykinson, Madrid. 2005, pp. 351-361.

FISCALÍA GENERAL DEL ESTADO (2005), *Circular 1/2005. Sobre aplicación de la reforma del Código Penal operada pora Ley Orgánica 15/2003, de 25 de noviembre.*

FRAILE COLOMA, C. (2010), En: GÓMEZ TOMILLO, M. (Dir.) (2010), *Comentarios al Código penal.* Ed. Lex Nova. Valladolid, 2010, pp. 1484-1510.

GARCÍA ARÁN, M. (1997), *.Fundamentos y aplicación de penas y medidas de seguridad en el Código penal español de 1995.* Ed. Aranzadi. Pamplona.

GIMBERNAT ORDEIG, E. (1980), *El sistema de penas en el futuro Código penal.* En, La reforma del Derecho penal. Ed. Servicio de publicaciones de la UAB, Bellaterra, Barcelona, 1980, pp. 181 ss.

GRACIA MARTÍN, L. / ALASTUEY DOBÓN, M.C. / BOLDOVA PASAMAR, M.A., (1998), *Lecciones de consecuencias jurídicas del delitoel sistema de penas, medidas de seguridad, consecuencias accesorias y responsabilidad civil derivada del delito.* Ed. Tirant lo Blanch. Valencia.

GRUPO DE ESTUDIOS DE POLÍTICA CRIMINAL (2005), *Una propuesta alternativa al sistema de penas y su ejecución, y a las medidas cautelares personales.* Ed. Grupo de Estudios de Política Criminal. Distrib. y venta electrónica, Tirant lo blanch. Valencia. http://www.gepc.es/web/sites/default/files/ficheros/gepc8.pdf

GUTIÉRREZ CASTAÑEDA, A. (2012), *Las penas privativas de derechos políticos y profesionales. Bases para un nuevo modelo regulativo,* Editorial Tirant lo Blanch, Valencia.

HANACK, E. W. (1996), § 70: Anordnung des Berufsverbots; § 70 a: Aussetzung des Berufsverbots. En: StGB: *Leipziger Kommentar; Großkommentar*, 11., neubearb. Aufl. Lfg. 23 §§ 69 – 72. Ed. Walter de Gruyter. Berlin. New York. 1996, pp. 211-272.

JESCHECK, H. H. (1978), *Tratado de Derecho penal, Parte General*, 3ª ed. (trad. MIR PUIG, S. y MUÑOZ CONDE, F.), Tomo II. Bosch casa Editorial, Barcelona, 1978.

JESCHECK, H. H. (1993), *Tratado de Derecho penal, Parte General*, 4ª ed. (trad. MANZANARES SAMANIEGO, J. L.), Ed. Comares, Granada. 1993.

JOECKS, W. / MIEBACH, K. –edtrs.– (2005), *Münchener Kommentar zum Strafgesetxbuch*. t. 2/1, §§ 52-79b StGB. Ed. Beck. München, 2005.

DE LAMO RUBIO, J. (1999), *Incidencia de la Ley Orgánica 14/1999, de 9 de junio en el sistema de penas del Código Penal de 1995*, Noticias jurídicas. Artículos doctrinales, Diciembre 1999, pp. 1-4. *http://noticias.juridicas.com/articulos/55-Derecho-Penal/199912-l14penas.html*

LLORCA ORTEGA, J. (1990), *Manual de determinación de la pena*. Ed. Tirant lo Blanch. 3ª ed. 1990. Valencia.

LUZÓN PEÑA, D. M. (1983), *Aplicación y sustitución de la pena en el futuro Código Penal*. En: RFDUC, monográfico nº 6, 1983, 413 ss.

LUZÓN PEÑA, D. M. (1991), *La aplicación y sustitución de la pena en el futuro Código Penal*. En: Estudios Penales, Barcelona, 1991, 281 ss.

LUZÓN PEÑA, D. M. (1991a), *Estudios penales*. Ed. Promociones y Publicaciones Universitarias, PPU, 1991.

LUZÓN PEÑA, D. M. (2012), *Lecciones de Derecho Penal, Parte General*, 2ª ed. Editorial Tirant. Valencia.

MAGRO SERVET, V. / SOLAZ SOLAZ, E. (2008), *Manual práctico sobre la ejecución penal. Las medidas alternativas a la prisión*. Ed. La Ley, Madrid.

MANZANARES SAMANIEGO, J. L. (1975), *Las inhabilitaciones y suspensiones en el Derecho positivo español*. ADPCP, 1975, pp. 175-228.

MANZANARES SAMANIEGO, J. L. (1981), *Las inhabilitaciones y suspensiones en el Proyecto del Código Penal*. ADPCP, I, 1981, 33-58.

MANZANARES SAMANIEGO, J. L. (2002), Las inhabilitaciones para cargo público. En DIEZ RIPOLLÉS, J.L. / ROMEO CASABONA, C. M. / GRACIA MARTÍN, L. / HIGUERA GUIMERÁ, J. F. (edts.) *La ciencia del Derecho Penal ante el nuevo siglo*. Libro homenaje al Prof. Dr. D. José Cerezo Mir. Ed. Tecnos. Madrid, 2002, pp. 1095-112.

MAPELLI CAFFARENA, B. (2002 a), *Penas accesorias*. En: (LUZÓN PEÑA, D. M.. Dir.) *Enciclopedia Penal Básica*. Ed. Comares. Granada, 2002, pp. 1004--1007.

MAPELLI CAFFARENA, B. (2002 b), *Penas privativas de derechos*. En: (LUZÓN PEÑA, D. M.. Dir.) *Enciclopedia Penal Básica*. Ed. Comares. Granada, 2002, pp. 1007-1017.

MAPELLI CAFFARENA, B. (2012), *La pena de inhabilitación absoluta ¿Es necesaria?*. CPC, nº 108 (2012), pp. 5-30

MAPELLI CAFFARENA, B. / TERRADILLOS BASOCO, J. (1996), *Las consecuencias jurídicas del delito*, 3ª ed. Civitas, Madrid.

DE LA MATA AMAYA, J. (1994), *Ejecución de penas restrictivas de libertad y no privativas de derechos*. Cuadernos de Derecho Judicial, nº. 15 (1994), pp. 141-195.

MIR PUIG, S. (2011), *Derecho Penal, Parte General*, 9ª ed. Ed. Reppertor. Barcelona.

NIETO MARTÍN, A. (2008), *La responsabilidad penal de las personas juríddicas: un modelo legislativo.*. Iustel. Madrid.

PAREDES CASTAÑÓN, J. M. (2003), *Los delitos de peligro como técnica de incriminación en el Derecho penal económico: bases político-criminales*. Revista de Derecho Penal y Criminología, 2ª época, nº 11 (2003), pp. 95-164.

PAREDES CASTAÑÓN, J.M. (2002), "La responsabilidad penal por productos defectuosos: problemática político-criminal y reflexiones de *lege ferenda*", en CORCOY VIDASOLO, M. (Dir.) / LARA GONZÁLEZ, R. (Coord.) *Derecho Penal de Empresa*. Universidad Pública de Navarra,. 2002, 403-431.

POZA CISNEROS, M. (1996), *Formas sustitutivas de las penas privativas de libertad*. Cuadernos de Derecho Judicial, CGPJ, XXIV, (1996), 186 ss.

POZUELO PÉREZ, L. (1998), *Las penas privativas de derechos en el Código penal*. Editorial Constitución y Leyes. Colex. Madrid. 1998

QUINTANA JIMÉNEZ, C. (1999), *Suspensión de la ejecución y sustitución de las penas privativas de libertad*. En, Estudios Jurídicos, Ministerio Fiscal III, 1999, pp. 331 ss.

QUINTANO RIPOLLÉS, A. (1966), *Comentarios al Código Penal. 2ª. ed*. Ed. Revista de Derecho Privado, Madrid.

QUINTERO OLIVARES, G. (Dir.) / MORALES PRATS, F. (Coord.) (2011), *Comentarios al Código Penal Español. Tomo I (Artículos 1 a 233)*. Ed. Aranzadi. Thomson Reuters. Pamplona, 2011.

SÁNCHEZ YLLERA, I. (1996), En: VIVES ANTÓN, T. (Coord.) *Comentarios al CP de 1995*, Valencia 1996, 479 ss.

SANZ MORÁN, A. (2010), Medidas de seguridad: régimen general,.En: ÁLVAREZ GARCÍA, F. J.. y GONZÁLEZ CUSSAC, J. L.. (Dirs.) *Comentarios a la Reforma Penal de 2010.*. Ed. Tirant lo Blanch, Valencia, 2010, pp. 139-143.

SANZ MORÁN, A. (2013), Medidas de seguridad,.En: ÁLVAREZ GARCÍA, F. J. (Dir.) y DOPICO GÓMEZ ALLER, J. (Coord.) *Estudio crítico sobre el anteproyecto de re-*

forma penal de 2012. (Ponencias presentadas al Congreso de Profesores de Derecho Penal "Estudio Crítico sobre el Anteproyecto deReforma Penal de 2012", celebradas en la Universidad Carlos III de Madrid los días 31 de eneroy 1 de febrero de 2013). Ed. Tirant lo Blanch, 3ª ed., Valencia, 2013, pp. 467-481.

SILVA SÁNCHEZ, J. M. (1999), La suspensión condicional de la ejecución de la pena principal privativa de libertad y la pena accesoria de inhabilitación para el ejercicio de profesión un oficio. Actualidad Penal, nº. 39 (1999), 751 ss.

SINN, A. (1996), § 70: Anordnung des Berufsverbots; § 70 a: Aussetzung des Berufsverbots. En: WOLTER, J. (ed.) *Systematischer Kommentar zum Strafgesetzbuch: SK-StGB*. Carl Heimanns Ed. [las citas del autor corresponden a la entrega 118, Julio 2009].

SOLAZ SOLAZ, E. (2010), *Manual práctico sobre la ejecución penal: Las medidas alternativas a la prisión: suspensión, sustitución y expulsión.* (MAGRO SERVET, V. (colab), 2ª ed. Revisada. Ed. La Ley. Madrid.

SUANZES PÉREZ, F. (1999), *Reflexiones en torno a las nuevas penas privativvas de derechos introducidas por las LO 11 y 14 / 1999, de modificación del Código Penal.* http://ruc.udc.es/dspace/bitstream/2183/2021/1/AD-3-28.pdf

TAMARIT SUMALLA, J. M. (2007), *Sistema de sanciones y política criminal. Un estudio de Derecho comparado europeo.* Revista Electrónica de Ciencia Penal y Criminología. RECPC 09-06 (2007), pp. 1-40. http://criminet.ugr.es/recpc/09/recpc09-06.pdf

TAMARIT SUMALLA, J. M. (2011), En: QUINTERO OLIVARES, G. (Dir.) / MORALES PRATS, F. (Coord.) (2011), *Comentarios al Código Penal Español.* Tomo I (Artículos 1 a 233). Ed. Aranzadi. Thomson Reuters. Cizur Menor. Pamplona, 2011.

TERRADILLOS BASOCO, J. (1995), *Derecho penal de la empresa.* Ed. Trotta. Madrid. 1995.

DE VICENTE REMESAL, J. (2002), *Rectificación postdelictiva: reparación y confesión.* En: (LUZÓN PEÑA, D. M.. Dir.) *Enciclopedia Penal Básica.* Ed. Comares. Granada, 2002, pp. 1088-1090.

DE VICENTE REMESAL, J. (2014 a), *Control de riesgos en la empresa y responsabilidad penal: la responsabilidad de la persona física (directivo, representante legal o administrador de hecho o de derecho de una persona jurídica) por infringir los deberes de vigilancia o control.* Revista Penal, nº 34 (julio, 2014), pp. 170-204.

DE VICENTE REMESAL, J. (2014 b), *La pena de inhabilitación profesional: consideraciones desde el punto de vista de los fines de la pena.* Cuadernos de Política Criminal, nº 113, II, Época II, septiembre 2014, pp. 45-104.

VIDAL CASTAÑÓN, A. (2003), *La Pena de Inhabilitación*. Noticias Jurídicas. Artículos doctrinales: Derecho Penal. Octubre 2003. http://noticias.juridicas.com/articulos/55-Derecho-Penal/200310-2855132381032265l.html

VILLACAMPA ESTIARTE, C. (2007), *El proceso de armonización de las penas de inhabilitación en el seno de la Unión Europea*. Revista de Derecho y Proceso Penal, nº 17 (2007), pp. 111-135,

VILLACAMPA ESTIARTE, C. (2009), Las penas de inhabilitación en la Unión Europea: regulación comparada y proceso de armonización. En: TAMARIT SUMALLA, J. M. (Coord.). *Las sentencias penales en Europa*. Ed. Aranzadi. Cizur Menor. 2009, pp. 251-300.

VV. AA. (2008), *Sistemas penales comparados: las medidas de seguridad*, Revista Penal. http://www.uhu.es/revistapenal/index.php/penal/article/viewFile/388/379

VV. AA. (2010) PLATAFORMA OTRO DERECHO PENAL ES POSIBLE, *Valoración de la plataforma "otro Derecho penal es posible", sobre la tramitación del Proyecto de Ley Orgánica de reforma del Código Penal.* (19 pp.) http://www.larevistilla.org/wp-content/uploads/2012/10/Valoraci%C3%B3n-del-C%C3%B3digo-Penal-por-la-Plataforma.pdf

WEDEKIND, V. E. (2006), *Die Reform des strafrechtlichen Berufsverbots (§§ 70-70b StGB)*. Inaugural Dissertation zur Erlangung der Doktorwürde der Juristischen Fakultät der Eberhard-Karls-Universität Tübingen. Druckerei Hans-Joachim Köhler Tübingen, 2006.

Estudio de derecho comparado sobre el consentimiento informado en los tratamientos médicos curativos

Virgilio Rodríguez-Vázquez*

Sumario: 1. Introducción. 2. El concepto unidimensional del bien jurídico protegido en el delito de lesiones. 2.1. El consentimiento informado como causa de justificación. 2.2. El tratamiento médico arbitrario: la solución del Código Penal en Portugal. 3. El concepto bidimensional del bien jurídico protegido en el delito de lesiones. 4. Crítica y toma de postura. 5. Conclusiones.

1. Introducción[1]

Los tratamientos médicos curativos se identifican con aquellas intervenciones sanitarias que inciden positivamente en la salud del enfermo, y en

---

* Profesor Titular de Derecho Penal de la Universidad de Vigo. Facultad de Derecho. Campus Universitario. Universidad de Vigo. 32004 Ourense. virxilio@uvigo.es

[1] El presente trabajo se inscribe en los proyectos de investigación "Responsabilidad de personas físicas y jurídicas en el ámbito médico-sanitario: estrategias para la prevención de errores médicos y eventos adversos", Ref. DER2011-22934, del que es investigador principal el Prof. Dr. Javier De Vicente Remesal, Catedrático de Derecho penal de la Universidad de Vigo, y de cuyo equipo investigador formo parte y "Las garantías penales como límite y guía en la solución de problemas penales complejos: la necesidad de evitar atajos" (Referencia: DER2013-47511-R, Ministerio de Ciencia e Innovación) del que es investigador principal el Prof. Dr. Miguel Díaz y García Conlledo, Catedrático de Derecho penal de la Universidade de León, y de cuyo equipo investigador formo parte.

DIREITO DA SAÚDE

un sentido amplio se pueden definir como "la acción llevada a cabo por un médico en el ejercicio de su actividad profesional, dirigida a favorecer las condiciones de vida de un ser humano viviente"[2]. Ante una definición como ésta parecen tener cabida todo tipo de intervenciones sanitarias; no obstante, existen supuestos que deben excluirse de la misma, al constituir claros ejemplos de intervenciones sanitarias no curativas, y otros cuya localización resulta más dudosa. Entre los tratamientos médicos no curativos se encuentra la extracción de órganos de una persona sana con la finalidad de trasplantarlos a un enfermo. Junto a éste se suele citar la investigación llevada a cabo mediante la experimentación en personas, si bien es necesario distinguir entre experimentación pura, cuyas características la convierten indudablemente en una forma de intervención sanitaria no curativa, y la experimentación terapéutica, que se ha reconocido como una posible vía de intervención curativa[3]. También se incluyen como tratamientos médicos no curativos la esterilización, la cirugía transexual y la cirugía estética, aunque tal decisión merece ser matizada, ya que intervenciones de este tipo pueden poseer un carácter curativo en determinados casos[4]. En definitiva, no es menor la dificultad de concretar en la práctica los casos de tratamientos curativos y no curativos. Aquí simplemente quiero dejar constancia de tales distinciones, advirtiendo que

[2] ROMEO CASABONA, C.M., El médico y el derecho penal I: la actividad curativa (licitud y responsabilidad penal), pról. CEREZO MIR, J., Barcelona, Bosch, 1981, 9 ss., 271; véase también, BERDUGO GÓMEZ DE LA TORRE, I., El delito de lesiones, Salamanca, Universidad de Salamanca, 1982, 29; ESER, A., Problemas de justificación y exculpación en la actividad médica, en: MIR PUIG (ed.), Avances de la Medicina y Derecho penal, Barcelona, PPU, 1988, 11; JORGE BARREIRO, Agustín, La imprudencia punible en la actividad médico-quirúrgica, Madrid, Tecnos, 1990, 17; VILLACAMPA ESTIARTE, C., Responsabilidad penal del personal sanitario. Atribución de responsabilidad penal en tratamientos médicos efectuados por diversos profesionales, Pamplona, Aranzadi, 2003, 52.
[3] Véase ROMEO CASABONA, C.M., La actividad curativa..., cit., 1981, 271; ESER, A., en: MIR PUIG (ed.), Avances de la medicina..., cit., 1988, 16; JORGE BARREIRO, Agustín, Actividad médico-quirúrgica..., cit., 1990, 21; DA COSTA ANDRADE, M., Consentimento e acordo em Direito Penal (Contributo para a fundamentaçao de um paradigma dualista), Coimbra, Coimbra Editora, 2004, 469 s.
[4] Entre otros, CARBONELL MATEU, J.C./GONZÁLEZ CUSSAC, J.L., en: VIVES ANTÓN, T. S. (coord.), Comentarios al Código Penal de 1995, t. I y II., Valencia, Tirant lo Blanch, 1996, 810; LÓPEZ BARJA DE QUIROGA, J., Derecho penal. PG. II. Introducción a la teoría jurídica del delito; IV. Las consecuencias jurídicas del delito. El Derecho penal de ejecución, Madrid, Marcial Pons, 172; VILLACAMPA ESTIARTE, C., Atribución..., cit., 2003, 49; DA COSTA ANDRADE, M., Consentimento..., cit., 2004, 470.

el valor del consentimiento del paciente será diferente, en mi opinión, según el supuesto ante el que nos encontremos. En el presente estudio me limito al análisis del mismo en el ámbito de los tratamientos médicos curativos, buscando soluciones a partir de la concreción del bien jurídico que se considera protegido en el delito de lesiones.

2. El concepto unidimensional del bien jurídico protegido en el delito de lesiones

2.1. El consentimiento informado como causa de justificación

Un sector de la doctrina considera que todo tratamiento médico curativo realiza, de entrada, el tipo de lesiones[5]. Y esto porque el bien jurídico protegido por el delito de lesiones se identifica exclusivamente con la integridad física (o la integridad y la salud), diferenciada intencionadamente de la salud. Desde este punto de vista, cuyo origen se sitúa en la jurisprudencia alemana[6], se parte de que toda intervención u operación

---

[5] Véase Arzt, G., Strafrecht. BT I (Delikte gegen die Person), Bielefeld, Ernst und Werner Gieseking, 102; Schwalm, FS-Bockelmann, 1979, 547; Bottke, W., Suizid und Strafrecht, Berlin, Duncker und Humblot, 1982, 144 s.; Schreiber, H-L., Zur Reform des Arztstrafrechts, en: FS-Hirsch, 1999, 713, 724. En la doctrina española Bajo Fernández, M., Manual de Derecho Penal. PE. Delitos contra las personas, 2º ed., Madrid, Ceura, 1987, 164; Moyano García, R., Consentimiento del paciente e imprudencia médica, CuadDJ 1993-I, 481 s.

[6] Desde que el RG en su sentencia de 31 de mayo de 1894 asumiese esta postura. Precisamente esta decisión judicial marca el inicio de una importante controversia entre la jurisprudencia y la doctrina alemanas en torno a uno de los aspectos más relevantes del tratamiento médico. Los primeros pronunciamientos doctrinales datan de finales del siglo XIX y principios del siglo XX sin que haya decaído el debate, que perdura en la actualidad. Así se puede ver, entre otros, Finger, A., Chirurgische Operation und ärztliche Behandlung, ZStW 20-1900, 12 ss.; Brückmann, A., Neue Versuche zum Problem der strafrechtlichen Verantwortlichkeit des Arztes für operative Eingriffe. Negatives und Positives, ZStW 24-1904, 657 ss.; Kahl, W., Der Arzt im Strafrecht, ZStW 29-1909, 351 ss.; Beling, E., Die strafrechtliche Verantwortlichkeit des Arztes bei Vornahme und Unterlassung operativer Eingriffe, ZStW 44-1924, 220 ss.; Engisch, K., Ärztlicher Eingriff zu Heilwechen und Einwilligung, ZStW 58-1939, 1 ss.; Grünwald, G., Die Aufklärungspflicht des Arztes, ZStW 73-1961, 5 ss.; Kaufmann, Arthur, Die eigenmächtige Heilbehandlung, ZStW 73-1961, 341 ss.; Bockelmann, P., Der ärztliche Heileingriff in Beiträg zur Zeitschrift für die gesamte Strafrechtswissenschaft im ersten Jahrhundert ihres Bestehens, ZStW 93-1981, 105 ss.; Eser, A., Medizin und Strafrecht: eine schutzgutorientierte Problemübersicht, ZStW 97-1985, 1 ss.; von Gerlach, A., Ärztliche Aufklärungspflicht und eigenmächtige Heilbehandlung, en: Kaufmann, Arthur (dir.), Moderne Medizin und Strafrecht. Ein Vademecum für Ärzte und Juristen über strafrechtliche Grundfragen ärztlicher Tätigkeitsbereich, Heidelberg, C.F.

médica sobre el paciente constituye una lesión corporal, en definitiva, es típica. Sin embargo, esta intervención típica puede quedar justificada y, por tanto, no ser antijurídica cuando concurra el consentimiento válidamente emitido por parte del paciente. El consentimiento del paciente se convierte así en una causa de justificación, de manera que estando presente ésta, el médico o personal sanitario en cuestión quedará exento de responsabilidad penal.

2.2. El tratamiento médico arbitrario: la solución del Código Penal en Portugal

Desde otro sector de la doctrina, crítico con el anterior, se ha defendido que la intervención médico-sanitaria, en principio, no realiza el tipo de lesiones, al no dañar el cuerpo ni la salud del paciente[7]. Entre quienes sostienen un concepto unitario de bien jurídico, identificado con un con-

---

Müller, 1989, 15 ss.; SCHREIBER, H-L., Zur Reform des Arztstrafrechts, en: FS-Hirsch, 1999, 713 ss.; ORBEN, S., Rechtliche Verantwortung für Behandlungsfehler, Heymanns, 2004, 5 s.
[7] En este sentido, ROMEO CASABONA, C.M., La actividad curativa..., cit., 1981, 137, 285 ss.; JORGE BARREIRO, Agustín, La relevancia jurídico-penal del consentimiento del paciente en el tratamiento médico-quirúrgico, CPC 1982, 12; el mismo, Actividad médico-quirúrgica..., cit., 1990, 72, 81; ANTÓN ONECA, J., Notas críticas al Código penal. Las lesiones, en: LH-Pereda, 1965, 791; BERDUGO GÓMEZ DE LA TORRE, I., Lesiones..., cit., 1982, 38; OCTAVIO DE TOLEDO Y UBIETO, E./HUERTA TOCILDO, S., Derecho penal. PG: Teoría jurídica del delito, 2ª ed., Madrid, Castellanos, 1986, 254 s.; LÓPEZ BARJA DE QUIROGA, J., El consentimiento informado, CPC 1995, 470 s.; el mismo, PG II..., cit., 2002, 172 s.; GARCÍA BLÁZQUEZ, M./MOLINOS COBO, J.J., Manual práctico de responsabilidad y defensa de la profesión médica (Aspectos jurídicos y médico-forenses), 3ª ed., Granada, Comares, 2011, 350 ss.; CHOCLÁN MONTALVO, J.A., Deber de cuidado y delito imprudente, Barcelona, Bosch, 1998, 175 s.; QUERALT JIMÉNEZ, J.J., Derecho penal español. PE, 6ª ed., Barcelona, Atelier, 2010, 50 s.; VILLACAMPA ESTIARTE, C., Atribución..., cit., 2003, 53; por todos, STOOS, R., Chirurgische Operation und ärztliche Behandlung: eine strafrechtliche Studie, Berlin, Liebmann, 1898, passim.; ENGISCH, K., ZStW 58-1939, cit., 5 ss.; SCHMIDT, E., Der Arzt im Strafrecht, Leipzig, Verlag von Theodor Weicher, 1939, 69 ss.; GRÜNWALD, G., ZStW 73-1961, cit., 1, 9; KAUFMANN, Arthur, ZStW 73-1961, cit., 341 s., 373 s.; BOCKELMANN, P., Strafrecht des Arztes, Stuttgart, Georg Thieme, 1968, 66 ss.; el mismo, ZStW 93-1981, cit., 105 ss.; NIESE, W., Ein Beitrag zur Lehre vom ärztliche Heileingriff, en: FS-Eb. Schmidt, 1971, 364 ss.; KRAUSS, D., Zur strafrechtlichen Problematik der eigenmächtigen Heilbehandlung, en: FS-Bockelmann, 1979, 565 ss.; ZIPF, H., Probleme eines Straftatbestandes der eigenmächtigen Heilbehandlung (dargestellt an Hand von § 110 öStGB), en: FS-Bockelmann, 1979, 577, 583; ZIPF, Problemas del tratamiento curativo realizado sin consentimiento en el Derecho penal alemán y austriaco. Consideración especial del transplante de órganos en: MIR PUIG (ed.), Avances de la medicina y Derecho penal, Barcelona, PPU, 1988, 155; ULSENHEIMER, K., Arztstrafrecht in

cepto amplio de "salud"[8], comprensivo de la salud en sentido estricto y de la integridad física, que jugaría así un papel instrumental respecto a aquélla[9], existen dos pareceres diferenciados. Algunos autores determinan la tipicidad o atipicidad de la conducta del médico en función del resultado del tratamiento, de manera que si existe desvalor de resultado, la conducta será típica (delito de lesiones), haciéndose necesario acudir a una causa de justificación para considerarlo lícito[10]. Otros, sin embargo, resuelven la cuestión de la tipicidad de la conducta en relación con el desvalor de acción, de manera que la intervención médica curativa, practicada según la *lex artis*[11], o para ser más exactos, conforme al deber de cuidado, excluyendo el carácter doloso e imprudente de la misma, no

der Praxis, 3ª ed., pról. BEULKE, Werner/SCHREIBER, Hans Ludwig, Heidelberg, C.F. Müller, 73 ss.; DA COSTA ANDRADE, M., Consentimento..., cit., 2004, 400 ss.

[8] Véase ROMEO CASABONA, C.M., La actividad curativa..., cit., 1981, 286; el mismo, Los delitos contra la integridad corporal y la salud, en: LH-Torío, 925; BERDUGO GÓMEZ DE LA TORRE, I., Lesiones..., cit., 1982, 22; JORGE BARREIRO, Agustín, Actividad médico-quirúrgica..., cit., 1990, 81; CARBONELL MATEU, J.C./GONZÁLEZ CUSSAC, J.L..., en: VIVES, Coment I..., cit., 1996, 788 s.; LÓPEZ BARJA DE QUIROGA, J., PG II..., cit., 2002, 171; VILLACAMPA ESTIARTE, C., Atribución..., cit., 2003, 51 s.; MUÑOZ CONDE, F., Derecho Penal. PE, 19ª ed., Valencia, Tirant lo Blanch, 2013, 107. Desde este punto de vista se asume el concepto de salud personal formulado por la OMS, como "el estado en el que una persona determinada desarrolla normalmente sus funciones, entendiendo por función el ejercicio de un órgano o aparato. Estado que, por otra parte, constituye una de las condiciones previas que posibilitan una concreta relación de participación en el correspondiente sistema social". Aunque ésta no es asumida, por ejemplo, por ROMEO CASABONA, C.M., LH-Torío, cit., 1999, 926.

[9] Así lo entienden, BERDUGO GÓMEZ DE LA TORRE, I., Lesiones..., cit., 1982, 20 s.; CARBONELL MATEU, J.C./GONZÁLEZ CUSSAC, J.L., en VIVES, Coment I..., cit., 1996, 789.

[10] Una relación detallada de los autores que sostienen esta postura en JORGE BARREIRO, Agustín, CPC 1982, cit., 8.

[11] Véase ANTÓN ONECA, J., LH-Pereda, cit., 1965, 791; ROMEO CASABONA, C.M., La actividad curativa..., cit., 1981, 9 ss., 273; el mismo, LH-Torío, cit., 1999, 927; JORGE BARREIRO, Agustín, CPC 1982, cit., 8; el mismo, Actividad médico-quirúrgica..., cit., 1990, 70; el mismo, Derecho a la información y el consentimiento informado, en: LAFARGA I TRAVER (coord.), IV Congreso "Derecho y Salud". Los Derechos de los usuarios de los servicios sanitarios (Donostia, 15, 16 y 17 de noviembre de 1995), Gasteiz, Servicio Central de Publicaciones del Gobierno Vasco, 1996, 167; BERDUGO GÓMEZ DE LA TORRE, I., Lesiones..., cit., 1982, 39.; ZIPF, H., en: MIR PUIG (ed.), Avances de la medicina..., cit., 1988, 156; CARBONELL MATEU, J.C./GONZÁLEZ CUSSAC, J.L., en: VIVES, Coment I..., cit., 1996, 807; CHOCLÁN MONTALVO, J.A., Cuidado..., cit., 1998, 175; VILLACAMPA ESTIARTE, C., Atribución..., cit., 2003, 58, 72; MUÑOZ CONDE, F., PE, cit., 16ª, 2007, 130; JESCHECK, H.H./WEIGEND, T., Tratado de Derecho Penal. PG, trad. 3ª ed. y adiciones MIR PUIG/MUÑOZ CONDE, Barcelona, Bosch, 1981; trad. 5ª ed. OLMEDO CARDENETE, Granada, Comares, 407; LÓPEZ BARJA DE QUIROGA, J., PG II, cit., 2002, 172.

DIREITO DA SAÚDE

constituye lesión típica aunque con ella haya empeorado el estado de salud del paciente, sólo atribuible, en tales circunstancias, a caso fortuito. Así pues, la intervención médica curativa no será constitutiva de un delito de lesiones, bien por razones objetivas, en aquellos casos en los que la acción médica ha tenido éxito, conforme a lo que la ciencia médica entiende por tal, o bien por razones subjetivas, cuando ha sido ejecutada de acuerdo con lo exigido por el estado de la ciencia, cumpliendo con el deber de cuidado y sin que quepa responsabilidad a título de imprudencia. Se concluye que el médico no lesiona sino que cura, con independencia de que haya mediado o no el consentimiento del paciente, pues la protección a su salud no se ve afectada por la presencia o ausencia de aquél[12]. Desde este punto de vista, el consentimiento del paciente resulta intrascendente en relación con el delito de lesiones, pues por una parte, la libertad de disposición sobre la propia salud, es decir, la autodeterminación personal, no se contempla como un bien jurídico protegido por el tipo de lesiones[13], y, por otra, porque desde el momento en el que se califica la acción médico-sanitaria como una conducta atípica, ya no es necesario acudir a una causa de justificación que excluya la antijuridicidad[14]. No obstante, esto no quiere decir que la actuación del profesional sanitario realizada de espaldas a la voluntad del paciente, permanezca ajena al Derecho penal. La conducta médica realizada en contra de la voluntad del paciente o en ausencia de la manifestación de su consentimiento

---

[12] Véase ROMEO CASABONA, C.M., La actividad curativa..., cit., 1981, 274, 286; el mismo, Responsabilidad médico-sanitaria y sida, Apen 1996, 464; JORGE BARREIRO, Agustín, CPC 1982, cit., 7 ss.; el mismo, en: LAFARGA I TRAVER (coord.), Usuarios de los servicios sanitarios..., cit., 1996, 164 ss.; BUENO ARÚS, F., El rechazo del tratamiento en el ámbito hospitalario, Apen 1991, 399; GÓMEZ PAVÓN, P., Tratamientos médicos: su responsabilidad penal y civil, 3ª, Barcelona, Bosch, 2013, 284 ss.; VILLACAMPA ESTIARTE, C., Atribución..., cit., 2003, 56.

[13] ROMEO CASABONA, C.M., La actividad curativa..., cit., 1981, 302 ss.; CHOCLÁN MONTALVO, J.A., Cuidado..., cit., 1998, 175; JESCHECK, H.H./WEIGEND, T., Tratado PG, cit., 2002, 403, 406.

[14] DÍAZ VALCÁRCEL, Revisión del CP, 1963, 181; ANTÓN ONECA, J., LH-Pereda, cit., 1965, 791; ROMEO CASABONA, C.M., La actividad curativa..., cit., 1981, 285 s., 304; JORGE BARREIRO, Agustín, Actividad médico-quirúrgica..., cit., 1990, 73; CARBONELL MATEU, J.C./GONZÁLEZ CUSSAC, J.L., en: VIVES, Coment I, cit., 1996, 808 s.; CHOCLÁN MONTALVO, J.A., Cuidado..., cit., 1998, 176; LÓPEZ BARJA DE QUIROGA, J., PG II, cit., 2002, 172.

supone un ataque a su libertad[15]. La mayoría de los que sostienen esta postura en España consideran que la intervención médica realizada sin contar con el consentimiento del paciente, fuera de los casos en los que su ausencia esté justificada, constituirá un delito de coacciones[16]. Algunos autores entienden que puede llegar a constituir un delito de detenciones ilegales[17], e incluso hay quien sugiere investigar la posible aplicación del delito de trato inhumano o degradante[18]. Son pocos los que proponen la introducción del "tratamiento arbitrario" como tipo específico que san-

---

[15] Díaz Valcárcel, L.M., La revisión del Código Penal y otras leyes penales: Decretos de 24 de enero y 28 de marzo de 1963, Barcelona, Nauta, 1963, 181 s.; Antón Oneca, J., LH-Pereda, cit., 1965, 791; Romeo Casabona, C.M., La actividad curativa..., cit., 1981, 286; Berdugo Gómez de la Torre, I., Lesiones..., cit., 1982, 32; Jorge Barreiro, Agustín, CPC 1982, cit., 16; el mismo, en: Lafarga i Traver (coord.), Usuarios de los servicios sanitarios..., cit., 1996, 164; Higuera Guimerá, J.F., El delito de coacciones, 2ª ed., pról. Cerezo Mir, José, Barcelona, Bosch, 1983, 219; López Barja de Quiroga, J., PG II, cit., 2002, 169; Gómez Rivero, P., Responsabilidad penal del médico, 2ª, Valencia, Tirant lo Blanch, 2008, 343 s.

[16] Véase Díaz Valcárcel, L.M., Revisión del CP..., cit., 1963, 182; Antón Oneca, J., LH-Pereda, cit., 1965, 791; Romeo Casabona, C.M., La actividad curativa..., cit., 1981, 287 s., 357; el mismo, El médico ante el Derecho, pról. Horno Liria, Madrid, Ministerio de Sanidad y Consumo, 1985, 48, 287 s.; Jorge Barreiro, Agustín, CPC 1982, cit., 16; el mismo, Actividad médico-quirúrgica..., cit., 1990, 81; el mismo, en: Lafarga i Traver (coord.), Usuarios de los servicios sanitarios..., cit., 1996, 167; Higuera Guimerá, J.F., Coacciones..., cit., 1983, 219 s.; Rodríguez Devesa, J.M./Serrano, A., Derecho penal español, PG, 18ª ed., Madrid, Dykinson, 1995, 517; López Barja de Quiroga, J., CPC 1995, cit., 465 s.; el mismo, El consentimiento informado, en: Martínez Martín (coord.), Responsabilidad del personal sanitario (actas del seminario conjunto sobre la responsabilidad del personal sanitario celebrado en Madrid los días 14, 15 y 16 de noviembre), Madrid, Consejo General del Poder Judicial, 1995, 295 ss.; el mismo, PG II, 2002, 169; Carbonell Mateu, J.C./González Cussac, J.L., en: Vives, Coment I, cit., 1996, 807 s.; García Blázquez, M./Molinos Cobo, J.J., Manual práctico de responsabilidad y defensa de la profesión médica (Aspectos jurídicos y médico-forenses), 2ª ed., Granada, Comares, 1997, 355; Palou Bretones, A., Responsabilidad del personal sanitario, LL 1999-6, 1939; Villacampa Estiarte, C., Atribución..., cit., 2003, 70; Cortés Bechiarelli, E., Ejercicio de las profesiones sanitarias y delitos imprudentes, CuadDJ 2005-XVI, 26.

[17] Véase Romeo Casabona, C.M., La actividad curativa..., cit., 1981, 287, 357; Jorge Barreiro, Agustín, Actividad médico-quirúrgica..., cit., 1990, 81; López Barja De Quiroga, J., CPC 1995, cit., 465 s.; el mismo, en: Martínez Martín (coord.), Personal sanitario..., cit., 1995, 295 ss.; el mismo, PG II, cit., 2002, 169 s.; Villacampa Estiarte, C., Atribución..., cit., 2003, 70.

[18] En este sentido, Villacampa Estiarte, C., Atribución..., cit., 2003, 70.

cione esta clase de intervenciones sanitarias[19], a diferencia de lo que sucede en otros países europeos en los que no sólo existe pronunciamiento doctrinal al respecto sino que incluso se ha tratado de incorporar este tipo al ordenamiento jurídicopenal, o se ha introducido finalmente[20].

En este orden de cosas, el modelo portugués destaca por su singular regulación positiva del Derecho penal médico, hasta el punto de constituir en esta materia una suerte de isla en el océano de los ordenamientos jurídicos europeos. El legislador portugués se adhiere a la doctrina según la cual el tratamiento médico indicado, realizado conforme al estado de la ciencia y con finalidad curativa, no puede ser comprendido como delito de lesiones, a pesar de que finalmente el resultado sea contrario a lo inicialmente esperado o no satisfaga las expectativas, con independencia, además, de que haya mediado o no el consentimiento del paciente. En el CP portugués el legislador, inmediatamente después de la tipificación del delito de lesiones (arts. 143 ss.), introduce un precepto, a través del art. 150 CP, dirigido exclusivamente a definir el concepto de trata-

---

[19] Así, ANTÓN ONECA, J., LH-Pereda, cit., 1965, 791, no llega a proponer la introducción de un tipo específico, pero deja entrever su valoración positiva; BAJO FERNÁNDEZ, M., PE, cit., 2ª, 1987, 164, para aquellos casos en los que la actividad médico-curativa obtiene un resultado exitoso que no implica menoscabo irreversible en la integridad física del paciente, pero que ha sido realizada sin su consentimiento, propone la creación de un "tipo intermedio"; JORGE BARREIRO, Agustín, Actividad médico-quirúrgica..., cit., 1990, 82 s.; el mismo, en: LAFARGA I TRAVER (coord.), Usuarios de los servicios sanitarios..., cit., 1996, 167 s.; RODRÍGUEZ DEVESA, J.M./SERRANO GÓMEZ, A., PG, cit., 18ª, 1995, 496; VILLACAMPA ESTIARTE, C., Atribución..., cit., 2003, 70. Contra la creación del delito de tratamiento arbitrario en el CP español se manifiesta ROMEO CASABONA, C.M., La actividad curativa..., cit., 1981, 288 s.

[20] En Alemania se muestran a favor de la creación e incorporación de un delito de tratamiento arbitrario, entre otros, GRÜNWALD, G., ZStW 73-1961, cit., 9; KAUFMANN, Arthur, ZStW 73-1961, cit., 374.; ESER, A., ZStW 97-1985, cit., 19; el mismo, en: SCHÖNKE, Adolf/SCHRÖDER, Horst, StGB, Kommentar, 27ª ed., a cargo de LENCKNER, Theodor/CRAMER, Peter/ESER, Albin/STREE, Walter/EISELE, Jörg/HEINE, Günter/PERRON, Walter/STEERNBERG-LIEBEN, Detlev/SCHITTENHELM, München, Beck, 2006, § 223 31; el mismo, en: MIR PUIG (ed.), Avances de la medicina..., cit., 1988, 15; el mismo, FS-Hirsch, cit., 1999, 482 s.; JAKOBS, G., Derecho Penal, PG, Fundamentos y teoría de la imputación, 2ª ed., trad. CUELLO CONTRERAS/GONZÁLEZ DE MURILLO, Madrid, Marcial Pons, 14/6; SCHREIBER, H-L., FS-Hirsch, cit., 1999, 713 ss., pone de manifiesto la oposición de la doctrina mayoritaria en Alemania a la posición adoptada por el BGH en relación con el tratamiento médico, y los continuos intentos por llevar a cabo una reforma del StGB para introducir el delito de tratamiento médico arbitrario; JESCHECK, H.H./WEIGEND, T., Tratado PG, cit., 2002, 407. Desde Austria, ZIPF, H., en: MIR PUIG (ed.), Avances de la medicina..., cit., 1988, 153.

miento médico y a consagrar positivamente su naturaleza atípica en lo que respecta a la protección de la salud e integridad física, cerrando las puertas de manera casi definitiva a las dudas y controversias que sobre el asunto se pudiesen plantear. El art. 150, incluido por primera vez en el CP portugués de 1982 (aprobado por Decreto-Ley nº 400/82, de 23 de Septiembre)[21], representa "una renovación del Derecho penal portugués, alejándose así, del entendimiento tradicional de la doctrina y jurisprudencia nacionales, que sostenían la calificación invariable de la intervención médico-quirúrgica como lesión corporal típica, cuya ilicitud sólo podría ser superada, en la vigencia del CP de 1852, invocando el 'ejercicio de un derecho' (art. 44.4), una causa de justificación que dependía, en concreto, del consentimiento del paciente"[22]. La revisión a la que el CP de 1982 se ve sometido por medio del Decreto-Ley nº 48/95, de 15 de Marzo, no afecta en lo sustancial al nº 1 del art. 150[23], que permanece invariable hasta la modificación introducida por la Ley nº 65/98, de 2 de Septiembre, quedando su redacción como sigue: "1. Las intervenciones y los tratamientos que, según el estado de los conocimientos y de la experiencia de la medicina, se mostrasen indicados y fuesen llevados

---

[21] El art. 150 CP portugués de 1982, en su primera versión, establece: "1. Las intervenciones y otros tratamientos que, según el estado de los conocimientos y de la experiencia de la medicina, se muestren indicados y fuesen llevados a cabo, de acuerdo con las leges artis, por un médico u otra persona legalmente autorizada para ejecutarlos con intención de prevenir, diagnosticar, vencer, o aminorar una enfermedad, un sufrimiento, una lesión o fatiga corporal o una perturbación mental no se consideran lesiones corporales. 2. Si de la violación de las leges artis resultare un peligro para el cuerpo, la salud o la vida del paciente, el agente será castigado con prisión de hasta 2 años. 3. El procedimiento criminal depende de queja".
[22] DA COSTA ANDRADE, M., Consentimento..., cit., 2004, 451, también señala que el art. 150 CP 1982 supone una reacción frente a los proyectos que lo anteceden. Sobre esta cuestión, MAIA GONÇALVES, M.L., Código Penal Português. Anotado e comentado e legislação complementar, 7ª ed., Coimbra, Livraria Almedina, 1994, 416; DA CUNHA GOMES RODRIGUEZ, A., Responsabilidade Médica en Direito penal. Estudo dos pressupostos sistemáticos, Coimbra, Livraria Almedina, 2007, 229 ss.; FIDALGO, S., Responsabilidade penal por negligencia no exercício da medicina m equipa, Coimbra, Coimbra editora, 2008, 37 s.
[23] El art. 150.1 CP portugués, tras la modificación introducida por Decreto-Ley nº 48/95, de 15 de Marzo, dispone: "Las intervenciones y los tratamientos que, según el estado de los conocimientos y de la experiencia de la medicina, se mostrasen indicados y fuesen llevados a cabo, de acuerdo con las *leges artis*, por un médico o por otra persona legalmente autorizada, con intención de prevenir, diagnosticar, vencer o aminorar enfermedad, sufrimiento, lesión o malestar corporal, o perturbación mental, no se consideran menoscabo de la integridad física".

a cabo, de acuerdo con las *leges artis*, por un médico o por otra persona legalmente autorizada, con intención de prevenir, diagnosticar, vencer o reducir una enfermedad, sufrimiento, lesión o malestar corporal, o perturbación mental, no se consideran menoscabo de la integridad física". Esta concepción del tratamiento médico no significa que la actividad de los profesionales sanitarios quede al margen del control jurídicopenal; al contrario, el legislador portugués contempla una serie de previsiones típicas que amplían considerablemente la intervención penal en este ámbito. Por una parte, en el marco de los delitos contra la integridad física y contra la vida, el art. 150.2 CP portugués dispone: "Las personas indicadas en el número anterior que, a la vista de las finalidades en él apuntadas, realizasen intervenciones o tratamientos violando las *leges artis* y creasen, de ese modo, un peligro para la vida o un peligro de grave lesión para el cuerpo o para la salud serán castigadas con la pena de prisión de hasta dos años o con la pena de multa de hasta 240 días, siempre que no les corresponda una pena más grave atendiendo a otra disposición legal"[24]. Este peculiar precepto, sometido a una importante controversia ya antes de su nacimiento[25], que carece de otros equivalentes en los CP de su entorno, supone adelantar las barreras punitivas hasta el punto de

---

[24] Se trata de un delito de peligro concreto que figuraba en el CP portugués de 1982. La reforma llevada a cabo por el Decreto-Ley nº 48/95, de 15 de Marzo suprime este delito, con lo que la infracción de la *lex artis* pasaba a ser típica sólo si producía un resultado lesivo para la salud del paciente, o su muerte. La reforma introducida por la Ley nº 65/98, de 2 de Septiembre lo recupera para incluirlo nuevamente en el CP portugués.

[25] Maia Gonçalves, M.L., Código Penal Português. Anotado e comentado e legislaçao complementar, 10ª ed., Coimbra, Libraria Almedina, 1996, 514, señala que "los nº 2 y 3 de la versión original del art. 150 del Código no constaban en el proyecto inicial (de 1966), pero ya se incluían en la Propuesta de Ley nº 221/I. Habían sido eliminados en la revisión mencionada anteriormente [*scil*. Dec.-Lei nº 48/95, de 15 de Março], y por razones fundadas: este artículo consagra un caso en que no es posible formular un juicio de censura y por eso el nº 2, subordinado a la intención de prevenir, diagnosticar, vencer o aminorar una dolencia, un sufrimiento, una lesión o malestar corporal o una perturbación mental no podía, dentro de la hermenéutica del Código y de principios indeclinables que perfiló, configurar ninguna infracción penal, siendo por eso aberrante". Posteriormente, la Ley nº 65/98, de 2 de Septiembre, lo recupera y vuelve a incluirlo en el CP portugués en términos prácticamente idénticos a la versión original recogida en el CP portugués de 1982. Un estudio detenido de este precepto se puede encontrar en Silva Dias, A., Direito penal. Parte especial. Crimes contra a vida e a integridade física, 2ª ed., Lisboa, aafdl, 2007, 113 ss.; Da Costa Andrade, M., Intervençoes e tratamentos médico-cirúrgicos, en: Figueiredo Dias, J., Comentário Conimbricense do Código Penal, Tomo I, Coimbra, Coimbra Editora, 1999, 302 ss.

abarcar los tratamientos médicos que no hayan llegado a producir un resultado lesivo o la muerte del paciente. Basta para su castigo con que "el médico u otra persona legalmente autorizada" hayan puesto en peligro la vida o la salud del paciente en el marco de un tratamiento médico, siendo relevante el hecho de apartarse en su actuación de las reglas incluidas en la *lex artis*. Se trata de un delito de peligro concreto reintroducido por la Ley nº 65/98, de 2 de Septiembre, mediante el cual, como señala VAZ RODRÍGUEZ, "el legislador quiere ampliar intencionadamente el arsenal de medios punitivos de los ilícitos imputables a los médicos. La exigencia se justifica en términos individuales y colectivos. En términos individuales, se salvaguarda la exigibilidad del empleo de diligencia en el desarrollo de la actividad. En términos colectivos, las necesidades sobre las que se extienden los servicios de salud implican, hoy en día, una progresiva complejidad que incluye medios humanos y estructuras de dimensiones crecientes. Uno de los efectos de esta realidad parece reflejarse en la relación entre el paciente y el agente médico. Ante aquél surge en menos ocasiones un agente médico visible y tutelar de la actuación profesional y cada vez más una pluralidad de personas que se suceden en el respectivo proceso. Frente al consecuente distanciamiento, el legislador ha querido oponer una creciente responsabilidad por los riesgos inherentes para el paciente"[26]. La duda que suscita este artículo es si exige el dolo del médico en la realización de la conducta o basta la imprudencia. Lo primero supondría, en mi opinión, limitar enormemente su aplicación al ser extremadamente difícil identificar en la práctica médica supuestos en los que el médico o el profesional sanitario infrinja, a sabiendas, la *lex artis*, con la finalidad, además, de situar al paciente en una situación de peligro para su vida o su salud. Por otra parte, resulta complicado, con el principio de legalidad en la mano, admitir la forma imprudente para su punición, pues el art. 150.2 CP portugués no tipifica expresamente la realización imprudente de esta conducta, cuando el art. 13 CP portugués consagra un sistema de *numerus clausus* en relación con los delitos imprudentes. Si el sujeto activo actúa dolosamente, lo que como ya he señalado es extraño en relación con tratamientos médicos curativos, será de aplica-

---

[26] VAZ RODRIGUES, J., O consentimento informado para o acto médico no Ordenamento Jurídico Português (Elementos para o estudo da manifestaçao da vontade do paciente), pról. DE OLIVEIRA, Guilherme, Coimbra, Coimbra Editora, 2001, 60.

DIREITO DA SAÚDE

ción el art. 143 CP portugués[27], cuando se trate de lesiones simples, el art 144 CP portugués[28] para las lesiones graves, y el art. 146 CP portugués[29] reserva una cualificación de la pena para supuestos especialmente graves. En el caso de que el tratamiento o la intervención médica que producen un resultado lesivo para el paciente fuesen realizados imprudentemente, será de aplicación el art. 148 CP portugués[30], en cuyo apartado 2 se recoge la posibilidad de que el tribunal dispense de pena al sujeto activo precisamente por su condición de médico cuando la lesión causada sea levísima. Por otra parte, la inclusión del art. 150 CP portugués relega al ostracismo cualquier intento de configurar el consentimiento del paciente como una causa de justificación del tratamiento o intervención médica curativa, pues ya el propio legislador se encarga de destipificar expresa-

---

[27] Art. 143 CP portugués establece: "1. Quien menoscabe el cuerpo o la salud de otra persona es castigado con la pena de prisión de hasta 3 años o con la pena de multa. 2. El procedimiento criminal depende de demanda, salvo cuando la lesión sea cometida contra agentes de las fuerzas y servicios de seguridad, en el ejercicio de sus funciones o por su causa. 3. El tribunal puede dispensar de pena cuando: a) Haya habido lesiones recíprocas y no se haya probado cual de los contendientes agredió primero; o b) El agente haya ejercido únicamente ejercicio del derecho de retorsión sobre el agresor".

[28] Art. 144 CP portugués: "Quien ofenda el cuerpo o la salud de otra persona de forma que: a) Lo prive de un órgano o miembro importante, o lo desfigure grave y permanentemente; b) Anule o afecte, de manera grave, la capacidad de trabajo, las capacidades intelectuales o de procreación, o la posibilidad de utilizar el cuerpo, los sentidos o el lenguaje; c) Le provoque enfermedad particularmente dolorosa o permanente, o anomalía psíquica grave o incurable; o d) Provoque un peligro para la vida; será castigado con la pena de prisión de 2 a 10 años".

[29] Art. 146 CP portugués: "1. Si las ofensas previstas en los artículos 143, 144 o 145 fuesen producidas en circunstancias que revelen conducta especialmente censurable o perversa del agente, éste es castigado con la pena aplicable al delito que le corresponda agravada en un tercio en sus límites mínimos y máximos. 2. Son susceptibles de revelar conducta especialmente censurable o perversa del agente, entre otras, las circunstancias previstas en el nº 2 del artículo 132".

[30] Art. 148 CP portugués: "1. Quien, por negligencia, lesione el cuerpo o la salud de otra persona, es castigado con la pena de prisión de hasta 1 año o con pena de multa de hasta 120 días. 2. En el caso previsto en el número anterior, el tribunal puede dispensar de pena cuando: a) El agente fuese médico en el ejercicio de su profesión y del acto médico no resultase enfermedad o incapacidad para el trabajo de más de 8 días; o b) De la lesión no resultase enfermedad o incapacidad para el trabajo de más de 3 días. 3. Si del hecho resulta lesión a la integridad física grave, el agente será castigado con pena de prisión de hasta dos años o con pena de multa de hasta 240 días. 4. El procedimiento criminal depende de la queja del lesionado".

mente esa conducta. Esta decisión legislativa, por sí sola, podría suponer desequilibrar la relación médico-paciente, a favor del primero, dejando a este último sometido a las decisiones de aquél, consagrando como supremo, en definitiva, el principio del "privilegio terapéutico", al desposeer al paciente de la única "arma" de protección que posee: su palabra. Tal peligro se ve más que conjurado cuando el legislador decide elevar a la categoría de bien jurídico protegido autónomo la libertad personal de decisión del paciente sobre su propio cuerpo y salud a través del art. 156 CP portugués[31].

La ubicación sistemática dentro del CP portugués del delito de tratamiento arbitrario, en el Capítulo IV, bajo la rúbrica *Dos crimes contra a liberdade pessoal* ("De los crímenes contra la libertad personal"), inmediatamente después del delito de coacciones (arts. 154 y 155 CP portugués) y antes del secuestro (art. 158 CP portugués), no deja lugar a dudas sobre el bien jurídico protegido en este delito, la libertad personal, si bien referida a la disposición de la salud y la propia vida, respecto de la cual, la manifestación del consentimiento para someterse a una intervención médica constituye el ejercicio de ese derecho, y la salvaguarda de aquel bien jurídico[32]. Las intervenciones y los tratamientos que se corresponden al ejercicio consciente de la actividad médico-quirúrgica no constituyen lesiones corporales, pero pueden ser incriminados como tratamientos arbitrarios. Este modelo doctrinal general, ha sido acogido en las más recientes codificaciones penales, destacando la austriaca (§ 110 öStGB) y la portuguesa (art. 150, 158 y 159 CP portugués), por ventura la tentativa más acabada de consagración legal[33]. En definitiva, como afirma Vaz Rodríguez, "la materia de la actuación médica posee en la redacción actualizada del CP portugués una regulación integrada y complementaria, cuyo resultado se manifiesta especialmente en un triángulo normativo constituido por los arts. 150, sobre intervenciones y tra-

---

[31] Véase Da Costa Andrade, M., Intervençoes e tratamentos médico-cirúrgicos, en: Figueiredo Dias, J., Coment I, cit., 1999, 302 ss.

[32] Maia Gonçalves, M.L., CP, cit., 10ª, 1996, 532 s.; Da Cunha Gomes Rodriguez, A., Responsabilidade Médica..., cit., 2007, 223.

[33] Véase da Costa Andrad, M., Consentimento..., cit., 2004, 418.

DIREITO DA SAÚDE

tamientos médico quirúrgicos; 156, sobre intervenciones y tratamientos médico-quirúrgicos arbitrarios; y 157[34], sobre el deber de información"[35].

3. El concepto bidimensional del bien jurídico protegido en el delito de lesiones

Frente a la concepción unidimensional del bien jurídico protegido en el delito de lesiones, otra postura lo entiende en una doble dimensión. Obviamente, la integridad física y/o la salud son objeto de protección, pero al mismo tiempo y de forma inseparable lo será el derecho de disposición sobre esos bienes[36]. Desde este punto de vista, el consentimiento

[34] Art. 157 CP portugués: "A efectos de lo dispuesto en el artículo anterior, el consentimiento sólo es eficaz cuando el paciente haya sido debidamente informado sobre el diagnóstico y la índole, alcance, envergadura y posibles consecuencias de la intervención o del tratamiento, salvo si eso implica la comunicación de circunstancias que, al ser conocidas por el paciente, pondrían en peligro su vida o fuesen susceptibles de causarle un grave daño a la salud, física o psíquica". Según MAIA GONÇALVES, M.L., CP, cit., 10ª, 1996, 534, "el texto de este artículo es resultante de la revisión del Código llevada a cabo por el Decreto-Lei nº 48/91, de 15 de Março. No introduce modificaciones relevantes respecto a su homónimo, el art. 159 de la versión original del CP portugués, de 1982, que tiene por fuente, a su vez, el apartado b) del art. 163.2 del Proyecto de PE de CP de 1966, discutidas en la 5ª sesión de la Comisión Revisora, el 26 de marzo del mismo año. Se trata de la regulación de más aspectos de las particularidades del consentimiento del paciente en los tratamientos e intervenciones médico-quirúrgicos, en donde el Código es más minucioso que la generalidad de la legislación comparada, reproduciendo en la Ley general las enseñanzas de la doctrina autorizada en la especialidad".

[35] VAZ RODRIGUES, J., O consentimento informado..., cit., 2001, 58.

[36] Cfr. LÓPEZ BARJA DE QUIROGA, J., CPC 1995, cit., 469; el mismo, PG II, cit., 2002, 171; BERDUGO GÓMEZ DE LA TORRE, I., Lesiones..., cit., 1982, 23, 36, 40; BAJO FERNÁNDEZ, M., La intervención médica contra la voluntad del paciente (a propósito del auto de la sala segunda del TS de 14 de marzo de 1979), ADPCP 1979, 499; BACIGALUPO ZAPATER, E., El consentimiento en los delitos contra la vida y la integridad física, PJ 12-1990, 151, 157; MOYANO GARCÍA, R., Consentimiento del paciente e imprudencia médica, CuadDJ 1993-I, 481 s.; DE LA GÁNDARA VALLEJO, B., Consentimiento, bien jurídico e imputación objetiva, pról. BACIGALUPO ZAPATER, Enrique, Madrid, Colex, 1995, 226 ss.; CORCOY BIDASOLO, M., Consentimiento y disponibilidad sobre bienes jurídicos personales. En particular: la eficacia del consentimiento del paciente en el tratamiento médico-quirúrgico, en LH-Torío, 1999, 268 s.; GUÉREZ TRICARICO, P., El tratamiento médico curativo y su licitud: el papel del consentimiento del paciente, pról. MOLINA FERNÁNDEZ, F., Cizur Menor (Navarra), Civitas Thomson Reuters, 2012, passim.; KRAUSS, D., Zur strafrechtlichen Problematik der eigenmächtigen Heilbehandlung, en: FS-Bockelmann, 1979, 572 ss.; MAURACH, R./GÖSSEL, K. H./ ZIPF, H., Derecho Penal. PG 2: Formas de aparición del delito y las consecuencias jurídicas del hecho, trad. de la 7ª ed. alemana BOFILL, supervisada por DONNA, Buenos

del paciente no se ubica entre las causas de justificación sino que se integra en el tipo. Así pues, el tratamiento curativo ejecutado conforme a las reglas técnicas constituirá un delito de lesiones si es realizado sin contar con el consentimiento del paciente.

A pesar de la aparente semejanza que esta solución pueda tener con la primera postura expuesta, hay que advertir que son netamente diferentes. En este caso, el punto de partida es radicalmente distinto, pues no se sostiene que toda intervención sanitaria sea típica, calificándola como un delito de lesiones, por el mero hecho de actuar sobre el cuerpo del paciente, y por lo tanto necesitada de justificación, sino que se volverá típica cuando no cumpla con el deber de cuidado requerido. Es decir, cuando o bien infrinja las reglas técnicas exigibles en el caso concreto o bien no cuente con el consentimiento del paciente. No obstante, el médico quedará exento de responsabilidad penal si concurre alguna causa de justificación, por ejemplo, estado de necesidad o cumplimiento de un deber. Desde este punto de vista se interpreta el delito de lesiones de una forma análoga a los delitos contra la propiedad en los que la toma de posesión de una cosa ajena contra la voluntad o sin contar con el permiso de su titular, no se califica como un atentado a la libre disposición del poseedor, sino que se incrimina como un delito de hurto o un delito de robo. Consecuentemente, esta postura tiende hacia la subjetivización del bien jurídico protegido, pues su titular es el que finalmente decide cuándo una determinada conducta atenta contra su salud o su integridad física. En este sentido, se advierte que el propio bienestar físico, o la salud, no pueden definirse con criterios puramente objetivos, sin tener en cuenta la representación que de los mismos posee su titular[37]. Partiendo de esta concepción, algunos autores, como ESER[38], introducen ciertos matices a la idea bidimensional del bien jurídico dentro del delito de lesiones,

---

Aires, Astrea, § 43 64; ROXIN, C., AT, t. I: Grundlagen. Der Aufbau der Verbrechenslehre, 3ª ed., München, Beck, 1997 (Derecho penal, PG, t.I: Fundamentos. La estructura de la teoría del delito, trad. de la 2ª ed. alemana y notas LUZÓN PEÑA, Diego-Manuel/DÍAZ Y GARCÍA CONLLEDO, Miguel/DE VICENTE REMESAL, Javier, Madrid, Civitas, 1997), § 13 24.

[37] Así, ROXIN, C., AT I, 3ª, 1997 (PG I, 1997), cit., § 13 19; CORCOY BIDASOLO, M., LH-Torío, cit., 1999, 265, 282.

[38] Cfr. ESER, A., ZStW 97-1985, cit., 4 ss.; en una línea semejante, KNAUER, C., Ärztlicher Heileingriff, Einwilligung und Aufklärung-überzogene Anforderungen an den Arzt?, en: ROXIN/SCHROTH (ed.), Medizinstrafrecht, 2ª, Stuttgart, München, Hannover, Berlin, Weimer, Dresden, Richard Boorberg, 2001 20 s.

DIREITO DA SAÚDE

al no conferir un valor absoluto a la libre autonomía de la voluntad del sujeto pasivo. Este autor diferencia los grados de afectación del cuerpo del paciente a través de la intervención sanitaria para determinar el valor de la disponibilidad y, por tanto, del consentimiento del paciente con el fin de concretar la tipicidad o atipicidad de la conducta. Así pues, si la intervención terapéutica no provoca una alteración sustancial o esencial en la materia corporal y mejora o, al menos, evita el empeoramiento del paciente, no se puede hablar de un delito de lesiones aunque no haya mediado consentimiento alguno. En cambio, si la afectación a la masa corporal es de tal calibre que sí supone una modificación sustancial de su cuerpo, entonces, aunque el acto médico-sanitario suponga mejorar objetivamente la salud del paciente, habrá que tener en cuenta también si su voluntad se vio o no afectada. De manera que, en el caso hipotético de que dicha operación se hubiese realizado sin su consentimiento, se exigirá responsabilidad penal por un delito de lesiones.

4. Crítica y toma de postura

Cada una de las posturas expuestas, que parten de una diferente interpretación del bien jurídico protegido en el delito de lesiones, conduce a distintas soluciones jurídicopenales, algunas diferenciadas sólo en el plano teórico pero otras con gran trascendencia práctica; ahora bien, todas ellas susceptibles de crítica.

La primera postura es criticable, en primer lugar, por suponer una criminalización generalizada de la actividad médico-sanitaria, ya que entiende que toda intervención médica constituirá un delito de lesiones por el mero hecho de incidir sobre la integridad física de una persona, independientemente de cuál sea el resultado alcanzado, de cómo se haya ejecutado la acción y de cuál haya sido la finalidad de su autor[39]. La calificación de la intervención sanitaria curativa como un daño corporal ha conducido a una grave desavenencia entre médicos y juristas, que incluso ha sido bautizada en la doctrina penal alemana con la expresión de "guerra fría" entre ambas disciplinas[40]. Los profesionales sanitarios se sienten

[39] Cfr. ESER, A., ZStW 97-1985, cit., 19; el mismo, en: MIR PUIG (ed.), Avances de la medicina..., cit., 1988, 14 s; ORBEN, S., Behandlungsfehler..., cit., 2004, 17; cfr. ROXIN, C., AT I, 3ª, 1997 (PG I, 1997), cit., § 13 24.

[40] Cfr. KUHLENDAHL, H., Ärztlicher Entscheidungsspielraum-Handlungszwänge, en: FS-Bockelmann, 1979, 469, quien recoge la expresión *Kalten Krieges*", como la utilizada

ESTUDIO DE DERECHO COMPARADO SOBRE EL CONSENTIMIENTO INFORMADO ...

agredidos al ver cómo su actividad, de carácter curativo, es identificada con actos delictivos que precisamente atentan contra el bien jurídico que ellos pretenden salvar. Por otra parte, esta concepción también supone una incorrecta representación del significado social y normativo de la intervención médica. En la percepción social, la intervención sanitaria curativa posee una connotación positiva, al entenderse como una acción que favorece a una persona. Las intervenciones médicas pueden afectar a la integridad corporal pero no parece adecuado una valoración aislada de actos individuales. Lo decisivo es que la intervención sea contemplada como un acto global, que sirva para la recuperación o mantenimiento de la salud[41].

En segundo lugar, se puede decir que la consideración aislada de cada concreto acto médico supone confundir ya en el plano dogmático el bien jurídico protegido por el delito de lesiones y el soporte material de ese bien jurídico. En numerosos casos, la protección de la salud exigirá llevar a cabo invasiones en la masa corporal del paciente, afectándola temporal o permanentemente. Desde el propio nacimiento, el hombre está permanentemente expuesto a traumas generadores de lesiones e incapacidades, viendo progresivamente limitadas sus capacidades como resultado del natural proceso de envejecimiento[42]. La relatividad del bien jurídico implica que no lesionan el bien jurídico las acciones que mejoran en sentido médico un estado físico disminuido o limitan un proceso de deterioro, y por eso, recuperan o garantizan total o parcialmente la salud[43]. Quien vence o previene un defecto físico no perjudica la integridad física,

---

tradicionalmente por la doctrina alemana para referirse a la relación existente entre ambas disciplinas a partir, fundamentalmente, de la ya expuesta sentencia del RG de 31 de mayo de 1894; von GERLACH, en: KAUFMANN, Arthur (dir.), Moderne Medizin..., cit., 1989, 30; también, ORBEN, S., Behandlungsfehler..., cit., 2004, 17.

[41] Cfr. DÍAZ VALCÁRCEL, L.M., Revisión del CP..., cit., 1963, 181; ANTÓN ONECA, J., LH-Pereda, cit., 1965, 791; ROMEO CASABONA, C.M., La actividad curativa..., cit., 1981, 9 ss., 273; DÍEZ RIPOLLÉS, J.L., La disponibilidad de la salud e integridad personales, CuadDJ 1995-XXXI, 137; QUERALT JIMÉNEZ, J., PE, cit., 6ª, 2010, 51; ORBEN, S., Behandlungsfehler..., cit., 2004, 18.

[42] Una reflexión semejante se encuentra en ROMEO CASABONA, C.M., La actividad curativa..., cit., 1981, 137; JORGE BARREIRO, Agustín, CPC 1982, cit., 12.

[43] Así, ROMEO CASABONA, C.M., La actividad curativa..., cit., 1981, 137; en el mismo sentido, BERDUGO GÓMEZ DE LA TORRE, I., Lesiones..., cit., 1982, 24 s., 28, 39; JORGE BARREIRO, Agustín, CPC 1982, cit., 7.

DIREITO DA SAÚDE

sino que aleja o reduce un perjuicio, es decir, realiza lo contrario de lo que sería una lesión corporal[44].

En tercer lugar, y siguiendo con la cuestión del bien jurídico, hay que apuntar que el intento de proteger la autodeterminación de la persona, o la autonomía de la voluntad respecto a su propio cuerpo y salud, a través de los delitos de lesiones es loable y necesario desde un punto de vista político-criminal, ante el vacío legal existente para hacer frente a conductas que atentan contra ese bien, en aquellos casos en los que no existen tipos específicos destinados a tal fin, o cuando los que existen para proteger la libertad personal se muestran insuficientes o inútiles en esta materia (delitos de coacciones, secuestros, detenciones ilegales, malos tratos, etc.)[45]. Sin embargo, esta solución choca aparentemente, al menos, con el Derecho positivo, ya que ni el art. 147 CP español[46], ni el § 223 StGB Alemán[47], ni tampoco el articulado de otros Códigos penales europeos[48], contemplan expresamente la libre autonomía de la voluntad del paciente o su derecho de autodeterminación como un bien jurídico protegido a través del delito de lesiones. También, en Alemania, la doctrina científica critica la posición dominante en la jurisprudencia del BGH –desde que a través de la sentencia de 10-7-1954 asumiera los postulados del RG en la materia– por suponer una ampliación del tipo (de lesiones), de manera que abandona la finalidad de la norma e introduce en el ámbito de protección bienes jurídicos ajenos a los delitos de lesiones[49]. Contra esa línea jurisprudencial, la doctrina argumenta que ante una intervención médica necesaria, realizada sin embargo sin el consentimiento del paciente, existe una laguna punitiva y su inclusión en el delito de lesiones entraría

---

[44] BERDUGO GÓMEZ DE LA TORRE, I., Lesiones..., cit., 1982, 28; CARDONA LLORENS, A., Estudio médico-penal del delito de lesiones, pról. MARTÍ LLORET, Juan, Madrid, Edersa, 1988, 36 s. Cfr. DA COSTA ANDRADE, M., Consentimento..., cit., 2004, 427.

[45] En este sentido, cabe recoger aquí la reflexión de ZIPF, H., en: MIR PUIG (ed.), Avances de la medicina..., cit., 1988, 152.

[46] El art. 147 CP español establece: "El que, por cualquier medio o procedimiento, causare a otro una lesión que menoscabe su integridad corporal o su salud física o mental (...)".

[47] El § 223 StGB dispone: "Quien inflija a otros malos tratos corporales o dañe su salud (...)".

[48] El art.143 CP portugués establece: "Quien lesione el cuerpo o salud de otra persona"; el art. 582 CP italiano, dispone: "Cualquiera que cause a alguien una lesión personal, de la que se deriva un menoscabo en el cuerpo o en la mente (...)".

[49] Véase ORBEN, S., Behandlungsfehler..., cit., 2004, 17.

en conflicto con el principio *nulla poena sine lege*, razón por la que se hace necesario buscar una solución legal[50].

En cuarto lugar, dado su punto de partida, la ubicación sistemática otorgada al consentimiento del paciente, como causa de justificación, resulta problemática. Por una parte, "implica afirmar con carácter general el carácter típico de la acción del médico, lo que supone, salvo en los casos en que se defienda la teoría de los elementos negativos del tipo, sostener, en contra de la realidad social, que en los casos de tratamiento exitoso estamos ante un comportamiento que el ordenamiento jurídico quiere evitar"[51]. Por otro lado, aplazar la validez de la manifestación del consentimiento a un momento posterior al de la intervención sanitaria supondría una inseguridad jurídica extrema para los profesionales sanitarios, quienes con independencia del modo en que realizaron la intervención podrían ser acusados de la comisión de un delito de lesiones.

La segunda postura, que parte también de una concepción unidimensional del bien jurídico protegido en el delito de lesiones, entiende, sin embargo, que el tratamiento curativo, realizado conforme al deber de cuidado, no supone en sí mismo un delito de lesiones que no protege ni directa (entendiéndola como bien jurídico protegido por el propio tipo de lesiones) ni indirectamente (exigiendo su concurrencia, mediante el consentimiento, como causa de justificación para excluir la antijuridicidad del acto médico) la voluntad del paciente. Esto hace que esta postura doctrinal se mantenga fiel al sentido social del acto médico y al principio de legalidad, al respetar la tipificación establecida en el Derecho positivo, eso sí, a costa de desguarnecer, en ocasiones de forma significativa, la protección de la autonomía del paciente. Precisamente, la fidelidad al Derecho positivo va a dar lugar a que la balanza que sostiene el difícil equilibrio entre la protección de la salud y el derecho de autodeterminación del paciente, se incline de tal forma que anule por completo este último, ya que en aquellos ordenamientos jurídicos en los que no se contempla la tipificación específica de un delito de tratamiento arbitrario, la posibilidad de incriminar al profesional sanitario que lleva a cabo una intervención curativa sobre el paciente sin su consentimiento a través de los delitos contra la libertad se encuentra con dificultades dogmáticas, en

---

[50] Véase KAUFMANN, Arthur, ZStW 73-1961, cit., 374; BOCKELMANN, P., Strafrecht des Arztes..., cit., 1968, 71; ORBEN, S., Behandlungsfehler..., cit., 2004, 17.

[51] BERDUGO GÓMEZ DE LA TORRE, I., Lesiones..., cit., 1982, 31 s.

muchos casos, insalvables. Esta vía de incriminación, así como las dificultades que pueda toparse, depende, en gran medida, de cómo hayan sido redactados los genuinos delitos contra la libertad en el Derecho positivo de cada país. En Alemania, por ejemplo, la doctrina[52] y la jurisprudencia han puesto de manifiesto la práctica imposibilidad de acudir a los delitos contra la libertad tipificados en el StGB para castigar al médico o al profesional sanitario que interviene sobre el paciente sin su consentimiento, dada la redacción actual, y las exigencias legales que de ella se derivan, de los artículos, que en principio, pudieran resultar de aplicación. En este sentido se advierte que en la actividad médica cotidiana, realizada con fines curativos, son infrecuentes o de muy rara aparición los supuestos en los que el tratamiento arbitrario pueda ser incluido en un delito de coacciones, tal y como aparece recogido en el § 240 StGB[53], y todavía más difícil y sorprendente sería la posibilidad de aplicar el delito de detenciones ilegales del § 239 StGB[54]. En España, a pesar de la amplitud con la que tradicionalmente se ha entendido el delito de coacciones, la doctrina también ha puesto de manifiesto las dificultades para encajar el tratamiento médico arbitrario en este delito[55]. Y es que la regulación en el CP actual de este tipo no difiere, en lo sustancial, de la contemplada en el respectivo artículo del StGB. El elemento típico que dificulta en extremo la inclusión del tratamiento arbitrario en el delito de coacciones del art. 172 CP es la exigencia de "violencia" como medio para impedir a otro ejercer libremente un derecho, ya que en los tratamientos médicos, la ausencia de manifestación de consentimiento se debe normalmente, en los casos más graves, a que el médico hace incurrir al paciente en un error, o le engaña, pero extraño parece que pueda crear una situación de confrontación tal en la que por medios violentos consiga doblegar la

---

[52] En este sentido, Roxin, C., AT I, 3ª, 1997 (PG I, 1997), cit., § 7 24.

[53] El § 239 StGB dispone: "(1) Quien encierre a otra persona o de otra manera la prive de su libertad, será castigado con pena privativa de libertad de hasta cinco años o con pena de multa".

[54] El § 240 StGB establece: "(1) Quien coaccione a una persona antijurídicamente con violencia o por medio de amenaza con un mal considerable, a una acción, tolerancia u omisión, será castigado con pena privativa de la libertad hasta tres años o con multa. (2) El hecho es antijurídico cuando la utilización de la violencia o la amenaza del mal para el fin perseguido se considere como reprochable".

[55] Cfr. Jorge Barreiro, Agustín, Actividad médico-quirúrgica..., cit., 1990, 82; De La Gándara Vallejo, B., Consentimiento..., cit., 1995, 226.

voluntad del paciente[56]. Más dificultades presenta todavía la posibilidad de enjuiciar al profesional sanitario en estos casos por un delito de detenciones ilegales, tipificado en el art. 163 CP. Ante esta situación legal, el tratamiento médico arbitrario podría ser reconducido a una falta de coacciones del art. 620 CP[57], pero esta posibilidad sería del todo insatisfactoria, ya que la reacción penal contemplada en dicho artículo no se corresponde con la gravedad del contenido de injusto que supone actuar contra o ignorando la voluntad del paciente.

Por otra parte, esta postura ha sido criticada por un sector de la doctrina al entender que la integridad física y la salud son bienes inseparables de la facultad de disposición sobre los mismos. La valoración de lo que es salud depende de cada sujeto, de manera que el médico no se puede aventurar a sustituir la concepción personal de cada cual, pues de lo contrario estaría atacando la propia integridad, salud, e incluso la vida. En definitiva, según esta postura, un tratamiento médico, por muy bien intencionado que sea, no puede sustituir las pretensiones del paciente sobre su salud, de manera que una intervención sin su consentimiento no debe quedar reducida a un mero atentado contra su libertad de disposición, ya que ataca algo más que la libertad, ataca la definición de salud dada por el propio sujeto y por lo tanto ataca, de alguna manera, a la misma salud o integridad física[58].

Por último, de la tercera postura se cuestiona el concepto bidimensional del bien jurídico protegido por el delito de lesiones, al considerar que no se puede incluir en el tipo de lesiones, además de la salud e integridad física, la libertad de decidir sobre los mismos, ya que son bienes diferentes que encuentran protección en tipos también diferentes. Entender que el tipo de lesiones, tal y como está redactado en el CP español, así

---

[56] En este sentido, VILLACAMPA ESTIARTE, C., Atribución..., cit., 2003, 70.

[57] El art. 620 CP dispone: "Serán castigados con la pena de multa de diez a veinte días: 1º Los que de modo leve amenacen a otro con armas u otros instrumentos peligrosos, o los saquen en riña, como no sea en justa defensa, salvo que el hecho sea constitutivo de delito. 2º Los que causen a otro una amenaza, coacción, injuria o vejación injusta de carácter leve, salvo que el hecho sea constitutivo de delito. (...)". Posibilidad, en todo caso, que desaparecerá una vez entre en vigor la recientemente aprobada reforma del CP español, conforme a la Disposición Derogatoria Única, LO 1/2015, de 30 de marzo, que deroga el Libro III del CP, en el que se contemplan las faltas, hecho que se producirá el 1 de julio de 2015.

[58] Véase BAJO FERNÁNDEZ, M., PE, cit., 2ª, 1987, 165; DE LA GÁNDARA VALLEJO, B., Consentimiento..., cit., 1995, 227 s.

DIREITO DA SAÚDE

como en el alemán[59], y otros de nuestro entorno, incluyen la protección de la integridad física y la autodeterminación, supone atentar contra el principio de legalidad.

Por otra parte, hacer depender la tipicidad de la conducta del médico respecto al delito de lesiones de la voluntad del paciente supone una subjetivización tal del concepto salud e integridad física, que puede acarrear efectos negativos como los expuestos en la crítica a la primera postura[60].

Además, esta concepción del bien jurídico da lugar a que en el caso de que la acción haya infringido la *lex artis*, al médico sólo se le podrán exigir responsabilidades por un delito de lesiones, aunque además hubiese realizado la conducta sin el consentimiento del paciente, sin que pueda apreciarse un concurso de delitos, como el expuesto (lesiones y coacciones), ya que coherentemente con la posición adoptada, en ambos casos se estaría infringiendo el mismo deber de cuidado. Una solución insatisfactoria desde el punto de vista de quienes defienden un concepto unidimensional del bien jurídico protegido en el delito de lesiones y que identifican la realización de la intervención médica sin consentimiento con un ataque a la libertad del individuo, es decir, con otra clase de delito. Pero insatisfactoria también porque se plantea la misma respuesta penal a dos supuestos de hecho diferentes, al apreciar un solo delito de lesiones tanto en el caso de que se haya cumplido con las normas técnicas en la ejecución del tratamiento pero sin contar con el consentimiento del paciente como en el supuesto de que además de no contar con el consentimiento se infrinjan las reglas técnicas aplicables. Parece que en esta segunda situación el desvalor de injusto es mayor que en la primera, sin embargo, las consecuencias penales serían prácticamente las mismas.

En mi opinión, la integridad física ha de ser concebida como instrumental respecto a la salud, hasta tal punto que en determinados supuestos puede ser contraria a la salud misma. Así, las intervenciones quirúrgicas que consisten en la extirpación de un órgano o miembro: tumores, un miembro gangrenado. En estos casos, la conducta de extirpar "atenta" contra la integridad corporal, pero no debe considerarse típica por cuanto no produce un perjuicio sino un beneficio para la salud[61]. La acti-

---

[59] Respecto al StGB, cfr. ESER, A., en: MIR PUIG (ed.), Avances de la medicina…, cit., 1988, 14.
[60] Cfr. VILLACAMPA ESTIARTE, C., Atribución…, cit., 2003, 66.
[61] Cfr. CARBONELL MATEU, J.C./GONZÁLEZ CUSSAC, J.L., en: VIVES, Coment I, cit., 1996, 789.

vidad médico-sanitaria no es atípica por el simple hecho de que se realiza con la intención de curar, sino porque se realiza de acuerdo con el deber de cuidado requerido en esa situación[62], algo que definirá el juez partiendo de datos proporcionados por la ciencia médica.

Todo esto no quiere decir que el médico, o el personal sanitario en general, puedan obrar con total libertad sobre el cuerpo, la mente o la vida del paciente, sin informarle y sin contar con su consentimiento. Decir que el consentimiento informado del paciente es irrelevante desde el punto de vista penal es exagerado y carece de sentido. Nadie postula esta solución, y tampoco aquellos que consideramos que la falta de consentimiento del paciente no se deba reconducir a un delito de lesiones. Al contrario, el consentimiento del paciente, y su premisa, la información otorgada por el personal sanitario, con todos los requisitos exigidos legalmente[63], constituyen el presupuesto de la intervención médica. Si el profesional sanitario no respeta este presupuesto, incurrirá en un ilícito penal por atentar contra la libertad del paciente, posiblemente en un delito de coacciones, del art. 172 CP.

No obstante, considero necesaria la inclusión de un delito de tratamiento médico arbitrario en el CP español[64], entre los delitos contra la libertad, que podría acompañarse de otro precepto relativo a la punición del tratamiento médico que imprudentemente causa un resultado lesivo al paciente, aunque este último no es tan necesario como el primero, ya que se trata de una conducta encajable en el delito de lesiones tal y como se encuentra redactado en la actualidad. A través de este tipo, el legislador zanjaría la polémica sobre la relación entre el delito de lesiones y el tratamiento médico, excluyendo explícitamente del marco de las lesio-

---

[62] En este sentido, VILLACAMPA ESTIARTE, C., Atribución..., cit., 2003, 49 ss.

[63] En España, establecidos en la Ley 41/2002, de 14 de noviembre, básica reguladora de la autonomía del paciente y de derechos y obligaciones en materia de información y documentación clínica.

[64] Junto con un sector de la doctrina en el que se incluyen, entre otros, ANTÓN ONECA, J., LH-Pereda, cit., 1965, 791, no llega a proponer la introducción de un tipo específico, pero deja entrever su valoración positiva al afirmar; HIGUERA GUIMERÁ, J.F., Coacciones..., cit., 2ª, 1983, 219; BAJO FERNÁNDEZ, M., PE, cit., 2ª, 1987, 164; JORGE BARREIRO, Agustín, Actividad médico-quirúrgica..., cit., 1990, 82 s.; el mismo, en: LAFARGA I TRAVER (coord.), Usuarios de los servicios sanitarios..., cit., 1996, 167 s.; VILLACAMPA ESTIARTE, C., Atribución..., cit., 2003, 70.

nes todo aquel tratamiento curativo que en su ejecución cumpliese con determinados requisitos objetivos, como, por ejemplo, ser realizado con indicación médica, conforme al estado de la ciencia y, en su caso, por un profesional sanitario, sin que fuese necesario acudir al consentimiento del paciente como expediente justificante de la actividad médica, al menos cuando nos encontramos en el marco de los delitos contra la salud y la integridad física. Además, esta solución pondría fin al peligroso proceso de criminalización que supone entender la actividad médica como una conducta inicialmente típica necesitada de justificación para su licitud. Este concepto siembra una sospecha permanente sobre la actividad médica, hecho que genera graves y perniciosos efectos para un sector clave de la sociedad como es éste. Por cierto, hay que señalar que la recientemente aprobada reforma del CP, a través de la LO 1/2015, de 30 de marzo, no contempla ninguna modificación en el sentido señalado, por tanto, otra oportunidad perdida.

En mi opinión, constituye un error tratar de resolver una supuesta laguna punitiva a través de un quiebro dogmático, incluyendo conductas que atentan contra la libertad en delitos que tratan de proteger la salud y la integridad física[65]. Además de ser una solución carente de coherencia con el sistema penal, resulta injusta con el propio paciente, dejando sin la respuesta penal que merecerían aquellos supuestos en los que junto a la actuación sin el consentimiento del paciente, se causa una lesión "real", por afectar negativamente a su salud. Por otra parte, no hay razón para afirmar que un delito de tratamiento médico arbitrario suponga una respuesta penal laxa frente a una conducta tan grave como la del médico que lleva a cabo una intervención sobre el cuerpo del paciente sin contar con su consentimiento. Esto es algo que dependerá de la consecuencia jurídicopenal que se establezca, y esta cuestión, como siempre, dependerá del valor jurídico que en el seno de una sociedad y en un momento histórico se le quiera atribuir a un determinado bien jurídico, en este caso, al derecho a decidir sobre la propia salud, como expresión especial del derecho a la libertad individual. Ésta es la solución adoptada en alguno de los Códigos penales que contemplan un delito de tratamiento médico

---

[65] En este sentido, Kaufmann, Arthur, ZStW 73-1961, cit., 374; BOCKELMANN, P., Strafrecht des Arztes..., cit., 1968, 71; ZIPF, H., en: MIR PUIG (ed.), Avances de la medicina..., cit., 1988, 152; ORBEN, S., Behandlungsfehler..., cit., 2004, 17.

arbitrario, que lejos de dejar impune o privilegiar la conducta del médico que realiza una intervención sin contar con la voluntad del paciente, establece un régimen punitivo extremadamente gravoso y restrictivo para el profesional sanitario que se atreve a emprender un tratamiento, una prueba diagnóstica o cualquier otra actuación sobre el paciente sin contar con su consentimiento. Por ejemplo, el art. 156 CP portugués señala que el médico que realice un tratamiento curativo sin el consentimiento del paciente podrá ser castigado con una pena de prisión de hasta 3 años, equiparándola así a la pena que le pudiera corresponder a cualquiera por cometer un delito de lesiones doloso, para el que el art. 143 CP portugués (tipo básico del delito de lesiones) también contempla una pena de prisión de hasta tres años y triplicando la gravedad de la respuesta penal frente al delito de lesiones imprudente, que en la mayoría de los casos sería el susceptible de aplicación para las intervenciones médicas, tipificado en el art. 148 CP portugués, y para el que se contempla una pena como máximo de 1 año de prisión.

5. Conclusiones

El elemento decisivo para resolver la cuestión del valor que el consentimiento informado posee respecto al análisis jurídicopenal de las actividades médico-sanitarias que inciden en el paciente ha de ser necesariamente la determinación del bien jurídico protegido, en este caso, en el delito de lesiones. Se parte de un concepto "unidimensional" del bien jurídico protegido a través del delito de lesiones, identificándolo con la "salud", entendida en un sentido amplio, incluyendo tanto la salud física como la psíquica. Desde este punto de vista, la integridad física se concibe con carácter instrumental respecto a aquélla, hasta tal punto que en determinados supuestos puede ser contraria a la salud misma.

La actividad médico-sanitaria no es atípica por el simple hecho de que sea realizada con la intención de curar, sino porque se realiza de acuerdo con el deber de cuidado requerido en esa situación, cuestión directamente relacionada con la *lex artis* médica, entendida como "conjunto de reglas técnicas que rigen en la actividad médico-sanitaria".

Para salvaguardar el bien jurídico libertad, entendida como libertad de decisión de la persona, existen tipos penales específicos. Esto no quiere decir que el médico, o el personal sanitario en general, puedan obrar con total libertad sobre el cuerpo, la mente o la vida del paciente, sin

DIREITO DA SAÚDE

informarle y sin contar con su consentimiento. Al contrario, el consentimiento del paciente y su premisa, la información otorgada por el personal sanitario, con todos los requisitos exigidos legalmente, constituyen el presupuesto de toda intervención médica. Si el profesional sanitario no respeta este presupuesto, incurrirá en un ilícito penal por atentar contra la libertad del paciente. La diferenciación de dos bienes jurídicos, salud y libertad, da lugar a distintas soluciones jurídicas según cuál haya sido el comportamiento del personal sanitario. En el caso de que se ejecute la intervención sanitaria sobre el paciente de acuerdo con el deber de cuidado requerido, y con el consentimiento válidamente emitido por el paciente, lo cual supone la previa información del médico en los términos estipulados legalmente, la conducta será atípica. Si la intervención sanitaria se realiza con el consentimiento del paciente, pero infringiendo el deber de cuidado y causándole un resultado lesivo, la conducta será constitutiva de un delito de lesiones imprudente. Si la conducta del médico no infringe el deber de cuidado, pero se realiza sin el consentimiento del paciente, bien por defectos en la información proporcionada, bien por vicios en el momento de otorgarla, bien porque simplemente no ha habido ningún consentimiento, o porque se realiza en contra de la voluntad expresa del paciente, entonces la conducta del médico será constitutiva de un delito contra la libertad. Por último, si falta el consentimiento y además el médico actuó sin el cuidado debido produciendo unas lesiones, existirá un concurso real entre un delito de lesiones imprudente y un delito contra la libertad.

Considero necesaria la inclusión de un delito de tratamiento médico arbitrario en el CP español, entre los delitos contra la libertad. A través de este tipo el legislador zanjaría la polémica sobre la relación entre el delito de lesiones y el tratamiento médico, excluyendo explícitamente del marco de las lesiones todo aquel tratamiento curativo que en su ejecución cumpliese con determinados requisitos objetivos, como, por ejemplo, ser realizado con indicación médica, conforme al estado de la ciencia y, en su caso, por un profesional sanitario, sin que fuese necesario acudir al consentimiento del paciente como expediente justificante de la actividad médica, al menos cuando nos encontramos en el marco de los delitos contra la salud y la integridad física. Además, esta solución pondría fin al peligroso proceso de criminalización que supone entender la actividad médica como una conducta inicialmente típica necesitada de justificación para su licitud. La introducción de un delito de tratamiento médico arbitrario la considero acertada desde el punto de vista dogmático, puesto que permitiría dar respuesta a una conducta delictiva en el ámbito médico-sanitario manteniendo la coherencia sistemática sobre la que se edifica el Derecho penal. En este sentido, la solución adoptada en el CP portugués constituye un modelo de referencia.

A consagração do direito ao consentimento informado na jurisprudência portuguesa recente

ANDRÉ GONÇALO DIAS PEREIRA[*]

Tive o privilégio de ser aluno do Senhor Prof. Doutor Guilherme de Oliveira no curso de Direito da Família e Sucessões, no 4º ano da Licenciatura em Direito (1995-96), e, por duas vezes, no Curso de Direito da Família do Mestrado em Ciências Jurídico-civilísticas: em 1999/2000 e em 2001/2002.

O que, porém, nesta obra quero – queremos – saudar é o Pioneiro, o Fundador e o Mobilizador de energias do Direito da Medicina e do Direito Biomédico.

Corria a primavera de 1999, quando comecei a frequentar os cursos do Centro de Direito Biomédico. Ao fim de poucos contactos, o Doutor Guilherme de Oliveira ofereceu-me uma bolsa para um Curso de Verão em Utrecht. Depois deste curso, a paixão pelo Direito médico foi crescendo e veio Helsínquia, Maastricht, Toulouse, Pequim, Leuven (Associação Europeia), Maceió, Bali e Coimbra (Associação Europeia) e sempre Coimbra (Associação Mundial)...

Nessa aprendizagem serena, nesse tempo em que o jovem Assistente estagiário e o Assistente tinha um salário... e tinha tempo.... fui aprendendo – num diálogo profícuo com o meu Mestre – a arte de problematizar os complexos e dinâmicos problemas do Direito da Medicina.

[*] Centro de Direito Biomédico/ Instituto Jurídico da Faculdade de Direito da Universidade de Coimbra (Grupo 2 – Vulnerabilidade e Direito, *Desafios Sociais, Incerteza e Direito*: UID/DIR/04643/2013).

DIREITO DA SAÚDE

Desde essa primavera do século passado, Guilherme de Oliveira tem sido sempre o meu mentor, o meu Mestre, o Professor que sempre me apoiou, que continuamente me incentivou no estudo, no pensamento e no fortalecimento de um conjunto de relações académicas de alto nível, a nível nacional e internacional, abrindo-me assim avenidas de progressão académica e científica, no desenvolvimento deste recente e deveras fascinante ramo do Direito, tendo sido co-orientador da minha tese de Doutoramento.

Em 1999 Guilherme de Oliveira disse-me que o consentimento informado seria tema para 20 anos... mais de 15 anos depois, a doutrina do consentimento informado, em grande medida, introduzida no Direito civil médico português pelo nosso Homenageado, finalmente logrou afirmar-se, com força plena, na jurisprudência do Supremo Tribunal de Justiça.

Uma vitória para os direitos dos doentes!

1. O Direito ao consentimento informado

Está já bem consolidado na nossa doutrina e na nossa jurisprudência que o paciente tem o direito a ser *devidamente esclarecido sobre o diagnóstico e a índole, alcance, envergadura e possíveis consequências da intervenção ou do tratamento* (art. 157 CP).

Acresce ainda que – com a Convenção de Oviedo (art. 5º) – a pessoa doente *deve receber previamente a informação adequada quanto ao objectivo e à natureza da intervenção, bem como às suas consequências e riscos.*

No **Ac. de 18 de março de 2010** (Relator: Pires da Rosa), o Supremo Tribunal de Justiça afirmou com clareza que pode haver responsabilidade civil pelos danos causados por uma intervenção médica não precedida da necessária informação, sejam os danos derivados da violação do bem jurídico *liberdade*, sejam os danos correspondentes à violação do bem jurídico *integridade físico-psíquica*.

Trata-se, neste aspecto, de um Acórdão muito importante e que saudamos vivamente. O STJ reconheceu que a *violação do dever de informar* conduz a um *consentimento inválido*, pelo que as lesões causadas à integridade física e à liberdade são ilícitas, donde gera-se uma obrigação de indemnizar os *danos patrimoniais* e *não patrimoniais* sofridos pelo doente.

No mesmo sentido decidiu o **Acórdão do Supremo Tribunal de Justiça de 16-06-2015** (Relator: Mário Mendes), acrescentando ainda que "a verificar-se uma situação de intervenção médico-cirúrgica não autorizada ou não validamente informada (consequentemente ilícita) estaremos desde logo, tout court e independentemente de outros danos ressarcíveis, perante um dano não patrimonial autónomo indemnizável." E acrescenta este aresto que "em princípio e independentemente de se fazer especial apelo ao princípio da colaboração processual *em matéria de prova, compete ao médico provar que prestou as informações devidas.*"

2. A Norma 15/2013 da DGS

No dia 14 de outubro de 2014, a Direção-Geral da Saúde publicou a Norma 15/2013 (atualizada a 04/11/2015) relativa ao *consentimento informado, livre e dado por escrito.*

Trata-se de uma *norma de caráter organizacional* que afirma ter como destinatários as Administrações Regionais de Saúde, dirigentes de unidades de saúde e profissionais de saúde do sistema de saúde.

Confiamos que esta Norma 15/2013 possa ter uma influência positiva na prestação de cuidados de saúde e que possa conduzir a uma maior implementação da prática de obter o consentimento do doente no âmbito das intervenções médicas, em especial médico-cirúrgicas. Desejamos, porém, que o consentimento dos doentes seja mais informado e mais livre e não se transforme num mero *formalismo burocrático.*

Numa análise muito breve deste documento, destaquemos os aspectos que nos parecem mais positivos:

- o facto de haver espaço disponível no formulário para que o médico insira a informação adequada ao procedimento concreto e que seja útil ao processo de esclarecimento que está a realizar (1-a);
- a obrigatória inserção do consentimento informado no processo clínico (1-b e 6);
- o facto de o doente poder ficar com uma cópia do formulário do CI (4-a);
- o facto de o doente poder identificar e guardar a informação acerca da instituição e do profissional que participou no processo de CI (4-b e c);
- a exigência da informação acerca dos riscos graves associados ao ato/ procedimento, bem como das alternativas de tratamento (4-f);
- a valorização do procurador de cuidados de saúde (7);
- a valorização da participação do menor que tenha capacidade de discernimento (Anexo: solicita-se a assinatura do menor).

Esta Norma da DGS poderá ter o condão de habituar os médicos a discutir com os seus doentes o processo terapêutico, com mais detalhe, com mais esclarecimento e com mais profundidade. Essa tomada de consciência dos riscos inerentes à intervenção, a escolha entre alternativas possíveis vai não só promover a autodeterminação das pessoas doentes e cimentar uma *relação mais democrática e transparente,*[1] mas vai ainda contribuir para a *segurança do tratamento,* pois o doente estará mais alerta para eventuais eventos adversos, e finalmente, vai contribuir para a *humanização dos cuidados de saúde* e conduz necessariamente a uma melhor relação pessoal e profissional entre o médico e o paciente: condição primeira para a adesão à terapêutica e consabidamente o melhor antídoto para problemas judiciais.

No entanto, não deve o médico descansar sobre o papel escrito, pois, como bem afirma o **Supremo Tribunal de Justiça em 9 de outubro de 2014** (Rel. Cons. João Bernardo): "*a referência num documento assinado por médico e doente a que aquele explicou a este de forma adequada e inteligível entre outras coisas os riscos e complicações duma cirurgia* não permite *ajuizar da adequação e inteligibilidade e bem assim dos riscos concretamente indicados* pelo que é manifestamente insuficiente".

Não deve pois o médico repousar numa assinatura, antes deve ativamente cumprir o seu dever de informar oralmente e, seguindo o comando da Norma 15/2013, deve registar *por escrito* no espaço próprio do formulário obrigatório um conjunto de informações relevantes.

Alguns dirão que esta Norma vem trazer uma grande burocratização do CI, uma vez que vai exigir muita informação escrita e um grande detalhe de registo. Dirão ainda que os médicos não têm tempo, visto estarem já demasiado ocupados com o atendimento aos pacientes...

Ora, este argumento tem em si algo de contraditório, pois, como vimos, o cumprimento do CI é um instrumento útil da própria consulta médica e do envolvimento dos doentes na terapêutica e contribui para o sucesso do tratamento.

O caminho imposto pela Norma parece-nos assim bem mais adequado do que a mera assinatura de um formulário que contenha cláusulas como

---

[1] A "*democracia sanitária*" – conceito que tem orientado as reformas do direito francês e do próprio direito europeu da saúde e que merece a nossa adesão. Cf. PEREIRA, André Gonçalo Dias, Direitos dos Pacientes e Responsabilidade Médica, Coimbra, 2015, p. 73 e 889.

a seguinte: *"o doente não deve hesitar em solicitar mais informações ao médico se não estiver completamente esclarecido"...* ressalva que, porém, o Supremo Tribunal de Justiça veio a considerar como excludente da responsabilidade, no aresto supracitado, de 9 de outubro de 2014, num caminho que pode vir a limitar gravemente um efetivo esclarecimento material.

Expliquemos melhor: para o STJ, se o formulário terminar com a cláusula: *"se tiver mais dúvidas, pergunte..."* isto seria suficiente para isentar o médico de responsabilidade. Parece-nos pouco; muito pouco...

Criticamos ainda este Acórdão do STJ de 9 de outubro de 2014, por negar a aplicação da lei das cláusulas contratuais gerais ao controlo dos formulários do consentimento informado. Não é objeto desta nossa intervenção aprofundar este problema hoje. Mas quero deixar público testemunho que não retiro uma vírgula ao que escrevi e publiquei no *Boletim da Faculdade de Direito*, ainda no século passado, sob o título: "Formulários para prestação do Consentimento: uma proposta para o seu controlo jurídico", onde defendi a solução diametralmente oposta, ou seja, a lei das cláusulas contratuais gerais é aplicável nesta sede.[2]

3. Limites ao dever de informar: os *riscos de verificação excecional ou muito rara mesmo que graves* nas intervenções terapêuticas

Um aspeto sempre controverso é o de saber se o médico tem o dever de **informar dos riscos graves ainda que raros ou excecionais.**

Em sentido negativo – no âmbito das **intervenções terapêuticas** – pronunciou-se o mesmo acórdão do STJ em 9/10/2014, ao afirmar que não se exige uma *"referência à situação médica em detalhe, nem a referência aos riscos de **verificação excecional ou muito rara** mesmo que graves ou ligados especificamente àquele tratamento."*

Por seu turno, a Norma da DGS, também de outubro do ano passado, deixa margem para diferentes interpretações, pois estatui que o médico deve indicar "os riscos frequentes e riscos graves associados ao ato/ procedimento".

Donde, podemos concluir que a chave da solução do problema deverá passar pela destrinça entre **intervenções voluntárias** (por exemplo,

---

[2] PEREIRA, André Gonçalo Dias, "Formulários para prestação do Consentimento: uma proposta para o seu controlo jurídico", *Boletim da Faculdade de Direito* da Universidade de Coimbra, 2000, pp. 433-472.

DIREITO DA SAÚDE

natureza estética) e as **intervenções médicas terapêuticas**, exigindo-se nas primeiras uma informação mais detalhada ou mesmo exaustiva dos riscos graves.

Era nesse sentido que se pronunciava o **Projeto de Lei nº 413/XI/2ª sobre Direito dos doentes à informação e ao consentimento informado**, no nº 5 do seu artigo 2º: *"A informação é tanto mais pormenorizada e extensa quanto menor for o intuito terapêutico da intervenção ou quanto mais graves forem os seus riscos."*[3]

Daqui resulta que, quando a intervenção não tem intuito terapêutico, o dever de esclarecer é mais exigente. Nesse sentido já se pronunciou o Supremo Tribunal de Justiça, no **Acórdão de 2 de junho de 2015** e no **Acórdão de 16 de junho de 2015**, no qual afirma: "entendemos que os riscos a informar devem ser os riscos tidos como previsíveis e sérios, admitindo ainda que em intervenções de particular grau de risco se comuniquem ao paciente os riscos graves dessa mesma intervenção (morte ou invalidez permanente) ainda que de ocorrência excepcional."

4. O Acórdão de 2 de junho de 2015 do Supremo Tribunal de Justiça: a responsabilidade civil por violação do consentimento informado

Antes de 2015, o direito ao consentimento informado havia sido afirmado pelo STJ em, pelo menos, duas ocasiões; todavia, nesses dois casos a decisão foi de absolvição do Réu. Ou seja, o doente que viu lesado o seu direito à informação não logrou obter uma justa reparação do seus danos nos tribunais portugueses. Haveria assim razão para temer que a Convenção sobre os Direitos do Homem e a Biomedicina que estabelece o direito à reparação pelo dano injusto (art 24º), incluindo pela violação do consentimento informado (art. 5º) estava a ser – em grande medida – mais um documento de *valor decorativo* do que verdadeiramente a gozar da força da *vigência em condenações judiciais*.

Daí a importância deste Acórdão de 2 de junho de 2015!

A partir desta decisão torna-se claro que a Jurisprudência reconhece todos os efeitos da violação do consentimento informado, condenando

---

[3] Sobre este Projeto-lei cf. OLIVEIRA, Guilherme/ MONIZ, Helena/ PEREIRA, André, "Consentimento Informado e Acesso ao Processo Clínico – Um Anteprojeto de 2010", *Lex medicinae – Revista Portuguesa de Direito da Saúde*, Ano 9, nº 18, Julho/Dezembro 2012, p. 13-33.

em indemnização por danos patrimoniais e não patrimoniais, decorrentes da violação do direito à autonomia nos cuidados de saúde e do direito à integridade física.

No Ac. do STJ de 2-6-2015 (Relatora: Maria Clara Sottomayor), o Supremo Tribunal de Justiça condena o cirurgião por violação do consentimento informado, afirmando: "O consentimento do paciente é um dos requisitos da licitude da atividade médica (artigos 5º da CDHB e 3º, nº 2 da Carta dos Direitos Fundamentais da União Europeia) e tem que ser livre e esclarecido para gozar de eficácia: se o consentimento não existe ou é ineficaz, a atuação do médico será ilícita por violação do direito à autodeterminação e correm por sua conta todos os danos derivados da intervenção não autorizada."[4]

Em suma: serão assim ressarcíveis não só os *danos não patrimoniais* causados pela violação do seu *direito à autodeterminação* e à *liberdade*, mas também por violação da sua *integridade física* (e, eventualmente, da *vida*) (arts. 70º e 483º CC), bem como os *danos patrimoniais* derivados do agravamento do estado de saúde.

Assim sendo, o montante das indemnizações resultantes de um processo de responsabilidade por violação do consentimento informado pode ser tão elevado como os casos de negligência médica.

5. O Acórdão do STJ de 18 de março de 2010: o instituto do "consentimento hipotético"

O Acórdão do STJ de 18 de março de 2010 pronuncia-se sobre a violação do dever de informação, não concedendo revista. Vejamos o essencial da matéria de facto do caso:

Uma mulher sofria de problemas na sua visão e consultou a sua médica oftalmologista, num consultório privado. Esta recomendou a realização de uma cirurgia a laser para tratar a miopia. Após a cirurgia, a paciente

---

[4] Os factos do caso falam por si: "No decorrer do processo da lipoaspiração programada com o consentimento da autora, tendo o Réu constatado que os tecidos sujeitos à intervenção não tinham a elasticidade que esperava, e não tendo com a referida intervenção logrado o ganho de tecidos que supunha vir a obter para a concretização da segunda intervenção planeada, decidiu o mesmo intra-operatoriamente aproveitar algum tecido adiposo que havia sido extraído da Autora e injectá-lo nos grandes lábios da mesma, concretizando, assim, e por este método, uma vulvoplastia, para cuja possibilidade de realização esta não fora sequer alertada, não prestando, assim, o seu consentimento."

DIREITO DA SAÚDE

começou a ver pior e uma semana depois foi operada novamente. Infelizmente a situação clínica agravou-se, visto que a retina ficou queimada pelo laser, conduzindo à sua cegueira. A paciente intentou ação contra a médica e contra a clínica, alegando negligência na realização da intervenção.

Como esta não logrou fazer **prova da violação das *leges artis* e da culpa** da cirurgiã, o processo foi orientado, já em sede de recurso, para a violação do dever de esclarecer. **A paciente alegou não ter sido devidamente informada dos riscos, nomeadamente do risco de que a intervenção poderia ser mal sucedida e de que havia um risco de cegueira.**

O STJ afirmou que a paciente não conseguiu fazer *prova de que se tivesse recebido mais informação* (a informação adequada acerca dos riscos graves – a cegueira), *teria recusado a operação.*

O tribunal considerou que a situação clínica era grave e de evolução imprevisível, com um prognóstico desfavorável e que a cirurgia deveria ser feita sem demora. Por isso, a paciente teve suficiente informação *da médica que ela havia escolhido...*

O Acórdão contém afirmações com as quais não podemos concordar, quais sejam:

"III –Tendo a autora escolhido livremente a clínica ré, estamos num domínio inteiramente privado, sendo que esta livre escolha induz uma tácita aceitação da orientação médica que na clínica receba: *isto é, alguém que escolhe previamente um determinado médico ou clínica privada porque confia nele, exigirá dele uma «informação menos informada», predispondo-se a aceitar as indicações médicas que receba nos mesmos termos, com o mesmo crédito de confiança com que firmou a sua escolha.*"

O Relator – entusiasmado com a sua própria linha de argumentação – vai mais longe e afirma: "Se a autora escolheu o seu médico, a sua clínica, é *impensável* aceitar a hipótese de *não consentir* no caminho terapêutico seguido."

Este Acórdão defendeu a absolvição da médica com base na figura do "consentimento hipotético" (embora não a mencione expressamente).

Concordo que este instituto deve ser acolhido como *defesa* legítima do médico perante uma ação de responsabilidade médica por *violação do dever de informação.*

Contudo, o 'consentimento hipotético' terá que ter um desenho justo e adequado, não podendo vingar a ideia peregrina de que *alguém que escolhe previamente um determinado médico ou clínica privada, exigirá dele uma "informação menos informada", predispondo-se a aceitar as indicações médicas que receba...*

Com efeito, e sem pretender fazer uma análise exaustiva do caso, devemos salientar um dos factos provados: perante a pergunta da paciente sobre se a intervenção tinha riscos, a médica afirmou que a operação *não tinha riscos*, pelo contrário, 'arriscado seria não fazer a intervenção cirúrgica.'

Ora, isto demonstra um incumprimento do dever de informação e revela ainda que a paciente tinha uma *dúvida razoável* sobre se valia ou não a pena submeter-se à dita intervenção.

Por outro lado, a paciente *não assinou nenhum formulário* do consentimento informado, nem consta que houvesse qualquer *procedimento ou guideline no sentido de se respeitar o direito ao esclarecimento e ao consentimento naquela clínica.*

Tal não constitui – *rectius, não constituía* – um requisito legal, mas a sua ausência ou a de um procedimento semelhante denuncia um desinteresse da clínica oftalmológica pela atividade de prestar informações e obter o consentimento livre e esclarecido, o que indicia uma *negligência grosseira* na omissão do dever de informar.

Ou seja, encontramos já dois fundamentos (1) **conflito de decisão da paciente** e (2) **culpa grave da médica** que, dentro do esquema dogmático que iremos apresentar, conduziria à **não** aplicação do instituto do consentimento hipotético.

Por outro lado, discordamos da tese do STJ no sentido de que tem que ser a paciente a suportar o *ónus da prova* de que teria recusado a intervenção, mesmo que tivesse sido devidamente informada.

Antes deve ser a médica a – querendo fazer valer um facto impeditivo do direito da Autora – a ter o *onus probandi* de que o consentimento hipotético seria aplicável *in casu*.

Em suma, este Acórdão – antes citado com louvor por ter enunciado com clareza o direito esclarecimento do paciente – acabou por se revelar titubeante e receoso de tirar as devidas consequências da afirmação de que existe o direito ao consentimento informado.

A justiça e o Direito impõem que os tribunais saibam dar o devido acolhimento às justas pretensões dos pacientes que, sendo lesados no decurso de uma intervenção médica para a qual não deram um consenti-

DIREITO DA SAÚDE

mento devidamente esclarecido, possam receber uma indemnização pelos danos patrimoniais e não patrimoniais causados.

Impõe-se também que, desde a petição inicial, sejam alegados e carreados os meios de prova dos factos que consubstanciam esta figura jurídica ainda pouco aplicada, no âmbito da responsabilidade civil médica em Portugal: o consentimento informado. Fica aqui, pois, um apelo aos Advogados!

6. O consentimento hipotético no direito comparado

O consentimento hipotético mergulha no chamado *comportamento alternativo lícito* – instituto da responsabilidade civil que – digamo-lo desde já – *em regra não é aceite como excludente da responsabilidade*.

Na Alemanha vem-se entendendo que, no caso de a informação prestada ter sido *insuficiente*, a intervenção médica é *ilícita* e acarreta responsabilidade do médico pelos danos produzidos.

O BGH admite, por princípio, a figura do *comportamento alternativo lícito* ou do *consentimento hipotético*. Se a jurisprudência antiga se bastava com a simples referência a uma violação do dever de informar em geral, hoje a posição processual do paciente está mais onerada: no caso de o paciente alegar que se tivesse recebido a informação adequada teria recusado a intervenção, é exigido que este demonstre que ficaria numa situação de **conflito de decisão** (*echter Entscheidungskonflikt*), ou seja que mostre ser ***plausível*** a sua recusa.

Sobre o médico, por seu turno, impende o *ónus da prova* de que o paciente teria realizado a operação mesmo que tivesse recebido toda a informação.[5] Esta inversão do ónus da prova justifica-se, uma vez que para o doente esta seria uma *prova de facto negativo e indefinido*.[6] Estamos perante uma situação de *causalidade psíquica*, pelo que o tribunal deve decidir com base em "balanços de verosimilhança".

---

[5] Deutsch, Erwin / Spickhoff, Andreas, *Medizinrecht, Arzneimittelrecht, Medizinprodukterecht und Transfusionsrecht*, 6. Auflage, Springer, 2008, p. 207.

[6] Sinde Monteiro, Jorge, *Responsabilidade por conselhos, recomendações ou informações*, Almedina, 1990, p. 290, pronuncia-se, em tese geral, sobre o ónus probatório, nos casos de causalidade virtual ou hipotética, e concorda com a doutrina dominante, que o faz incidir sobre o *lesante*. "Isto sobre a base de que ele agiu ilicitamente, colocando uma condição equivalente para o dano". Mas, relativamente ao comportamento alternativo lícito não apoia uma solução unitária.

O doente só tem que provar que ficaria numa situação de conflito de decisão, não tem de provar como na realidade decidiria. E o juiz não deve ser muito exigente quanto à plausibilidade dos fundamentos apresentados pelo paciente. Por outro lado, no direito alemão, o comportamento hipotético do paciente deve ser analisado não de acordo com o paciente razoável *("vernünftigen Patienten")*, mas sim tendo em conta a situação de *decisão pessoal*, ou seja, prevalece o critério do *paciente concreto*.[7]

Não basta, pois, provar que um doente aceitaria uma intervenção médica que com grande probabilidade melhoraria a sua qualidade de vida com poucos riscos ou uma intervenção urgente que visasse evitar consequências graves para a saúde do paciente. É necessário provar que se verificam as condições que corresponderiam à *vontade daquele concreto paciente*.

Deve notar-se que, em termos processuais, o paciente só é obrigado a apresentar esta argumentação relativa aos fundamentos plausíveis do conflito de decisão, se o Réu (médico) tiver apresentado a defesa do consentimento hipotético. *O tribunal não pode oficiosamente levantar essa questão.* Por outro lado, o juiz não deve colocar demasiadas exigências no que respeita à fundamentação das razões plausíveis do paciente para o conflito de decisão. A essência e a finalidade do esclarecimento é assegurar um *espaço de decisão individual,* este deve ser garantido e *o médico deve suportar o ónus da prova do consentimento hipotético.*[8]

Em suma, na Alemanha, pode surgir a questão de o paciente ter aceite a intervenção médica, mesmo que tivesse sido devidamente informado acerca dos riscos. Se não for improvável que o paciente teria tido um conflito de decisão, se tivesse recebido a informação de forma inteiramente adequada, *o paciente tem direito à indemnização na sua totalidade.*[9]

Pelo contrário, a responsabilidade é excluída se o médico convincentemente indicar que, se tivesse dado a informação necessária, o paciente teria consentido no procedimento médico e o paciente não consegue

---

[7] Cf. ENGLJÄHRIGER, Daniela, *Ärztliche Aufklärungspflicht vor medizinischen Eingriffen*, Verlag Orac, Wien, 1996, p. 118.

[8] KATZENMEIER, Christian, *Arzthaftung*, Tübingen, Mohr Siebeck, 2002, p. 348-349.

[9] Cf. síntese de BARENDRECHT/JANSEN/LOOS/PINNA/CASCÃO/VAN GULIJK, *Principles of European Law, Study Group on a European Civil Code, Service Contracts*, Chapter 7, Sellier, 2007, p. 778.

DIREITO DA SAÚDE

tornar plausível que ele teria ficado em dúvida (em situação de conflito de decisão), ou seja, aplica-se o *consentimento hipotético*.

Seguindo esta doutrina , a Lei de 2013 – "Lei para a Melhoria dos Direitos das Doentes e dos Doentes, de 20 de Fevereiro de 2013 – prevê, no § 630h referente ao *Ónus da prova na responsabilidade por erro de tratamento ou erro de esclarecimento:*

> (2) O prestador de cuidados de saúde tem de provar que obteve o consentimento, de acordo com o § 630d, e prestou os esclarecimentos, em conformidade com os requisitos do § 630e. *No caso de a prestação de esclarecimentos não estar em conformidade com os requisitos do § 630e, o prestador de cuidados de saúde pode alegar que o doente teria consentido no tratamento, caso houvesse sido adequadamente esclarecido.*[10]

Em França, a *Cour de Cassation* admitiu que, caso se demonstre *com toda a probabilidade* que o paciente não informado teria autorizado a intervenção, mesmo que se lhe tivesse informado previamente dos riscos existentes, não haverá lugar a qualquer responsabilidade civil do médico. Com efeito, neste país, na circunstância de violação do dever de informar, haveria responsabilidade pelos danos totais sofridos pelo paciente, mas os tribunais podem tomar em conta qual a *probabilidade* para o paciente de recusar um tratamento, se tivesse recebido a informação adequada. Ou seja, aplica-se a teoria da *perda de chance* no domínio da responsabilidade civil por violação do dever de informação.[11] Se tal probabilidade puder ser aceite em juízo, o paciente pode receber uma proporção dos danos efetivamente sofridos, pela *perda da chance* de recusar o tratamento que conduziu aos danos. A dimensão da *chance perdida* depende inteiramente dos factos provados caso a caso.[12]

No direito inglês, este problema surge no âmbito do pressuposto da "causation". O direito da *common law* opera com delitos tipificados.

---

[10] Tradução do Doutor Luís Vasconcelos de Abreu.

[11] GALÁN CORTÉS, Júlio César, *Responsabilidad Médica y Consentimiento Informado*, Madrid, Civitas, 2001, p. 224. Neste contexto a jurisprudência francesa costuma lançar mão do instituto de *"perte de chance"*.

[12] BARENDRECHT/JANSEN/LOOS/PINNA/CASCÃO/VAN GULIJK, *Principles of European Law, Study Group on a European Civil Code, Service Contracts*, Chapter 7, Sellier, 2007, p. 777. Essa tese tem também seguidores em Espanha, ARCOS VIEIRA, Maria Luísa, *Responsabilidad Sanitaria por Incumplimiento del Deber de Información al Paciente*, Navarra, Thomson Aranzadi, 2007, p. 59 ss..

No domínio da responsabilidade médica, há dois fundamentais: (1) *battery* e (2) *negligence*.

O *tort of battery* consiste numa interferência intencional no corpo de outra pessoa sem causa de justificação. Uma ação por *battery* tem lugar quando o Autor foi 'agredido' de qualquer forma pelo Réu e **não houve consentimento**, expresso ou tácito, para tal intervenção, valendo, natural-mente, também, para os casos e que o Autor *recusou* a intervenção, mas o médico, não obstante, a realizou. Não é necessário estabelecer qualquer prejuízo como consequência desse dano e, portanto, não há qualquer problema de causalidade.[13] Trata-se de um tort *per se*, o que significa que o Autor tem direito a *nominal damages* (mesmo que não haja um dano real) e se teve algum prejuízo real, tem direito a ser indemnizado.[14]

Uma ação por *negligence* é adequada quando o paciente deu o seu consentimento para um ato da natureza daquele que foi praticado pelo médico, mas houve um vício no consentimento por *falta de esclarecimento adequado*.[15] Numa ação pelo *tort* de *negligence*, o paciente tem não só que demonstrar que a informação revelada se encontra abaixo do que era exi-gido por lei, mas também que **ele não teria autorizado o tratamento se estivesse informado desses mesmos riscos**.[16] Neste ordenamento jurídico, o paciente tem o *ónus da prova* no "tort of negligence". Assim, incumbe ao paciente provar num juízo de *"balance of probabilities"* que ele não teria realizado a intervenção, se tivesse recebido a informação adequada.[17]

---

[13] HERRING, Jonathan, *Medical Law and Ethics*, 2012, p. 85 descreve ainda a ação criminal de battery que acontece muito raramente, "unless she or he was acting maliciously, for example, where the act involved a sexual assault, como aconteceu no caso *R v. Healy* [2003] 2 Cr App R (S) 87.

[14] RIBOT IGUALADA, Jordi, La responsabilidad civil por la falta de consentimiento informado, *Revista de Derecho Privado*, Noviembre-Diziembre 2007, 29-62 (35); HERRING, p. 86 indica que pode ainda haver lugar a *punitive damages*.

[15] Cf. MASON, J. K./LAURIE, G. T., *Mason & McCall Smith's Law and Medical Ethics*, 8th ed. Oxford, Oxford University Press, 2010.

[16] *Chatterton v. Gerson*, [1981] QB 432. Se a demanda for baseada no tort de negligence, o Autor tem que provar não apenas a violação do dever de informar mas também que se o dever não tivesse sido violado, o paciente não teria optado por consentir na operação. Isto implica que o paciente tem que provar que se tivesse sido informado (dos riscos e consequências secundárias, por exemplo), ele teria tomado outra decisão.

[17] DAVIES, Michael, *Textbook on Medical Law*, 1998, p. 174.

Há causalidade, portanto, quando o paciente razoável – partilhando as características do paciente concreto que poderiam afectar a decisão do consentimento – se soubesse do risco, teria declinado a operação se fosse informado.

Todavia, a House of Lords com a decisão *Chester v Afshar* [2004] UKHL 41 veio atenuar o rigor desta perspetiva sobre a causalidade no âmbito da violação do dever de informar. Consagrou-se a jurisprudência segundo a qual, se a paciente não foi informada dos riscos de uma cirurgia (neste caso risco de *paralisia* na sequência de uma cirurgia à coluna) que se vieram a verificar na sequência da mesma, provando-se que a paciente *"at that time"* não teria aceite submeter-se à operação, *tanto basta para condenar o médico pelos danos causados.*

Não é necessário que a paciente prove que *nunca* teria aceite aquela intervenção. Apenas que não a aceitaria naquele momento e que a operação (que conduziu aos danos) *não se teria realizado se ela tivesse sido devidamente informada.*

No caso tratava-se de uma intervenção de neurocirurgia à coluna com o risco de 1 a 2% de paralisia, que se veio a verificar. Tendo-se provado que o médico não informou desse risco, mas que a paciente teria aceite a intervenção, mas mais tarde, foi o primeiro condenado.

Foi intenção dos juízes reforçar o dever de informação, que de outro modo sairia fragilizado.[18]

Que diferença face ao que se tem passado nos nossos tribunais...

7. O consentimento hipotético: sua aplicabilidade no Direito português e o Acórdão do STJ de 2/6/2015...

O problema do consentimento hipotético, numa primeira leitura, afigura-se como sendo dogmaticamente um problema de causalidade, onde o legislador adotou a *teoria da adequação*. Todavia, seguindo uma interpretação *objetivista atualista*, beneficiamos de horizonte hermenêutico para concluir que o nosso direito é, nesta sede, aberto às inovações da doutrina e da jurisprudência, já que o art. 563º parece ir no sentido de consagrar que *não* são apenas critérios naturalísticos que presidem à imputação objetiva.

---

[18] HERRING, *Medical Law and Ethics*, p. 49 e 106.

Por outro lado, a moderna doutrina aceita, dentro de um apertado enquadramento, que o lesante se possa defender invocando a exceção de comportamento alternativo lícito.[19]

Este é um expediente adequado e justo para quiçá amenizar um pouco a pressão indemnizatória sobre o prestador de saúde.

Defendemos, portanto, que este instrumento poderá ser aplicado, mas apenas se respeitar um conjunto de requisitos, que deverão ser analisados casuisticamente e que se regem pelos seguintes parâmetros:

Em primeiro lugar, não deverá ser admitido quando estão em causa *violações graves* dos deveres de conduta do médico. Este conceito é também ele complexo e pode abranger:

a gravidade objetiva da violação em si (ex: ausência de consentimento – será o caso de uma histerectomia, feita com indicação médica, aquando de um parto por cesariana, não precedido de consentimento da mulher), ou

a gravidade subjetiva da violação, por exemplo, o *grau de culpa do médico*, ou seja, este omite informações de forma dolosa ou com negligência grosseira, por exemplo com *intuitos comerciais* ou para *não perder clientes....*[20]

Também a *violação de formalidades essenciais* pode configurar um caso de violação grave: será o caso da ausência de consentimento escrito para a participação num *ensaio clínico de medicamentos,* mas já parece duvidoso nos casos de prática de uma interrupção voluntária da gravidez ou de uma esterilização. É que – se, no segundo grupo de casos, é difícil configurar uma situação de total ausência de consentimento –, já no primeiro, qualquer pessoa pode, contra a sua vontade, ser levado a participar num ensaio clínico de medicamentos, pelo que as *cautelas* e exigências da lei têm uma dimensão de formalidade *ad substantiam.*

É ainda impeditivo de aplicação da figura do consentimento hipotético, a omissão de *informações fundamentais (por exemplo, risco de paralisia, risco de cegueira, risco de impotência)* para que o doente se autodetermine.[21]

---

[19] DEUTSCH/ AHRENS, *Deliktsrecht, Unerlaubte Handlungen – Schadenersatz –Schmerzensgeld,* 4., völlig überarbeitete und erweiterte Auflage, Carl Heymanns Verlag KG, 2002, p. 37-38.

[20] Helmut KOZIOL, "Rechtsmässiges Alternativverhalten –Auflockerung starrer Lösungsansätze", in *Festschrift für Erwin DEUTSCH*, Carl Heymanns Verlag KG, 1999, p. 187.

[21] Cf. KOZIOL, *Haftungspflichtrecht,* 1997, p. 278.

DIREITO DA SAÚDE

Pelo contrário, julgamos que podem ser consideradas *violações leves* do dever de esclarecimento, a omissão de formalidades secundárias ou a não revelação de informações não essenciais, casos em que será de admitir esta defesa – o consentimento hipotético.

No caso de aceitarmos esta defesa, deveremos, seguidamente resolver o problema de saber se o tribunal deve lançar mão do critério do *paciente razoável* ou do *paciente concreto.*

Quando se apela ao juiz para que faça um juízo sobre processos psicológicos de um agente jurídico, normalmente o Direito Civil lança mão de critérios objetivistas, como por exemplo no critério do *bonus pater familias* para aferição da culpa (art. 487, nº 2) ou do *declaratário normal* (art. 236º e 247º).

Porém, perante valores como a liberdade, a integridade física e a saúde, devemos respeitar a idiossincrasia e as opções fundamentais de cada cidadão, pelo que o critério do juízo deve ser o do **paciente concreto**.

Em terceiro lugar, o *ónus da prova* deve impender sobre quem se pretende fazer valer de um "facto impeditivo do direito invocado" (art. 342º, nº 2 CC), ou seja, o <u>médico</u>. [22] Como vimos, para o doente tratar-se-ia da *prova de factos negativos (provar que não teria aceite a intervenção médico-cirúrgica, caso tivesse sido devidamente informado).*

Finalmente, em caso de fundada dúvida sobre se o paciente aceitaria a intervenção ou a recusaria, no direito português não tem que valer o princípio *tudo-ou-nada,* dada a fecundidade hermenêutico-prática do art. 494º.[23] Assim, o juiz poderá perante as circunstâncias do caso, *v.g.,* graves dúvidas de avaliação da prova produzida, o carácter *irrazoável* do juízo hipotético do paciente, o grau de culpa do médico, etc., *atenuar* a responsabilidade, procurando a justiça material no caso concreto.[24]

---

[22] Neste sentido, *vide* a proposta do *Study Group on European Civil Code,* cujo art. 6:109, sobre causalidade (*Causation*).

[23] Assim SINDE MONTEIRO, Jorge, "Aspectos Particulares de Responsabilidade Médica", *Direito da Saúde e Bioética,* p. 152, em nota.

[24] Aceita-se assim o pensamento de Helmut KOZIOL, "Rechtsmässiges Alternativverhalten – Auflockerung starrer Lösungsansätze", in *Festschrift für Erwin DEUTSCH,* Carl Heymanns Verlag KG, 1999, p. p. 187 e, aparentemente, *de jure condendo,* de DEUTSCH, Erwin/AHRENS, Hans-Jürgen, *Deliktsrecht, Unerlaubte Handlungen – Schadenersatz – Schmerzensgeld,* 5. völlig überarbeitete und erweiterte Auflage, Carl Heymanns Verlag KG, 2009, p. 38: "In einem solchen Fall sollte der Ersatzanspruch *ermässigt* werden." Esta solução parece-nos preferível à

Para além do art. 494º, o fundamento jurídico-positivo poderá encontrar-se no art. 570º[25] Acresce, aliás, que este último artigo não é mais do que uma expressão, centrada na culpa, de uma regra de geral do direito da responsabilidade civil, segundo a qual, no caso de existência de uma conduta ou atividade concorrente do lesado que contribui para o dano, a responsabilidade pode ser *reduzida* ou *excluída*.[26]

Essa flexibilidade ou maleabilidade em sede de montante de indemnização está também patente no art. 566º, nº3, segundo o qual "o tribunal julgará equitativamente dentro dos limites que tiver por provados".

Todas estas normas demonstram que o Direito Civil português aceita que o juiz – em função das circunstâncias do *caso decidendo* e da complexidade dos fatores a tomar em consideração na avaliação do montante de indemnização – a possa reduzir ou limitar.[27]

Assim, uma oftalmologista que não informa a sua paciente do risco de cegueira; um neurocirurugião que não informa o seu doente do risco de paralisia; um cirurgião plástico que não informa o seu paciente do risco de insucesso ou de necrose e infeção – *nenhum destes médicos merece a proteção do consentimento hipotético.*

---

solução da jurisprudência alemã do *"echte Entscheidungskonflikt"*, até porque tempera a também exigente carga probatória que impende sobre o médico, ademais se – como nós defendemos – se optar pelo critério do paciente concreto.

[25] MOTA PINTO, Carlos, *Teoria Geral do Direito Civil* (4ª Edição por António PINTO MONTEIRO e Paulo MOTA PINTO), Coimbra, Almedina, 2005, p. 217.

[26] Veja-se, neste sentido, o regime proposto pelos Princípios Europeus de Responsabilidade Civil, no Art. 8:101. Contributory conduct or activity of the victim (1) Liability can be excluded or reduced to such extent as is considered just having regard to the victim's contributory fault and to any other matters which would be relevant to establish or reduce liability of the victim if he were the tortfeasor. Versão portuguesa disponível em: MONTEIRO, Jorge Ferreira Sinde/ PEREIRA, André Gonçalo Dias, "Translations of the Principles of European Tort Law, Portuguese translation", EUROPEAN GROUP ON TORT LAW, *Principles of European Tort Law*, 2005, p. 251-257.

[27] Em alternativa a este enquadramento, podemos falar de uma "concorrência alternativa de causas", dominante na doutrina austríaca, com Franz Bidlinsky e Helmut Koziol, e que veio a ter acolhimento nos *Princípios Europeus de Direito da Responsabilidade Civil*, quer no já referido artigo 8, mas também no art. 3:106. *Causas incertas no âmbito da esfera do lesado:* "O lesado deverá suportar o prejuízo na medida correspondente à probabilidade de este ter sido causado por uma atividade, ocorrência ou qualquer *outra circunstância* que *se situe no âmbito da sua própria esfera*, incluindo eventos naturais."

Pelo contrário, o oncologista que olvida informar do risco de perda de libido na sequência de um tratamento de quimioterapia; um ortopedista que não informa do risco de dor temporária a um doente operado na sequência de um acidente de viação; o dentista que não informa do risco de abcesso numa extração dentária de um dente que causa agudo sofrimento e que é irrecuperável; o anestesiologista que não informa de eventuais e raras perdas de memória causadas pela anestesia geral a um doente com mais de 80 anos e reformado... em todos estes casos, mesmo que se considere que se omitiram *informações necessárias e devidas*, pode o médico invocar e provar que o doente (muito provavelmente) teria consentido na operação, *de qualquer modo*. Ou seja, nestes casos a defesa do consentimento hipotético deve proceder e a indemnização, nos termos das disposições anteriormente referidas, será *diminuída* ou *excluída*.

O Jurisprudência, no já citado Acórdão de 2 de junho de 2015, explica com clareza que:

"O ónus da prova do consentimento hipotético, doutrina oriunda da jurisprudência alemã, pertence ao médico e obedece aos seguintes requisitos:

1) que tenha sido fornecida ao paciente um mínimo de informação;
2) que haja a fundada presunção de que o paciente não teria recusado a intervenção se tivesse sido devidamente informado;
3) que a intervenção fosse:
   i) medicamente indicada;
   ii) conduzisse a uma melhoria da saúde do paciente;
   iii) visasse afastar um perigo grave;
4) a recusa do paciente não fosse objetivamente irrazoável, de acordo com o critério do paciente concreto."

Por isso, também no caso decidido, que consistia numa intervenção cirúrgica suscetível de causar riscos graves, como dores intensas e incapacidade para manter relações sexuais, andar e trabalhar, concluiu-se que a autora, se soubesse dos riscos da mesma, teria recusado o consentimento, logo não se aplicou o instituto do consentimento hipotético e condenou-se o réu a pagar uma indemnização pelos danos patrimoniais e, sobretudo, não patrimoniais causados, no valor de €26.000 (dos quais €25.000 por danos não patrimoniais). Como se escreve no aresto: *"A paciente sofreu, assim, danos existenciais, biológicos, sexuais, psicológicos e físicos, resultantes, não só das consequências da operação, mas também da falta de assistência do réu no período pós-operatório."*[28]

1968: Estatuto Hospitalar – Decreto-Lei nº 48 357 de 27 de Abril de 1968: no Capítulo VII reconhece-se aos doentes o direito de recusarem a assistência, salvo se houver disposição legal em contrário, e o de recusarem exames ou tratamentos desnecessários ao diagnóstico e tratamento que precisem.[29]

1982: ano em que o legislador introduz o tipo legal de crime de intervenções médico-cirúrgicas arbitrárias (artigos 156º e 157º do Código penal).

1995: Guilherme de OLIVEIRA publica "O Fim da "Arte Silenciosa" (o dever de informação dos médicos), na *Revista de Legislação e Jurisprudência* (ano 128).

2015: 20 anos depois, o direito ao consentimento informado fez-se ouvir no Supremo Tribunal de Justiça!

---

[28] Igualmente não é aplicável a figura do consentimento presumido. Afirma, com razão, o Acórdão do STJ de 2/6/2015: "Em relação às operações estéticas reconstrutivas, porque se repercutem na imagem da pessoa e na relação consigo mesma e com os outros, porque relacionadas com o corpo e com a identidade, e, no caso *sub judice*, com a vida sexual e íntima, não é possível que se verifiquem os pressupostos do consentimento presumido."

[29] Prescrevia o art. 80º: 2 do Estatuto Hospitalar. Os doentes podem recusar a assistência, salvo quando a lei dispuser o contrário. Este direito não pode ser exercido pelo representante ou tutor do assistido. 3. Os doentes não podem ser submetidos, sem seu consentimento, a exames ou tratamentos, nem ser retidos nos serviços hospitalares, contra a sua vontade, por período superior ao estritamente necessário para diagnóstico e tratamento de que precisem, salvo nos casos expressamente previstos na lei.

Do exercício da medicina: dos «*médicos escravos para escravos e (dos) médicos livres para os homens livres.*»*

João Vaz Rodrigues**

I. Introdução: sobre o Mestre.

Existem momentos inesquecíveis plenos de singular pedagogia, como no vetusto conto japonês em que um monge, desafiado por um samurai para lhe explicar em que redundava afinal a diferença entre o inferno e o céu, afirmou com desdém ser espúrio justificar tal sofisticação a uma reles personagem; o guerreiro enfureceu-se e lançou mão da sua espada: – como te atreves? A resposta foi pronta: – já sentes o inferno, oh nobre senhor? A evidência gelou o samurai, que, envergonhado, embainhou a *katana* pedindo perdão, ao que o monge retorquiu com serena bonomia: – meu nobre senhor, mostrais agora o céu!

Tantas e tantas vezes, com análoga simplicidade nesta arte de propiciar uma *metacognição*, mas com superior elegância, ouvi similitudes ao Professor Doutor Guilherme de Oliveira, dando atenção muito especialmente às tiradas sobre a *indecisão crónica* e os passos difíceis dos juristas

---

* Platão, *Leis, Livro IV.*
** Professor Auxiliar na Escola de Ciências Sociais da Universidade de Évora. Advogado.

DIREITO DA SAÚDE

entre séculos em matéria dos dilemas jurídicos da medicina[1]; dificuldades a que, sem exclusividade, dedicou elevada reflexão.

Mais recentemente, no dia 27 de Março de 2015, na Sala dos Actos do Colégio do Espírito Santo de Évora, ouvi meu Mestre tecer alguns comentários, no cadinho que me importa salientar, sobre o *percurso da Academia*. As leituras em avaliação, afirmou, recordaram-lhe uma Universidade (a um tempo: a ganhar e a não perder) cuja existência e rumo traçou livre de cronogramas, de freios, de correias a reter liberdades e prazeres que se reflectem no que se estuda, no que se escreve e no que se aprende e se busca ensinar. Em suma, emprestou e retirou valias com indicação de gostos. O rumo, é bom de ver, permite uma ou outra nostalgia mas sobretudo a consciência da oportunidade de não ser demais dar *aviso à navegação*. Rumar adiante é inevitável; e a viagem impõe boas companhias. Sem com isto me pretender libertar das responsabilidades: da investigação, do acerto dos compromissos ou do empenho na pedagogia, sublinho que a mera produção quantitativa, forçada que não espontânea, reescrita tantas vezes não pela prudência ou pela (re)descoberta mas outrossim por razão simples de que confrontar-se uma alma com precipitações constitui o dia-a-dia do expoente das grelhas das burocracias, onde a sombra da valia individual se pode formar menos pela desejável luz natural do que pela artificial[2]. E depois? Inquirirá o leitor; depois será o inferno, o paraíso e acrescento o purgatório. É liberdade da escolha das lentes.

---

[1] Para quem pretenda regozijar-se com um superior momento –literário– deste tipo de pedagogia cf. *Introdução ao Colóquio sobre Transplantações*, 25/03/1993, org. CDBM|FDUC, in *Temas de Direito da Medicina* (CDBM 1, 2ª ed.), Coimbra Ed., 2005, pp. 73-79. Neste, como em muitos outros *Temas* –Mãe só há ~~uma~~ duas; *Estrutura jurídica do acto médico; Genoma; DPN; Fim da* arte silenciosa; *Menores; O Erro; A vulnerabilidade; O cuidado e a aliança terapêutica* sem esgotar, evidentemente – sublinho a prudência de quem vê longe e lê o decurso dos tempos, antecipando e prevenindo problemas e alvitrando prudentes soluções; tantos *golpes-de-asa*. A estória *japonesa* foi recolhida e parafraseada em Daniel GOLEMAN, *Inteligência Emocional*, Sábado, 2006 (Dep Leg B-39891), p. 69.

[2] A propósito, mostrando aspectos perniciosos da voracidade académica e científica (o que já apelidei de *histerismo de produção científica*, e que se materializa em listas infindáveis de micro artigos e bizarros mecanismos de publicação) cf. Susan HAACK, *The Integrity of Science: what it means, why it matters*, in AA.VV. (coord. José de OLIVEIRA ASCENSÃO), *Estudos de Direito da Bioética*, vol. II, Almedina, 2008, pp. 183-209, máx., 193-201. Com laivos de um humor extraordinário relata Paloma GARCÍA PICAZO, sobre acelerações indesejadas, ter ouvido a seguinte *estória* a seu Mestre, Don António TRUYOL Y SIERRA, –rindo a propósito– quando este integrou já para o fim de sua longa vida um júri para uma das disputadíssimas Cátedras

Sendo pressuposto dar contorno panegírico ao perfil do Doutor Guilherme Freire Falcão de Oliveira, não pretendo aqui hastear um pau de bandeira sem bandeira, se bem que o mesmo lhe oferecesse o sentido de patentear o protesto de fidelidade de um «soldado» munido de bastão ao serviço, pronto para erguer o seu tecido de linha fina, preciosa. Uma das características que apraz sublinhar entre as virtudes reside na capacidade presciente dos seus escritos. Depois de analisar os escolhos do Direito ditado, eleva-se por regra dos realismos jurídicos e aponta os prudentes caminhos das *vias do meio* até às soluções que, tarde ou cedo, os tempos confirmam. Não se inibe em oferecer soluções, se bem que estas venham usualmente envolvidas em interrogações que a sabedoria entrevê como possíveis no nevoeiro dos tempos seguintes. Muito do rame-rame do nosso quotidiano representou em algum momento um controverso trampolim a prenunciar *perigos* e *fracturas sociais*. Outras vezes, verificou-se a inversa. Uma leitura bem-humorada da História permite afirmar que *no Mundo se vive com este a passar a vida a chegar ao Fim*!

Muitos dos problemas suscitados pela relação entre o paciente e os profissionais de saúde que agora começam verdadeiramente a engrossar as tarefas dos nossos Tribunais mereceram-lhe o seguinte diagnóstico[3]:

«Parece adequado, por fim, dizer que há uma outra linha de reforma que traria vantagens para a criação de um ambiente pacífico, favorável à diminuição do erro médico – refiro-me à prática do *consentimento informado*. (...) Creio que –um dia– os Sistemas de Saúde vão distinguir-se uns dos outros não tanto pela sofisticação das máquinas ou pela diferenciação e capacidade dos médicos, quanto pela sua

---

universitárias espanholas (comentário a um muito nutrido *curriculum*): «*Observo que viaja usted mucho; que ha asistido a muchos congresos, conferencias y simposios, incluso internacionales; que ha ocupado usted una cantidad notable de cargos académicos y de outro tipo, todos de grande responsabilidad e importancia; que son incesantes los cursos que imparte, y los seminarios y conferencias que ha dictado, supongo que acompañados de una actividad docente regular en su asignatura... Son, asimismo, numerosos los artículos que ha publicado e incluso libros; su actividad es verdaderamente prodigiosa. Es usted una persona muy atareada y productiva. Le felicito por ello, pero a la vez me pregunto con preocupación, ¿y usted,* **cuándo lee?**», cf. *Teoría Breve de Relaciones Internacionales*,Tecnos Ed., 2010, p. 17.

[3] Fundamentando a afirmação, apenas no que foi objecto de apurada investigação no campo da responsabilidade civil, cf. Mafalda MIRANDA BARBOSA, *A Jurisprudência portuguesa em matéria de responsabilidade civil médica: o estado da arte*, in Cadernos de Direito Privado, 38, Abril|Junho de 2008.

DIREITO DA SAÚDE

capacidade de organização e pela cultura de segurança que conseguirem atingir. Vamos esperar que o sistema português tenha iniciado a sua caminhada.»[4]

Tenho em memória ter ouvido o vaticínio no dia 2 de Março de 1996, no decurso da primeira aula proferida pelos Professores Doutor Orlando de Carvalho e Doutor Guilherme de Oliveira, de abertura do 1º Curso de pós-graduação em Direito da Medicina, na FDUC. Pensei estar perante «um *clip*»; a simplicidade de um arame que torcido de forma engenhosa se transforma em uma *mola* mais do que útil, essencial, para prender e organizar papéis. A necessidade prática de obtenção e manutenção do consentimento esclarecido para e no decurso da intervenção médica foi, durante esses anos e os seguintes, objecto de vigorosas oposições e discussões e *apoucamentos,* presenciados e participados em fóruns onde *os da sua Escola* transmitiram a *ideia.* Hoje, vejo, oiço e leio antigos cépticos a defenderem – e bem – a necessidade e a conveniência. Significa isto que se venceu um «teste da recusa»? Seria uma alegria ouvir dizer que sim, mas temo que a lição tenha sido apenas insuficientemente compreendida para *um primeiro momento prévio,* consagrado formalmente.

Foi ainda a imagem de um «*clip*» que me ocorreu quando, em 1999, consegui inventariar –sobre a sua tolerante orientação– os casos em que o legislador impõe o registo por escrito da declaração do consentimento do paciente. Os sectores da medicina foram-se multiplicando e os requisitos do consentimento também. Actualmente, a «Norma O15|2013|DGS» dificilmente deixa algum procedimento médico ou medicamentoso fora desse *título de crédito médico.* Mais: ao balcão de qualquer farmácia após avio medicamentoso, cada um de nós outorga ou vê outorgar, por regra *cegamente,* uma *declaração informada* (esclarecida?).

Já em 2015, com a simplicidade de sempre, culminou-me mais uma orientação com céptica discussão (permanente) sobre a circunscrição de um teste restrito que credito como a solução para o *meta-consentimento* que espreita: o da recusa para intervenções médicas, a permitir salvaguardar redutos daquela dignidade indomesticável aos extremismos de

---

[4] Cf. Guilherme de OLIVEIRA, *O Erro em medicina,* in *Temas...* 2ª ed., p. 305.

uma *pacta sunt servanda*[5] ou a necessidades sociais crescentes. Agradecer não me basta.

II. O paciente e a sua vulnerabilidade: limites de uma *escravatura*

A doutrina em torno do consentimento esclarecido propende a fornir a imagem do paciente como um *credor* de informação. Um *credor* que deverá ser satisfeito até aos parâmetros equitativos do respectivo esclarecimento de forma a amenizar a qualidade de parte fraca na relação. Intoleravelmente fraca, pois perde o domínio sobre o que lhe podem fazer. Acresce um catálogo evidente de vulnerabilidades para alguns: a criança, o geronte, o pobre, a vítima e o iliterato ocupam com facilidade as cinco quinas do *estandarte*. São aqueles a quem o exercício de uma «vivência» como componente integrante do «direito à vida»[6] encontra dificultada a manufactura de uma:

> «verdadeira afirmação jurídica da autonomia pessoal no contexto de uma certa comunidade –no quadro, portanto, de uma certa comunidade jurídica– e que se traduz na titularidade ou na pretensão *pessoal* (*proprium:* como seu), *impositiva* (imposta ou exigida de outrem com o carácter de *facultas ac potestas* e que para os outros destinatários se traduz num dever ou numa imposição) e *dispositiva* (cabendo de qualquer modo na disposição pessoal do titular), *jurídico-normativamente válida* de certos valores ou bens jurídicos»[7]

Este carácter marcadamente pessoal com que o ser humano se imprime no seu *ser e dispor* é também uma projecção para os demais e o seu reflexo. Para o emissor faculta poderes de facto sobre si próprio, sobre o

---

[5] A persistente faculdade de recusa inata ou subsequente –tendencial radicalidade da liberdade de revogação da manifestação de vontade– que dá cunho ao exercício dos direitos e deveres em torno da personalidade é exactamente a que permite circunscrever sempre como estranha a respectiva limitação, sobrepondo a projecção individual perante a insegurança e a incerteza da uma manifestação produzida. Neste preciso sentido, cf. H. Ewald Hörster, *A Parte Geral do Código Civil Português – Teoria Geral do Direito Civil*, Coimbra Ed., 1992, p. 272.

[6] Que constitui um «ius excludendi alios» enquanto integrante inalienável da personalidade humana, algo que afasta as intromissões indesejadas nas componentes protegidas das esferas endógenas da personalidade, mas que dificilmente poderá deixar de invocar a solidariedade quando, carente, vai bulir com os equilíbrios mínimos adequados à esfera físico-psíquica--ambiental.

[7] Cf. António Castanheira Neves, *Introdução ao Estudo do Direito*, Coimbra (1971/72), p. 395.

seu destino, mas invoca a protecção dos que o circundam nos sucessivos círculos de proximidade perante a contracção dos requisitos equilibrados da inteligibilidade, da volição, do bem estar-estar. A vulnerabilidade exorta –e bem– uma permanência dogmática que consiste em um feixe de retorno concreto de solidariedade a ser projectado da *obrigação passiva universal* sobre o *respeito* que emana da dignidade da existência. Tentando concretizar: a contrapartida ao aspecto potestativo que contém o âmbito dos direitos de personalidade é uma garantia de não interferência, que está na plena disponibilidade do titular. Sou *senhor* de mim e respeitarei a soberania dos demais sobre si próprios. Esta garantia a exigir aos e dos demais contém, todavia, uma tensão ainda onto-axiológica fundante: eu apenas poderei manter essa soberania na justa medida em que, por um lado, esta me seja reconhecida. Por outro lado necessito de exercer efectivamente a disponibilidade que integra a garantia (liberdade vivenciada reciprocamente nas esferas dos outros e na minha). É um efeito da solidariedade que se activa perante a *vulnerabilidade*. É fácil indicar matérias exemplificativas: a violação dos direitos humanos pode despertar a resistência (quando se entorpece a inteligência e se esgota a diplomacia); a reacção à catástrofe restringe a liberdade para garantir cuidados; o internamento e tratamento do doente inconsciente beneficia-lhe a integridade físico-psíquica, etc. Já em extremo, a reivindicação sobre certos níveis de *mutilação* (cuja auto consecução é possível) exorta a delimitação de uma cláusula aberta: o contexto *terapêutico* (cujo conteúdo atravessa permanente mutação | adaptação *actualística*).

1. O paciente credor? Devedor?

A solidariedade tem preço, carece de sustentabilidade. Assim se perspectivam alguns comportamentos de risco: é questão de *cobranças* do *cobrador*. Podem ou devem exigir-se posturas saudáveis aos cidadãos? Trata-se de um discurso sempre perigoso pela sedução moralista (até falaciosa) que acalenta. As prestações sociais são sinalagmáticas e os prevaricadores podem *perder,* podem ser sancionados pelos respectivos comportamentos desviantes. A medicina preventiva *ensina* cautelas. Quem não possua *certificação de boa conduta em dia*, poderá acalentar uma expectativa de que a projecção da solidariedade deva suprir a respectiva vulnerabilidade? Até onde e até quando? Bem está de ver a ruinosa sedução do silogismo. Se mirarmos em torno surge sensível o abuso da recriminação na justificação das frustrações: é o paroxismo da exortação das virtudes da *formiguinha* e da condenação da *cigarra*. Mas antes deste excesso reside um núcleo conceptual salvífico: a *concretização dos deveres de respeito impostos pela ordem jurídica para a organização individual das garantias individuais da dignidade humana, em vista da tutela de um interesse determinado ou de um núcleo de interesses decorrentes do entrelaçamento das esferas da personalidade humana*[8]. Assim, pior não será repensar estas *impressões* sobre o que apelidarei *conta-corrente* do paciente. Em boa verdade este não deve ser tido como um *pedinte com a palma em riste*. Qualquer ser humano carece de auxílio, desde o nascimento até à morte, tanto mais premente quanto maior for o factor terapêutico a justificar *estenderem-se as mãos*. A generalidade dos valores e bens sociais relevantes em termos comunitários devem ser acarinhados na cidadania na sua dupla vertente: como direitos e como deveres. Não espanta a proclamação no art. 64º, nº 1 da CRP: «... todos têm direito à protecção na saúde *e o dever de a defender e promover.*». Vulnerável mas não inimputável; carente mas não pedinte; e detentor de uma *conta-corrente* onde os créditos e débitos sociais não se inscrevem com preito mercantilista. Recordo KARL JASPERS:

---

[8] João CASTRO MENDES, *Teoria Geral do direito Civil*, II. Vol, AAFDL, 1999, p. 24; cf. ainda Rabindranath CAPELO DE SOUSA, *O Direito Geral de Personalidade*, Coimbra Ed., 1995, p. 612, que cito: «Indubitável é a subsunção do direito geral de personalidade no conceito de direito subjectivo de João de Castro Mendes, como *o poder concedido pela ordem jurídica para tutela de um interesse ou de um núcleo de interesses de uma ou mais pessoas*. É que o titular de um direito geral de personalidade detém uma posição pessoal de vantagem, advinda da disposição de diversos meios jurídicos, para tutela da relação de interesse entre ele a sua personalidade.». Se assim for, e assim é, nada impede o retorno, i.e., o reflexo que as vantagens implicam na teia actual das prestações sociais alargadas, onde aos custos crescentes da saúde se associam os do ensino, da solidariedade social, do ambiente, dos transportes, etc. Daqui à formulação de uma *consolidação* do preenchimento de requisitos para aspirar a merecer as contraprestações de solidariedade vai um passo; um passo fácil de mais de justificar perante carências na progressiva distribuição de bens escassos. A sociedade tardo moderna é coeva de uma modificação generalizada do esquema de prestações sociais fundadas no trabalho: o que vai sendo substituído pela precisão tecnológica da maquinaria que avoluma vagas de pessoas desempregadas (o sistema necessita permaneçam como consumidoras); mas as necessidades de laboração manual e intelectual encontram satisfação em um número crescente dos números da população mundial e nas assimetrias existentes, cf. Boaventura SOUSA SANTOS, *A Crítica da Razão Indolente. Contra o desperdício da experiência*, Afrontamento Ed., 2000, pp. 258-264. Silvério da ROCHA-CUNHA, *Crítica da Razão Simplificadora*, Húmus, 2015, pp. 28 e ss.; 54 e ss.; 111-166; e *passim*.

DIREITO DA SAÚDE

«... a doença é um processo natural que ataca o corpo. O doente tem de saber lidar com ele (...) O paciente é instruído, sabe, pois, do que se trata e coopera na execução da terapia conveniente. Anui, deixa-se convencer em caso de dúvida, ou repudia a intervenção médica proposta.»[9].

2. A combinação poderes | deveres da cidadania

A premissa «instrução» não é um dado adquirido mas uma aspiração individual e societária permanente da cidadania. O pressuposto de uma decisão reside na certificação do discernimento do paciente, o que valoriza a construção de uma órbita de deveres no campo informacional. Tal como a circulação na *cidade* é o resultado de um dédalo de vias que não se querem obstruídas sob pena de se criar um tráfego caótico, destruidor, também a aspiração à saúde reclama a comparticipação da segurança, da educação, do trabalho, da quota-parte do financiamento organizacional... Para se integrar plenamente no *sistema* o paciente deve revelar e inquirir; deve avaliar e entender, na medida possível, o que se lhe oferece por diante. E isto significa detectar e exercer um dever de colaboração a par de um dever de colher e de transmitir informação. Mais a mais porquanto a medicina encontra hoje como *pontes* entre os vários agentes e a(s) nosologia(s) o conjunto de informações reveladas pelo processo clínico (um elemento histórico de hermenêutica individual[10]) e as que o próprio paciente consiga desvelar ao desvelar-se pela interacção dos vários especialistas cujas actuações invoca. Retomo JASPERS para assentar em um pressuposto inverso ao que o levou a afirmar:

«... o doente não quer, de facto, dever, mas obedecer. A autoridade de um médico é para ele o ponto mais firme e desejado que o isenta de reflexão e responsabilidades próprias. 'O meu médico ordenou' é a libertação mais confortável[11]».

O paternalismo acarreta a inércia do que a *piedade* facilita, todavia, outra realidade se sobrepõe: a dignidade humana tem lastro fundo na

---

[9] Cf. Karl JASPERS, *O Médico na Era da Técnica*, Ed. 70, tradução de João Tiago Proença, 1986, pp. 7 e ss.

[10] Desenvolvimentos em Carla BARBOSA, *Aspectos Jurídicos de Acesso ao Processo Clínico*, in *MedLex*, Ano 7, nº 13, 2010, pp. 107-140.

[11] Cf. ID, *ibid, p. 10*.

DO EXERCÍCIO DA MEDICINA: DOS «*MÉDICOS ESCRAVOS PARA ESCRAVOS ...*

responsabilidade individual (DWORKIN) e esta, em sentido geral e abstracto (jus filosófico), permite recolocar o homem hodierno perante um dever, também geral: de decidir, de não se *encostar, de* obter informação ao invés de aguardar que a mesma se lhe deposite no regaço, e, sobretudo, tem de actuar em relação a si e tem de actuar na correnteza de acção em relação à qual a comunidade lhe dita encargo de responsabilidade... A responsabilidade é inter geracional e fica forçosamente imposta na solidariedade concomitante. Existem sequelas remotas cujas realidades são perfeitamente previsíveis: pode o ser humano hodierno agir na pressuposição de que a evolução da técnica dará resposta? Eis a dificuldade das teses que afastam a responsabilidade pelas gerações futuras. E tanto mais me surge esta evidência quanto desejo que a autonomia persista na espiral crescente de biliões de pessoas[12] cujas necessidades hão-de forçar alterações perante a finitude de recursos em que nos encontramos por ora enclausurados. Há que analisar de forma nua e crua a *fotografia* de Hans JONAS, segundo a qual já existe na Terra demasiada gente que não quer (pode?) prescindir do uso da tecnologia disponível[13]. Com efeito, a possibilidade de se verificarem compressões de valores justificadas na massificação e na escassez de recursos constitui um sério e evidente problema. A finitude da natureza postula alterações inevitáveis com novas premissas plenas de maleabilidade, como lucidamente explica Gilbert HOTTOIS[14]. Nos edifícios dos Hospitais o que antecede é corolário corrido ao paroxismo. A massificação é notória e o que é notório dispensa comentários. Por seu turno existem mais premissas a intersectarem o raciocínio e a produzirem fantasmas gerando outros silogismos. Por ex°, até ao recente início da «era do antibiótico»[15] a escassez dos recursos pendia para a

---

[12] Aceitando a informação recolhida em www.nato.int/docu/review/2011/ Climate-Action/.../ index.htm, a perspectiva ascende a números em torno dos 9,5 mil milhões de seres humanos vivos para o último quartel do séc. XXI.

[13] Cf. Hans JONAS, *El Principio de Responsabilidad. Ensayo de una ética para la civilización tecnológica* (Introduction de Andrés Sánchez Pascual), Herder Ed., 1ª ed. digital, loc. 913; 973; 5442-5446

[14] Cf. Gilbert HOTTOIS, *El Paradigma Bioético: Una Ética para la Tecnociência,* Ed. Anthropos, Barcelona, 1991, pp. 27 e ss.

[15] A investigação de medicamentação sintética antibiótica está associada tradicionalmente a nomes como Paul Ehrlich ou Alexander Fleming, no início do séc. XX, com «época de ouro», milagrosa, entre os anos 50 e 70 do século passado, mas encontraram-se resíduos de tetraciclina em esqueletos humanos oriundos do Sudão e datados entre 350 e 550 dC

coluna do leque da oferta médica e científica. Hoje, os recursos escassos situam-se com escândalo nos cabedais dos candidatos. Existe um abismo entre os recursos individuais e mesmo os recursos sociais disponíveis face aos custos estruturais e tecnológicos e medicamentosos. Um Mundo em desequilíbrio, finito, perfeitamente «abarcável» e reciprocamente dependente quanto a um «destino comum», inexoravelmente partilhado, com milhões de pessoas que poderiam encontrar solução para padecimentos caso possuíssem o que se esbanja. A medicina também alargou o espectro da actuação. A ideia de que se trata de uma ciência que se concretiza na satisfação de necessidades na esfera físico-psíquica das pessoas humanas no sentido da obtenção da saúde, já não é um conceito pleno[16]. O homem, na sua humanidade, vive no *fio da navalha* da doença[17]. As *doenças* reclamam o simples atraso da decrepitude mas prosseguem até à especialidade de *alfaiate do corpo*. A morte enquanto confronto implica uma inevitável derrota, sempre eivada de precocidade. Um embate cujo encontro justifica todos os atrasos possíveis? Temível interrogação. Pelo lado da comunidade é possível responder afirmativamente: desde o humanismo às forças de um mercado que necessita de seres vivos e contentes que, como marabuntas, se atestam de bens e serviços que alimentam

---

(a «dieta» alimentar de então, naquele local, deveria conter o produto activo). No Egipto (Oásis de Dakhleh: *The Daklheh Oasis Project*: DOP, cf. http://artsonline.monash.edu.au/archaeology/excavations-in-dakhleh-oasis-egypt), com referência ao período romano tardio encontrou-se tetraciclina em análises ósseas. Cf. Rustam I. Aminov, *A brief history of the antibiotetic era: lessons learned and challenges in the future,* in *Frontiers in Microbiology,* Dezembro 2010, acessível in http://www.scielo.br/scielo.php?script=sci_arttext&pid=S1415-790X1998000300009. Também a medicina tradicional chinesa terá uma centenária utilização vg. da *artemisinina*, retirada de planta *Artemisia annua,* (contra a malária). Os problemas actuais resultam em uma luta contra a resistência aos medicamentos, como refere expressamente Aminov. O problema assume foro de grande preocupação uma vez que a utilização antibiótica na nossa alimentação (agrícola e pecuária) *desactiva* os efeitos úteis dos produtos e permite criar resistências no mundo microbiano envolvente, colocando-se hoje inúmeras interrogações sobre causas que expliquem a compreensão do aumento das resistências de sorte a permitir uma eficácia que se revelou como um «milagre» científico no século passado.

[16] O sentido segue agora até ao conceito de *metaconsentimento* (um consentimento genérico que incluirá limites por traçar –recusa?!– e que integra a solidariedade que alinha os deveres sociais com a dupla função terapêutica e de ensaios incluindo a utilização de dados), cf. Dal-Re, R.; Carné, X. y Gracia, D. (2013). *Luces y sombras en la investigación clínica.* Madrid: Triacastela; Fundació Víctor Grífols I Lucas, *passim.*

[17] Cf. Jaspers, *O médico na era da técnica,* p. 12.

DO EXERCÍCIO DA MEDICINA: DOS «MÉDICOS ESCRAVOS PARA ESCRAVOS ...

o processo de criação de riqueza e revelam felicidade na existência pacífica que consigam construir e manter. Em termos individuais, é já dado adquirido a bipolaridade da (in)disponibilidade jurídica da pretensão a prestações alheias radicais na esfera própria. Mas existem *nuances* onde a liberdade possui reivindicações possíveis à solidariedade, que inquire. A *vulnerabilidade* permite que alguém disponha outrem a aliviar-lhe a vida; mas até ao limite de causar-lhe a morte? Não poderei intervir em termos de experimentação pura sem vantagem própria? Mas os benefícios causados habilitam uma relevância do consentimento que desvenda, por si, o benefício para o próprio e, até, defende-se a terceiros (os custos são parcelas justificadas da disponibilidade da vida). O contrato de gestação reifica? Mas a liberdade de disposição permite retardar o momento da reificação até onde ainda se justifique não o efeito *pacta sunt servanda* mas o exercício libertário da revogabilidade e a abstracta composição de responsabilidades parentais não biológicas. A autonomia presumida (vg. solução da oposição para a disponibilidade de órgãos, etc.) não constitui um exercício responsável de reconhecimento perante uma preguiça intolerável ao desaire alheio?

A medicina extravasa o leito e invade os demais ambientes tecnológicos, científicos, etc. Existem muitas outras disciplinas que não podem deixar de lhe prestar a devida vassalagem. Da alimentação à habitação, dos usos à cosmética, tudo passa a ser objecto de atracção pelo íman que a medicina possui em catálogo. A opção de Diógenes em estar sossegado e tranquilo, pretendendo apenas da generosidade de Alexandre, o Magno, que este se desviasse dos raios solares é já difícil[18]. Ficando em silêncio recolhe-se o que possa ser útil a terceiros... e existe um mercado ilícito a conviver com outros meramente despudorados quanto a este trato, quanto a este «comércio». Em rigor temo ressuscitar-se como defensável dispensar o consentimento, estabelecendo-se prévia grelha de delimitação do que é aceitável como decisão (má? boa?) em matéria de integridade física, e psíquica. E tanto vale um sentido como o outro: dos agentes médicos para o paciente; do paciente para os agentes médicos. Sobra sempre a persuasão, rememoração, confiança e, sobretudo, informação das contingentes disponibilidades. Nesta perspectiva, ao paciente, a tarefa fulcral do

---

[18] Recolhi o lendário episódio, de sedução juvenil, em Ernst H. GOMBRICH, *Uma Pequena História do Mundo* (trad. Raquel Moura), Publico|Tinta-da-china Ed., 2010, p. 85.

agente médico pode acabar apenas em viabilizar-lhe escolhas. Mas isto não lhe afasta a posição de devedor. Antes de optar entre contingências, fará prova de ter prosseguido uma *vida boa,* adequada a evitar intervenções terapêuticas e a interagir para um ambiente sustentável que habilite a comunidade a recatar-se sobre o mesmo desiderato moralmente funcional. Pergunto-me se não retomei uma platónica asserção dicotómica: *médicos escravos para escravos e médicos livres para homens livres?* Arredada a liberdade em um ambiente pleno de mecanicismo onde a ministração eficiente da descoberta científica pode redundar em mero «acto de Fé», fica subserviente esta profissão com risco de uma retoma escatologicamente *religiosa*, senão pior. Pior? É consabido que os charlatães sempre exerceram uma concorrência desleal, mas com assinaláveis êxitos, e não foi a coexistência com os verdadeiros «salvadores de almas» que afastaram aqueles dos ganhos da crendice. As soluções psicossomáticas ou a mera sorte são sempre ampliadas e tornadas fantásticas.

3. O ambiente tecnocrático e empresarial: de profissional de saúde a empreiteiro

A evolução tecnológica da medicina tem efeitos colaterais importantíssimos, aos quais se não empresta importância devida[19]. Em primeiro lugar a dispersão de especializações médicas pulveriza o conceito de agente médico e cria forças sociológicas contrárias que esbatem os «perfis profissionais». É o «agente-que-está-de-serviço» que, com sorte, deixa o seu «rasto» em um processo clínico retomado pelo «agente-que-se-segue». Em segundo lugar, a actividade médica de cariz eminentemente terapêutico lida com estremos a roçar o puramente cosmético. Em terceiro lugar, as descobertas científicas propendem a empurrar o agente médico para uma prestação de serviços que se aproxima progressivamente da empreitada, sobrando a explicação do desvio (exactamente se acredita ser determinável). Em quarto lugar, as pressões da rentabilidade invadem uma área em que se verifica um embate entre a medicina assistencial e os aspectos mais negros das regras de mercado. Os profissionais de saúde contratam carreiras e salários mercê de resultados estatísticos com

---

[19] Cf. Graça CARAPINHEIRO, *Saberes e poderes no Hospital...*, Afrontamento Ed., CES, 1988, Cap. IV; pp. 207 e ss; Helena SERRA, *Médicos e Poder...*, Almedina, Coimbra, 2008, cap. II, pp. 255-347.

pagamentos «à peça», por exemplo, em um Sistema Integrado de Gestão de Inscritos para Cirurgia» (SIGIC), de que tratarei adiante. Em quinto lugar, as relações entre profissionais de saúde e pacientes encontram-se sob o foco de discursos por construir que dão azo a novos «espaços» de responsabiliade, onde, muito naturalmente, tudo esmorece. Se o paciente se satisfaz, então é aceitável concluir que o agente médico cumpriu as «*leges artis*». Se o paciente não está satisfeito, «as *legis artis ad* hoc» serão esgrimidas para aferir eventuais negligências, que pesam por vezes, muitas vezes, no mercado noticioso como «presunção» de culpa.

Acresce que o discurso será a breve trecho univocamente internacional (pressente-se a vertigem nesta asserção). Os «Estados-Nação» desconfiguram as delimitações geográficas. A produção convencional deslocaliza-se e vai a internacionalizar-se[20]. As populações estão a vocacionar-se para diásporas. Toda esta movimentação aspira a traçar perfis universais para a medicina. Talvez tenha chegado a hora de devolver parte dos deveres ao ambiente, às posturas correctas de saúde, às informações[21], ao próprio paciente.

Os deveres dos pacientes merecem reponderação, tanto mais ingente quanto existe uma «narrativa» a sublinhar os direitos. A autonomia, o elogio da esfera intocável da incolumidade será preservada na intersecção com a seguinte. Cada esfera persistirá com foro de autonomia porque se inicia em uma outra, como o resultado de uma interacção que nos acompanhará ao longo da vida –inter-relacionados e interdependentes. O exercício de uma opção esclarecida pelo paciente constituirá, a meu ver, a primeira linha nítida da responsabilidade possível para que o saber--fazer da medicina seja certificável e se não misture nem confunda com a esperança, com as meras promessas, quando não com a patranha. O que

---

[20] Cf. Boaventura Sousa Santos, *A Crítica da Razão Indolente... cit.*, pp. 269-281: direito estatal, direito territorial, direito sistémico (sistema inter-estatal das relações internacionais); que permitem várias órbitas de superação dos domínios dos Estados territoriais para os estados periféricos e usam linguagens e, sobretudo, práticas ampliadas com significação reconhecível e reproduzida, cf. pp. 281 e ss.: « hoje em dia, as campanhas para a vacinação das crianças» ou para a autodeterminação gestacional, «em toda a periferia são constelações desse tipo. (...)» Através da interpenetração ou da contaminação tudo assume características dos demais conhecimentos –, máx 286 e ss. Tudo a conduzir a propostas para a expansão do jurídico e do político, cf. pp. 291 e ss. e capítulo 6º: «não disparem sobre o utopista».

[21] Perdoe-se-me a vírgula de *Oxford*.

distinguirá o correcto desempenho do profissional de saúde consiste, em primeira linha, na informação: se a deficiência desta alimentar uma recusa, que não a confiança, então torna-se válida a presunção por inferência lógico-dedutiva óbvia de que o esclarecimento atraiçoou o declaratário. Quebrou-se a aliança e inverte-se o percurso probatório objectivo em que o apuramento da responsabilidade depende menos de adequações específicas com lesões exógenas do que com a falha intercalar de deveres que viabilizassem outras decisões.

4. A confiança

A confiança constitui um dos princípios vectores para a matéria disciplinar do Direito da Medicina (Guilherme de OLIVEIRA) e que urge ressuscitar plenamente. É requisito da sobrevivência humana para ultrapassar a respectiva incompletude. A confiança constitui a base essencial para a construção moral, ética e jurídica, designadamente para a formação, existência, interpretação e concretização das manifestações relevantes da vontade[22].

4.1. A confiança pública

Parece pontificar uma *confiança pública*. Neste aspecto é fulcral regular e garantir o acesso efectivo à informação tendente à adopção de atitudes saudáveis. O esclarecimento é terapêutico. Cria e estimula a prevenção de eventos adversos que minimizam o erro, impõe mecanismos que solucionam litígios... e, organizacionalmente, sem esgotar, permite associar

---

[22] A confiança resulta de um alicerce fundamental nas relações sociais, designadamente das relações jurídicas e que consiste no princípio da boa-fé. A boa-fé, enquanto modelo e parâmetro da motivação e da actuação constitui um cânone axiológico de primeira água, sempi-presente em todo o tráfego social, além de ser um princípio ético-social fundamental, a viabilizar ao intérprete ou ao juiz uma margem larga de delimitação para a aferição de uma caso concreto. Serve, claro, as fases fulcrais do negócio jurídico (formação, interpretação e execução, cf. arts. 227º, nº 1; 239º; 762º C.Civ), pode servir a exclusão da culpa em acto formalmente ilícito ou acentuar ou rarear a dosimetria de uma sanção até à respectiva exclusão; pode ser a raiz de específicos deveres; pode qualificar as condutas exigíveis, pode limitar ou excluir um poder jurídico, designadamente um direito subjectivo ou potestativo (cf. arts. 243º, nº 1 e nº 2; 612º a contrario sensu; 1294º a 1296º; 1298º e 1299º C.Civ); o abuso de direito, (cf. art. 334º do C.Civ); como influi no valor jurídico dos usos (cf. art. 3º do C.Civ). Sobre esta matéria pontifica, por todos, António MENEZES CORDEIROS, *Da Boa Fé*, Almedina, para onde remeto os convenientes desenvolvimentos sobre esta matéria.

e envolver todos os sujeitos em interacção proactiva. Trata-se como afirma muito assertivamente Guilherme de OLIVEIRA: «a palavra-chave»[23]. Seguindo de perto o Mestre, trata-se de todo um fenómeno de paciência, de um moroso e cuidadoso processo cheio de avanços e de recuos. A confiança pública obriga muitas vezes a esquemas agressivos de actuação, como sejam exemplos os fortes condicionamentos no que concerne ao consumo de tabaco[24] ou de estupefacientes[25], as medidas de segurança na condução de veículos rodoviários (excesso de velocidade, transporte de crianças, etc.)[26], a notificação obrigatória de doenças[27], as medidas de protecção da saúde reprodutiva; a participação voluntária na doação de material genético para investigação[28]. E não são apenas as resistências a mecanismos mais agressivos que são disponibilizados para o exercício defensivo[29] da medicina como sejam os DGPI ou para a solução de pro-

---

[23] Cf. Guilherme de OLIVEIRA, *Medicina preventiva... cit.*, p. 9

[24] Cf. a Lei nº 37/2007, de 14 de Agosto

[25] Cf. o DL nº 15/93, de 22 de Janeiro (versão da Lei nº 77/2014, de 11/11, podendo as sucessivas alterações serem analisadas e confrontadas in http://www.pgdlisboa.pt/leis/lei_mostra_articulado.php?nid=181&tabela=leis)

[26] Código da Estrada, DL nº 114/94, de 03 de Maio, sucessivamente alterado, cuja versão mais recente é a 17º (Lei nº 73/2013, de 10/09), cf. http://www.pgdlisboa.pt/leis/lei_mostra_articulado.php?nid=349&tabela=leis.

[27] As doenças de declaração obrigatória constam de listas normativamente actualizadas, cf. Lei nº 81/2009, de 21 de Agosto, DR, I, nº 162 e as respectivas estatísticas podem ser consultadas, v.g. através do levantamento PORDATA que revelam um decréscimo significativo na primeira década do séc. XXI quanto às doenças tidas como mais representativas, das quais escolho a Tuberculose ea aHipatite B, cf. os dados in http://www.pordata.pt/Portugal/Doenças+de+declaracao/obrigatoria+casos+notificados-773. Cf. ainda SINAVE (sistema social de vigilância epidemiológica).

[28] Cf. a Lei nº 12/2005, de 16/01 sobre «informação genética pessoal e informação de saúde»; no que concerne à criação de biobancos, cf. o portal informativo http://www.biobanco.pt/faq. Cf, ainda o Parecer 68/CNECV/2012, acessível in http://www.google.pt/url?sa=t&rct=j&q=&esrc=s&frm=1&source=web&cd=6&ved=0CEcQFjAF&url=http%3A%2F%2Fwww.cnecv.pt%2Fadmin%2Ffiles%2Fdata%2Fdocs%2F1354037643_Parecer%2520CNECV%252068%25202012%2520testes%2520geneticos%2520final.pdf&ei=Zd3TU6uHLvOa0QXRx4CIDA&usg=AFQjCNGYJkgTRANGNT6o2fmIMR-0KyDNgg&sig2=LP8Eyxzuz7VTGNRwANX-PA, cf. ainda a Lei nº 12/2009, de 26/03 (regime jurídico da qualidade e segurança relativa à dádiva, colheita, análise, processamento, preservação, armazenamento, distribuição e aplicação de tecidos e células de origem humana), transpõe as Directivas nº 2004/23/CE, do PE e do Conselho, de 31/03; nº 2006/17/CE, da Comissão, de 08/02; e nº 2006/86/CE, da Comissão, de 24/10.

[29] Quanto à expressão medicina defensiva, cf. *O Consentimento...*, p. 32.

DIREITO DA SAÚDE

blemas de carácter individual ou de natureza familiar, *insondáveis*, como a cessação voluntária da gravidez até às dez semanas sem fundamento outro que não o do alvitre da grávida ou do respectivo representante legal se for menor. O próprio paciente pode oferecer resistência: está ou sente--se são, e, portanto, menos predisposto a angústias que afasta *para o dia seguinte*. Obviamente que se terá por inimiga a iliteracia na sua infinidade de dramas. De qualquer modo, será muitíssimo interessante analisar a *contabilidade* entre o funcionamento, custos e eficácia de serviços preventivos (vg. urgência e gestão de intervenções), por exº, entre Portugal e a Finlândia, confrontando sistemas de saúde que se vocacionam exactamente para promover uma gradação preventiva e defensiva (esta com o sentido específico de uma actuação intermédia da confiança, com referência a um carácter preventivo)[30].

4.2. A confiança *privada:* aliança

Em termos iconográficos, a relação do paciente com os profissionais de saúde pode ser perfeitamente representada por uma aliança em que a álea das consequências de uma actuação correcta por parte dos profissionais é perfeitamente assumida pelo paciente como possível, porque não pode deixar de ser parceiro ciente do que lhe pode acontecer. Os factores adversos a esta configuração foram, por um lado, os séculos de progressiva aprendizagem das surpresas do corpo humano e as investigações

---

[30] Cf. Lauri Vuorenkoski, *Finland. Health System Review,* in Health Systems in transition, vol. 10, nº 4, 2008, Philipa Mladovsky|Elias Massialos Ed., *European Observatory on Health Systems and Policies* (pp. 1-168), vol 10 nº 4, p. 134, que cito: «Emergency care is provided by health centres and hospital districts. Normally, every health centre has at least one physician on call for emergencies. It is common that a large proportion of physicians work on call in health centres is not genuinely medically urgent as many times patients have difficulties in getting ordinary daytime appointments. This is especially the case in municipalities with physician shortages. Currently, it is very common to lease physicians from private firms for out-of-office hour care, so they are different physicians than those working during the day (see section 3.5.2.1). Normally, patients should first go to the health centre emergency care to receive a referral to hospital if needed. In hospitals there are several physicians of different specialties on call. The arrangement for emergency care differs greatly between hospital districts as their size varies considerably.», acesso in http://www.google.pt/url?sa=t&rct=j&q=&esrc=s &frm=1&source=web&cd=10&ved=0CHMQ_xMwCQ&url=http%3A%2F%2Fwww.euro. who.int%2F__data%2Fassets%2Fpdf_file%2F0007%2F80692%2FE91937.pdf&ei=UurTU 63lMoOm0QWX0ICwCA&usg=AFQjCNGVEhRgeVvkXcytwh9R2oj6mZJdDg&sig2=Eg 08fDOW3YVgxukY3lCtQw

sobre os efeitos de novas técnicas médico-medicamentosas. Estamos em uma era de clarificação progressiva da ignorância. Este véu (RAWLS) persiste ainda, mas parece revelar um optimismo crescente fundado em uma fé tecnológica que anuncia conquistas sem fim. A sofisticação de meios também alimenta a crença de que a medicina correcta é a medicina eficaz, e sendo possível aquela há que exigir dos profissionais de saúde esta última eficácia. Eis o paradoxo. E o paradoxo aumenta a vulnerabilidade dos pacientes, incrementando a sua incompreensão e revolta perante um desígnio (mito) a modificar, mas também grassa, por identidade de razões, entre as hostes dos profissionais de saúde pois a negligência é progressivamente menos tolerada, convocando receios e a prática de uma medicina receosa. Daqui ao encarniçamento percorre-se apenas mais um caminho paralelo. Um minuto mais de vida? É menos um processo possível. Eis o resultado de uma conquista reivindicada e uma vulnerabilidade cavada de diferente forma: a de um véu de eficácia insustentável. Pois se durante séculos foi a ignorância que lançou nos braços dos profissionais de saúde as debilidades dos pacientes que queriam esperança, talvez agora seja exactamente o brilho galvanizado dos materiais, o ambiente asséptico e as máquinas de *design* ajustado a ficção científica... o que produz a precipitação (a todos). Hoje como antigamente subsistem ganas em castigar o profissional de saúde pelas contrariedades fisiológicas e psíquicas. Antigamente porque não se repetiu um êxito; hoje porque o êxito é possível ser repetido, assim tivesse...

5. A recusa propriamente dita

Para o paciente o dissentimento resulta como faculdade para manifestar livremente a sua autodeterminação, livre de peias formais e em princípio até ao limite da sua radicalidade absoluta. Sejam *más decisões,* seja nada querer saber, seja prevenir uma futura inconsciência, etc. Noutra perspectiva mais benévola revela a faculdade de escolher soluções[31] que se adaptem menos à prossecução da saúde mas privilegiem as aspirações individuais a uma conformação da própria vida, de acordo com as alternativas que se ofereçam menos *eficazes* mas desejáveis. É a recusa parcial

---

[31] Para uma perspectiva alternativa, cf. Eduardo DANTAS, *When Consent is not enough: The construction and development of the modern concept of autonomy,* in *Medicine and Law,* vol. 30, nº 4, Dez 2011, pp. 461-475.

DIREITO DA SAÚDE

por oposição à recusa integral, actual ou prospectiva; pessoal ou por representação. Tanto se extrai da lei em matéria de informações a prestar, e repito: garantindo-se a compreensão do essencial para que tome uma decisão livre e consciente, o paciente deve (tem de) ser *devidamente esclarecido sobre o diagnóstico e a índole, alcance, envergadura e possíveis consequências da intervenção ou do tratamento,* porém, recusando, terá de apurar as sequelas. Eis o que se oferece, enquanto argumento apagógico, por exemplo, na necessidade imposta pelo legislador penal em sede de uma *decisão substituída* configurar um *teste de recusa* (cf. 156º, nº 2, al. *b*), *in fine,* CP), isto é, a necessidade de se certificar da ausência de *sinais* que afastem a conjectura presumida tal como os factores de *urgência.* Se vale para a decisão substituída do profissional de saúde valerá igualmente para a decisão substituída sobre o apuramento de responsabilidade a realizar pelo juiz em sede de julgamento. O dissentimento mostra-se um mecanismo que permite diminuir a ignorância do paciente como reflexo da intensificação dos deveres de informação que se condensam na esfera do agente médico, e, logo, diminuir a ignorância dos profissionais de saúde também.

6. Entre os incapazes, um oximoro: os menores *adultos*

Uma questão de particular delicadeza prende-se com o *peso* da recusa dos menores[32]. Dita o legislador dever o agente médico certificar-se se o menor (16 anos) tem o «discernimento necessário para avaliar o sentido e alcance» da sua decisão (cf. art. 38º, nº 3 CP). A convicção sobre a maturidade parece conferir legitimidade para atender à vontade? Tenho naturais dúvidas sobre se o profissional de saúde terá postura análoga à que assume perante a recusa de um adulto, especialmente se a decisão sobre a maturidade lhe pertencer. Será madura uma decisão que troca um benefício para a saúde pela – usando aqui um velho exemplo – participação num torneio de xadrez?[33] Tudo leva a crer que a análise do problema

---

[32] Para os demais incapazes existem igualmente especialidades e dúvidas. Para os respectivos desenvolvimentos, por todos, cf. Geraldo Rocha Ribeiro, *A Protecção do Incapaz Adulto no Direito Português,* CDF|Coimbra Ed., 24, 2011, *passim;* André Dias Pereira, *O Consentimento...* CDBM|Coimbra Ed., 9, 2004, pp. 214 a 289. Em relação aos menores, ID. *Ibid,* pp. 289 e ss.; e Guilherme de Oliveira, *O acesso...*Temas, CDBM|Coimbra Ed.; *e* João Vaz Rodrigues, *Consentimento...* pp. 209 e ss. Rosa Martins |Paula Távora Vítor in AA.VV: *O Cuidado Como Valor Jurídico,* Ed. Forense (coord. Guilherme de Oliveira | Teresa da Silva Pereira).
[33] Será falacioso querer responder com o respeito pela vontade de um adulto nas mesmas circunstâncias. A reacção excepcional em termos de autonomia é a de aceitar como tributo

DO EXERCÍCIO DA MEDICINA: DOS «*MÉDICOS ESCRAVOS PARA ESCRAVOS ...*

passa pela distinção entre as medidas que envolvem o consentimento e o dissentimento. São diferentes. A intervenção de saúde constitui um meio para tentar averiguar e/ou obter as condições prévias do estado físico-psíquico do paciente (Orlando de CARVALHO). Pressupondo a necessidade da intervenção para a melhoria do estado de saúde do paciente, no caso do consentimento as informações visam dissipar dúvidas e confirmar a actuação proposta, ao passo que na recusa, perante a mesmíssima intervenção, acentuam-se os cuidados a ter com a manifestação de vontade e a decisão do médico terá logo, logo, a *sombra receosa*. A tentação do médico será a de acatar a decisão do menor se esta coincidir com a sua. As dúvidas agravam-se pelo facto de a relevância a atribuir à decisão dos representantes legais dos menores não se afigurar definitiva nesta matéria. E explico: é cristalina a perplexidade do agente médico a quem se afirma o dever de agir contra o dissentimento paternal como acontece (situações já clássicas) perante convicções religiosas; e, simultaneamente, se possa configurar uma censura por ter ultrapassado a autonomia do menor *com discernimento* quando, em análogas condições de protecção da saúde, a actuação recusada tiver o beneplácito dos representantes legais[34] (penso na cessação voluntária da gravidez). O problema é que, perante a negativa, o agente médico não recebe, como acontece com o consentimento, uma colaboração do visado ou do seu representante e a institucionalização judicial *vive* em menos de *um terço do horário hospitalar* e, com o devido respeito, louva-se por regra em opiniões de profissionais de saúde. Em suma: pragmaticamente, o agente médico encontra-se investido na

da autodeterminação. Mas não poderá ser exigido ao médico que se reporte a uma bitola de normalidade, à sensatez do homem comum?

[34] A questão colocou-se já perante a jurisprudência inglesa, aceitando-se que a decisão capaz de um menor – devendo ser respeitada se for afirmativa e se confrontar com o dissentimento paternal – poderá ser ultrapassada pelo consentimento paternal para uma intervenção médica, que aquele repudiou. Face aos valores em conflito e, sobretudo, à enorme responsabilidade depositada no agente médico, alguma doutrina recomenda para tais casos o suprimento judicial. A decisão a tomar deverá acatar os desejos do menor, tendo por pressuposto os seus *melhores interesses*. Cf. John EEKELAAR, *White Coats or Flak Jackets?...* pp. 182-187. Idênticas dificuldades colho em Daniel SERRÃO, cuja aceitação parece ficar restringida às decisões tomadas por menores com 16 anos ou mais, verificando-se discernimento e as matérias em causa não impliquem perigo de vida, exemplificando com uma decisão aceitável de um menor sobre a não utilização de um aparelho de correcção dentária (cf.: *Riscos em recusar tratamentos, in* AA.VV. *Bioética*, Verbo Ed., 1996, p. 82). Sobre esta matéria, por todos, remeto para Guilherme de OLIVEIRA, *O acesso...* in Temas., pp. 16 e ss..

DIREITO DA SAÚDE

responsabilidade da decisão e esta levará em consideração a prossecução dos melhores interesses do paciente. Uma opção solitária e sempre casuística. Confirmo por esta via que a diferença entre as manifestações de vontade positiva e negativa se manifestará sobretudo nas maiores cautelas que rodeiam uma materialização da decisão negativa objectivamente divergente dos interesses do paciente. Na verdade, investido na responsabilidade, o agente médico que decida não atender a recusa de um menor ou de um incapaz quando entenda a actuação médica como decisiva e fundamental ficará fora de censura e só receará a compulsividade. A decisão sobre capacidade e incapacidade acidental pertence-lhe, mercê de uma concretização da *teoria normativa dos factos*. Mas a recusa pode ser considerada independentemente da incapacidade do paciente que a manifeste, como seja no caso da oposição à experimentação[35]. Este regime não revela igualmente a existência de um campo relativamente alargado, em que a eficácia a atribuir à recusa convoca a protecção de bens jurídicos, como a saúde, que poderão colidir com a protecção da autonomia? Reclamando-se aquela protecção, acredito ser possível e desejável a compressão desta outra, salvaguardando os bens jurídicos fundamentais. E não se diga que ressuscito o paternalismo perante as dificuldades e o enterro logo que estas se esvanecem. A opinião dos intervenientes é contingente, mas deverá ser tomada em consideração pelo agente médico[36]. Neste mesmo preceito parece residir uma válvula de segurança que consiste em prever a possibilidade de a autorização dada pelos representantes dos pacientes incapazes, ou *pelas autoridades em sua substituição*, ser revogada quando se prossiga o «... interesse da pessoa em causa»[37]. Então por que não exigir ao legislador a constituição eficaz dessas *autoridades* para facultar ao médico a possibilidade de junto destas recolher auxílio para a dúvida sobre a maturidade da decisão do menor em dissentir? É uma hipótese que agrada, até pelo facto de respeitar uma solução *ad hoc*[38].

---

[35] Cf. art. 17º, nº 1, al. *e*) da CDHB.
[36] Cf art. 6º, nº 2 e nº 3, da CDHB.
[37] Cf. o citado art. 6º, nº 5 da CDHB.
[38] Por todos cf. João LOUREIRO, *Pessoa e Doença Mental*, in BFDUC, vol. LXXXI, 2005, p. 172.

7. Intervenções em que se justificam restrições à liberdade e à auto-determinação.

Existem *terrenos* em que se constata uma *belicosidade* entre a *vontade* e a *saúde*. E para além desta *fragmentação*, outras circunstâncias se envolvem na *briga*: penso nas limitações individuais exigíveis aos próprios pacientes (na raia da contenção da esfera de personalidade). Considero os direitos e os interesses de terceiros envolvidos (entre os quais os próprios profissionais de saúde), os interesses sociais que justifiquem a intervenção da Administração Pública no âmbito da prossecução da garantia constitucional da protecção da saúde (cf. art. 64º da CRP) ou mesmo em outros âmbitos (*v.g.* a descoberta da verdade material). As limitações imanentes ou as colisões entre direitos fundamentais exigem uma avaliação permanente das *fronteiras* a traçar entre as compressões que os bens jurídicos subjacentes convoquem e o apuramento da prevalência abstracta ou concreta dos valores individuais *versus* valores sociais[39]. Não é a hierarquia que me interessa colocar em discussão, se bem que se trate de um tema para cuidada atenção e debate, progressivamente premente perante: a *velocidade do tempo*; a *crise* que parece instalada no que de tardo moderno revelam os *tempos que correm*; algum *comunitarismo* emergente, etc. Quanto à generalidade de cruzamento de valores e de bens constitucionalmente protegidos afirma Manuel da Costa Andrade:

«De uma forma ou de outra, as decisões da pessoa 'irritam' o sistema social e projectam sobre ele uma complexidade que este é chamado a reduzir, segundo legitimação e critérios próprios. *Brevitatis causa*, segundo uma lógica de auto-referência.»[40].

Daqui retiro uma configuração autónoma da recusa: face a intervenções arbitrárias, o que fica colocado em crise é a desvalorização da faculdade de repúdio ou de não adesão a uma intervenção ou constrição na esfera da liberdade ou da autonomia. Só a recusa revela a crise aberta pelo embate dos valores constitucionais em causa, até caso a caso. O con-

---

[39] Sobre esta matéria não será de somenos indicar a consulta: da obra de VIEIRA DE ANDRADE, *Os Direitos Fundamentais...*, Almedina, 1987, pp. 213 e ss.; das anotações à *CRP Anotada* de Jorge MIRANDA e Rui MEDEIROS (entre outras as relativas aos arts. 24º, pp. 222 e ss.; e 64º, pp. 652 e ss.); João LOUREIRO, *Constituição e Biomedicina* (dissertação de doutoramento, Coimbra); Carla AMADO GOMES, *Defesa da Saúde vº Liberdade individual...*, AAFDL, 1999, entre outros.

[40] Cf. Manuel da COSTA ANDRADE, *Direito Penal Médico*, Coimbra Ed., 2004, p. 44.

DIREITO DA SAÚDE

sentimento torna-se, em regra[41], irrelevante; pelo contrário, o dissentimento – mais não sirva – *inquire por controvérsia* a norma que o constrange.
O elenco dos tratamentos compulsivos e das intervenções arbitrárias é
extenso e apresenta inúmeros aspectos controvertidos, pelo que previno
a incompletude do que se segue. Por tratamento compulsivo ou intervenção arbitrária denomino o exercício potestativo da faculdade de actuação
médica invasiva da esfera físico-psíquica de uma pessoa, prosseguida com
o objectivo da protecção social da saúde, ou seja, de acautelar os interesses *superiores* da colectividade *perante a dignidade individual*, garantindo o
direito fundamental à saúde, a nível colectivo e ou individual, em caso
urgente; ou protegendo outro direito ou bem jurídico fundamental, mas
sempre em cumprimento de uma norma jurídica ou de uma decisão judicial proferida a coberto de legislação específica habilitante[42].

[41] Quero acautelar, mesmo em sede do consentimento, as eventuais sequelas da adesão a um
ditame normativo que venha a ser reputado como ilegal ou a uma decisão que não encontre
estribo na formulação legal aparentemente habilitante, que suscitem ulteriormente ao visado
que a acatou a possibilidade de, sentindo-se lesado, reagir.

[42] Assim decanto a noção que avancei em o *Consentimento...*, pp. 290 e ss., tendo em mente
o sentido e alcance da pertinente advertência – e recorrendo à expressão utilizada – de
Paulo da MOTA PINTO na sua «declaração de voto», proferida no Ac. do TC nº 228/2007,
de 28/03 (Rel.: Maria Fernanda PALMA), cf. http://www.tribunalconstitucional.pt.
E aproveito para reler o que deixei explanado em sede de *testes para aferição de perfis de ADN*
(cf. o *Consentimento...*, pp. 326 e s.), aderindo à restrição – todavia com a divergência que
antecede em que secundo Paulo da MOTA PINTO – que o Ac. TC *supra* citado (na sequência do
fundamentante Ac. TC nº 155/2007, de 02/03 (Relator: GIL GALVÃO) introduz na interpretação
do preceituado no art. 172º, nº 1, do CPP, de onde se retira que a sujeição compulsiva a exame
(colheita compulsiva de vestígios biológicos) carece de autorização do juiz competente; Ac.
este último de onde retiro apenas a seguinte passagem (da longa e profunda fundamentação
que merece toda a atenção), esclarecedora do que está em *jogo*: «Assim, admite-se que, em si
mesmo, não existirá desproporcionalidade na utilização de tais meios invasivos» – colheita
de saliva através de *zaragatoa* bucal – «do corpo da pessoa (mas não lesivos da integridade
física), da sua liberdade e privacidade, como único meio para obtenção da prova em situações
(tal qual a do presente caso) de extrema gravidade dos factos perpetrados, com base numa
ponderação de todas as circunstâncias a efectuar por um juiz imparcial que não tem a seu
cargo ou sob o seu domínio a investigação do processo, e sendo assegurado o controlo de
todo o aproveitamento possível dos resultados de tal intervenção.». O sublinhado pertence-
-me. Neste sentido, cf. igualmente Helena MONIZ, in *Parâmetros Adjectivos, Constitucionais e
de Direito Comparado, na estrutura das soluções legais previstas na Lei nº 5/2008, de 12 de Fevereiro*,
in AA.VV: *Bases de Dados Genético Forenses* (coord. Helena MACHADO e Helena MONIZ),
Coimbra Ed., 2014., pp. 47 e ss., onde a respeito da Lei 05/2008, de 12/02, que consagra
a possibilidade de colheita de material biológico com a teleologia da identificação civil e

DO EXERCÍCIO DA MEDICINA: DOS *«MÉDICOS ESCRAVOS PARA ESCRAVOS ...*

Aqui se incluem os serviços de polícia sanitária para vacinações e rastreios; a despistagem de doenças infecto-contagiosas; os serviços que lutam contra epidemias; os serviços para internamento e tratamento de

da investigação criminal inclina-se para que essa viabilidade não esteja assegurada para mero suspeito, o que leva a A. e Ilustre Conselheira do STJ a propender pela necessidade de decisões judiciais (que não de mero MP). Dando ainda nota concomitante do direito comparado. Os Ac. do TC em referência acabam por iniciar um processo de *solvência* das dúvidas suscitadas pela Jurisprudência do TRC (Acórdãos ali citados), que culminou com o Ac. TRC de 13/09/2006 (Relator: Luís de ALMEIDA GODINHO, cf. http://www.dgsi.pt), cuja transcrição parcial pode igualmente ser encontrada em *RMP*, ano 27, nº108, pp. 239 e ss. e que resultou assim corrigido. Devo sublinhar aqui o comentário crítico de Mário FERREIRA MONTE, cf. *ibid*, pp. 250-262, cuja argumentação não deve de todo ser desconsiderada, especialmente quando concebe que o próprio exame por *zaragatoa* «pode ocorrer mediante a utilização de força» e que todas estas diferenças podem e devem ser relevantes para a decisão a tomar, concluindo pela aludida necessidade – prevenida também por Paulo da MOTA PINTO, como disse já – da *prévia regulamentação*. Eis o plano distintivo (casuístico, é verdade), que me levou a considerar e que mantenho (em sede de testes para a detecção de álcool no âmbito das infracções rodoviárias) que, no estado corrente da legislação em vigor, a existência de soluções alternativas (*desobediência*, etc.) seriam suficientes para ultrapassar o que a lei parece não prever: o dissentimento efectivo, radical, ainda que ilegítimo e, até ilícito (cf. *O Consentimento...*, pp. 328 e ss., neste aspecto – parece – secundadas por Jorge MIRANDA e Rui MEDEIROS, *CRP Anotada...*, I, p. 277). Pesam aqui, sempre, os ensinamentos de Guilherme de OLIVEIRA, *Implicações...* p. 328. E sendo certo que a ponderação dos valores e bens se altera muito significativamente perante os ilícitos em confronto, a verdade é ser inegável (para lá da justiça do caso concreto) que a obrigatoriedade dos exames e a sua efectivação compulsiva à custa da violação da integridade física constituem planos diferentes, a merecer este último uma competência legislativa para ser dirimido, com respeito pela proporcionalidade entre o exercício da força e o que a justifica. Bem compreendo a tentação da *descoberta a verdade material,* como entendo a tentação que sofrerá o médico ou o cientista no decurso de uma actuação ou de uma investigação importantíssimas para o combate de uma doença ou uma descoberta singular... Mas a verdade é que os princípios fundamentais, quando fragmentados sob a premência de uma *topoi* que os contradiga, não podem ser pulverizados, sem mais, sem o avisado e prévio *império da Lei*, à custa de inferências particulares não tipificadas. Subsiste sempre o perigo de revelarem, mais tarde, consequências chocantes, a jusante ou a montante, no edifício ético *codificante* do tecido social. Começo por afirmar que a colheita de saliva é uma invasão insignificante da esfera físico-psíquica de uma pessoa e acabo embasbacado perante uma queixada quebrada por um alicate cirúrgico... São as consequências da aludida «banalidade do mal» que impressionou Hannah ARENDT. Cabe por fim ressuscitar o que pertinentemente dá eco Manuel da COSTA ANDRADE, sobre o princípio *nemo tenetur...* na lúcida anotação ao Ac. TC nº 340/2013 cuja «ressonância constitucional» ultrapassa a temática fiscal e se alcandora a uma reintegração axiológica do que sejam «restrições não desprezíveis», cf. *RLJ*, Ano 114, nº 3989, Nov|Dez 2014, pp. 121-158, máx, 129 e ss.

DIREITO DA SAÚDE

doenças mentais[43]. E devem ainda ser consideradas as medidas decorrentes da declaração do *estado de calamidade pública*[44]. E o mesmo se diga para os tratamentos em detidos e manutenção da ordem e da segurança nos estabelecimentos prisionais, *v.g.* casos de greve de fome ou tentativa de suicídio[45]; exames médicos em medicina do trabalho[46], a prática de actividades desportivas, etc. Outros aspectos devem ainda ficar referenciados: o tratamento coactivo para evitar a tentativa de suicídio, pelo menos a partir da inconsciência[47]; os limites da eutanásia[48]; as já afloradas intervenções de perícia no campo do direito processual, penal e civil, determinadas por decisão judicial habilitante[49]; as DAV quanto à «solução de oposição», relativa à colheita de órgãos e de tecidos para fins de transplante ou disposição do corpo após decesso; e o mesmo digo dos Testamentos Vitais que possuam indicações negativas para prever a impossibilidade de manifestar a vontade face a quadros futuros previsíveis.

Escreveu Guilherme de Oliveira em Janeiro de 2001:

«Tenho para mim que o 'consentimento informado' vai ser uma dor de cabeça para os profissionais da saúde, nos próximos anos. Há muitas normas legais a falar dele e há pouca tradição de o praticar; os médicos sabem que têm de fazer alguma coisa, mas não sabem até que ponto as leis os obrigam; há doentes que querem exercer o direito de consentir e outros que o não querem. Os juristas também não estão habituados ao conceito. É certo que os instrumentos gerais lhes permitem saber, com relativa precisão, do que se trata; mas não é fácil

---

[43] Cf. Base XIX da LBS e art. 5º do DL nº 336/93, de 29/09 e, ainda, LSM: Lei nº 36/98, de 24/07. Sobre este aspecto e ressuscitando questões conexas com alguma da matéria aflorada na nota anterior, cf. o comentário crítico de André Dias Pereira ao Ac. TRP, de 06/02/2002 (Internamento compulsivo de doente tuberculoso), in *LM*, I, 1, 2004, onde se pode analisar igualmente os extractos relevantes do Aresto. Cf. ainda Maria João Antunes, *O internamento...*, *BFDUC, Stvdia Iuridica 2*, Coimbra ed., 1993, André Dias Pereira, *Direitos dos Pacientes...*, CDBM 22, Coimbra ed., 2015, pp. 541 e ss.

[44] Cf. art. 19º, nº 2, da CRP.

[45] Cf.: Costa Andrade, *Consentimento e Acordo...*, p. 408; Anabela Miranda Rodrigues, *Novo Olhar..., Coimbra ed.*, 2000, pp. 101-128; e o que escrevi in *O Consentimento...*, pp. 304 e ss.

[46] Cf. art. 19º do CT. Cf. Carlos Lopes do Rego, *Comentário ao Ac. TC nº 368/02, 25/09*, e este aresto, in *RMP*, Ano 23, nº 92, pp. 117 e ss.

[47] Cf., por todos, André Dias Pereira, *O Consentimento...*, pp. 508 e s.

[48] ID, *ibid*, pp. 509 e ss. e Luísa Neto, *Direito Fundamental à Disposição do Próprio Corpo...* Coimbra Ed. 2004.

[49] Para outros desenvolvimentos, cf. o que escrevi in *O Consentimento...*, pp. 324 e ss.

ter uma noção precisa do que se pode exigir dos médicos na vida real da prática clínica.»[50].

A recusa revela-se uma pedra de toque que suscitará eventualmente as soluções para o *confronto* que vou pressentindo crescer, por força dos sucessivos pontos de fricção entre a *célula* individual do ser humano e a sua esfera de protecção com as esferas de protecção da sociedade e a intervenção, ao menos tutelar, do Estado.

8. Quando o legislador (não?) ajuda: um esforço que não pode ser escondido

O desempenho técnico que usualmente se associa às *leges artis* significa poder exigir ao profissional de saúde que se mantenha *à tona* no que é o caldo de procedimentos operacionais normalizados (PON), de *guidelines,* de conhecimentos que o habilitam a exercer tecnicamente as suas funções. Neste sentido, não espantará que submeta a carreira a um escrutínio de aferição de que essas competências se encontram actualizadas. Eis o que sucede igualmente em muitas outras profissões e que desemboca em processos de avaliação[51]. Actividades como a docência, as magistraturas ou a advocacia são meros exemplos onde as estruturas de auto-regulação e ou de autotutela visam máximos de autonomia e simultaneamente contribuem para construir uma rastreabilidade individual que certifica a confiança no desempenho profissional. São ainda mecanismos preventivos: em rigor, classicamente, o reconhecimento profissional acaba por oferecer o *selo de garantia* em como as qualidades individuais reduzem a verificação de riscos indesejados e, pelo contrário, facultam o sucesso possível. A cada profissional se associa uma *aura* e uma *sombra* que oferecem atracção ou retracção, admiração e rotas para os demais. Sempre existiram *escolas práticas,* mentores. Já a massificação propende a diluir mas exacerba a prevenção. Muito bem ou menos bem, pouco importa. O que me interessa aqui sublinhar é que as *leges artis* deixaram de ser apenas o conjunto de conhecimentos técnicos disponíveis para um caso concreto: elas imiscuem-se com o caso concreto, e quando assim ocorre,

---

[50] Cf. *op cit, supra,* na nota anterior: «Apresentação».
[51] Já a burocratização metodológica que se aplica em regra aos processos de avaliação merece análise e aprofundamento que não cabe aqui aprofundar,

DIREITO DA SAÚDE

outras componentes se associam. Não pretendo que um tirocinante possa prosseguir o seu percurso de aprendizagem com um tutor que dispensa o esforço pedagógico por um número excessivo de aprendizes em um número excessivo de horas de ensino. Não pretendo que um cidadão veja os seus interesses patrimoniais e os pessoais entregues à decisão de um magistrado que não poderá dispensar-lhes mais do que 20 ou 30 minutos de esforço intelectual para ponderar e decidir. Finalmente, não pretendo que a um profissional de saúde se permita ou exija uma disponibilidade de tempo –ou se lhe faculte uma disponibilidade de gestão do tempo– que exponencie riscos de cansaço ou repetição. Submeter ou permitir que um profissional de saúde exceda o que cada profissional deverá ter como uma *taxa média máxima de esforço* adequada constitui um requisito mínimo de segurança que não pode deixar de ser levado em consideração. No tráfego rodoviário os condutores dos transportes pesados encontram--se forçosamente delimitados quanto ao tempo de condução máxima contínua: possuem discos tacógrafos que medem o índice de esforço máximo associado a uma actividade que se pretende segura[52]. No tráfego aéreo, os pilotos e a tripulação possuem uma regulamentação específica destinada a assegurar a segurança das pessoas na respectiva assistência, incluindo o facto de estarem monitorizados os tempos máximos de função. E assim por diante, será desnecessário prosseguir o óbvio[53].

No campo da medicina desconheço a existência de PON ou *guidelines* para este efeito, e encontro aqui uma urgência. É necessário proceder a uma certificação –sobretudo no SNS– dos tempos individuais, da rastrea-

---

[52] Cf. o Reg. CE nº 3821/85, do Conselho, de 20 de Dezembro de 1985 (aparelho de controlo no âmbito dos transportes rodoviários) e Reg. CE nº 561/2006, de 15 de Março de 2006, Parlamento Europeu e Conselho (harmonização das disposições em matéria social nos transportes rodoviários), onde, evidentemente, se contemplam regras e excepções (cf. art. 3º), acessível in http://eur-lex.europa.eu/legal-content/PT/TXT/?uri=CELEX:32006R0561 e cf. ainda as Lei nº 27/2012, de 30808 o DL nº 117/2012, de 05/06 (transposição da Directiva nº 2002/15/CE do PE e Conselho, de 11 de Março (organização do tempo de trabalho das pessoas que exercem actividades móveis de transporte rodoviário).

[53] Sem necessidade de grandes desenvolvimentos cf. parecer do Conselho Consultivo da PGR (Relator ESTEVES REMÉDIO), sobre aviação civil; pessoal de voo, funções e segurança, com remissões para a legislação aplicável, etc,), 16-12-2005, Parecer nº P000932005, acessível in http://www.dgsi.pt/pgrp.nsf/0/c2918dd6d148427680257084004bc81b?OpenDocume nt#_ftn3,. Segue menção da legislação relativa aos limites dos tempos de serviço de voo e de repouso para a tripulações da aviação civil, cf. DL nº 139/2004, de 5 de Junho – Transpõe a Directiva nº 2000/79/CE, de 27 de Novembro.

DO EXERCÍCIO DA MEDICINA: DOS «MÉDICOS ESCRAVOS PARA ESCRAVOS ...

bilidade individual do *índice de esforço* de cada profissional de saúde, etc.. O paciente não embarca em uma viagem menos perigosa do que um passageiro rodoviário ou aéreo quando penetra as paredes de uma instituição de saúde. Ulteriormente necessário será fixar *os máximos das taxas de esforço*. Por seu turno, as instituições devem revelar os índices em referência com o mesmo rigor com que elaboram os panegíricos ou os rogatórios relatórios sobre as estatísticas atingidas (seja para atrair elogios, seja para reclamar recursos). São informações sem as quais a opção do paciente fica comprometida: não é indiferente depositar *caução ao barqueiro* em instituição hospitalar onde não existam consultas prévias de anestesia ou onde o ou os profissionais de saúde tenham semanas de trabalho com 50 e mais horas de trabalho ou em listas de intervenções que prossigam com a mesma equipa *sem mudança de lençóis*, etc. Eis o que entendo também dever incluir a *confiança pública* e as *opções*. Estou perante um leque de condutas habilitantes de responsabilidades seja em termos individuais, seja em termos institucionais e, sobretudo, elementos com que o decisor, ou o juiz, procederá a uma livre apreciação sobre a influência destes factores enquanto fonte adequada da violação das *leges artis (também ad hoc)*. E falo dos profissionais de saúde que não apenas das instituições de saúde.

Obstar-se-á com a drástica redução do tempo de serviço e com a impossibilidade de «erguer-os-braços» na cirurgia ao «toque-do-sino»... Não impugnarei especificadamente, «taco-a-taco», com exemplos de «dobras» ou com os incidentes possíveis no decurso das intervenções. Deixarei apenas uma menção para a necessidade de planificação comum às profissões *mais sofisticadas*, e entre estas, aquelas em que o desempenho assume maior risco de verificação de danos (negligência, efeitos adversos, erros, etc.). Neste sentido, para pesar bem a distinção do que tenho pela frente, reproduzo o que no esteio do Mestre de novidade e síntese pondera André DIAS PEREIRA:

«Também o Direito da reparação de danos pessoais, que abrange o direito rodoviário, o direito dos acidentes de trabalho e das doenças profissionais, não abrange, com a subtileza necessária a especificidade do Direito da Medicina. Trata-se de objetos de estudo jurídico que partem de um ponto de vista distinto. No Direito Médico, o paciente tem interesse na relação social e jurídica e o médico visa "cuidar" do doente e não o mero lucro económico. Numa palavra: o Direito da Medicina deve considerar o *plus* de solidariedade existencial que deve

DIREITO DA SAÚDE

caracterizar a relação médico-paciente e que ultrapassa a mera primacial ontoantropológica relação de cuidado-perigo do direito dos acidentes rodoviários e laborais».[54]

9. A burocracia: efeitos perniciosos da regulamentação: SIGIC

Afirmei que aos profissionais de saúde muito depressa se lhes acena com pagamentos «à peça», seduzindo-os para comportamentos utilitaristas que os aproximam de regimes análogos aos da empreitada. Tratarei em seguida de elaborar uma análise sumária do Sistema Integrado de Gestão de Inscritos para Cirurgia» (SIGIC), onde a redução das listas de espera de pacientes implica escalas e intervenções que em termos quantitativos e qualitativos deviam ser objecto de estudo para medição de «esforço», capacidade de resposta dos serviços, avaliação do incremento de riscos, cumprimento das *leges artis* e das *leges artis ad hoc*, etc.[55]. Procurarei situar-

---

[54] Cf. André Dias Pereira, *Direitos dos pacientes e Responsabilidade médica* CDBM|Coimbra Ed., 22, 2015, p. 42, onde faz referência igualmente importante às reflexões que sobre Ética médica foram concebidas por José de Faria Costa, *Um olhar, eticamente comprometido, em redor da ética médica*, in RLJ, Coimbra, Ano 140, nº 3965, (Nov-Dez 2010), p. 70 ss.

[55] O SIGIC foi criado em Junho de 2004, por uma Resolução de Conselho de Ministros (nº 79/2004, in *DR* nº 147, I-B, de 24/06), no seguimento de uma política de combate aos atrasos constatados em listas de espera que se mostrava inclemente para casos de emergência ou carências críticas de doentes (O Programa Especial de Combate às Listas de Espera cirúrgicas: PECLEC, cf. Res. CM nº 100/2002, de 26/04, in *DR*, I, 25/05). O PECLEC, com carácter temporário (2 anos) foi tido como medida de êxito e permitiu ponderar a construção informática de um sistema para aferir, gerir e limitar os tempos entre a inscrição de um doente e a intervenção que lhe foi determinada. Este sistema (SIGLIC: sistema informático de apoio...) foi desenvolvido no âmbito do Instituto de Gestão Informática e Financeira da Saúde (IGIF). O sistema visava a generalização a todas as instituições e a contratação com os sistemas de saúde de natureza não pública, associando-os nesse esforço nacional de «redução do tempo de espera admissível», cf. III|5 da Res. nº 79/2004, de 24/06; a partir daqui sucederam-se os despachos Ministeriais para a consecução do SIGIC, designadamente o DespMS nº 24 110/2004, in *DR*, II, de 23/11 (minuta tipo das convenções entre a ARS e sistemas e subsistemas do sector social e privado, incluindo serviços médicos, enfermagem, técnicos e hoteleiros), em um propósito ambicioso de investimento social, como o demonstra a cláusula 2ª, nº 2: «Os valores globais constantes do despacho compreendem todos os cuidados e serviços prestados desde a fase de preparação para a cirurgia até dois meses após a alta hospitalar sem que sejam identificadas complicações, nos termos do Regulamento do SIGIC, e inclui hotelaria, consumíveis, medicamentos, meios complementares de diagnóstico e terapêutica e tudo o mais que for necessário.». Acresce a título de curiosidade contratual que «a recusa de um procedimento cirúrgico disponibilizado pela entidade quando indevidamente injustificado» dava azo a uma «desconformidade grave», que, por

DO EXERCÍCIO DA MEDICINA: DOS «*MÉDICOS ESCRAVOS PARA ESCRAVOS ...*

-me no campo de que trato neste trabalho, confirmar a materialização do «objectivo» traçado sobre o «consentimento informado» na Resolução do CM nº 79/2004 [56], e que preceitua (cf. I, al. *b*)): «*Envolver o utente de uma forma activa no processo de formalização do consentimento para a realização da cirurgia*, cujos procedimentos deverão ser objecto de larga divulgação junto daqueles». Mais tarde, pela Portaria nº 45/2008, de 15/01[57], o SIGIC passou a estar dotado de DAV, cf. Parte II, nº 6:

«Para efeitos do disposto no presente Regulamento, dá-se o nome de «lista de inscritos para cirurgia» ao conjunto das inscrições dos utentes que aguardam a realização de uma intervenção cirúrgica, independentemente da necessidade de internamento ou do tipo de anestesia utilizada, proposta e validada por médicos especialistas num hospital do SNS ou numa instituição do sector privado ou do sector social que contratou com aquele Serviço a prestação de cuidados aos seus beneficiários e *para a realização da qual esses mesmos utentes já deram o seu consentimento expresso*.».

Explicando-se de seguida no nº 7:

«Entende-se por «nota de consentimento» o documento que reco-lhe a concordância do utente com a proposta de intervenção cirúrgica

---

seu turno, penalizava as «unidades» em «50% do valor total devido pelos cuidados prestados ao utente...», cf. cláusula 19ª, nº 1, al. *b*), da minuta convencional. O DespMS nº 6263/2005, in *DR*, nº 58, II, de 23/03 (admissibilidade de os hospitais recorrerem aos profissionais de saúde vinculados à instituição); até à Portaria nº 45/2008, in *DR*, nº 10, I, de 15/01 (que veio colocar em vigor um novo Regulamento, em que se reconhece a respectiva institucionalização, generalização e alargamento às entidades contratadas no âmbito do SNS, na sequência da Lei nº 41/2007, de 24/08, que garante os «tempos máximos de espera a todos os seus beneficiários» e que se encontra já revogada pela LDDUS que introduziu uma uniformização nos conceitos de TME); Portaria nº 1306/2008, in *DR*, nº 219, I, de 11/11: alarga o reg. do SIGIC às cirurgias de oftalmologia (cataratas) e consultas (introduz uma nova sigla HPD e os respectivos TME e prevê 30 000 cirurgias em um ano); Portaria nº 1529/2008, in *DR*, nº 249, I, de 26/12 (Fixa os tempos máximos garantidos TMRG para cuidados não urgentes e publica a CARTA DOS DIREITOS DE ACESSO AOS CUIDADOS DE SAÚDE PELOS UTENTES DO SERVIÇOS NACIONAL DE SAÚDE); Portaria nº 271/2012, in *DR*, nº 171, I, de 04/09 (Tabelas de preços revista em vista do programa «troika» de contenção financeira, alterando a portaria nº 852/2009, 07/08); Portaria nº 45/2008, in *DR*, nº 10, I, de 15/01 (1ª alteração ao programa contra a obesidade: Portaria nº 1454/2009, 29/12).

[56] Cf. *DR*, nº 147, de 24/06, pp. 3846 e ss.

[57] Cf. *DR*, I, nº 10, 15/01.

DIREITO DA SAÚDE

e com a sua inscrição na LIC[58] e a aceitação do conjunto de normas do Regulamento do SIGIC que servirão de base para a gestão da proposta cirúrgica.».

A questão da DAV (*consentimento antecipado?*) foi minuciosamente objecto de definição em matéria de «registos», cf. Parte II, nº 23 a 27, sem prejuízo de ulterior «readmissão» e «reinscrição»[59]. Esta antecipação prospectiva foi igualmente prevista no diploma em referência, cf. Parte V (procedimentos de gestão de inscritos...). Até à aprovação da portaria que estabeleça os *tempos máximos de espera* (TME), os níveis de prioridade são os estabelecidos, em princípio, pelos níveis aludidos no nº 74, que vão desde o nível 4: 72 horas ou o período de internamento até ao nível 1: nove meses, sempre que seja admissível o TME, dependendo as dilações (5 a 15 dias) por via da gestão mais eficiente do funcionamento do bloco, cf. nº 75. A partir daqui o legislador entra em um emaranhado de fundamentos e justificações para protelamentos, cheques-cirúrgicos, transferências, procedimentos burocráticos, reinscrições, agendamentos e reagendamentos, de acordo com as intervenções possíveis das orgânicas e modelos regulamentares e de procedimentos que envolvem um sistema

[58] LICir – Lista de Inscritos em Cirurgia.

[59] «23 – Dá -se o nome de «registo provisório» ao registo de um utente na LIC que se encontra ainda por validar ou *não foi ainda objecto de consentimento por escrito.* / 24 – Dá-se o nome de «registo activo» ao registo de um utente na LIC, provisoriamente inscrito, após validação da proposta cirúrgica *e obtenção do seu consentimento escrito,* que não se encontra pendente ou suspenso administrativamente. / 25 – Entende -se por «registo cancelado» a anulação do registo de um utente na LIC determinado por motivos supervenientes à inscrição, clínicos ou outros, que impedem a realização da cirurgia. / 26 – Entende– se por «registo pendente» uma alteração temporária do registo de um utente na LIC que, a seu pedido, fundado em motivo plausível, ou a pedido do médico proponente da cirurgia, decorrente de uma situação clínica que o impede temporariamente de ser operado, *fica pendente por um período definido de tempo, findo o qual é novamente activado, mantendo– se o interesse do utente em submeter -se a uma intervenção cirúrgica no hospital.* / 27 – Um «registo suspenso administrativamente» é uma alteração temporária do registo de um utente na LIC, decorrente de problemas técnicos ou de insuficiência de informação, por um período máximo de 5 dias úteis consecutivos ou 10 dias úteis interpolados, que o impede de ser movimentado, mas não interrompe a contagem do tempo de espera. / 28 – Uma «readmissão» consiste na reincorporação em LIC de um utente indevidamente cancelado, relevando o tempo já decorrido para efeito de contagem de tempo de espera. / 29 – Uma «reinscrição» consiste no recomeço, a partir de zero, da contagem do tempo de espera para um dado utente que a seu pedido, mantendo– se a indicação cirúrgica, é inscrito de novo na LIC.»

simplificado para assegurar os TME, com ou sem renovação dos MCDT, assim os HO e os HD estejam em sintonia para que os serviços da ACSS, por via do seu CA, assegurem o cumprimento do MGIC, via os competentes serviços do CA da UCGIC que tutelará a hierarquia das URGIC e UHGIC, que, por sorte de um bom funcionamento do SIGLIC fará com que o SIGIC atalhe as LIC. UF! Se porventura o TME for ultrapassado no HO o doente é transferido (cf. nº 89) ou não (cf. nº 91 e ss.), tendo sempre a hipótese de requerer (3 vezes) a pendência de inscrição em LIC até um período total de tempo equivalente à prioridade para que foi classificado. Caso contrário, terá sempre o respeito do seu «consentimento expresso» ou garantindo-lhe a sua «recusa», caso este último em que terá de o fazer por escrito e sair do «sistema» LIC (cf. Parte VI, nº 139); os outros motivos encontram-se previstos na Parte VI, nº 136:

«Os motivos de saída do utente da LIC são os seguintes: a) Realização da cirurgia; / b) Perda de indicação para cirurgia; / c) Desistência; / d) Incumprimento das normas do Regulamento do SIGIC; / e) Pendência da inscrição, a pedido do utente, por um período total de tempo superior ao tempo máximo de espera garantido; / f) Óbito.»

Retomando uma permanência em LIC, e avançando já até à proposta de cirurgia, esta (cf. Parte V. nº 62 e ss.) respeitará os formalismos do SIGLIC e será preenchida pelo «médico proponente» com «ao menos a seguinte informação»:

«a) Identificação completa do utente; / b) Identificação dos diagnósticos pré-operatório, principal, secundário e associado e respectiva nomenclatura; / c) Identificação das patologias ou problemas associados devidamente especificados; / d) Identificação da cirurgia proposta e respectiva nomenclatura; / e) Indicação do nível de prioridade, fundamentado de acordo com o MGIC; / f) Identificação das necessidades de suporte perioperatório.»

E segue, encaminhada «pelo médico que realizou o atendimento» para o «responsável pelo serviço cirúrgico» e para o «utente», cf. nº 63. Por via enunciativa, retiro que a mesma deverá chegar ao utente com uma «nota de consentimento», cujo teor me deixa muitas dúvidas sobre se destina a aprovar todo o processado incluindo os actos médico e medicamentosos

DIREITO DA SAÚDE

além de, obviamente, «aprovar o registo informático». Rezam os §§ em causa o seguinte:

«64 – A nota de consentimento visa esclarecer o utente sobre os seus direitos e deveres e recolher a sua aprovação relativamente ao registo informático da proposta de intervenção cirúrgica e o seu compromisso pelo cumprimento das normas do Regulamento do SIGIC. / 65 – A nota de consentimento não dispensa a entrega de outras declarações exigidas para a realização de uma intervenção cirúrgica, nos termos da lei em vigor. / 66 – A nota de consentimento é obrigatoriamente assinada pelo utente que, se não puder assinar, se *pode fazer substituir por representante legal*. / 67 – Quando o consentimento por escrito for dado em momento posterior ao da proposta cirúrgica, a nota de consentimento é entregue na UHGIC do hospital onde foi feito o atendimento, no prazo de 2, 5 ou 10 dias a contar da inscrição provisória na LIC, consoante se trate de utentes classificados respectivamente nos níveis 3, 2 e 1, de acordo com o nº 74 deste Regulamento.»

Fico com receio sobre o mecanismo de esclarecimento. Além do peso burocrático que este *novelo* regulamentar pressupõe, resta-me ainda sublinhar que nos aludidos prazos de 2, 5 ou 10 dias, prazos estes mais dilatados consoante a menor urgência da intervenção, verificar-se-á uma certificação do «responsável do serviço cirúrgico» sobre a conformidade da cirurgia proposta com as *leges artis*[60], e verificando-se divergência de opinião:

«69 – Caso o responsável do serviço cirúrgico conclua que a cirurgia proposta não está conforme nos termos do número anterior, deverá fazer constar essa indicação no campo do documento destinado para o efeito e comunicar essa decisão ao médico proponente que, no prazo de dois dias, convoca o utente *para consulta para redefinição de orientação terapêutica*.».

---

[60] Registo a letra da lei: § «68 – O responsável pelo serviço cirúrgico deverá, nos prazos referidos no número anterior, conferir se a cirurgia proposta está de acordo com a *legis artis* e *com a orientação do serviço*, e, em caso afirmativo, validar a indicação de cirurgia por assinatura electrónica autenticada ou através da aposição da sua assinatura em documento que entrega na UHGIC.». O sublinhado pertence-me e sem prejuízo de retomar a questão creio que o procedimento demonstra que o «responsável» não possui nenhum contacto com o paciente.

A expressa indicação regulamentar que afasta o médico responsável do contacto directo com o paciente contempla ainda uma «redefinição de orientação terapêutica» que terá de contemplar –por interposta pessoa tecnicamente hierarquizada e subalternizada– a satisfação de um consentimento esclarecido sobre a índole, alcance, alternativas possíveis, sob pena de «sair do sistema». Com efeito.

«70 – *A falta de entrega da nota do consentimento ou a sua entrega extemporânea, assim como a não validação pelo responsável de serviço da proposta cirúrgica determinam o cancelamento do registo provisório do utente na LIC.* 71 – O registo do utente na LIC pressupõe uma proposta de cirurgia validada e consentida nos termos deste Regulamento e é activado pela UHGIC quando é emitido o certificado de inscrição que é enviado ao utente nos prazos referidos no nº 67.»

De toda a sorte, existem entre os deveres do paciente, cf. Parte II:

«45 – Os utentes, para efeito do disposto no presente Regulamento, estão obrigados ao cumprimento dos seguintes deveres: a) Formalizar o seu consentimento por escrito para a inscrição em LIC, de acordo com uma proposta cirúrgica e aceitar as normas do presente Regulamento».

Determinações *normativas* cuja *economia* parece estar em flagrante e frontal violação dos mais elementares princípios consignados em normas hierarquicamente superiores: sobre a dignidade, sobre a garantia da autonomia e da autodeterminação esclarecida... tudo em uma *linha recta* até aos preceitos constitucionais e normas internacionais vigentes, cujo elenco seria fastidioso esmiuçar. Sem grande rigor, o legislador colocou no SNS, por via desta portaria, um regime de excepção (privilégio) terapêutico altamente burocratizado, com custos directos e indirectos que a mais elementar curiosidade gostaria de apurar e sem uma expressa regulação sobre o cerceamento dos limites temporais das prestações por técnico, das delimitações dos riscos de efeitos adversos directos ou colaterais, etc.

O utente poderá reclamar. Tanto está no elenco dos seus direitos, cf. Parte III:

«Direitos e deveres dos utentes 44 – Para efeitos do disposto no presente Regulamento, são reconhecidos aos utentes os seguintes direitos:

a) Obter um certificado comprovativo da sua inscrição em LIC; / b) Invocar motivo plausível para a não comparência à cirurgia ou às consultas, exames e tratamentos associados ao procedimento cirúrgico proposto, para os quais tenha sido convocado; / c) Dispor de uma garantia de tratamento dentro do tempo máximo de espera garantido por nível de prioridade, por patologia ou por grupo de patologias; / d) Aceder a todo o tempo junto da unidade hospitalar de gestão de inscritos para cirurgia (UHGIC) do seu hospital e a seu pedido aos dados que lhe respeitem registados na LIC, nomeadamente o nível de prioridade que lhe foi atribuído e o seu posicionamento relativo na prioridade atribuída; / e) Escolher, quando haja lugar a transferência, de entre os hospitais indicados para a realização daquela cirurgia; / f) Recusar a transferência do seu hospital para outros hospitais para realização da cirurgia de que carece; / g) Requerer até ao máximo de três vezes a pendência da sua inscrição na LIC, invocando motivo plausível, por um período total de tempo inferior ao tempo máximo de espera garantido / h) Requerer por escrito a sua saída da LIC; / i) Apresentar reclamação escrita sempre que se verifique alguma irregularidade em alguma das fases do processo.»

Em matéria de autodeterminação, para os direitos, sublinho a recusa de transferência hospitalar prevista na al. *f*), seguida do eufemístico requerimento escrito para «a saída da LIC.». O regime de reclamação administrativo privativo do «sistema» resulta do preceituado no nº 46 e merece igualmente transcrição:

«46 – A reclamação prevista na alínea i) do nº 44 deve conter a identificação completa do utente e do seu processo, bem como a exposição clara da situação verificada e ser entregue, no prazo de 20 dias úteis sobre a ocorrência ou o seu conhecimento, à Unidade Central de Gestão de Inscritos para Cirurgia ou à Unidade Regional de Gestão de Inscritos para Cirurgia da respectiva Administração Regional de Saúde que remeterá cópia à primeira.»

É com surpresa que vislumbro na norma sobre deveres do paciente, como já referi, a concretização da autodeterminação, exactamente em um exemplo da consagração legal da medicina receosa (defensiva), a saber:

«45 – Os utentes, para efeito do disposto no presente Regulamento, estão obrigados ao cumprimento dos seguintes deveres:

a) **Formalizar o seu consentimento por escrito para a inscrição em LIC, de acordo com uma proposta cirúrgica e aceitar as normas do presente Regulamento;** / b) Manter actualizados os dados constantes do seu registo na LIC, informando a UHGIC do seu hospital das alterações de quaisquer elementos que constam do seu processo, designadamente dos contactos pessoais (residência, telefone, correio electrónico); / c) Comparecer na data marcada para a realização da cirurgia e aos actos que lhe estão associados e para os quais seja convocado, nomeadamente consultas, exames e tratamentos; / d) Informar a UHGIC do seu hospital, se possível antecipadamente, de qualquer situação que impossibilite ou determine o adiamento da realização da intervenção cirúrgica ou dos actos referidos na alínea anterior e justificar a sua ausência nos termos deste Regulamento.»

Eis consignado um dever do paciente em prestar o consentimento, por escrito, independentemente de estar informado ou esclarecido, sob pena de não se concretizar o seu acesso a um sistema nacional que se encontra institucionalizado para viabilizar a prestação de cirurgias reputadamente submetidas a *tempos máximos de resposta garantidos* (TMRG). O SNS no âmbito desta cobertura parece incluir nas respectivas tabelas de preços e contratualização com entidades hospitalares de natureza pública, mista e particular a facturação de intervenções com indicação terapêutica reduzida (cosmética?) ou (in)existente[61], como sejam a esterilização masculina e feminina, a cirurgia à obesidade (estética?) ou intervenções mamárias sem indicação de doença, entre outros exemplos[62]. Todavia, tanto significará evidentemente uma indicação médica, cuja natureza será seguramente terapêutica.

---

[61] Refiro-me a uma perspectiva médica pura face aos interesses físico-psíquicos do paciente, para quem a intervenção se afigura como preenchimento de um desequilíbrio ou melhoria das suas condições de vida.

[62] Cf. Portaria nº 271/2012, in *DR*, nº 171, I, de 04/09: Tabelas de preços revistas em vista do programa «troika» de contenção financeira, art. 7º, nº 4, eventualmente mais prótese, nº 15; e art. 8º, nº 1.

DIREITO DA SAÚDE

10. Uma excepção: o regime de «Cirurgia Segura Salva Vidas»

Generalizada a todos os blocos operatórios do SNS existe uma *Norma* DGS nº 02/2013, de 12/02/2013, actualizada em 25/06/2013, que visa estabelecer um conjunto de procedimentos tidos por essenciais para reduzir os elevados riscos de verificação de «complicações cirúrgicas» e da respectiva contribuição para indesejados índices de mortalidade. Trata-se da constatação da necessidade de inserir mecanismos de reciprocidade na certificação dos procedimentos na equipa cirúrgica, entre os quais a aplicação do índice de APGAR Cirúrgico[63], e que são actualmente obrigatórios em todos os blocos operatórios nacionais do SNS. Assim integrou-se definitivamente na *leges artis ad hoc* para as cirurgias o registo informático do prévio cumprimento da «Lista de Verificação de Segurança Cirúrgica»[64]. Esta certificação recíproca decorre em três momentos

[63]A Norma DGS nº 02/2013 pode ser consultada in http://www.google.pt/url?sa=t&rct=j& q=&esrc=s&frm=1&source=web&cd=2&ved=0CCcQFjAB&url=http%3A%2F%2Fwww. dgs.pt%2Fdirectrizes-da-dgs%2Fnormas-e-circulares-normativas%2Fnorma-n-0022013- de-12022013-atualizada-a-25062013-jpg.aspx&ei=TynXU9elJYiQ0AXapYCoCQ&usg=AF QjCNGXk2W-oYQe3ZVSH-W52akfxB7Ngg&sig2=C8zJXVKf4KAvHZVCPyYXDQ e veio revogar a Circular nº 16/DQS/DQCO, de 22 de Junho de 2010 pode ser acedida in https:// www.google.pt/?gws_rd=ssl#q=indice+de+apgar+dgs. O índice de Apgar (Vírgina APGAR) foi inicialmente congeminado para avaliar cinco sinais vitais aos recém-nascidos com o escopo de avaliar as condições de saúde destes, criando uma escala simples de pontuação que acompanha e sinaliza o paciente. O índice de Apgar Cirúrgico resulta desta fonte inspiradora que se generalizou (cf. Anexo II da norma DGS 02/2013) e reconduz-se ao seguinte: O ÍNDICE DE APGAR CIRÚRGICO: Cálculo do "Índice de Apgar cirúrgico", com avaliações intra-operatórias de perda de sangue estimada, da menor frequência cardíaca e da menor tensão arterial média.

[64] De acordo com a norma em questão: «I – NORMA 1. A implementação do projeto "Cirurgia Segura, Salva Vidas" de acordo com o manual "Orientações da OMS para a cirurgia segura 2009" publicado no sítio desta Direção-Geral é obrigatório em todos os blocos operatórios do Serviço Nacional de Saúde e das entidades com ele contratadas, sendo considerado o padrão mínimo de qualidade clinica. 2. Em todas as cirurgias deve proceder-se ao registo da utilização da "Lista de Verificação da Segurança Cirúrgica" e do Apgar Cirúrgico nos sistemas de informação locais, que tenham interface com a Plataforma de Dados da Saúde (PDS) ou diretamente na própria PDS. 3. Todas as organizações hospitalares devem, no final de cada semestre, enviar ao Departamento da Qualidade na Saúde, a monitorização do nível de implementação do projeto, de acordo com formulário, disponível no sítio desta Direção-Geral. 4. A presente Norma revoga a Circular Normativa nº 16/DQS/DQCO, de 22/06/2010. / II – CRITÉRIOS A. A Lista de Verificação de Segurança Cirúrgica e o Índice de Apgar Cirúrgico (ANEXOS I e II), bem como o Manual de Implementação da Lista de Verificação de Segurança Cirúrgica da OMS e as Orientações da OMS para a Cirurgia Segura

e pela inserção informática das respostas a três questionários simplificados[65], a saber: antes da cirurgia, na «presença ao menos do enfermeiro e do anestesista», se «o doente confirmou a sua identidade, o local, o procedimento e deu consentimento»[66]. É com natural aplauso que confirmo que o consentimento, mercê desta norma *procedimental* de natureza administrativa, foi reconhecido e passou inequivocamente a integrar no campo *regulamentar* cirúrgico a integração das *leges artis ad hoc,* melhor: não apenas um consentimento, mas uma certificação de que o mesmo foi aflorado em termos *suficientes,* exactamente em um *ambiente* em que a imediação entre o paciente e cada um dos intervenientes da equipa médica operatória é *viva,* já que estão presentes e têm conhecimento *de viva voz,* assistindo directamente ao respectivo registo.

11. A afirmação dos procedimentos no sentido de uma plenitude da aplicação do consentimento: Um futuro breve

A análise dos procedimentos em referência na norma DGS nº 02/2013 –com óbvios graus de simplificação– através das plataformas informáticas, devem passar em curto prazo a incluir a confirmação da existência de DAV|PCS pelo que, desse momento em diante, nas salas de cirurgia de Portugal (dando-se cumprimento ao *Manual OMS* correspondente) pode afirmar-se uma consolidação concreta e pragmática da autonomia do paciente, plenamente garantida e certificada tão logo a DAV|PCS seja inserido no sistema. Com efeito, a confirmação pela negativa de existência ou inexistência de uma DAV trará o que é pragmaticamente possí-

---

2009, disponibilizados no sítio da DGS (www.dgs.pt), fazem parte integrante desta Norma, e devem ser considerados como referenciais para a implementação do projeto "Cirurgia Segura, Salva Vidas". B. A implementação do projeto "Cirurgia Segura, Salva Vidas" deve ter em conta o desenvolvimento de estratégias de dinamização e melhoria do trabalho em equipa, com uma ênfase primordial na comunicação interprofissional, das equipes cirúrgicas. C. Todas as organizações hospitalares, através da sua estrutura de garantia e monitorização da Qualidade, devem garantir a adequada implementação do projeto de acordo com a Orientação nº 030/2011 de 31/08/2011, bem como a realização de auditorias internas de acompanhamento e avaliação. / III – AVALIAÇÃO A. A avaliação da implementação da presente Norma é contínua e executada através de processos de auditoria interna e externa. B. A efetividade da implementação da presente Norma e a emissão de diretivas e instruções para o seu cumprimento é da responsabilidade das direções clínicas dos hospitais. (...)»

[65] Cf. Anexo I à norma em referência, p. 6.

[66] O sublinhado pertence-me.

DIREITO DA SAÚDE

vel aspirar, ou seja, ter sido dado cumprimento aos deveres de prestação de informação e de esclarecimento e obtenção da anuição (confirmativa ou revogatória).

Faltam ainda mais dois pormenores: O primeiro é que esta norma significará uma natural desnecessidade –fora dos casos em que o período de maturação se revele de molde a exigir especial atenção– da prestação do consentimento em papel, reduzindo a respectiva burocratização. Por seu turno, mesmo para as intervenções mais delicadas, objecto de legislação avulsa: PMA; Genoma; CVG (IVG); Transplantes; Investigação Clínica, etc. reabre-se a possibilidade de uniformizar em matéria da autodeterminação e do processo clínico, a construção de uma legislação de protecção da esfera do paciente que viabilize igualmente a inserção de um regime uniformizado de responsabilidade civil com a eventual *ressarcibilidade* dos danos não subjectivados em culpa do agente médico (deixando esta negligência para direito de regresso e para as *esferas* criminais e disciplinares aplicáveis): como será a ponderação, *vg.*, em volta de um regime *no-fault* já apontada como possível no ensino de Guilherme de OLIVEIRA e de André DIAS PEREIRA. O segundo, será o de dar o *pequeno passo de gigante* para a generalização da «aplicação informática» para todas as intervenções de saúde invasivas. Sucede que este mecanismo possui a enorme virtude de registar temporalmente –e de forma inequívoca– os sucessivos passos dados no decurso da interacção entre os vários profissionais de saúde envolvidos e o paciente. Neste sentido, à luz do «estado da arte» constitui o melhor «espelho» para a inserção e prática de um «manual de procedimentos» técnicos «da esfera do exercício da medicina» para que seja possível aceder à esfera físico-psíquica ambiental de um ser humano e aí deixar fluir um discurso que têm necessariamente de passar a ser o quotidiano da *vida* da medicina.

12. O papel diferenciador da recusa: *a prova dos nove*

À simplicidade está muitas vezes reservado um papel essencial no panorama do correcto funcionamento do(s) sistema(s). Concretizado e ampliado o que antecede, após três anos de «teste», fica agora à disponibilidade do paciente colocar uma garantia suplementar para o caso de se reservar um cepticismo contra a «confiança» que lhe é oferecida pelo «sistema». A elaboração de uma DAV terá o condão de permitir promover na «Lista de Verificação de Segurança... Cirúrgica» (que, espero, se generalizará às intervenções invasivas) a confirmação da conformidade dos procedimentos com as informações obtidas e com as manifestações de vontade proferidas. É óbvio que os procedimentos se podem burocratizar e as «teses da conspiração» persistirem em nublar os cépticos mais *pirrónicos*[67] de sorte a se avançarem hipóteses em que a autonomia e respectivos procedimentos são contornados. Mas esses são os receios que a *confiança* deve e pode afastar e o procedimento dos «três passos» previstos se adequa a sublimar, através de meras confirmações no registo informático do processo clínico do paciente a saber (concentrando-me no requisito do consentimento nas *leges artis ad hoc* para o procedimento clínico cirúrgico:

Passo I: Antes da indução da anestesia (na presença ao menos do anestesista e enfermeiro) com a certificação de consentimento e confirmação de informação que permite aferir «a orientação» e discernimento do paciente (identidade e procedimentos);

Passo II: Antes de incisão (na presença de toda a equipa): confirmação da identificação (e no futuro: de eventual DAV?), antecipação de eventos críticos; e

Passo III: Antes da saída do paciente (na presença do cirurgião, anestesista e enfermeiro): para além das contagens de equipamentos o registo de que existe (ou não) «informação relevante a transmitir à equipa de recobro e as principais preocupações/necessidades do doente). Em rigor, se estes «passos» se tornaram obrigatórios para as cirurgias em vista da despistagem de factores de morbilidade, então, por maioria de razão se devem impor onde se verifiquem análogos riscos de eventos adversos de morbilidade, i.e., nas demais actuações invasivas onde o registo informático facilmente será ampliado.

12.1. Os resultados

Da mesma forma que a epistemologia exercita nos dias que correm as *teorias dos jogos*, mediante os quais se afirmam testar as consistências e as fra-

---

[67] Refiro-me a PIRRO de Eleia (Élis ou Élida: 365-275 a.C), a quem se atribui as raízes do cepticismo (admirado por Voltaire). Eis um tipo de céptico que dá solução aos paroxismos inevitáveis dos exageros; pugna pela ataraxia (despreocupação) e, curiosamente mas não por acaso– o cito aqui, já que a sua *épogé* é reinventada por Peter SLOTERDJICK: *Muerte Aparente el Pensar... , passim*). Sobre Pirro de Eleia (ou Elis), cf. Denis HUISMAN e André VERGUÉZ (org.): *Historia de los Filósofos*, Tecnos ed., 2007, pp. 75-81.

gilidades das *topói*, muitas das tarefas e justificações legislativas assentam nos *relatórios de contabilidade: as teorias dos números.* O mais recente relatório do SIGIC oferece a indicação de que o sistema de que venho tratando, tem determinado uma redução das listas de espera e um aumento significativo do número de cirurgias, com excepções, como é o caso do cancro, que se sinalizam para correcção[68]. Creio que seria fundamental encontrar o *grau de esforço* em tempo disponibilizado por profissional de saúde que consta do SNS para a totalidade das suas tarefas. Por esta linha de investigação seria possível encontrar dados importantes para aferir a possibilidade de incidência de erro por *cansaço* e a interactividade informacional (terapêutica e de autodeterminação) entre os profissionais de saúde e os pacientes.

Existem apenas Homens livres, pelo que importa sobretudo recordar o *parágrafo* de Platão para que a descrição alerte os homens contra si e

---

[68] O relatório relativamente a 2013, publicado em Junho de 2014, recebeu a seguinte síntese da qual expurgo alguns aspectos que se me oferecem desajustados nesta nota: «O relatório síntese do (...) SIGIC relativo ao ano de 2013 (...) revela que, até Dezembro, foram operados 544.377 doentes, mais 1,9% que no ano anterior./ O número de doentes com cancro operados num ano, em todo o universo de prestadores (públicos, privados e protocolados), foi (...): 44.264 doentes (+6,1% face ao ano anterior). Apesar dos números (...) que caracterizam o aumento de actividade, o tempo de espera para cirurgias com cancro aumentou, o que reforça a necessidade de prevenir o aparecimento destas doenças, continuar a melhorar a articulação entre os cuidados de saúde primários e a intervenção hospitalar, e encetar novas medidas para aumentar a resposta do SNS face à estimativa de aumento da incidência deste flagelo./ No total das patologias com intervenção cirúrgica, verificou-se um aumento de 3,2% nas entradas em (LIC) e do número de inscritos para cirurgia em 5,6% face ao ano anterior. No final de 2013, a mediana de tempo de espera atingiu os 2,8 meses (-4,5% face a 2013 *–a gralha deve respeitar a 2012–*), o tempo de espera mais reduzido de sempre no SNS. Em termos da percentagem de inscritos que ultrapassaram o Tempo Máximo de Resposta Garantida (TMRG), o valor atingido no final de 2013 foi de 12,8%, também o mais baixo resultado de sempre no SNS». O texto *supra* e o relatório podem ser consultados e analisados em: http://www.acss.min-saude.pt/artigo/tabid/98/xmmid/896/xmid/6564/xmview/2/Default.aspx. Os indicadores cruzados permitem comparar os anos entre 2006 e 2013 e mostram que a síntese omitiu a componente de utentes inscrito LIC e a inflexão de TMRG em 2011 e 2013, pelo que talvez a comparação de melhoria deva ser feita em relação ao ano de 2010 (entendendo até à moratória da crise). A pp. 18 e ss., encontro os valores por operados nos HD nos hospitais das várias regiões e se cruzar esses valores com o total mais de meio milhão das intervenções cirúrgicas e ponderar a incidência das benignas (p. 13), tenho a possibilidade de especular em termos de resultados de medicina defensiva, mas não encontro a fórmula que me permite ponderar o grau de esforço dos profissionais de saúde. Em suma, *leituras.*

DO EXERCÍCIO DA MEDICINA: DOS *«MÉDICOS ESCRAVOS PARA ESCRAVOS ...*

contra os profissionais de saúde a quem a escravatura serve uma servidão humana.

E ao recordar assim, presto singela homenagem a quem sempre pretendeu libertar desta "escravatura" os parentes e os profissionais de saúde, o Professor Doutor Guilherme Freire Falcão de Oliveira. Mestre Meu.

Meirinho, 31 de Maio de 2015

Informed consent in aesthetic treatments: remarks on a recent judgment of the Italian Supreme Court

VITULIA IVONE[*]

SUMMARY: 1. The case. – 2. The normative core of informed consent in Italy. – 3. Information and consent in cosmetic surgery. – 4. The judgment of the Supreme Court of June 6, 2014, n.12830. – 5. Conclusions.

[*] Department of Legal Sciences (School of Law)
University of Salerno
Email: vituliaivone@unisa.it
http://www.unisa.it/docenti/vituliaivone/index
[*] Prof. Vitulia Ivone is Associate Professor of Private law, Faculty of Law, University of Salerno; Lecturer of Civil law at the Specialization School for Legal Professions; Chairman of the Scientific Committee of the *Fondazione Scuola Medica Salernitana;* Member of the academic board and professor in the Ph.D. Programme on "Legal Sciences", University of Salerno; Member of the Patent Commission of the University of Salerno; Member of the Scientific Committee of the *Observatory on Human Rights: Bioethics, Health, Environment*; Member of the Scientific Board of the journals Biodiritto (Aracne Rome) and Cuadernos de Bioética (UMSA, Buenos Aires); Recipient of a scholarship for the international mobility of researchers granted by the Province and the University of Salerno; Co-director of the International Summer School on Law, Bioethics and Health 2015, School of Law, University of Salerno.
This stance, similar to the one already taken by the Court of Appeal in Perugia, does not absolve the practitioner and, reiterating some points on the subject of informed consent in the particular field of cosmetic surgery, exceeds the path already traced by earlier judgments. In other words, in terms of medical liability, the professional is subject to liability for damage to health even when derived from an intervention performed with skill, but based on an absent or flawed consensus, for the objective reason that he has withheld information of a medical nature to the patient undergoing surgery.

1. The case.

In the field of cosmetic surgery, the content and scope of the physician's obligation to provide information, as the basis of a truly informed consent and expression of the patient's a conscious adherence of to medical treatment, is obviously a topic of crucial importance. This assumption requires the physician to reflect – on a basis of logical and statistics probability – on the possibility of an effective improvement of aesthetic conditions of the patient.

The Italian case concerns a girl, no longer satisfied with a tattoo, who decides to remove it: to do this, she goes to the doctor to undergo an intervention of plastic surgery, to make an epidermal excision of the interested part. The removing of the tattoo from the shoulder involves the creation of a quite extended scar (about 6 cm).

Despite the perfect intervention, the patient finds a worsening of the physical condition of her body because of the scar: therefore she sues the doctor, in order to obtain compensation for damages.

The patient sues the doctor because of her disappointment for the outcome of the aesthetic treatment. The doctor, despite a conduct fully respectful of the rules of the medical art, had not provided all the necessary information to enable her to develop a free and informed choice. After the first two sets of proceedings, which ended with diametrically opposed results, the judges of the Supreme Court – by judgment of 6 June 2014, n.12830 – rejected the appeal filed by the doctor, sentencing him to compensation for the damage suffered by the girl.

2. The normative core of informed consent in Italy.

In general terms, the patient is entitled to receive a complete and adequate information about the conditions of therapeutic treatment, in order to make an informed choice and decide whether or not to consent to medical procedures[1]. Informed consent, as an expression of conscious adherence to medical treatment proposed by the physician, represents a real right of the person and is grounded in the principles expressed in article 2 of the Constitution, which protects and promotes fundamental

---

[1] The failure by the doctor of the obligation to require informed consent to the patient is violation of the inalienable right to self-determination: artt. 2 e 3 Cost., e art. 32 Cost., comma 2 (see v. Cass., sez. un., 11 novembre 2008, n. 26972; Cass. 9 febbraio 2010, n. 2847).

rights, and in articles 13 and 32 of the same fundamental Charter, which stipulate, respectively, that "personal liberty is inviolable", and that "no one can be forced to a specific medical treatment unless required by law.[2]"

Besides the presence of several international dispositions that provide the necessity of the patient's informed consent in the context of medical treatment[3], the principle that the patient is placed in a position to know the course of treatment can be seen from different national laws governing specific medical activities, including the Italian law establishing the National Health Service[4].

The fact that informed consent has its foundation in articles 2, 13 and 32 of the Constitution, emphasizes its function of synthesis of two fundamental human rights: the right to self-determination and the right to health, because if it is true that every individual has the right to be taken

---

[2] B. Pezzini, Il diritto alla salute: profili costituzionali, in Dir. e soc., 1983, I, pp. 50; A. Santosuosso, Autodeterminazione e diritto alla salute: da compagni di viaggio a difficili conviventi, in Notizie di Politeia, 1997, pp.47-48; A. Santosuosso, Corpo e libertà. Una storia tra diritto e scienza, Milano, 2001; D. Morana, La salute nella costituzione italiana, profili sistematici, Milano, 2002, p.143; R. Romboli, Atti di disposizione del proprio corpo, Pisa, 2007; P. Veronesi, Il corpo e la Costituzione. Concretezza dei casi e astrattezza della norma, Milano, 2007; G.U. Rescigno, Dal diritto di rifiutare un determinato trattamento sanitario secondo l'art.32, co.2° Cost., al principio di autodeterminazione intorno alla propria vita, in Dir.pubbl., 2008; D. Carusi, Tutela della salute, consenso alle cure, direttive anticipate: l'evoluzione del pensiero privatistico, in Riv.crit.dir.priv., 2009; S. Rodotà, La persona costituzionalizzata e la sua autodeterminazione, in S. Rodotà, M. Tallacchini (a cura di), Ambito e fonti del Biodiritto, in S. Rodotà, P. Zatti (diretto da), Trattato di Biodiritto, Milano, 2010, pp. 169 e ss.; N. Posteraro, Evoluzione del diritto alla salute e riconoscimento dell'autonomia del paziente tra tecnologia, spersonalizzazione e crisi valoriale, in Dìke kai nòmos, n.4/2013, pp. 115 e ss.

[3] Art. 24 of the Convention on the Rights of the Child, signed in New York on 20 November 1989, ratified and implemented by Law 27 May 1991, n. 176; art. 5 of the Convention for the Protection of Human Rights and Dignity of the Human Being with regard to the Application of Biology and Medicine: Convention on Human Rights and Biomedicine, signed in Oviedo on 4 April 1997 and ratified by Italy with Law 28 March 2001, n. 145; art. 3 of the Charter of Fundamental Rights of the European Union.

[4] L.26 giugno1967 n. 458, Trapianto del rene tra persone viventi; L.22 maggio 1978, n. 194, Norme per la tutela sociale della maternità e sull'interruzione volontaria della gravidanza; L. 23 dicembre 1978, n. 833, Istituzione del servizio sanitario nazionale; L. 14 aprile 1982, n. 164, Norme in materia di rettificazione di attribuzione di sesso; L. 19 febbraio 2004, n. 40, Norme in materia di procreazione medicalmente assistita; L. 21 ottobre 2005, n. 219, Nuova disciplina delle attività trasfusionali e della produzione nazionale degli emoderivati.

care of, he has also the right to receive relevant information on the nature and possible developments in the course of treatment that can be applied, as well as any alternative therapies. Such information has to be the most comprehensive possible, precisely in order to ensure free and conscious choice by the patient and, therefore, his own personal freedom, in accordance with article 32, paragraph 2, of the Constitution.

It follows that informed consent should be considered a fundamental principle in the field of health protection, in addition to defending the dignity of every human being, which is protected in art. 1 of the Additional Protocol to the Convention on Biomedicine. The transition from the conception of the manifestation of consent – understood as removing an obstacle to the exercise of a right to freedom – the idea that it constitutes the exercise of a freedom, represents a new approach[5]. At the center of

---

[5] D. Callahan, Bioethics, in W.T. Reich (chief ed.), Encyclopedia of Bioethics, New York, Simon & Schuster – MacMillan, 1995; J. Loureiro, "Bioethical Legislation in Portugal", in: Proceedings of the First Meeting on "Basic Ethical Principles in Bioethics and Biolaw" at the Centre for Ethics and Law, Copenhagen, 1996; N. Lenoir, B. Mathieu, Les normes internationales de la bioéthique, Paris, PUF, 1998, p. 16; P. Borsellino, Bioetica tra autonomia e diritto, Milano, 1999; A. DONATI, Consenso informato e responsabilità da prestazione medica, in Rass. Dir. Civ., n.2, 2000; T. Feola, P. Antignani, C. Durante, M. Spalletta, Consenso Informato, Torino, 2001, p. 2; D. Beyleveld, R. Brownsword, Human Dignity in Bioethics and Biolaw, Oxford, Oxford University Press, 2002, p. 11; A. G. Dias Pereira, O Consentimento Informado na Relação Médico-Paciente – Estudo de Direito Civil, Coimbra, 2004; R. Andorno, Dignity of the person in the light of international biomedical law, in Medicina e morale, n.1, 2005; G. Toscano, Informazione, consenso e responsabilità, Milano, 2006; F. D'Agostino, L. Palazzani, Bioetica. Nozioni fondamentali, Brescia, 2007, p. 15; S. HURST et al., Ethical Difficulties in Clinical Practice: Experiences of European Doctors, in Journal of Medical Ethics, 2007; Guilherme de Oliveira, Medicina Preventiva – será assim tão diferente da... Medicina?, in Lex Medicinae – Revista Portuguesa de Direito da Saúde, n.10, 2008; C. Casonato, Introduzione al biodiritto, Torino, Giappichelli, 2009; ; L. Nivarra, Autonomia (bio) giuridica e tutela della persona, in Eur. Dir. Priv., 2009, pp. 719 e ss.; M. Graziadei, Il consenso informato e i suoi limiti, in L. Lenti, E. Fabris, P. Zatti (a cura di), I diritti in medicina, in S. Rodotà, P. Zatti, Trattato di Biodiritto, Milano, 2010, pp. 191 e ss.; G. Marini, Il consenso, in S. Rodotà, M. Tallacchini (a cura di), Ambito e fonti del Biodiritto, in S. Rodotà, P. Zatti (diretto da), Trattato di Biodiritto, Milano, 2010, pp. 361 e ss.; A.G. Dias Pereira – C. Barbosa, Partilha de informação de saúde, in Lex Medicinae – Revista Portuguesa de Direito da Saúde, n.16, 2012; M. Bobbert, 20 Jahre Ethikunterricht im Medizinstudium: Eine erneute Lehrziel– und Curriculumsdiskussion ist erforderlich, in Ethik in der Medizin, n.4, 2013; F. De Montalvo Jääskeläinen, El paradigma de la autonomía en salud pública ¿una contradicción o un fracaso anticipado? El caso concreto de la política de vacunación, in Derecho y salud, n.24,

the relationship of "therapeutic alliance" the protagonist is not the doctor but the patient, who has the right to dispose of his own health.

The evolution undergone by the doctor-patient relationship, which changed from a relationship traditionally set in "paternalistic" terms[6] into a relationship between two ideally equal persons, led to the configuration of a direct relationship to overcome, at least potentially, both the congenital asymmetry of information that characterizes this type of relationship, and the inevitable position of the patient's emotional awe, through, essentially, two instruments: a health service performed diligently and the fulfillment of informed consent[7].

The case-law has expanded the range of cases in which these obligations must be met: if in the past the need of the physician to inform the patient was limited to the cases in which life or the subject's physical integrity were put in jeopardy[8], today judges assert that the requirement subsists whenever there is not only the need for a devastating and complex intervention, but also in the case of a simple medical activity involving some kind of risk. Doctors must inform patients not only in the case of surgery, but also when he intends to take diagnostic or instrumental tests. The obligation to provide information by the physician is extended only to foreseeable risks and not to abnormal findings, on the edge of the fortuitous.

2014; S. SEMPLICI, Social responsibility and health. In H. ten Have, & B. Gordijn (a cura di), Handbook of global bioethics, p.187, Dordrecht.

[6] M. GORGONI, Libertà di coscienza v. salute; personalismo individualista v. paternalismo sanitario, in Resp. civ. e prev., 2009, p.126 ss.

[7] A. DONATI, Consenso informato e responsabilità da prestazione medica, in Rass. dir. civ., 1980, p.1 ss.; D. VINCENZI AMATO, Tutela della salute e libertà individuale, in Giur. cost., 1982, I, p.2462 ss.; U.G. NANNINI, Il consenso al trattamento medico, Milano, 1989, spec. 455 ss.; A. SCALISI, Il consenso del paziente al trattamento medico chirurgico, in Dir. fam. e pers., 1993, p.442 ss.; R. DE MATTEIS, La responsabilità medica. Un sottosistema della responsabilità civile, Padova, 1995, p.50; A. SANTOSUOSSO, Il consenso informato, Ancona, 1996; G. FERRANDO, Consenso informato del paziente e responsabilità del medico, principi, problemi e linee di tendenza, in Riv. crit. dir. priv., 1998, p.53 ss.; P. PERLINGIERI, Il diritto civile nella legalità costituzionale, Napoli, 2006, p.374 ss.; S. CACACE, Il consenso informato del paziente al trattamento sanitario, in Danno e resp., 2007, p.283 ss.; M. DE LUCA, La responsabilità medica, Milano, 2011, p.58.

[8] Cass. 25 luglio 1967 n. 1950; Cass. 18 giugno 1975 n. 2439, in *Foro it.* 1976, I, p.745; Cass. 29 marzo 1976 n. 1132, in *Foro it. Rep.* 1976; Trib. Genova 20 luglio 1988; Cass. 6 dicembre 1968 n. 3906, in *Resp. civ. prev.* 1970, p.389.

3. Information and consent in the cosmetic surgery.

Following the remarks above, informed consent has a special importance, so as to constitute a fundamental element of the contract between doctor and patient, which is necessary for the lawfulness of the medical treatment. The obligation to inform, placed on health professionals, is very detailed because the patient has the right to obtain complete, timely and detailed information concerning the different values that come into play with the medical treatment[9].

According to the case-law, the health professional should provide all possible information on the medical care or surgery at issue, and has a duty to inform the patient about the nature of the intervention, the scope and extent of its results, as well as on possibility and probability of the results achieved.

This obligation refers only to foreseeable risks and not to abnormal results, which are not relevant according to the id quod plerumque accidit principle, and extends to the various phases of the same taking of their own managerial autonomy.

Informed consent – provided by the patient or a family member – in view of a surgery or other specialized therapy, does not regard only the objective and technical risks in relation to the subjective situation and state of the art, but it is even related to the concrete, even temporarily, hospital situation in relation to the facilities, equipment and their proper functioning, so that the patient can decide not only to undergo surgery or not, but also to do this in that structure or another[10].

Moving from the assumption that the information has the scope of putting the patient in a position to decide whether or not to undergo surgery, it seems appropriate to evaluate whether the information to be provided, where the intervention is not necessary, has the same content

---

[9] M. GRAZIADEI, Il consenso informato e i suoi limiti, cit., p. 208 e C. CARTONI, Il giudice civile e la responsabilità sanitaria, in Giust.civ., 2013, p.536 ss.

[10] Cass., 30 luglio 2004, n. 14638, in Resp. civ., 2007, 688 ss., F. Zauli, Mancato consenso informato: danno conseguenza di per sé non oggetto di risarcimento, e in Giur. it., 2005, 1395 ss., M. D'Auria, Consenso informato: contenuto e nesso di causalità; Cass., 16 maggio 2000, n. 6318, in Danno e resp., 2001, 154 ss. con nota di G. Cassano, Obbligo di informazione, relazione medico-paziente, difficoltà della prestazione e concorso di responsabilità and in Resp. civ. prev., 2000, 940 ss., M. Gorgoni, L'incidenza delle disfunzioni della struttura ospedaliera sulla responsabilità "sanitaria".

as that offered in case of treatments with therapeutic purpose. This is certainly not a new problem, but to consider the content of the information in aesthetic treatments nowadays means to reflect on the position assumed in our society by cosmetic surgery. Moreover, in this field, aiming to achieve benefits of especially exterior nature, the medical act doesn't seem to have purely therapeutic purposes[11]. However, it should be clear that there are different types of not purely therapeutic surgery: if, on the one hand, there is a cosmetic surgery intended to correct imperfections, on the other hand, there is another interested in treatment of congenital or acquired pathology[12]. Therefore, recourse to this branch of medicine is not always the result of a "whim" of the patient.

If you refer only to purely aesthetic interventions, it must be considered that this industry has had a lower value than the other branches of medicine.

In fact, according to legal literature[13] and jurisprudence[14], the cosmetic surgeon, acting on a "healthy" body, is bound to a disclosure obligation stronger than that of other doctors. Reflections have led to say that there is not enough information about the benefits, foreseeable risks, methods of intervention and alternative techniques, but the specialist of cosmetic surgery has to be taken "to envisage to the patient, in terms of logical probability and statistics, the opportunity to achieve a real improvement in physical appearance, which is also reflected positively in professional and relational life"[15].

---

[11] F. Mangili, I. Graffuri, Sulla responsabilità professionale nelle prestazioni chirurgiche a finalità estetica, in Arch. med. leg. ass., 1979, p.131 ss.; R. De Matteis, La responsabilità medica. Un sottosistema della responsabilità civile, Padova, 1995, pp.50-90; G. Iadecola, Potestà di curare e consenso del paziente, Padova, 1998, p.225; M. Galli, Osservazioni a Corte d'appello 10 gennaio 2012, in Riv. it med. leg., 2013, p.475 ss.

[12] V. Pinchi, M. Focardi, G.A. Norelli, Deontologia ed etica in chirurgia plastica: una analisi comparativa, in Riv. it. med. leg., 2010, p.903 ss.

[13] A. Bertocchi, La responsabilità contrattuale ed extracontrattuale del medico libero professionista, in U. Ruffolo (a cura di), La responsabilità medica,Milano, 2004; A. Lo Duca, Il consenso informato nella chirurgia estetica, in www.filodiritto.com, 17 marzo 2013; L. Mattina, Chirurgia estetica: la Cassazione tra consenso informato e "dissenso presunto"del paziente, in Danno e resp.,n.3, 2015, p.253.

[14] Cass.civ., 8 agosto 1985, n.4394.

[15] Cass. 6 giugno 2014, n. 12830.

The result desired by the patient is the improvement of aesthetics and the health professional must take this into account when providing information, a fundamental moment for the evaluation of the patient who has to decide whether or not to undergo a cosmetic surgery treatment or not. This, however, is not enough, because the particular objectives pursued require the practitioner to inform his patient not only on the actual improvement achieved, but also the risks of deterioration of existing aesthetic conditions. Therefore, the information is functional to the patient's choice to refuse or accept the intervention.

In the branch of cosmetic surgery, the only source of legitimacy and the foundation of the medical act is valid consent and it is not relevant if the act has been properly executed. In the absence of a truly informed consent and in the presence of a blemish more serious than the one to be "cured", the doctor's responsibility for the resulting damage to health is obvious. It was stressed that health, as a right recognized and guaranteed by our Constitution, must be understood in a broad sense, not only in terms of physical, but also mental well-being[16]. Accepting this idea, cosmetic surgery would have equal "dignity" as that which characterizes the other areas of medicine. Although there are no foundations in a specific pathology, surgery aims to treat the individual well-being and, therefore – even indirectly – to protect the health, which becomes a notion encompassing both physical and psychological well-being.

All this would overcome the peculiar obligation to provide information placed on the cosmetic surgeon. According to this reading, the information would assume the same extent regardless of the type of intervention; otherwise you run the risk – as it in fact happens – to differentiate, making it more onerous, the obligation to provide information which is placed on the specialist of cosmetic surgery. Assuming that cosmetic surgery is a branch of medicine, to date, it seems now time to assess whether this particular requirement is still justified, not only because health assumes broad meaning, but also, and above all, because the obligation of any medical information is already very detailed in all other branches of medicine, as noted previously.

---

[16] Cass., 16 ottobre 2007, n. 21748, cit., 421 ss.

4. The judgment of the Supreme Court, June 6, 2014, n.12830.

The decision of the Supreme Court of 6 June 2014, n.12830 follows suit with the jurisprudence on the obligation of disclosure of the cosmetic surgeon, characterized by an idea – now overcome – of health restricted solely to physical integrity.

Previously, the Supreme Court affirmed the principle that any medical intervention which is not necessary, "made without valid consent loses any source of legitimacy", even if well executed. In the judgment of 2014, the Supreme Court again tackles some issues – very delicate – related to the theme of informed consent and, in particular, the content of the obligation to provide information in cosmetic surgery.

In fact, it reaffirms the distinction between functional surgery and cosmetic surgery in terms of content of its " informed consent ", reasserting it especially in "unnecessary" interventions.

As it has been said, "in terms of surgical treatment, the burden of the duty to inform placed on health professionals is functional to the conscious exercise by the patient of the right, enshrined in articles 13 and 32, paragraph 2, of the Constitution (with the exception of cases of medical treatment required by law or state of necessity), to choose whether or not to undergo a therapeutic intervention. In particular, the special nature of the voluntary health treatment comes at the end of a valid expression of consent by the patient, needing for the practitioner to inform him of the benefits, of ways and means, for any choice of different surgical techniques and, finally, of the foreseeable risks in the post-operative phase. This necessity is believed to be particularly meaningful in the field of cosmetic surgery (where demand is the existence of concrete possibility for the patient to achieve a real improvement in the physical appearance that may impact positively on his professional or relational life), with the result that the omission of such information generates for the doctor, in case of the occurrence of the damaging event, two forms of liability, namely contract and tort liability".

Unnecessary interventions are those operations carried out for the removal of blemishes and not for the care of the individual's health state resulting from trauma or disease. These actions, according to the Supreme Court, should be subject to relevant and detailed information concerning the real ameliorative effects of the proposed treatment. The need for a timely, complete and capillary information would therefore be functional to the choice of the patient to accept the intervention even if informed of the risk of worsening his/her aesthetic conditions[17].

The ruling affirms the responsibility of the surgeon who, while performing the lex artis in the execution of the operation, has not adequately informed the patient as to the possibility that a persistent blemish (extensive scar) results from the cosmetic surgery aimed at removing a tattoo[18].

5. Conclusions.

The attention paid to the issue of consent in aesthetic treatments grew every day more and more. Today, health professionals know that they must provide full and exhaustive information, because informed consent allows the patient to take the decisions they deem most appropriate for their own health.

Returned after some time to deal with the role of information in cosmetic surgery treatments, the judges of the Supreme Court pointed out that the failure to provide information regarding the possible worsening of the aesthetic conditions, that then in fact occurred, allows to assume that the patient – like any normal, rational person – would not have consented to the treatment. Therefore, the lack of timely information and the presence a blemish more serious than the one to be cured engage the responsibility of the professional. It is even unnecessary to ascertain the "determinations to which the patient would have befallen if he had been informed of the possible risks", an ascertainment that would ho-

---

[17] R. Pozzato, Aspetti di responsabilità professionale nella chirurgia plastica e nella chirurgia estetica: il consenso dell'assicurato, la colpa a livello di informazione ed esecuzione di trattamento, in AA.VV., Chirurgia plastica ricostruttiva e chirurgia estetica. Aspetti etici, giuridici e medico-legali, Milano, 1988, pag. 41; I. Guidantoni, Chirurgia estetica e culto della bellezza nella società contemporanea, in Med. Mor., 1, 1995, p.59; E. Scoditti, Chirurgia estetica e responsabilità contrattuale, in Foro it., 1995; R. Barale, La responsabilità del chirurgo estetico, in Riv. trim. dir. e proc. civ., 2005, p.1368; L. D'Alessandro, Il risarcimento del danno nel caso di intervento di chirurgia estetica mal riuscito, in La resp.civile, 8-9, 2005; L. Klesta Dosi, La chirurgia estetica tra consumerismo e valore della persona, in La nuova giur.civ.comm., n.3, 2010; L. Mattina, Chirurgia estetica: la Cassazione tra consenso infromato e "dissenso presunto" del paziente, in Danno e resp., n.3, 2015.

[18] R. Barale, La responsabilità del chirurgo estetico, in Riv. trim. dir. e proc. civ., 2005.

wever be essential to shift the responsibility in case of necessary medical treatments[19].

According to the Supreme Court, the particularities of the result desired by the patient, and the instinct present in every human being, to maintain the current health status, help eliminate the investigation to which the judge is bound on the possible course of events, thus giving the responsibility of the damage to the health professional[20]. According to the judges of the Supreme Court it is not necessary to analyze the motivations of the patient, who voluntarily went to a plastic surgeon, nor any investigation on causation between omitted information or consent: from the omissive conduct of the health professional follows ordinarily his responsibility. This reasoning, thus elaborated and limited only to cosmetic surgery treatments, seems to expressly sanction within our legal system what could be called as "alleged dissent": in other words, it could be assumed that a person, informed of the possible worsening of their aesthetic conditions, would not have given their consent.

The alleged dissent to the aesthetic treatment, rom which follows the responsibility of the physician, seems to refer to an "objective" responsibility of the health professional, who would be responsible tout court even when the patient has anyway agreed to take the risk of undergoing the treatment[21]. Considering that type of setting valid only in this area, the judgment of 2014, rather than being a victory of the right to self-determination of the patient, seems almost to take a step backwards as compared to the most recent case-law, reiterating the position of cosmetic surgery and professional operators of such specialization, who, on the one hand, would seem to be bound, even today, to a particularly challenging disclosure obligation and, secondly, would become ordinarily responsible if they have not informed the patient of the imperfection that has in fact occurred. By doing so, there is the risk – apparently permissible only in this area – always to shift to the doctor, who has "exhaustively" informed, the consequences of a failure of treatment, even if well executed.

---

[19] R. De Matteis, La responsabilità medica. Un sottosistema della responsabilità civile, Padova, 1995, p.82.

[20] L. Mattina, Chirurgia estetica: la Cassazione tra consenso informato e "dissenso presunto" del paziente, in Danno e resp., n.3, 2015.

[21] Cass. 9 febbraio 2010, n. 2847, in *Danno e resp.*, 2010, p.685 ss.

O cuidado médico transfronteiriço e o consentimento informado: as suas repercussões em sede de direito internacional privado. Um primeira abordagem

GERALDO ROCHA RIBEIRO*

I. INTRÓITO

O presente artigo é um trabalho exploratório ao problema do cuidado médico transfronteiriço e às suas implicações para as relações jurídico--privadas internacionais. Ainda que o grau de desenvolvimento dos temas não seja tanto quanto o autor do presente artigo gostaria de apresentar, não poderia deixar de lhes fazer uma abordagem preliminar, por o conhecimento e interesse por estas temáticas se dever ao homenageado e nosso Mestre, o Prof. Doutor Guilherme de Oliveira.

Posto isto, vamos tentar abordar as várias dimensões dos cuidados médicos transfronteiriços, em particular a determinação dos direitos dos pacientes e dos médicos, quando o cuidado médico tem contacto com mais de um ordenamento jurídico.

O objecto do nosso trabalho não será tratar das considerações de direitos substantivo, mas de direito internacional privado, em particular,

---

* Centro de Direito Biomédico/ Instituto Jurídico da Faculdade de Direito da Universidade de Coimbra (Grupo 2 – Vulnerabilidade e Direito, *Desafios Sociais, Incerteza e Direito*: UID/DIR/04643/2013).

DIREITO DA SAÚDE

a coordenação entre diferentes ordenamentos jurídicos, ressalvando a diversidade normativa, mas sem perder o norte de garantir a protecção individual dos sujeitos envolvidos: pacientes e médico.

II. Problema: a internacionalização do cuidado médico

A. O turismo médico

Existem vários casos em que que a circulação de pacientes e profissionais demonstra que a prestação de cuidados de saúde há muito que deixou de ser uma questão interna da cada país.

No processo *Rosenthal c. Warren,* a viúva de um médico de Nova Iorque solicita uma indemnização no valor de 1 milhão de dólares, afirmando que o seu marido foi morto em virtude de um tratamento negligente em Massachusetts (Nova Inglaterra). O marido havia sido operado em Nova Inglaterra, Boston, e 8 dias após a operação morreu. Em causa esta aferir se o direito a aplicar seria o de Nova Iorque ou o de Massachusetts. Este ordenamento jurídico local limita o dano por morte em 50 mil dólares e além disso conhece especiais limitações da responsabilidade médica, o que não sucede de acordo com o direito de Nova Iorque. O Tribunal de recurso de Nova Iorque, decidiu que o local da prática habitual só por si não constitui uma ligação suficiente para determinar a aplicação da lei e que também não se pode falar de uma vontade hipotética ou concludente das partes porque o médico e o paciente não teriam, por regra, cogitado aquela situação. O facto do médico ser conceituado neste campo, é frequentemente um factor para ser procurado por pacientes estrangeiros e o motivo porque uma parte dos doentes vem de Nova Iorque (8% dos doentes); o que faz com que a actividade do médico perca o carácter local. Por isso mesmo, entendeu o Tribunal que é o interesse do estado de Nova Iorque que prevalece e deve ser aplicado, pelo que não foram aplicados os limites à indemnização estipulados na legislação de Nova Inglaterra[1].

Outro caso mediático ocorreu em 1997 quando o *Court of Appeal* Inglês decidiu reconhecer à senhora *Blood* o direito a recorrer a serviços

---

[1] Cfr. Erwin Deutsch & Andreas Spickhoff, Medizinrecht – Arztrecht, Arzneimittelrecht, Medizinprodukterecht und Transfusionsrecht (Springer 6. Auflage ed. 2008), p. 513.

de procriação medicamente assistida no estrangeiro, mais propriamente na Bélgica, com vista a realização de inseminação artificial com esperma do marido falecido[2]. Ao contrário da lei inglesa, o ordenamento jurídico Belga permitia tais técnicas.

Veja-se ainda o caso *Leichtle*[3] julgado pelo Tribunal de Justiça da União Europeia (TJUE), no qual um cidadão de nacionalidade alemã requereu, junto da sua Caixa de Saúde, o reembolso do tratamento termal e despesas de alojamento, alimentação, viagem, diária e elaboração de um relatório médico final realizado na Itália. *Leichtle* invocou perante o Tribunal o princípio da livre prestação de serviços e pedia que se considerasse que o regime de comparticipação que regulava os fundos de saúde dos funcionários alemães violava o direito da União Europeia. O TJUE, dando razão ao senhor *Leichtle*, afirmou que os artigos 49º CE e 50º CE devem ser interpretados no sentido de que "se opõem a uma regulamentação de um Estado-Membro que faz depender a assunção de despesas referentes ao alojamento, à alimentação, à viagem, à diária e à elaboração de um relatório médico final, realizadas com um tratamento termal efectuado noutro Estado-Membro, da obtenção do reconhecimento prévio de elegibilidade para a comparticipação, que só é concedido desde que seja provado, através de parecer dos serviços de saúde pública ou de um médico assessor, que o tratamento previsto é imperiosamente necessário, por serem substancialmente maiores as probabilidades de êxito nesse outro Estado-Membro."

Daí que a ideia de turismo médico traga consigo diferentes realidades e objectivos. Podemos falar na possibilidade de procurar tratamentos inovadores ou permitidos, como será o caso de transplantes[4], interrupção voluntária da gravidez, técnicas de procriação medicamente assistida[5],

---

[2] Cfr. Blood (R. v. Human Fertilisation and Embriology Authority, ex parte Blood [1997])

[3] Cfr. Acórdão *Leichtle*, C-8/02 (os acórdãos do TJUE estão disponível no sítio www.curia.eu).

[4] No quadro europeu esta questão não se coloca com tanta pertinência em virtude da sintonia em termos de adopção de critério de morte cerebral e regulação harmonizada em matéria de transplantação, mas por exemplo o turismo médico no Japão é uma realidade no que tange aos transplantes por não ser admitido neste país o critério da morte cerebral.

[5] Cfr. Hazel Biggs & Caroline Jones, *Tourism, in* THE GLOBALIZATION OF HEALTH CARE (I. Glenn Cohen ed. 2013).

eutanásia, ou simplesmente no acesso a cuidados de saúde mais baratos ou simplesmente indisponíveis no Estado de origem[6].

B. Europa: entre o património de valores comum e a construção de um direito à saúde

1. Conselho da Europa: Direito à saúde – direito fundamental europeu?

No quadro regional europeu, no âmbito do Conselho da Europa, a primeira nota diz respeito à omissão expressa do direito à saúde na Convenção Europeia dos Direitos do Homem (CEDH)[7]. Nesta apenas é consagrado o direito à vida (artigo 2º CEDH), invocando-se a saúde e sua protecção no âmbito de interesse público, enquanto fundamento à limitação dos direitos fundamentais (artigos 2º, nº 3, 8º, nº 2, 9º, nº 2, 10º, nº 2 e 11º, nº 2)[8]. Este direito é, porém, invocado amiúde no âmbito de outros instrumentos aprovados sob a égide do Conselho da Europa ou pelo Tribunal Europeu dos Direitos do Homem (TEDH). Assim sucedeu na decisão do caso *Enhorn c. Suécia*[9]. Neste, o Tribunal reconheceu o direito à saúde individual tendo em conta os riscos de doenças contagiosas com HIV/ /SIDA apreciando correspectivamente os limites do direito à liberdade e justificação de internamento compulsivo[10].

No caso *Pretty v. The United Kingdom* é afirmada a protecção da saúde enquanto garantia do direito à vida (negando-se o direito à morte). Bem como é reconhecida a obrigação dos Estados protegerem a saúde individual de pessoas em situação vulnerável, como é o caso de pessoas privadas de liberdade nos termos do artigo 3º da CEDH. Neste foi ainda

---

[6] Sobre o problema da globalização e cuidados transfronteiriços ver AA.VV., THE GLOBALIZATION OF HEALTH CARE (I. Glenn Cohen ed., Oxford University Press. 2013).

[7] Sobre a evolução ver Toma Birmontiene, *The development of health law as a way to change traditional attitudes in national legal systems. The influence of international human rights law: what is left for the national legislator?*, 17 EUROPEAN JOURNAL OF HEALTH LAW (2010).

[8] Numa abordagem sobre a demência e o Conselho da Europa, ver Nicole Kerschen, *Are legal systems in Europe fit for the Dementia Challenge? Approach of the Council of Europe, in* COMPETENCE ASSESSMENT IN DEMENTIA (Gabriela Stoppe ed. 2008).

[9] Cfr. (Enhorn c. Suécia, 2005).

[10] O Tribunal afirmou que a privação de liberdade, para ser justificada por causa de doenças contagiosas, deve prosseguir as finalidades de protecção da saúde pública, mas igualmente a protecção da saúde individual, de forma a justificar a proporcionalidade da medida. Cfr. (Enhorn v. Sweden, 2005), pp. 17-18.

reconhecido expressamente o direito à autodeterminação nos cuidados de saúde através do consentimento informado[11]. No caso *Keenan c. Reino Unido*[12] é referido que os Estados têm um obrigação positiva de intervir em situações que esteja em causa o direito à vida nos termos do artigo 2º CEDH. No entanto o Tribunal deixa claro que tal obrigação positiva apenas pode existir quando não represente uma obrigação desproporcional para os Estados ("impossible or disproportionate burden on the authorities") e, para isso, a situação de risco de violação do direito à vida tem que ser conhecida ou cognoscível para as autoridades. Por isso conclui que para as pessoas vulneráveis, em especial as privadas de liberdade, há uma obrigação de protecção da saúde ao impor-se a remoção do perigo de suicídio e auto-lesão, estando por isso (assim se infere da decisão) obrigado a prestar os cuidados médicos adequados e necessário ao estado da pessoa[13]. Podendo, inclusive a negação de cuidados configurar uma violação do artigo 3º[14]. Igualmente se pronunciou o TEDH a respeito do consentimento informado no caso *VC c. Eslováquia* em situações de esterilização e da obrigação de assegurar uma adequada informação, de modo ao paciente se poder pronunciar de forma livre e esclarecida sobre os riscos e consequências, concluindo pela violação do artigo 8º CEDH[15].

Sobre descontinuação terapêutica e obstinação terapêutica e respeito pelos artigos 2º, 3º e 8º CEDH veja-se o recente caso *Lambert e outros c. França*. Neste, e na sequência da decisão do *Conseil d'État*[16], foi considerado como obstinação terapêutica, e por isso desproporcional, a manutenção da alimentação e hidratação artificial de alguém que se encontra em estado vegetativo persistente e sofreu danos cerebrais irreversíveis.

---

[11] Cfr. (Pretty c. Reino Unido, 2002).

[12] Cfr. (Keenan c. Reino Unido, 2001).

[13] Cfr. (Keenan c. Reino Unido, 2001), pp. 28-31.

[14] Cfr. (H. c. Suíça, 1993), §79. Em sentido convergente ver ainda o caso *İlhan v. Turkey*, no qual o Tribunal concluiu que é obrigação das autoridades de um Estado prestarem o cuidado médico adequado, aqui se incluindo a prestação deste em tempo útil (İlhan v. Turkey, 2000, p. 22).

[15] Cfr. (V.C. c. Eslováquia, 2012), p. .Sabine Michalowski, *Comentary on article 3º (Right to the Integrity of the Person) of the EU Charter, in* THE EU CHARTER OF FUNDAMENTAL RIGHTS. A COMMENTARY (Steve Peers, et al. eds., 2014)., p. 48. Sobre a jurisprudência do TEDH e a doença mental, ver PEDRO CORREIA GONÇALVES, O ESTATUTO JURÍDICO DO DOENTE MENTAL COM REFERÊNCIA À JURISPRUDÊNCIA DO TRIBUNAL EUROPEU DOS DIREITOS DO HOMEM (Quid Iuris. 2009).

[16] Cfr. (Lambert e outros c. França, 2015), pp. 14-16.

DIREITO DA SAÚDE

Os meios de alimentação e hidratação artificial foram vistos como fins em si mesmo e não como uma terapêutica ou associados a uma, com vista à melhoria das condições e saúde do paciente[17].

A construção da protecção à saúde tem neste âmbito como destinatários os Estados e não os indivíduos, pelo que se tende a recusar o reconhecimento individual de um direito subjectivo[18]. Segundo XAVIER BIOY os direitos humanos na Europa, no que à protecção à saúde diz respeito, desenvolvem-se de forma parcelar, mediada e penosa[19]. No entanto, apesar da ausência de referências expressas na Convenção, verificamos que a interpretação feita aos instrumentos, em particular pelo TEDH, demonstram que a saúde é protegida e que se enquadra, pelo menos no que diz respeito às pessoas vulneráveis, como uma obrigação positiva a cargo dos Estados, conferindo-lhes, desta forma, um efectivo direito subjectivo, ainda que integrado no âmbito de outros direitos expressamente previstos na Convenção como é o caso dos artigos 2º, 5º, 8º e 12º CEDH.

A isto acresce a relevância dos instrumentos de *soft law* ou, nas palavras de ERIK JAYME, de normas-narrativas[20], como a Recomendação 1418 (1999)[21]. Apesar da sua natureza não poderão estas normas deixar de relevar juridicamente[22]. Um dos exemplos resulta da Convenção Europeia dos Direitos do Homem e Biomedicina CEDHB que, apesar de não ter sido ratificada por todos os Estados-membros, não deixa de ser invocada e corporizada em outros instrumentos normativos como sucedeu em matéria de normas de qualidade e segurança dos órgãos humanos-

---

[17] O Tribunal, depois de recusar a legitimidade dos queixosos, apreciou a questão somente quanto à existência de uma obrigação activa do Estado francês de protecção de vida de *Lambert* e se esta foi violada nos termos do artigo 2º CEDH, tendo concluído, por maioria, que tal não sucedeu (Lambert e outros v. France, 2015), p. 36 ss.

[18] Cfr. NATHALIE DE GROVE-VALDEYRON, DROIT EUROPÉEN DE LA SANTÉ (L.G.D.J. 2013), p. 31.

[19] Cfr. Xavier Bioy, *Le droit fondamental à l'accès aux soins en Europe. Vers un standard de conciliation entre libertés économiques et droits du patient?*, REVUE DES AFFAIRES EUROPÉENNES (2011)., p. 495.

[20] Cfr. ERIK JAYME, NARRATIVE NORMEN IM INTERNATIONALEN PRIVAT– UND VERFAHRENSRECHT (Eberhard – Karls – Universit¨åt Tübingen. 1993), pp. 16.

[21] Para além desta existem muitas outras onde a saúde é directamente tutelada conforme se pode constatar por consulta ao sítio da internet do Conselho da Europa http://www.coe.int/t/dg3/healthbioethic.

[22] Cfr. DOMINIQUE BUREAU & HORATIA MUIR WATT, DROIT INTERNATIONAL PRIVÉ § II – Partie spéciale (Presses Universitaires de France 2.e édition mise à jour ed. 2010), p . 31.

destinados a transplantação[23]. Destarte, ainda que não se possa afirmar, numa fase inicial, de um autónomo direito à saúde, a verdade é que o mesmo não deixa de ter tutela no quadro jurídico europeu. Até porque tal direito não deixou de ser referido na protecção à saúde em domínios específicos como a protecção do trabalhador (artigos 10º, 34º e 49º do Código Europeu de Segurança Social) e o regime dos medicamentos e produtos de saúde (Convenção Relativa à Elaboração de Uma Farmacopeia Europeia e Convenção contra o Doping).

Neste enquadramento, é com naturalidade que surge a aprovação da CEDHB[24]. Esta Convenção pretende promover uma *standard* mínimo de regulação dos problemas de natureza bioética, com vista a promover a convergência mais do que uniformização[25]. Nela são regulados e reconhecidos diversos direitos dos pacientes integrantes do cuidado de saúde: consentimento, respeito pela vida privada e familiar e direito à informação, controlo genético, ensaios clínicos, proibição de discriminação, colheita de órgãos e tecidos em dadores vivos para fins de transplante. Bem como, por intermédio de Protocolos adicionais, se regulam as questões de clonagem, transplantação e investigação biomédica[26]. Através da CEDHB são ainda consagrados os princípios da autonomia, a proibição de práticas eugénicas, o princípio da não obtenção do lucro com base na utilização de partes do corpo humano, a proibição da clonagem, e o princípio do acesso equitativo aos cuidados de saúde[27].

---

[23] Veja-se a integração no artigo 13º da Directiva 2010/45/UE, do Parlamento Europeu e do Conselho, de 7 de Julho de 2010, relativa a normas de qualidade e segurança dos órgãos humanos destinados a transplantação, do princípio da gratuitidade alinhado com o artigo 21º da CEDHB. Cfr. Jean Mchale, *Fundamental rights and health care*, in HEALTH SYSTEMS GOVERNANCE IN EUROPE. THE ROLE OF EUROPEAN UNION LAW AND POLICY (Elias Mossialos, et al. eds., 2010)., p. 300. A respeito da ligação do artigo 3º da Carta de Direitos Fundamentais da União Europeia e a CEDHB ver Michalowski, Comentary on article 3º (Right to the Integrity of the Person) of the EU Charter. 2014.

[24] Convenção que ainda não foi capaz de obter uma elevada adesão, continuando a não ser ratificada por países como a Alemanha, França, Itália, Reino Unido, entre outros. Sobre o quadro de países vinculados à Convenção consultar http://www.coe.int/.

[25] Um dos objectivos da Convenção é, nas palavras de André Dias Pereira, evitar a criação de "paraísos (ou, melhor dizendo, infernos) bioéticos" (cfr. André Gonçalo Dias Pereira, *Um Direito da Saúde para a Europa?*, DEBATER A EUROPA (2010), p.29).

[26] Cfr. Mchale, Fundamental rights and health care. 2010, p. 285.

[27] Cfr. Pereira, DEBATER A EUROPA, (2010), p. 32. Sobre a Convenção ver AA.VV., DIREITOS DO HOMEM E BIOMEDICINA (Universidade Católica Editora. 2003).

Este quadro normativo vale, mesmo para os países não vinculados, a título de normas-narrativas essenciais na resolução de conflitos e balizamento das linhas da ordem pública nacional face às liberdades fundamentais europeias. Torna-se, por isso, necessário estabelecer um *standard* de garantias comuns a todos os Estados, quer de informação, quer de protecção de dados que assegurem subjectivamente os interesses jurídicos do paciente. O que será mais fácil de assegurar atendendo à natureza negativa ou defensiva de tais direitos[28].

Todavia, o reconhecimento do direito ao consentimento informado, acompanhado do reconhecimento da relevância da vontade manifestada num momento anterior à incapacidade (artigo 9º CEDHB) mostram o caminho para a construção de um estatuto jurídico transfronteiriço do paciente. Estatuto que lhe confere a garantia mínima de protecção onde quer que se encontre e que prevê a relevância de uma vontade prospectiva, ainda que não vinculativa[29].

2. União Europeia

a) *Evolução das competências da UE*

A União Europeia (UE) não tem competência geral directa para regular questões relativas à saúde. Reservaram os Estados Membros a soberania sobre estas matérias, apenas transferindo competência à UE em pontos específicos e expressamente previstos no TFUE. Será o caso das questões de saúde pública expressamente previstas (artigo 4º, nº 2 al. k) e artigo

---

[28] Para este standard não deixa de ser relevante o previsto Carta Social Europeia, de 18 de Outubro de 1961, onde é referido expressamente o direito à protecção da saúde. Quer enquanto direito na Parte I nº 11: "Todas as pessoas têm o direito de beneficiar de todas as medidas que lhes permitam gozar do melhor estado de saúde que possam atingir", quer, para efectivar tal direito, como obrigação imputada aos Estados no artigo 11º da Parte II ao impor como objectivos: eliminar, na medida do possível, as causas de uma saúde deficiente (1); estabelecer serviços de consulta e de educação no que respeita à melhoria da saúde e ao desenvolvimento do sentido da responsabilidade individual em matéria de saúde (2); evitar, na medida do possível, as doenças epidémicas, endémicas e outras (3). Cfr. Henriette D. C. Roscam Abbing, *Health Law: Facing the European Challenges (Editorial)*, 10 EUROPEAN JOURNAL OF HEALTH LAW (2010), p. 3.

[29] Cfr. Salla K Lötjönen, *Medical Research on Patients with Dementia – the Role of Advance Directives in European Legal Instruments**, 13 EUROPEAN HUMAN RIGHTS LAW REVIEW (2006), p. 243 e Tito Ballarino, *Is a conflict rule for living wills and euthanasia needed?*, VIII YEARBOOK OF PRIVATE INTERNATIONAL LAW (2006), p. 7.

168º), ou a título complementar como meio de concretização de outras políticas comunitárias como é o caso do ambiente (artigo 191º, nº 1), da protecção e melhoria da saúde humana (artigo 6º, nº 1 *al.* a)), em especial na protecção laboral (artigo 153º, *al.* a)), definição de políticas europeias (artigo 9º *in fine*) e política de harmonização (artigo 114º, nº 3)[30] [todos do TFUE].

Já quanto ao âmbito de integração europeu a referência ao direito à saúde como direito subjectivo encontra-se expressamente referido na Carta dos Direitos Fundamentais da União Europeia (CDF). Não obstante as dificuldades históricas iniciais, e hoje dissipadas, na qualificação jurídica deste instrumento – uma vez que foi adoptado enquanto recomendação e texto de referência complementar à Convenção Europeia dos Direitos do Homem –, é indiscutível que a Carta consagra um direito à saúde (artigo 35º[31]).

Hoje, tendo finalmente adquirido uma natureza vinculativa para vinte e oito Estados Membros[32] assume-se como pilar unificador dos valores e direitos fundamentais europeus e em última instância concretizador da ordem pública europeia. Existem duas dimensões no direito ora consagrado no espaço europeu: o reconhecimento de um direito subjectivo e a imposição de uma verdadeira obrigação de resultado por conta dos Estados como meio de efectivar tal direito.

Como já foi referido, o ponto de entrada da saúde no contexto comunitário deu-se essencialmente pela necessidade de protecção dos trabalhadores e da sua liberdade de circulação. Como nota NATHALIE DE GROVE-VALDEYRON a saúde tem duas dimensões no quadro europeu[33]. Uma negativa enquanto cláusula de salvaguarda dos Estados Membros que lhes reconhece a faculdade para imporem obstáculos às liberdades

---

[30] A preocupação com os cuidados de saúde, não obstante a recusa de atribuição de competência directa à União Europeia, vem dos primórdios da formação das então chamadas Comunidades Económicas e inicialmente centrada na protecção dos trabalhadores (artigos 46º, 55º TCECA, artigos 117º e 118º TCEE e artigo 30º e seguintes TCEEA) acabando por evoluir a reboque de uma concepção mais ampla de cidadania.

[31] "Todas as pessoas têm o direito de aceder à prevenção em matéria de saúde e de beneficiar de cuidados médicos, de acordo com as legislações e práticas nacionais. Na definição e execução de todas as políticas e acções da União é assegurado um elevado nível de protecção da saúde humana".

[32] O Reino Unido e a Polónia beneficiam da derrogação da sua aplicação.

[33] Cfr. GROVE-VALDEYRON, Droit européen de la santé. 2013, p. 22.

DIREITO DA SAÚDE

comunitárias do então mercado comum e uma positiva tendente à afirmação da liberalização do acesso e exercício de profissões do sector da saúde (médicos, paramédicos, farmacêuticos) (actual artigo 53º, nº 2 TFUE).

Como também mencionado, a União Europeia não tem competência directa (*Kompetenz-Kompetenz*), logo carece de base legitimadora em matéria de saúde a não ser por mediação dos Estados-membros e a título complementar. Contudo há uma intervenção oblíqua em matérias da saúde, como é o caso das politicas anti-tabaco. que constituem verdadeiras «zonas cinzentas»[34] dentro da repartição de competências. Um dos exemplos que podemos apontar foi a adopção de Directivas já em 1965 e 1975 sobre medicamentos à base de sangue ou de plasma humano (Directivas 65/65/CEE e 75/318/CEE) por recurso ao antigo artigo 100º TCEE. Dando aqui nota que uma concretização plena da integração europeia não pode ser feita sem atingir domínios que *ab initio* e *individualmente* estariam excluído do foro de competência da União.

Com o Acto Único Europeu prevê-se a interferência em matéria de saúde quando tenha por base a política ambiental (actual artigo 191º, nº 1 TFUE), alargando-se ainda (mais) quanto à política social e protecção dos trabalhadores (artigo 153º, nº 1 *al.* a TFUE), identificando-se ainda a saúde pública como um dos objectivos da integração europeia (actual artigo 114º, nº 3 TFUE). Objectivo que foi identificado no Livro Branco da Comissão para conclusão do mercado interno de 1985, como necessidade de promover a harmonização legislativa entre Estados-Membros[35].

Mas foi com o Tratado de Maastricht que se deu o impulso decisivo na criação de um mercado interno em matéria de saúde ao ter sido autonomizado o capítulo respeitante à saúde pública e que ainda hoje se mantém (actual artigo 168º TFUE). Contudo esta autonomização não lhe confere a natureza de uma política europeia em sentido estrito (à semelhança, p.ex., do ambiente), tanto mais que a actuação da União pressupõe uma intervenção estadual. Todavia não deixa de ser uma porta que legitima a actividade legiferante da União Europeia, ainda que limi-

---

[34] Cfr. Pierre-Henri Teitgen & Colette Megret, *La fumée de la cigarette dans la "zone grise" des compétences de la C.E.E.*, 17 REVUE TRIMESTRIELLE DE DROIT EUROPÉEN (1981).

[35] Cfr. Comissão das Comunidades Europeias, "Completing the Internal Market: White Paper from the Commission to the European Council." COM (85) 310 FINAL. Bruxelas, 14 de Junho de 1985, p. 19.

tada, prevendo-se a possibilidade de iniciativa de acções de incentivo e de recomendação (artigo 129º, nº 4)[36].

A partir do Tratado de Amesterdão foi alargado o domínio de competência da União legitimando-se uma intervenção directa, ainda que complementar, em matéria de saúde pública[37]. As competências da União, então Comunidade, eram autolimitadas, o que já não sucede a partir do Tratado de Amesterdão. A versão dada ao artigo 129º legitima uma intervenção directa ao se ter eliminado a expressão "contribuirá", reforçando o carácter complementar como meio de suprir as insuficiências de uma intervenção meramente nacional[38]. Igualmente são completadas as funções a desempenhar pela União, nomeadamente a título de prevenção onde se acrescentaram as afecções humanas e se legitimou a intervenção da União na luta e prevenção dos grandes flagelos não se limitando, como o fazia na versão de Maastricht, à luta contra a droga (autonomizada num parágrafo).

Outra nota prende-se com explicitação dos objectivos das acções de incentivo e recomendação em matéria de saúde pública: "proteger e melhorar a saúde humana". Bem como reforçando a competência para garantia de *elevada* qualidade e segurança dos órgãos e substâncias de origem humana, do sangue e dos derivados do sangue como resposta aos episódios de sangue contaminado[39] e à protecção de saúde pública no domínio veterinário e fitossanitário[40]. Este novo quadro jurídico adop-

---

[36] Pode-se dizer que foi consagrada de forma expressa em matéria de saúde uma competência específica, de meios limitada, mas ainda assim uma competência integrada (cfr. GROVE-VALDEYRON, Droit européen de la santé. 2013., p. 26).

[37] Na versão do tratado de Maastricht o artigo 129º (actual artigo 168º TFUE) era referido: "A Comunidade **contribuirá** para assegurar um elevado nível de protecção da saúde humana, incentivando a cooperação entre os Estados-membros e, se necessário, apoiando a sua acção" [sublinhado nosso].

[38] Cfr. Symeon Karagiannis, *La politique communautaire de santé publique et le traité d'Amsterdam, premières impressions (et premières interrogations)*, in ÉTUDES EN L'HONNEUR DE PIERRE SANDEVOIR: SERVICE PUBLIC, SERVICES PUBLICS (Xavier Vandendriessche ed. 2000)., pp. 240-241. De acordo com este autor, a *actuação comunitária, não se pondendo substituir à actuação nacional, tem contudo a vantagem de ter passado a existir por completo. Não ganhou a sua independência; mas tornou-se autónoma* (cfr. Id. at., p. 241).

[39] Cfr.GROVE-VALDEYRON, Droit européen de la santé. 2013., p. 29.

[40] Uma das consequências desta alteração foi a validação da Directiva 2002/2/CEE no caso Fratelli Martini (C-11/04) e a legitimidade para a aprovação do Regulamento (CE) nº 999/2001 de 22 de Maio.

DIREITO DA SAÚDE

tado reforça o princípio de integração, ao ponto de se poder falar na previsão de uma obrigação de resultados para protecção da saúde pública: "Na definição e execução de todas as políticas e acções da Comunidade será assegurado um elevado nível de protecção da saúde" (artigo 129º, nº 1 na versão vigente do Tratado)[41].

Do Tratado de Amesterdão até ao Tratado de Lisboa não ocorreram alterações de fundo, reforçando-se apenas as competências da UE, que acabaram por justificar a regulação do mercado interno de cuidados de saúde através da Directiva nº 2011/24/UE que vem corporizar, por fonte legislativa, a jurisprudência do TJUE[42]. Entre nós a directiva foi transposta e regulada pelas Lei nº 52/2014, 25/8 e Portaria nº 191/2014, 25/9[43].

Actualmente encontramos o artigo 168º TFUE que corporiza as atribuições e competências em matéria de saúde, estabelecendo como obrigação da UE prosseguir nas suas políticas e acções um elevado nível de protecção da saúde. No entanto tais competências surgem enquadradas pelo princípio da subsidiariedade, ao dar primazia a políticas de cooperação e harmonização (artigo 168º, nº 2), pressupondo, ainda assim, que todas as intervenções, quer por mediação da UE, quer a nível nacional, assegurem elevados *standards* de qualidade. Esta são os fundamentos e critérios que haviam já levado à aprovação das Directivas 2002/98/CE (relativa à qualidade e segurança ao sangue), 2004/23/CE e 2010/45/UE (relativas à qualidade e segurança na colheita e transplante de órgãos e tecidos humanos).

b) Carta de Direitos Fundamentais da UE: o direito fundamental ao consentimento informado

É relevante darmos conta que o quadro jurídico europeu abarca hoje um componente substantiva que tende a fixar um *standard* de garantias a respeito do direito à autodeterminação, ao consagrar o consentimento informado no artigo 3º da Carta dos Direitos Fundamentais da União Europeia. Este é sem dúvida o grande marco e de grande repercussão na

---

[41] Cfr.GROVE-VALDEYRON, Droit européen de la santé. 2013, p. 30.

[42] Para uma resenha histórica dos cuidados médicos transfronteiriços ver Miguel Gorjão--Henriques, *A Directiva 2011/24/UE e o Mercado Interno da prestação de cuidados de saúde: da proposta Bolkenstein à próxima transposição. Alguns pressupostos e desafios*, 31-32 TEMAS DE INTEGRAÇÃO (2011).

[43] Cfr. http://diretiva.min-saude.pt/direitos/.

definição de um patamar mínimo de direitos e garantias do cidadão europeu. Na senda da incorporação de valores e interesses já consagrados nas normas-narrativas, o artigo 3º da CDF incorpora os valores e interesses já consagrados na CEDHB e Protocolos Adicionais[44], bem com o artigo 9º CEDHB e a relevância da vontade prospectiva[45]. É, contudo, pouco, tendo em conta a margem de discricionariedade conferida aos Estados-Membros para concretizarem o conteúdo e garantias do consentimento informado[46]. Todavia, existem instrumentos do Conselho da Europa e da própria União Europeia que nos permitem deslindar as linhas mestras do conceito europeu de consentimento informado[47].

Na verdade a relevância do consentimento, como critério para a licitude da colheita e transplante de órgãos e tecidos humanos, já era mencionado nas Directivas 2004/23/CE e 2010/45/UE. Contudo não era concretizado qual o conteúdo mínimo de informação necessário, remetendo para a diversidade das ordens jurídicas comunitárias (*vide* considerando 21 e artigos 4º, nº 2, *al.* b) e 14º da Directiva de 2010).

O que já não sucede na regulamentação sobre os ensaios clínicos através do Regulamento nº 536/2014/UE[48]. Neste é definido e estabelecido o conteúdo mínimo do dever de informação e validade do consentimento prestado[49]. Dos requisitos para a validade do consentimento informado

---

[44] Cfr. Michalowski, Comentary on article 3º (Right to the Integrity of the Person) of the EU Charter. 2014, p. 39.

[45] A este respeito são relevantes as resoluções do Parlamento Europeu onde é afirmada a relevância do artigo 9º CEDHB e a necessidade de ratificação da Convenção por todos os Estados membros (Resolução do Parlamento Europeu, de 14 de Janeiro de 2009, sobre a situação dos direitos fundamentais na União Europeia (2004-2008) (2007/2145(INI))) e, mais recentemente, o direito à autodeterminação prospectiva (Resolução do Parlamento Europeu, de 27 de fevereiro de 2014, sobre a situação dos direitos fundamentais na União Europeia (2012) (2013/2078(INI))). Ver ainda Stefania Negri, *The right to informed consent at the Convergence of International Biolaw and International Human Rights Law, in* SELF-DETERMINATION, DIGNITY AND END-OF-LIFE CARE. REGULATING ADVANCE DIRECTIVES IN INTERNATIONAL AND COMPARATIVE PERSPECTIVE (Stefania Negri ed. 2011), pp. 70-71.

[46] Neste sentido Herman Nys, *The Right to Informed Choice and the Patients' Rights Directive (Editorial)*, 19 EUROPEAN JOURNAL OF HEALTH LAW (2012), p. 329.

[47] Cfr. Michalowski, Comentary on article 3º (Right to the Integrity of the Person) of the EU Charter. 2014, pp. 47-48.

[48] Cfr. Guilherme de Oliveira, *Direito Biomédico e Investigação Clínica, in* TEMAS DE DIREITO DA MEDICINA (2005).

[49] No artigo 2º, *al.* j) consentimento informado é definido como "a expressão livre e voluntária por parte de um sujeito do ensaio da sua vontade de participar num ensaio clínico específico,

DIREITO DA SAÚDE

destaca-se ainda o seu regime jurídico que, independentemente das leis nacionais, pode ser livremente revogável (artigo 28º, nºs 2 *in fine* e 3 do Regulamento), bem como o direito de participação e informação dos pacientes sem capacidade para consentir (artigos 31º, nº 2 e 3 e 32º, nº 2 do Regulamento). Ao contrário do que sucedia com a Directiva 2001//20/CE, não é mencionada a vontade presumida como critério de decisão do representante (artigo 5º, *al.* a)), contudo não deixará a mesma de relevar e vincular o representante, em especial atento o direito de co-consentimento e de veto reconhecido ao paciente incapaz[50].

Esta conexão material de valores entre os direitos fundamentais reconhecidos pela CEDH e CEDHB e o direito da UE verifica-se ainda no âmbito do co-consentimento e direito de veto do paciente vulnerável. O artigo 17º, nº 1 v) CEDHB consagra do direito de recusar a participação num ensaio clínico, direito que é também reconhecido pelos artigos 31º, nº 2 *al.* c) e 32º, nº 1 *al.* c) e do Regulamento. Também o artigo 17º, nº 2 da CEDHB encontra correspondência, em matéria de ensaios clínicos, com os artigos 31º, n. 1 *al. g)* e 32º, nº 1 *al.* g) do Regulamento. O mesmo sucede com as disposições previstas no Protocolo Adicional relativo à investigação biomédica, nos artigos 15º e 19º, em especial este último quanto às intervenções de urgência (artigo 35º do Regulamento).

Deve ainda ser destacado o artigo 35º CDF, integrado no capítulo IV referente à solidariedade, que consagra o direito de protecção à saúde: Todas as pessoas têm o direito de aceder à prevenção em matéria de saúde e de beneficiar de cuidados médicos, de acordo com as legislações e práticas nacionais. Na definição e execução de todas as políticas e acções da União é assegurado um elevado nível de protecção da saúde humana. Contudo não é claro que do artigo 35º se possam assacar efeitos directos. Ainda que, no Caso C-444/05, *Stamatelaki*, o Advogado-Geral tenha afirmado o direito individual do cidadão europeu no acesso a cuidados de

---

depois de ter sido informado de todos os aspectos do ensaio clínico que sejam relevantes para a sua decisão de participar, ou, no caso de um menor ou de um sujeito incapaz, uma autorização ou a concordância do seu representante legalmente autorizado sobre a sua inclusão no ensaio clínico".

[50] Sobre as directivas antecipadas e a ligação entre a CEDHB e a Diretiva 2001/20/CE ver Lötjönen, European human Rights Law Review, (2006), pp. 246-250.

saúde, o que pode pressupor o exercício da sua liberdade de circulação como meio dos obter[51].

Um dos campos de desenvolvimento prende-se com *o tempo útil* para acesso ao cuidado de saúde, em especial nas situações em que o Estado de origem do paciente fazia depender a concessão de uma autorização para recorrer a tratamento transfronteiriço. Conforme já havia sido decidido noutros casos[52] e confirmado no caso *Inizan*, o TJUE conclui que, para concretizar o conceito de tempo útil, é necessário que a instituição competente atenda "ao conjunto das circunstâncias que caracterizam cada caso concreto, tendo devidamente em conta não apenas a situação médica do paciente no momento em que a autorização é solicitada e, eventualmente, o grau de dor ou a natureza da deficiência deste último, que possa, por exemplo, tornar impossível ou excessivamente difícil o exercício de uma actividade profissional, mas igualmente os seus antecedentes"[53]. Concretizando depois no caso *Watts* que o direito de acesso a cuidados de saúde não só terá que ser garantido em tempo útil enquanto condição para autorização de tratamento transfronteiriço, como igualmente permite o acesso imediato a esse mesmo cuidado, se se justificar à luz do artigo 22º do Regulamento nº 883/2004/CE relativo à coordenação dos sistemas de segurança social[54], assegurando-se assim a plena autonomia e complementaridade de regimes[55].

---

[51] Transcrevendo: "é a do direito dos cidadãos aos cuidados médicos, proclamado no artigo 35º da Carta dos Direitos Fundamentais da União Europeia, pois «[s]endo encarada como um bem superior, a saúde não pode ser considerada exclusivamente do ponto de vista das despesas sociais e das dificuldades económicas latentes». Este direito reveste carácter pessoal, à margem da relação entre o sujeito e a segurança social, sem que o Tribunal de Justiça possa ignorar tal aspecto" (cfr. § 40, Conclusões do Advogado-Geral, p. I-3197). Ou seja, é equacionável a possibilidade de invocação do artigo 35º, não só como direito subjectivo do cidadão europeu, como o quadro de valores e objectivos da política da UE (cfr. Tamara K Hervey, *The 'Right to Health' in European Union Law, in* ECONOMIC AND SOCIAL RIGHTS UNDER EU CHARTER OF FUNDAMENTAL RIGHTS (Hart Publishing ed. 2006)., p. 202).

[52] C-157/99 *Smits e Peerbooms* e *Müller-Fauré* e C-385/99 *Van Riet*.

[53] Cfr. C-56/01 *Inizan* §46.

[54] Cfr. C-372/04 *Watts* §60.

[55] Cfr. LEIGH HANCHER & WOLF SAUTER, EU COMPETITION AND INTERNAL MARKET LAW IN THE HEALTH CARE SECTOR (Oxford University Press. 2012)., pp. 202-204.

DIREITO DA SAÚDE

c) Liberdades comunitárias: o direito à saúde como corolário da liberdade de circulação

(1) Liberdade de circulação de pacientes e profissionais de saúde

Em termos de liberdades comunitárias, a liberdade de circulação pressupõe a liberdade de entrar e permanecer num outro Estado-Membro e aqui se inclui a liberdade do paciente se deslocar no mercado interno e aceder a cuidados de saúde prestados noutro Estado-Membro. Isto significa que as restrições a esta liberdade terão que ser fundadas nas excepções previstas nos tratados e concretizadas por direito derivado (ordem pública, segurança pública e saúde pública) e que podem implicar expulsão ou não admissão de um cidadão em território nacional. Certo é que qualquer decisão carece de justificação proporcional e circunscrita (pelo menos no que à moral e segurança diz respeito) ao comportamento pessoal do cidadão.

O conflito entre a competência exclusiva dos Estados-Membros em relação à organização e prestação de serviços de saúde e a livre circulação de mercadorias e prestação de serviços tem sido objecto de exaustiva análise por parte do TJUE. Aliás a questão dos cuidados de saúde entrou pela porta do Tribunal muito antes da discussão da Directiva 2011/ /24/UE[56].

A Directiva 2011/24/UE, que, como já foi referido, foi transposta pela Lei nº 52/2014 de 25 de Agosto e regulada pela Portaria nº 191/2014 de 25 de Setembro, quanto aos actos médicos sujeitos a prévia autorização, define como cuidados de saúde aqueles que são prestados por profissionais de saúde aos doentes com o objetivo de avaliar, manter ou reabilitar o seu estado de saúde, incluindo a prescrição, a dispensa e o fornecimento de medicamentos e dispositivos médicos[57].

---

[56] Alguns dos acórdãos mais relevantes nesta matéria são os seguintes: Acórdão C-158/96 *Kohll*; C-120/95 *Decker*; C-157/99 Geraets-*Smits and Peerbooms*; C-368/98 Van Braekel; C-385/99 *Müller Fauré and Van Riet*; C-8/02 *Leichtle*, C-444/05 *Stamatelaki*; C-255/09 *Comissão Europeia c. Portugal*.

[57] Num abordagem sobre os problemas e vantagens da Directiva 2011/24/UE ver AA.VV., Unionsbürgerschaft und Patientenfreizügigkeit. Citoyenneté Européenne et Libre Circulation des Patients. EU Citizenship and Free Movement of Patients (Springer. 2014).

A Directiva deixa vincado que os cuidados de saúde devem assegurar elevados padrões de qualidade[58] – artigos 1º e 4º, nº 1 –, mas nada dispõe sobre os direitos do paciente para além da óptica de consumidor, nomeadamente sobre o consentimento informado. Se é certo que no quadro de valores temos a CEDHB que consagra o consentimento informado (e como vimos serve de norma-narrativa), tal não permite a afirmação do seu carácter vinculativo. Ainda assim podemos socorrer-nos da interpretação do artigo 8º da CEDH e sua interpretação feita no caso *Pretty* e confirmada no caso *Lambert*, bem como do artigo 3º, nº 2 *al.* a) CDF.

Certo, porém, é que não se pode retirar da Directiva a consagração expressa de um direito à informação e consequente consentimento informado. O artigo 4º, nº 2 *al.* b) da Directiva ao reconhecer a obrigação de informação dos Estados pressupõe o acesso aos cuidados de saúde e informação necessária a fazer essa escolha e não ao cuidado médico per se. Numa perspectiva de acesso aos cuidados de saúde isso pressupõe o dever de informação sobre as ofertas em termos de cuidados de saúde, tipos de serviço, qualidade, custos, quer para os cuidados transfronteiriços, quer a nível interno[59]. Contudo tal dever de informação assenta na oferta disponível de cuidados médicos e não na relação interna médico-paciente[60].

(2) Liberdade de exercício de actividades médicas (os médicos em especial)
A relevância da actividade exercida pelos profissionais de saúde ou a ela conexas desde cedo trouxe consigo preocupações à UE sobre a liberdade de circulação, prestação de serviços e estabelecimento. A importância da actividade desenvolvida teve como consequência o reconhecimento

---

[58] Cfr. Considerandos 10, 11, 20, 39 50, 54, 58.

[59] Cfr. Diana Delnoij & Wolf Sauter, *Patient information under the EU patients' rights Directive*, 21 European Journal of Health Law (2011), pp. 271-272.

[60] Cfr. Herman Nys, *The Right to Informed Choice and the Patients' Rights Directive (Editorial)*, 19 see id. at (2012), p. 329. Daí uma autora afirmar que o direito de informação tem como destinatários a colectividade de pacientes e não o paciente individual (cfr. Nathalie de Grove-Valdeyron, La directive sur les droits des patients en matière de soins de santé transfrontaliers. Véritable statut juridique européen du patient ou simple clarification d'un régime de mobilité?, 47 Revue Trimestrielle de Droit Europeen (2011)., p. 318).

DIREITO DA SAÚDE

de limites às liberdades comunitárias[61]. Contudo as actividades do sector saúde, em particular os médicos, depende do reconhecimento de qualificações e inscrição na respectiva ordem profissional. Assim o é para Portugal e para os demais países que integram o espaço europeu. Em Portugal, e cingindo-nos à actividade médica, esta é regulada pelo Estatuto da Ordem dos Médicos aprovado pelo Decreto-Lei nº 282/77, de 05/07 (com a última alteração do Decreto-Lei nº 217/94, de 20/08) e pelo Código Deontológico[62]. De acordo com o artigo 8º do EOM "o exercício da medicina depende da inscrição na Ordem dos Médicos". Desta norma decorre que para o exercício da actividade médica em território português, o médico tem que estar inscrito na Ordem dos Médicos portuguesa, independentemente da sua nacionalidade. Trata-se por isso de uma norma que, pela sua natureza e função, estabelece uma autolimitação espacial quanto ao seu âmbito de aplicação.

Numa actividade tão técnica e com tanta proeminência social, os poderes conferidos às associações profissionais confere-lhes o monopólio de regulação da conduta dos profissionais que exerçam a actividade médica num determinado país[63]. Quer impondo a prévia inscrição na ordem profissional, quer vinculando o médico que temporariamente actua noutro país. Em qualquer uma das variantes, a responsabilidade exigível ao profissional de saúde é conectada ao local onde exerce a sua actividade, seja com carácter duradouro ou permanente, seja a título temporário ou ocasional.

O artigo 9º do EOM dispõe que só estão em condições de validamente se inscreverem licenciados em Medicina por escola superior portuguesa ou estrangeira, desde que, neste último caso, tenham obtido equivalência oficial de curso devidamente reconhecida pela Ordem dos Médicos. Daqui resulta que não há qualquer discriminação em razão da nacionalidade, pelo que os direitos de nacionais e estrangeiros são por princípios iguais no acesso e exercício da carreira médica em Portugal (artigo 14º,

---

[61] Assim defendia o advogado-geral Mayras no caso Reyners (cfr. J. M. Coutinho de Abreu & Miguel Gorjão-Henriques, *Livre Circulação de Médicos na Comunidade Europeia e Conhecimentos Linguísticos*, 3 TEMAS DE INTEGRAÇÃO (1998), p. 201).

[62] Regulamento nº 14/2009, da Ordem dos Médicos, Diário da República nº 8, II Série, de 11 de Janeiro de 2009.

[63] Sobre a auto-regulação profissional dos médicos ver Guilherme de Oliveira, *A auto-regulação profissional dos médicos, in* TEMAS DE DIREITO DA MEDICINA (2001).

nº 1 do Código Civil, de ora em diante designado por CC). Dizemos em princípio na medida em que pode ser recusada a inscrição se o cidadão estrangeiro ou nacional, cuja a formação de origem seja num Estado não membro da UE e da Espaço Económico Europeu (Noruega, Islândia e Liechtenstein) e simultaneamente não reconheça idêntica pretensão dos cidadãos nacionais (artigo 14º, nº 2 CC).

Este enquadramento interno exige a verificação da sua compatibilidade em relação às liberdades da União Europeia, não tanto no que diz respeito ao reconhecimento da liberdade da actividade médica, mas na liberdade de estabelecimento e reconhecimento das habilitações médicas, como instrumentos de concretização daqueles. Como resulta da leitura do artigo 9º EOM é reservado à competência da Ordem dos Médicos o poder discricionário de reconhecimento dos cursos lecionados por escolas superiores estrangeiras. Com vista a garantir a liberdade de circulação e estabelecimento, a União Europeia, em 2005, aprovou um nova Directiva, a 2005/36/CE do Parlamento e do Conselho (revogando a Directiva 93/16/CEE), e que foi transposta pela Lei nº 9/2009 de 4 de Março. No entanto e no quadro da directiva torna-se em primeiro lugar decisivo distinguir liberdade de prestação de serviços de liberdade de estabelecimento.

O artigo 45º TFUE estabelece no seu nº 1 o princípio geral da liberdade de circulação dos trabalhadores (implica a abolição, entre os Estados-membros, dos obstáculos à livre circulação de pessoas e de serviços), consagrando uma liberdade fundamental constituinte do mercado interno, atributiva de um direito fundamental[64]. E enquanto tal é uma norma produtora de efeito directo, logo pode ser directamente invocada pelos trabalhadores.

No entanto, esta liberdade pode ser objecto de restrições. Para além das restrições enunciadas no nº 3 do artigo 45º (ordem pública, segurança pública e saúde pública), o nº 4 afasta a liberdade de circulação a respeito dos empregos na administração pública. Ora, a questão que se podia colocar é se um médico ou outro profissional de saúde de nacionalidade estrangeira estaria impedido de concorrer e aceder a um hospital ou unidade de saúde pública integrada no serviço nacional de saúde. Contudo, trata-se de uma falsa questão na medida em que o Tri-

---

[64] Cfr. Acórdão *Unectef c. Heylens*, C-222/86.

DIREITO DA SAÚDE

bunal de Justiça fez prevalecer uma noção funcional de administração pública. No caso Comissão c. Bélgica (C-149/79) o Tribunal considerou que estavam abrangidos na noção de administração pública "os empregos que comportam uma participação, directa ou indirecta, no exercício do poder público em funções que tenham por objecto a salvaguarda de interesses gerais do Estado ou de outras coletividades públicas", o que significa que aos médicos de cidadania europeia é reconhecida a liberdade de circulação e consequente acesso a concursos ou contratação por hospitais públicos[65].

Outro componente essencial do mercado interno é a liberdade de circulação dos serviços (artigo 26º, nº 2 TFUE). Esta liberdade é ambivalente na medida em que se destina aos prestadores e aos destinatários de uma prestação de serviço, desdobrando-se no direito ao estabelecimento (artigo 49º-55º TFUE) e livre prestação de serviços (art. 56º a 62º TFUE). Com vista a assegurar o mercado interno e a eliminar obstáculos à circulação dos respectivos profissionais entre os Estados membros foi aprovada a Directiva 2006/123/CE e Directiva 2005/36/CE.

A respeito do direito de estabelecimento, o artigo 49º TFUE dispõe que a liberdade de exercício deste direito compreende tanto o acesso às actividades não assalariadas e o seu exercício, como a constituição e a gestão de empresas e designadamente de sociedades, na acepção do segundo parágrafo do artigo 54º, nas condições definidas na legislação do país de estabelecimento para os seus próprios nacionais.

As principais notas que caracterizam o direito de estabelecimento são estabilidade e permanência, por oposição à livre prestação de serviços, cujo 57º TFUE refere o carácter temporário da actividade. Esta distinção é de assaz pertinência, porque o direito de estabelecimento vai depender de prévia inscrição e autorização para o exercício da actividade médica em Portugal. Prévia inscrição de que se prescinde no caso da prestação de serviços.

Outra nota relevante é autonomia da liberdade de prestação de serviços face ao direito de estabelecimento: aquela não preclude este, antes pode constituir pressuposto para o mesmo. De acordo com o Acórdão *Gebhard*: "as disposições relativas ao direito de estabelecimento visam o acesso às actividades e ao seu exercício (...). Com efeito, a pertença a

---

[65] Cfr. Abreu & Gorjão-Henriques, TEMAS DE INTEGRAÇÃO, (1998), pp. 205-206.

uma ordem profissional inclui-se nas condições aplicáveis ao acesso às actividades e ao seu exercício e não pode, portanto, ser considerada um elemento constitutivo desse estabelecimento"[66].

Concluindo, nos termos do artigo 52º segundo parágrafo TFUE, a liberdade de estabelecimento é exercida nas condições definidas na legislação do país de estabelecimento para os seus próprios nacionais. A imbricação entre estas liberdades implica, como dispõe os artigos 50º, 52º, nº 2 e 53º, nº 1 TFUE, a coordenação das disposições nacionais relativas ao acesso ou ao exercício das actividades num Estado-membro (53º, nº 1 *in fine* TFUE) e o reconhecimento mútuo dos diplomas, certificados ou outros títulos (artigo 53º, nº 1 1ª parte TFUE). Assume tanto maior importância estes objectivos quando nos centramos nas profissões médicas, (paramédicas e farmacêuticas), na medida em que as directivas são condição prévia para a eliminação progressiva das restrições

De acordo com o caso *Factortame*[67], o direito de estabelecimento *pretende tutelar a prossecução efectiva de uma actividade económica, através da instalação estável noutro Estado-Membro, por período indefinido.*

No que aos médicos diz respeito, a diferença entre estabelecimento, prestação de serviços ou liberdade de circulação será centrada, em termos especiais, com a exigibilidade do reconhecimento de qualificações e inscrição em entidades públicas de que depende o exercício da actividade médica. A relevância do carácter transitório ou pontual da prestação de serviços será determinante para aferir da exigibilidade ou não do reconhecimento de qualificações e da prévia inscrição para exercer a actividade médica. E, neste campo, mais do que a nacionalidade, a relevância prende-se com o reconhecimento de qualificações, quer de formação médica, quer da especialidade feitas num outro Estado-membro que não o de destino.

É pressuposto para este reconhecimento a existência de uma conexão plurilocalizada entre Estados-Membros distintos: Estado de origem distinto do Estado de destino. É esta conexão internacional que, associada à cidadania europeia, justifica a invocação das liberdades comunitárias, mesmo que o interessado seja nacional de um Estado-Membro de destino. Assim foi decidido no caso *Knoors*[68], no qual o TJUE reconhece a

---

[66] Cfr. C-55/94, §31.
[67] Cfr. C-221/89.
[68] Cfr. C-115/78.

DIREITO DA SAÚDE

liberdade de circulação aos próprios nacionais, quando em causa a residência ou sede seja estabelecida em Estado que não o da nacionalidade.

Como vimos, o reconhecimento de habilitações e liberdade de exercício da actividades no sector da saúde, em especial os médicos, farmacêuticos, médicos dentistas estão condicionados à inscrição prévia na respectiva associação profissional, quando a actividade médica seja exercício com carácter duradouro ou permanente, conforme artigo 4º *a contrario* com os artigos 17º e seguintes e 21º e seguintes da Lei nº 9/2009 estando com estes alinhados os artigos 8º e 9º do EOM.

No entanto se a actuação for temporária ou ocasional, o artigo 7º da Directiva e artigos 3º, nº 3 e 4º, nº 1 da Lei nº 9/2009, estipulam que o médico estrangeiro é livre de a exercer no Estado Membro de destino, desde que tenha habilitações reconhecidas no seu país de origem. Atendendo ao teor da lei portuguesa, vale a jurisprudência fixada no Acórdão *Cassis-Dijon*, que o TJUE, através do Acórdão *Van Binsberg*[69], alargou à prestação de serviços. Neste campo este princípio que se o interesse geral invocado é suficientemente protegido por regulamentação nacional de um Estado-Membro de origem equivalente então impõe-se que ocorra o reconhecimento mútuo, pelo que a norma nacional invocada seja *ineficaz*. Exige-se por isso uma estrita proporcionalidade entre o interesse nacional e o interesse comunitário, pelo que a regulamentação nacional não poderá ir para lá do estritamente necessário atendendo ao interesse comunitário do mercado interno e os objectivos por si tutelados. No entanto a liberdade de prestação de serviços, aparentemente sem restrições, pode ser condicionada à prévia comunicação às entidades competentes no Estado-Membro de destino.

É o que sucede quanto aos médicos, onde o médico estrangeiro está obrigado a declarar o local onde serão prestados os serviços médicos, a duração previsível e o início depende, de acordo com o artigo 3º da Directiva e artigos 3º, 4º e 5º do Lei nº 9/2009, da comunicação do exercício da actividade médica em Portugal junto da Ordem dos Médicos. Apesar de não se exigir a inscrição na Ordem dos Médicos e autorização prévia ou inscrição, a natureza e função da actividade médica, pressupõe como précondição para o seu exercício a comunicação prévia. Só não é exigível se se tratar de um caso de urgência, estando o médico obrigado a comunicar

---

[69] Cfr. C-33/74.

posteriormente à prestação de serviços efectuada (artigo 6º Directiva e artigo 4º, nº 4 *in fine* da Lei nº 9/2009).

Só nos casos em que não esteja assegurado o reconhecimento automático se exige que o interessado tenha que comunicar, com uma antecedência mínima de 30 dias, que pretende prestar cuidados de saúde no Estado de destino (6º, nº 6 Lei nº 9/2009). A previsão de mera comunicação mostra que o legislador europeu parte do princípio que uma intervenção na limitação da liberdade de prestação de serviço por necessidade de licença ou de registo ou integrar a ordem dos médicos não seria justificada por considerações de bens gerais ou interesse público, pois todos os modelos de formação médico e desta maneira a qualificação médica tem igual valor. Assim decorre do princípio de mútua confiança, na medida em que se parte da habilitação para exercer a actividade médica no Estado-Membro de origem. Contudo a comunicação permite o exercício dos poderes de fiscalização atribuídos à Ordem dos Médicos, nomeadamente assegurar a qualidade do serviço prestado e licitude da actuação do médico. Tanto mais relevante quando as regras aplicáveis à *legis artis* são as portuguesas (artigos 5º, nº 3 da Directiva e 3º, nº 2 Lei nº 9/2009). A liberdade de exercício não afasta a aplicação imperativa das normas do Estado onde são prestados os cuidados de saúde (artigo 3º, nº 2 da Lei nº 9/2009)[70].

C. Conclusão Intermédia

Como constatámos, a liberdade de circulação pressupõe por um lado uma ideia de garantia de acesso de cuidados de saúde, mas simultaneamente coloca em risco as garantias à liberdade e autonomia pessoal, em especial do paciente, a respeito do consentimento informado. É aliás, ao homenageado Prof. Doutor Guilherme de Oliveira, a quem devemos o grande contributo para o estudo e caracterização da relação médico-paciente e a relevância do consentimento informado[71]. Centrando-nos no carácter transfronteiriço da relação médico-paciente e do regime conflitual do

---

[70] Entretanto a Directiva de 2006 foi alterada pela Directiva 2013/55/UE cujo prazo de transposição termina a 18 de Janeiro de 2016.

[71] Cfr. Oliveira, Estrutura Jurídica do Acto Médico, Consentimento Informado e Responsabilidade Médica. 2005.. Ver ainda ANDRÉ GONÇALO DIAS PEREIRA, DIREITOS DOS PACIENTES E RESPONSABILIDADE MÉDICA (Coimbra Editora. 2015), pp. 397-599 e VERA LÚCIA RAPOSO, DO ATO MÉDICO AO PROBLEMA JURÍDICO (Almedina. 2014). pp. 213-248.

DIREITO DA SAÚDE

consentimento informado, é de notar que a mera deslocação de fronteiras pode significar a incapacidade do paciente para consentir ou soluções mais ou menos paternalistas. Por exemplo, no caso português, a ausência de um representante para cuidados de saúde ou um testamento vital coloca na esfera de decisão do médico muitas vezes a decisão a tomar, quer ao abrigo do instituto do consentimento presumido (artigo 340º, nº 3 do CC 39º do Código Penal) ou da gestão de negócios para actos pessoais (artigo 464º e ss. CC). Ou como no caso da Espanha (artigo 9º da Ley 41/2002) onde, perante a incapacidade do paciente, é atribuída a capacidade decisória à família ou, no caso do Japão, em que tal capacidade é reconhecida ao médico e à família, de acordo com os melhores interesses do paciente[72]. Isto significa que a diversidade cultural, social e consequentemente jurídica não oferece um estatuto unitário do paciente, cabendo por isso ao direito internacional privado assegurar a convergência ou pelo menos a concordância de interesses entre os sujeitos intervenientes no cuidado médico, quer os pacientes, quer os responsáveis pelos cuidados de saúde, quer o próprio interesse público inerente à definição dois limites da autodeterminação do paciente[73].

A evolução é notória. Contudo, a ausência de regulamentação que concretize os direitos do paciente no quadro europeu, deixa ainda grande espaço aos Estados-Membros para concretizar quais os âmbitos de protecção colectivos e individuais.

O consentimento informado apresenta-se como prerrogativa da soberania do paciente sobre a sua esfera pessoal, de que depende a licitude do cuidado médico prestado. Uma decisão que desconsidere os interesses e vontade do paciente estaria assim contrária ao quadro de valores comuns europeus, violando o artigo 8º CEDH[74] e artigo 9º CEDHB[75].

---

[72] Cfr. CRISTIANO VEZZONI, THE LEGAL STATUS AND SOCIAL PRACTICE OF TREATMENT DIRECTIVES IN THE NETHERLANDS (s.n. 2005)., p. 25.

[73] Cfr. Ballarino, YEARBOOK OF PRIVATE INTERNATIONAL LAW, (2006)., pp. 22-23. A respeito do ordenamento espanhol, e com destaca para a regulação autonómica, ver CRISTINA LÓPEZ SÁNCHEZ, TESTAMENTO VITAL Y VOLUNTAD DEL PACIENTE (CONFORME A LA LEY 41/2002, DE 14 DE NOVIEMBRE) (Dykinson. 2003).

[74] Como julgou o TEDH no caso *Pretty*: "In the sphere of medical treatment, the refusal to accept a particular treatment might, inevitably, lead to a fatal outcome, yet the imposition of medical treatment, without the consent of a mentally competent adult patient, would interfere with a person's physical integrity in a manner capable of engaging the rights protected under Article 8 § 1 of the Convention. As recognised in domestic case-law, a person may

Apesar da delimitação do quadro jurídico europeu , não podemos deixar de dar conta da Convenção das Nações Unidas sobre os Direitos das Pessoas com Deficiência que vinculam os Estados-Membros[76]. Em especial o artigo 3º *al.* a) que consagra o direito à autodeterminação, bem como artigo 12º, nº 4, no qual se impõe aos Estados contratantes a obrigação de assegurem "que todas as medidas que se relacionem com o exercício da capacidade jurídica fornecem as garantias apropriadas e efectivas para prevenir o abuso de acordo com o direito internacional dos direitos humanos". Nomeadamente, quanto ao processo de decisão respeitante às esferas de interesse pessoal e patrimonial das pessoas vulneráveis, consagrando o princípio da proporcionalidade enquanto critério de decisão[77].

claim to exercise a choice to die by declining to consent to treatment which might have the effect of prolonging his life", conclui do que "The very essence of the Convention is respect for human dignity and human freedom. Without in any way negating the principle of sanctity of life protected under the Convention, the Court considers that it is under Article 8 that notions of the quality of life take on significance. In an era of growing medical sophistication combined with longer life expectancies, many people are concerned that they should not be forced to linger on in old age or in states of advanced physical or mental decrepitude which conflict with strongly held ideas of self and personal identity" (cfr. (Pretty v. The United Kingdom, 2002), p. 34).

[75] Sobre o direito ao consentimento informado e os direitos fundamentais Negri, The right to informed consent at the Convergence of International Biolaw and International Human Rights Law. 2011, pp. 42-60.

[76] A Convenção foi aprovada e ratificada por Portugal através Resoluções da Assembleia da República nº 56/2009 e nº 57/2009 e Decretos do Presidente da República nº 71/2009 e nº 72/2009. Quase todos Estados-Membros ratificaram a Convenção (até à presente data apenas a Irlanda, Países Baixos e Finlândia não o fizeram). De realçar que no espaço lusófono só não ratificaram até ao momento São Tomé e Príncipe e Timor-Leste. Para a lista completa veja http://www.un.org/disabilities/countries.asp?navid=12&pid=166). De realçar que a própria União Europeia integrou a Convenção na sua estratégia «Estratégia Europeia para a Deficiência 2010-2020» (cfr. EILIONÓIR FLYNN, FROM RHETORIC TO ACTION. IMPLEMENTING THE UN CONVENTION ON THE RIGHTS OF PERSONS WITH DISABILITIES (Cambridge University Press. 2011), pp. 74-76).

[77] Cfr. UNITED NATIONS, FROM EXCLUSION TO EQUALITY. REALIZING THE RIGHTS OF PERSONS WITH DISABILITIES (s.n. 2007). pp. 101-102, FLYNN, From Rhetoric to Action. Implementing the UN Convention on the Rights of Persons with Disabilities. 2011., p. 16. e ANDREAS DIMOPOULOS, ISSUES IN HUMAN RIGHTS PROTECTION OF INTELLECTUALLY DISABLED PERSONS (Ashgate Publishing Limited. 2010), pp. 73-74 .

III. O CONSENTIMENTO INFORMADO: PROBLEMÁTICA DE UMA QUESTÃO PESSOAL TRANSFRONTEIRIÇA

A. Quadro normativo e delimitação do âmbito de eficácia dos instrumentos internacionais, europeus e nacionais

O quadro normativo em vigor em Portugal caracteriza-se pela fragmentariedade de fontes legais, porquanto hoje encontram-se em vigor não só as Regras de Conflitos previstas no Código Civil como também Regulamentos Comunitários, nomeadamente o Regulamento Roma I aplicável às obrigações contratuais e o Regulamento Roma II relativo à lei aplicável às obrigações extracontratuais[78], bem como a Convenção da Haia de 2000 relativa à protecção de adultos.

De realçar, desde já e perante esta complexidade de fontes (nacionais, europeias e internacionais), que a assunção de competências da UE em matéria de direito internacional acaba por desagregar e fraccionar o sistema de DIP interno português na medida em que não procede a uma substituição integral deste[79], isto em especial perante a interpretação do artigo 1º *al.* g) do Roma II, no que diz respeito ao conceito de "direitos de personalidade"[80].

A alteração do Tratado da União, através do Tratado de Amesterdão, reconheceu à União Europeia a competência directa para regulação das questões de direito internacional privado com vista a assegurar a liberdade de circulação dentro do espaço comunitário (artigo 73º-O do Tratado de Amesterdão). Competência que foi confirmada e reforçada com o Tratado de Lisboa na reformulação dada pelo artigo 81º e que passou a fazer parte do Título V do TFUE. Neste foi reforçado o objectivo de realização de um Espaço Europeu Comum que garanta a livre circulação das pessoas e assegure uma protecção jurídica eficaz. Isto coloca problemas em termos metodológicos na interpretação e aplicação dos regulamentos,

---

[78] O Regulamento Roma II entrou em vigor, conforme dispõe os artigos 31º e 32º, em 11 de Janeiro de 2009, aplicando-se regulamento aos factos danosos que ocorram após a entrada em vigor. Isto significa que os factos ocorridos em data anterior, aplica-se o artigo 45º do Código Civil.

[79] Cfr. Fausto Pocar, *La Comunitarizzazione del Diritto Internazionale Privato: una «European Conflict of Laws Revolution»*, XXXVI RIVISTA DI DIRITTO INTERNAZIONALE PRIVATO E PROCESSUALE (2000), p. 883.

[80] Sobre o problema da delimitação do âmbito material do Roma II e a interpretação autónoma do conceito direitos de personalidade ver *infra*.

desde logo pelo risco de frustrarem os objectivos de uma regulamentação que deseja ser uniformemente aplicável em todos os Estados-membros[81].

Posto isto, cabe determinar o âmbito de aplicação dos artigos 25º, 27º, 40º e 45º do CC que regulam o estatuto pessoal, direitos de personalidade, prescrição e caducidade e estatuto delitual face ao âmbito de aplicação dos Regulamentos Roma I e Roma II[82]. As estas normas ainda devem ser acrescentadas, para efeitos de medidas de protecção, a Convenção da Haia sobre a Protecção de Adultos de 2000[83].

B. Delimitação do âmbito de aplicação dos instrumentos. A questão dos direitos de personalidade (artigo 1º, nº 2 al. g) Roma II)

No artigo 1, nº 2, do Regulamento Roma II, conforme já referido, é delimitado o âmbito de aplicação material do Regulamento. Na sua alínea g) é excluído do Regulamento Roma II as violações da reserva da vida privada ou direitos de personalidade. Tal significa que se mantém quanto a estes direitos ou interesses as regras do Código Civil, nomeadamente os artigos 45º e 40º do CC, cuja relevância dependerá dos artigos 25º e 27º do CC.

No entanto não fica respondido o que se entende pelo conceito de direitos de personalidade para efeitos do Roma II. Apegados ao elemento literal e num exegese nacional diríamos que estariam excluídos todos os direitos de personalidade tal como a ordem jurídica portuguesa os qualifica (artigos 70º e ss. CC[84]). Contudo, a ser assim, a depender a interpretação do conceito quadro do direito de cada Estado, estaríamos perante um instrumento comunitário que não alcançaria a uniformização das regras de conflitos. A interpretação deste conceito terá, por isso, que ser

---

[81] Sobre a questão da interpretação e qualificação ver o nosso Geraldo Rocha Ribeiro, *A europeização do direito internacional privado e direito processual internacional: algumas notas sobre o problema da interpretação do âmbito objectivo dos regulamentos comunitários*, 23 Julgar (2014), pp. 269-277.

[82] Sobre os antecedentes históricos à aprovação e entrada em vigor do Roma II ver Jan von Hein, *Of Older Siblings and Distant Cousins: The Contribution of Rome II Regulation to the Communitarisation of Private International Law*, 73 RabelsZ (2009), pp. 463-466.

[83] Para uma exposição sobre a Convenção ver o nosso Geraldo Rocha Ribeiro, *A Convenção de Haia de 2000 relativa à protecção dos Incapazes Adultos*, 32 Revista do Ministério Público (2011).

[84] Cfr. Rabindranath Capelo de Sousa, O Direito Geral de Personalidade (Coimbra Editora. 1995).

realizada de forma autónoma aos direitos internos dos Estados Membro. É esta, aliás, uma exigência do primado do direito da UE e da sua interpretação uniforme[85]. O que significa que o conteúdo e função de direitos de personalidade referidos no artigo 1º, nº 2 *al.* g) Roma II não é equivalente ao conceito de direito de personalidade previsto no artigo 70º, nº 1 do CC. Em particular porque foram razões políticas as que estiveram por detrás desta alínea e não razões substantivas[86].

A interpretação autónoma pressupõe ainda uma caracterização jurídica dos conceitos a partir das concepção individual de cada Estado integrando-os depois no âmbito do ordenamento jurídico comunitário. Mais do que a natureza do conceito de acordo com a *lex fori* ou a *lex causae*, interessa aferir da sua função reconhecida pelos instrumentos jurídicos comunitários e é à luz desta que se circunscreve o chamamento operado por aqueles[87]. Uma vez feita esta operação, o conceito assume um sentido próprio, mas sem que se possa falar de uma independência absoluta, antes uma relação de interdependência do direito da união face aos direitos nacionais. O fim visado é a fixação de conceitos com suficiente abstracção que permitam a adesão dos direitos nacionais e de acordo com uma consciência jurídica geral da europeia. O resultado interpretativo

---

[85] Assim já afirmou e reiterou o TJUE. Veja-se por exemplo, reforçando a jurisprudência, o disposto no Acórdão *Toccani*: "de acordo com jurisprudência assente (...), os conceitos de «matéria contratual» e «matéria extracontratual» (...) devem ser interpretados de forma autónoma, por referência principalmente ao sistema e aos objectivos dessa Convenção de [Bruxelas]. Estes conceitos não podem, portanto, ser entendidos como meras remissões para o direito interno de um ou outro dos Estados contratantes em causa. Com efeito, esta interpretação é a única que permite assegurar a aplicação uniforme da Convenção de Bruxelas, cujo objectivo consiste, designadamente, em uniformizar as regras de competência dos órgãos jurisdicionais dos Estados contratantes e em reforçar a protecção jurídica das pessoas domiciliadas na Comunidade, permitindo simultaneamente ao requerente identificar facilmente o órgão jurisdicional a que se pode dirigir e ao requerido prever razoavelmente aquele perante o qual pode ser demandado" (Cfr. C-344/00, §§19 e 20).
[86] Cfr. Abbo Junker, *Rom II-VO Anwendungsbereich, in* Münchener Kommentar zum Bürgerlichen Gesetzbuch (2015), Anotação ao artigo 1º, Rn. 43.
[87] No fundo está aqui em causa a transposição da posição nacional sobre a operação de qualificação doutrinalmente defendida e a solução legal vertida no nosso artigo 15º do Código Civil. Sobre o problema da qualificação ver, entre outros, Isabel Magalhães Collaço, Da qualificação em Direito Internacional Privado (s.n. 1964), António Arruda Ferrer Correia, Direito Internacional Privado – Alguns problemas (s.n. 4ª reimpressão ed. 1985), pp. 199-243, João Baptista Machado, Lições de Direito Internacional Privado (Almedina. 2002), pp. 102-144.

que se obtenha terá que ser próximo da construção de um conceito de direito comparado validado pelos fins e valores prosseguidos pela União Europeia. Os conceitos terão por isso que ter uma dose de abstracção que lhes confira flexibilidade e operatividade no quadro jurídico da União.

Ainda assim fica por determinar quais os interesses e critérios normativos que permitem aferir qual o âmbito de aplicação do Roma II, dito de outra forma, qual é o objecto de regulação das regras de conflito do Roma II quando estejam em causa interesses intrínsecos à esfera pessoal do lesado. Para isso é necessário, atender, no caso particular, à discussão do processo legislativo a respeito da alínea g) e a polémica entre a protecção da liberdade de expressão e liberdade de impressa que levaram à sua consagração[88].

Os direitos de personalidade resultam da manifestação da personalidade individual das pessoas, pelo que seria natural a sua integração nas matérias ditas pertencerem ao estatuto pessoal[89]. Contudo, se se aceita a sua integração com vista à existência e determinação do direito de personalidade na esfera jurídica privada, já a sua tutela e garantias deslocam o centro do problema para o estatuto da responsabilidade. Há particularidades, nas várias dimensões da personalidade, que levam a uma consideração distinta em sede de protecção desses direitos e lei aplicável aos mesmos. A autonomia do conceito pressupõe não só a construção de um conceito operacional e com suficiente plasticidade para integrar as dife-

---

[88] Ver *inter alia* ANDREW DICKINSON, THE ROMA II REGULATION. THE LAW APPLICABLE TO NON--CONTRACTUAL OBLIGATIONS *(1ª Reimpressão ed. 2013)*, pp. 234-240. Como nota este autor a discussão e sensibilidade da matéria levou à reformulação da proposta inicial da Comissão, tanto mais que aquando do Tratado de Amesterdão os Estados-Membros a ele vinculados emitiram uma Declaração onde "as medidas adoptadas em aplicação do artigo 73º-M [*actual artigo 81º do TFUE*] do Tratado que institui a Comunidade Europeia não impedirão que os Estados-Membros apliquem as suas normas constitucionais em matéria de liberdade de imprensa e de liberdade de expressão noutros meios de comunicação social." (cfr. Id. at., p. 234). Entre nós ver LUÍS DE LIMA PINHEIRO, DIREITO INTERNACIONAL PRIVADO. DIREITO DE CONFLITOS. PARTE ESPECIAL § II (Almedina 3ª Edição Refundida ed. 2014), pp. 389--390, Elsa Dias Oliveira, *Algumas considerações sobre a responsabilidade civil extracontratual por violação de direitos de personalidade em Direito Internacional Privado*, 5 CUADERNOS DE DERECHO TRANSNACIONAL (2013); PINHEIRO, Direito Internacional Privado. Direito de Conflitos. Parte Especial. 2014.

[89] Cingimo-nos às pessoas singulares atento o objecto do nosso trabalho. No entanto as considerações aqui tecidas serão extensíveis, com as devidas adaptações às pessoas colectivas, atenta a natureza conflitual da nossa abordagem.

rentes regulações nacionais, como a sua interpretação conforme os interesses pressupostos na regulação europeia e respectivas finalidades.

Olhando para a proposta inicial da Comissão Europeia, em particular para o artigo 6º e a discussão que se seguiu e desembocou na *al.* g) do nº 2 do artigo 1º Roma II, podemos mesmo concluir uma forte ligação entre o conceito direitos de personalidade e o artigo 8º da CEDH e a criação de um meta-conceito de direitos de personalidade especial[90] ou, pelo menos, um alinhamento entre o conteúdo e função dos direitos de personalidade e o direito fundamental consagrado no artigo 8º. Como nota ANDREW DICKINSON, a ligação restringe-se, em parte por força do argumento histórico, às dimensões aos direitos à honra e reserva da vida privada associados com as liberdades de impressa e de expressão e à protecção de dados[91]. Pelo que se deve fazer uma leitura limitada destes direitos tomando ainda por referência outras disposições do Conselho da Europa, ainda que de *soft law* ou as denominadas normas-narrativas, como a Resolução da Assembleia Parlamentar do Conselho da Europa nº 1165 de 26 de Junho de 1998, relativa ao direito à privacidade das pessoas públicas.

Neste sentido, conjuntamente com a própria discussão inerente ao processo legislativo de aprovação do Roma II, é comum interpretar direitos de personalidade como dizendo respeito à honra, intimidade e dados pessoais (neste sentido o artigo 30º, nº 2 Roma II). Interesses cujos limites e âmbito de protecção podem chocar com a liberdade de impressa e de expressão e cuja proteção depende em exclusivo da tutela jurisdicional. São direitos, acompanhando ABARCA JUNCO, cuja relevância jurídica só se verifica quando são lesados, por isso carecendo de *conteúdo positivo*[92].

Acabam, dentro do conceito-quadro assim delimitado, por bulir com a reserva de soberania dos Estados-Membros, em especial as liberdades de imprensa e expressão, bem como questões respeitantes à reserva da

---

[90] Entre nós ver ELSA DIAS OLIVEIRA, DA RESPONSABILIDADE CIVIL EXTRACONTRATUAL POR VIOLAÇÃO DE DIREITOS DE PERSONALIDADE EM DIREITO INTERNACIONAL PRIVADO (Almedina. 2011), pp. 235-236.

[91] Cfr. DICKINSON, The Roma II Regulation. The Law Applicable to Non-Contractual Obligations. 2013, pp. 239-240.

[92] Cfr. ALFONSO-LUIS CALVO CARAVACA & JAVIER CARRASCOSA GONZÁLEZ, LAS OBLIGACIONES EXTRACONTRACTUALES EN DERECHO INTERNACIONAL PRIVADO: EL REGLAMENTO "ROMA II" (Comares. 2008), p. 187.

vida privada, ou seja, interesses associados aos *delitos de imprensa*[93]. Para estes mantêm-se em vigor os artigos 40º e 45º CC. Isto significa que a exclusão dos direitos de personalidade, tal como são configurados na alínea g) do artigo 1º, nº 2, é feita em função da origem da violação ou possível violação de interesses, servindo esta como causa de pedir (ou objecto do pedido) e consequente delimitação material de competência.

Destarte estarão incluídos no âmbito matéria do Roma II as violações à integridade física e vida[94], assim como estão incluídas, no que ao objecto do presente trabalho diz respeito, violações à saúde do paciente, mas igualmente a responsabilidade por violação do dever de informação e regras sobre consentimento informado.

Em síntese, ressalvadas as questões das bases de dados que serão relevantes em termos de regras sobre os processos clínicos e para as quais se mantém em vigor o artigo 45º CC, a sede da responsabilidade médica em termos de direito internacional privado será feita à luz das regras de conflitos do Regulamento Roma II (e também Roma I, quando exista uma relação contratual).

C. Particularidades metodológicas. A dépeçage e a questão prévia

No presente trabalho apenas trataremos do problema da lei aplicável e delimitação do estatuto pessoal, delitual e negocial face às especificidades da relação jurídica de cuidados de saúde a respeito do consentimento informado e seu suprimento. Não iremos tratar por isso de questões respeitantes à competência jurisdicional, nem propriamente das relações contratuais ou legais emergentes dos cuidados de saúde no que toca à tutela de interesses jurídicos como vida, integridade física e saúde. Limi-

---

[93] Cfr. Junker, Rom II-VO Anwendungsbereich. 2015., Rn 43 e ANNA-LUISA LEMMERZ, DIE PATIENTENVERFÜGUNG: AUTONOMIE UND ANKNÜPFUNGSGERECHTIGKEIT (Mohr Siebeck. 2014)., p. 162. Este é aliás a interpretação defendida entre nós por Elsa Dias Oliveira e Lima Pinheiro, ainda que com argumentos diferentes, para aquela autora trata-se da concretização da interpretação autónoma, enquanto que para este último deveria ser feita uma interpretação restritiva do conceito de direitos de personalidade. No entanto, como aponta Elsa Dias Oliveira a interpretação restritiva partiria do pressupostos entre a identidade dos conceitos previstos no regulamento com a *lex causae*, no caso a portuguesa (Cfr. OLIVEIRA, Da Responsabilidade Civil Extracontratual por Violação de Direitos de Personalidade em Direito Internacional Privado 2011., pp. 224-240, em especial p. 225. Ver ainda PINHEIRO, Direito Internacional Privado. Direito de Conflitos. Parte Especial. 2014., pp. 389-390).

[94] *Vide* considerandos nº 17, 30 e 33 do Roma II.

DIREITO DA SAÚDE

tar-nos-emos portanto a enquadrar juridicamente o direito à autodeterminação, em especial o consentimento informado, e consequências em sede de tutela da mesma quando os cuidados de saúde pressuponham o contacto com mais do que um ordenamento jurídico[95].

Uma das notas que caracteriza o actual método conflitual é a sua especialização. Desta resulta a fragmentariedade das regras de conflito e a adopção de um sistema analítico da situação jurídica plurilocalizada. Atendendo aos interesses que subjazem as relações jurídicas de direito privado e os fins de DIP (segurança e estabilidade das relações jurídicas) a especialização das regras de conflito oferecem a certeza (pelo menos assim é o intento do legislador) de que a lei que regula a situação jurídica seja, conforme as suas diferentes componentes, a adequada. Todavia, desta opção pode resultar a aplicação de mais do que uma lei à mesma situação e desta forma potenciar o risco de existirem contradições normativas da solução material ao caso concreto[96].

Não podemos contudo confundir o desmembramento resultante da especialização das regras de conflito com o problema da questão prévia ou da referência pressuponente[97]. Esta, segundo BAPTISTA MACHADO, refere-se "àquele tipo de hipóteses em que, segundo um dado direito material, a preexistência, a constituição, a admissibilidade ou a extinção duma situação jurídica (situação jurídica condicionante) repercute certas consequências sobre o conteúdo, a admissibilidade, a constituição, modificação ou extinção doutra situação jurídica (situação jurídica condicionada)"[98]. O problema centra-se por isso na determinação dos

---

[95] No entanto não podemos deixar de realçar a relevância, em sede de competência jurisdicional, Bruxelas I, em especial a sua jurisprudência (aqui se incluindo também a Convenção de Bruxelas) a respeito da distinção entre obrigação contratual e não contratual.

[96] Cfr. António Arruda Ferrer Correia, *O Novo Direito Internacional Privado Português*, *in* ESTUDOS VÁRIOS DE DIREITO (1982), p. 13.

[97] Sobre esta ver, *inter alia*, Paul Lagarde, *La Règle de conflit applicable aux questions préalables*, REVUE CRITIQUE DE DROIT INTERNATIONAL PRIVÉ (1960), FERNANDO M. AZEVEDO MOREIRA, DA QUESTÃO PRÉVIA EM DIREITO INTERNACIONAL PRIVADO (s.n. 1968), Allan Ezra Gotlieb, *Incidental Question Revisited – Theory and Practice in the Conflict of Laws*, 26 INTERNATIONAL & COMPARATIVE LAW QUARTERLY (1977), JOÃO BAPTISTA MACHADO, ÂMBITO DE EFICÁCIA E ÂMBITO DE COMPETÊNCIAS DAS LEIS (Almedina. 1998), pp. ; 315-374. Mais recentemente CARMEN CHRISTINA BERNITT, DIE ANKNÜPFUNG VON VORFRAGEN IM EUROPÄISCHEN KOLLISIONSRECHT (Mohr Siebeck. 2010).

[98] Cfr. MACHADO, Lições de Direito Internacional Privado. 2002., p. 108.

efeitos jurídicos de que depende a outra situação jurídica, não se con-
fundindo com as situações em que uma situação condicionante integra
a hipótese legal da situação condicionada. Continuando a acompanhar
este autor, temos que distinguir entre a aplicação do direito estrangeiro
como *pressupostos de regulamentação* (verdadeira questão pressuponente)
das situações em que se tratem de *critérios de regulamentação*, pois neste
caso o que está em causa é a aplicação do *direito a quo* e não *ad quem*[99].
Resumindo, o problema centra-se na interpretação da norma material
reguladora da questão dita principal[100].

O carácter prejudicial da situação condicionante deve conservar a sua
autonomia ou ser consumido pela *lex causae* da situação condicionada?[101]
Seja qual for a resposta é indiscutível que o problema da questão prévia
se centra na interpretação da norma material prejudicial à situação condicionada. Serão três os requisitos para estarmos perante uma questão
prévia: a questão principal é regulada por uma lei estrangeira; a situação
condicionante tem que ter foros de autonomia e susceptível de se determinar a lei competente, as regras de conflito do foro determinam a
aplicação de um lei diferente da que regula a questão condicionada[102].

Na prática, e no que diz respeito ao nosso objecto do presente trabalho, os diferentes estatutos que regulam uma mesma situação jurídica
podem determinar a aplicação de leis diferentes. Antecipando algumas
considerações *infra* avançadas, veremos que o reconhecimento e exercício do direito de autodeterminação e a incapacidade serão regulados pelo
artigo 25º, 27º e 30º CC, o artigo 36º CC regula a forma das directivas
antecipadas, os meios de protecção serão regulados pela Convenção de
2000[103], os deveres de informação e outras prestação de natureza contratual pelo Regulamento Roma I, e a tutela delitual pelo Regulamento
Roma II. A isto acresce a possibilidade de reconhecimento de directivas
antecipadas à luz do artigo 31º, nº 2 CC.

---

[99] Cfr. João Baptista Machado, Âmbito de Eficácia e Âmbito de Competência das Leis
(Limites das Leis e Conflitos de Leis) (Almedina Reimpressão ed. 1998), p. 315.

[100] Cfr. Albert Ehrenzweig, Private International Law (A.W. Sijthoff. 1967), p. 169 ss

[101] Cfr. Machado, Lições de Direito Internacional Privado. 2002., pp. 288-289. Para um visão
histórica sobre o problema da questão prévia ver Gotlieb, International & Comparative
Law Quarterly, (1977).

[102] Cfr. Gotlieb, International & Comparative Law Quarterly, (1977), p. 737.

[103] Que se espera que entre em vigor muito em breve tendo em conta a data da ratificação pelo
Estado Português: Decreto do Presidente da República nº 44/2014 de 19 de Junho.

DIREITO DA SAÚDE

Daqui resulta a distribuição de competências entre possíveis leis competentes chamadas por diferentes regras de conflitos, quer quanto ao seu conceito-quadro, quer quanto à sua origem (nacional, convencional ou comunitária). E desta aplicação distributiva pode advir a aplicação de soluções materiais cujo resultado seja incompatível e antinómico, portanto inconciliável nos seus pressupostos e efeitos. Como também pode suceder que, perante os mecanismos de flexibilização previstos, p. ex. cláusulas de excepção (artigo 4º, nº 3 Roma II), se promova a unidade da regulação através de aplicação de uma lei em conexão com situação que regule todos os aspectos da situação jurídica plurilocalizada. É neste ponto que nos encontramos, em particular quanto à qualificação do consentimento. Em especial porque a possibilidade de ser invocada uma conexão autónoma a um determinada parte da situação plurilocalizada através do funcionamento da cláusula excepção prescrita no nº 3 do artigo 4º não é admitida. Não é possível o fraccionamento dos elementos da situação jurídica que se reportem ao estatuto delitual (*issue-to-issue*). O Regulamento impõe a regulação unitária por um única lei do âmbito das questões suscitadas pelo estatuto delitual (artigo 15º)[104].

Contudo, mesmo que tenha sucesso a unificação da lei aplicável a uma situação plurilocalizada, continuarão a existir situações que não se encontram abrangidas pelo estatuto delitual, em especial as questões referentes às normas de aplicação necessária e imediata (artigo 16º) e regras de segurança e de conduta (artigo 17º), para além das questões prévias, entre elas, as inerentes às relações de família (responsabilidades parentais, p.ex.) e cuidado de adultos (representação legal ou voluntária)[105]. A existência, extensão e limitações destes direitos é também regida pela

---

[104] O Conselho rejeitou a proposta do Parlamento Europeu de permitir a *dépeçage* quanto ao funcionamento da cláusula de excepção (cfr.). Ver Hein, Rabelsz, (2009), p. 483 e Dickinson, The Roma II Regulation. The Law Applicable to Non-Contractual Obligations. 2013, p. 342. Não obstante a versão final, não deixa de existir um instrumento de flexibilização com vista a *corrigir* o resultado que decorre do normal funcionamento das regras de conflitos. É no fundo um instrumento corrector que visa equilibrar a tensão entre *law making* e *law application* (cfr. Peter Hay, Flexibility versus Predictability and Uniformity in Choice of Law: Reflections on Current European and United States Conflict Law § 226 (Martinus Nijhoff Publishers. 1992), p. 221).

[105] Numa posição crítica da rigidez das normas do Roma II Symeon C. Symeonides, *Rome II and Tort Conflicts: A Missed Opportunity*, 56 American Journal of Comparative Law (2008). pp. 184-186.

O CUIDADO MÉDICO TRANSFRONTEIRIÇO E O CONSENTIMENTO INFORMADO ...

lei pessoal, sendo esta que define se o bem jurídico personalidade humana é tutelável ou não antes do nascimento (artigo 27º do CC). No entanto, e no que às formas de tutela diz respeito, apenas se admitem aquelas que foram reconhecidas pela lei portuguesa, quer procedimentais, quer processuais (pense-se na figura dos *punitive damages* que não é reconhecida pelo direito português e pela maior parte dos direitos continentais[106]), artigo 27º, nº 2 ss. CC. Contudo, e como vimos, as consequências da violação destes direitos são regidas pela lei indicada pelo artigo 45º CC (para os direitos de personalidade referidos no artigo 1º, nº 2 *al.* g) do Roma II) e Roma II, atinente à responsabilidade civil extracontratual[107].

D. Conclusão Intermédia

O quadro metodológico actual do DIP encontra-se em franca ebulição, em especial porque carece o direito de conflitos europeu de uma parte geral uniforme que agregue as suas normas e assegure a uniformidade na sua aplicação. Aparentemente continua a caber a cada Estado-Membro o método de aplicação das regras de conflitos, nomeadamente quanto à qualificação propriamente dita, à questão prévia, à condição do direito estrangeiro e ao efeitos da excepção de ordem pública internacional[108].

No entanto, mesmo sem parte geral, um princípio regulador das relações plurilocalizadas será a paridade de tratamento das diferentes ordens jurídicas que integram a UE. Este princípio significa que tanto a lei do foro como a lei estrangeira têm de ser tratadas no mesmo plano de igualdade, ou seja a lei estrangeira tem que ter o mesmo tratamento e valor que a lei do foro. Logo, o direito da união deve conceber o sistema como autónomo que prima sobre o direito nacional, não impondo diferenciação formal entre estes, mas assumindo-se como meio de impor interesses

---

[106] Aliás a obrigação de indemnização, quer nos fundamentos, quer no quantum pode encontrar limites em termos de ordem pública internacional prevista nos artigos 26º e 32º Roma II (cfr. ANABELA SUSANA DE SOUSA GONÇALVES, DA RESPONSABILIDADE EXTRACONTRATUAL EM DIREITO INTERNACIONAL PRIVADO (Almedina. 2013)., pp. 388-389). 107 Cfr. MACHADO, Lições de Direito Internacional Privado. 2002., pp. 343-344 e 375-376. [108] Cfr. CLEMENS TRAUTMANN, EUROPÄISCHES KOLLISIONSRECHT UND AUSLÄNDISCHES RECHT IM NATIONALEN ZIVILVERFAHREN (Mohr Siebeck. 2011)., p. 411 e Ribeiro, JULGAR, (2014), pp. 270-272.

DIREITO DA SAÚDE

e políticas próprias que se sobrepõe aos interesses individuais de cada Estado-membro[109].

Os problemas que se colocam a respeito do consentimento informado, veremos, prendem-se com a concretização da obrigação de informação, justificação do cuidado médico, e desta feita da concretização da ilicitude ou culpa.

IV. Lei aplicável às causas de justificação: o consentimento informado

A. Lei pessoal versus estatuto delitual

Na senda da escola estatutária holandesa, estatuto diz respeito a um conjunto unitário de matérias que se pretendem que sejam reguladas pela mesma lei. O conjunto de matérias jurídicas, quando falamos de estatuto pessoal, dizem respeito ao foro pessoal, à intimidade da pessoa. Por dizerem respeito à pessoa, as exigências de *estabilidade* e *permanência* das situações jurídicas plurilocalizadas é mais intensa do que em quaisquer outras situações[110]. Assim, não só há particular cuidado na escolha da conexão relevante – a conexão mais próxima da pessoa – como se pretende que este conjunto de matérias seja tendencialmente regulado por uma só lei com vista a garantir unidade e coerência na regulamentação do estatuto pessoal[111]. Para além destes valores, decorre ainda a necessidade de

[109] Segundo Baptista Machado, cujas considerações são transmutáveis para o direito europeu de conflitos há um "princípio geral de direito, imanente a todos os ordenamentos jurídicos positivos: o princípio da tutela das expectativas legítimas, emanação directa daquela função essencial do direito que é a de estabilizar expectativas, garantindo a previsibilidade necessária aos planos de vida de cada um e a uma ordem de convivência operativa" (cfr. João Baptista Machado, *Contributo da Escola de Coimbra para a Teoria do Direito Internacional Privado*, 59 Boletim da Faculdade de Direito da Universidade de Coimbra (1985), p. 163).

[110] Assim nos diz Nuno Ascensão Silva quando fala no estatuto pessoal, apesar de todas as suas variações de sentido e conteúdo que possa assumir nos diferentes sistemas jurídicos, como resultado da "crença ma existência de um conjunto unitário de matérias ou questões – todas àquelas intimamente ligadas ao indivíduo – que deverão ser submetidas à aplicação de uma *lei constante, única e que as pessoas sintam como sua de modo a assegurar a permanência do seu estatuto individual e relacional* no contexto das relações plurilocalizadas", sublinhado nosso (cfr. Nuno Ascensão Silva, *Do Estatuto Pessoal – Unidade e Dispersão (Algumas notas a propósito da comemoração dos 35 anos do Código Civil), in* Comemorações dos 35 anos do Código Civil e dos 25 da Reforma de 1977 (2006), p. 552).

[111] O estatuto pessoal relaciona-se com a necessidade de determinação de uma lei pessoal, "cujos preceitos e permissões formem como que a «magna charta» dos direitos civis

garantir a harmonia jurídica interna, com vista a evitar desarticulações ou incoerências resultantes do desmembramento da regulação das situações plurilocalizadas. Pretende-se atribuir ao estatuto pessoal uma vocação universal com vista a garantir a necessária continuidade da lei aplicável relativa à pessoa enquanto tal.

As exigências na regulamentação unitária das matérias que integram o estatuto pessoal não são todavia encontradas na definição e configuração deste conceito, o que compromete as finalidades de estabilidade e previsibilidade pretendidas. Não só pela diferente opção em termos de conexão relevante (nacionalidade ou residência habitual), como na própria identificação das matérias que compõem o estatuto pessoal. No ordenamento jurídico português, o conceito de estatuto pessoal encontra-se definido de forma ampla no artigo 25º CC, que o define pela enunciação do âmbito das matérias que são regidas pela lei pessoal, sejam elas atinentes ao estado individual ou à esfera relacional da pessoa[112]. O mesmo abrange as questões relativas do "estado dos indivíduos, capacidade das pessoas, as relações de família e as sucessões por morte".

O âmbito de uma regulação global das matérias que recaem no estatuto pessoal é, porém, limitada a uma função residual pela decorrência da especialização das regras de conflitos quanto a particulares matérias jurídicas[113]. Não só sucede quanto à regulação material das mesmas, como às questões de forma a elas relacionadas, pautando-se por finalidades que não apenas a ideia de regulação pela lei mais próxima, mas antes com vista à validação dos actos, dando relevo à *lex loci actum*, utilizando-se conexões

do indivíduo – uma espécie de passaporte, em que todos os Estados da comunidade internacional se obriguem a pôr o visto" (cfr. António Arruda Ferrer Correia, *Unidade do estatuto pessoal*, XXX Boletim da Faculdade de Direito da Universidade de Coimbra (1954), pp. 107-108).

[112] Cfr. Rui Manuel Moura Ramos, *Linhas Gerais da evolução do Direito Internacional Privado Português posteriormente ao Código Civil de 1966, in* Comemorações dos 35 anos do Código Civil e dos 25 anos da Reforma de 1977: A Parte Geral do Código e a Teoria Geral do Direito Civil (2006)., p. 509; Dário Moura Vicente, *Lei pessoal das pessoas singulares, in* Direito Internacional Privado. Ensaios (2002). e id. at; Silva, Do Estatuto Pessoal – Unidade e Dispersão (Algumas notas a propósito da comemoração dos 35 anos do Código Civil). 2006.

[113] Cfr. António Arruda Ferrer Correia, Lições de Direito Internacional Privado (s.n. 1969). p. 770 e Silva, *Do Estatuto Pessoal – Unidade e Dispersão (Algumas notas a propósito da comemoração dos 35 anos do Código Civil). 2006*, p. 583, n. 104. Veja-se a título de exemplo, os artigos 26º, 27º, 30º, 47º, 52º, 53º, 62º CC.

DIREITO DA SAÚDE

múltiplas alternativas como sucede no artigo 36º CC. Conforme já verificamos, será no quadro do Roma II que determinaremos a lei aplicável ao estatuto delitual e não o artigo 45º CC[114].

De acordo com o artigo 4º, nº 1 Roma II, a lei competente para regular o estatuto delitual é o lugar do dano[115], ao contrário do que se verifica no artigo 45º, nº 1 CC (lugar da conduta). Será competente a lei do Estado onde se verificou o dano, independentemente, do Estado onde se verificou o facto lesivo ou onde se verificaram as consequências indirectas. Todavia apesar da aparente diferença, em termos práticos, o artigo 4º, nº 1 refere-se ao *dano directo* e nesta medida tenderá corresponderá ao lugar da conduta causadora do dano[116]. Isto significa, portanto, que as ofensas à pessoa ou património coincidirão entre o facto lesivo e o dano daí resultante[117]. Neste sentido a noção adoptada pelo Roma II acaba por ser coincidente com a avançada por BAPTISTA MACHADO: "quando tenhamos que aplicar o nº 2 do art. 45º, atenderemos, portanto, ao 'lugar da lesão' (...) pelo menos quando possa entender-se que nesse lugar ocorreu um primeiro dano"[118].

Posto isto e tendo em consideração o artigo 15º Roma II, verificamos que existe um paralelo com o conceito-quadro do artigo 45º CC, ao estarem integrados no estatuto delitual de ambos todas as questões respei-

---

[114] Será também o Roma II a regular a relação jurídica de gestão de negócios no âmbito de prestação de cuidados de saúde. Sobre a obrigação de prestar cuidados de saúde em situações plurilocalizadas em casos de emergência ver o *Landgericht Görlitz* (cfr. *LG Görlitz: Grenzüberschreitender Einsatz eines Notarztes*, in Medizinrecht, 23. Jahrgang, Heft 3, März 2005, pp. 172-173) que concluiu que não existe uma obrigação internacional de prestação de cuidados de saúde do médico fora do Estado onde exerce a actividade médica (o caso envolvia um médico com sede na Alemanha e um paciente localizado na Polónia). O tribunal não condenou o médico por omissão de prestação de cuidados de saúde com o argumento de que, tratando-se de uma actividade *pública*, não existe nenhuma obrigação para actuar para lá das fronteiras do Estado onde o médico exerce a sua actividade médica (cfr. LEMMERZ, Die Patientenverfügung: Autonomie und Anknüpfungsgerechtigkeit. 2014.p. 160).

[115] Cfr.Junker, Rom II-VO Anwendungsbereich. 2015., anotação ao artigo 4º, Rn. 3 e 4, Luís de Lima Pinheiro, *Choice of Law on Non-contractual Obligations between Communitarization and Globalization. A First Assessment of EC Regulation Rome II*, XLIV RIVISTA DI DIRITTO INTERNAZIONALE PRIVATO E PROCESSUALE (2008), p. 17, Hein, RABELSZ, (2009), p. 475.

[116] Cfr. Gerhard Wagner, *Die neue Rom-II-Verordnung*, IPRAX (2008). P. 4 e Oliveira, CUADERNOS DE DERECHO TRANSNACIONAL, (2013). p. 150.

[117] *Vide* Considerando 17.

[118] Cfr. MACHADO, Lições de Direito Internacional Privado. 2002., p. 372.

tantes concretização da ilicitude, dos direitos e interesses tutelados e das formas de violação contra as quais são tutelados, enquanto concretizadores do pressuposto da ilicitude[119], formas de violação[120], imputabilidade[121], culpa[122], nexo de causalidade entre facto e dano, modalidades de indemnização, titularidade, transmissibilidade e prescrição do direito de indemnização, taxa de juro, etc. Integram ainda o estatuto delitual as causas de justificação por dizerem respeito à determinação do desvalor jurídico do facto danoso, desde que não qualificáveis como questões prévias (p.ex. decorrentes da relação de família). A conexão relevante será por isso a referente ao local do resultado da actuação delitual quanto ao consentimento actual. Desta forma, face à normal coincidência local da conduta-local do dano acautela-se o regime unitário da responsabilidade, evitando o reconhecimento de um privilégio unilateral do lesado por referência à conexão pessoal deste.

No que diz respeito à responsabilidade médica, no caso de um erro de tratamento, a lei competente corresponderá ao país onde o cuidado de saúde prestado produziu o dano de saúde ao paciente por ofensa à sua integridade ou vida. No caso de se tratar de uma omissão, o local do dano corresponderá ao país onde foi violado o interesse jurídico para cuja protecção existiu uma obrigação de evitar o resultado danoso[123]. Já quanto à violação do consentimento informado, não estaremos a falar propriamente de um dano à integridade física e saúde, pelo que se podem colocar questões sobre se o dano resulta da violação do dever de informação ou se as repercussões lesivas por causa da incorrecta informação. Tendo em conta a noção de dano directo, a lei competente corresponderá ao local onde foi realizada a intervenção ilícita e não o local onde se encon-

---

[119] No entanto a existência do direito deverá ser regulado autonomamente e à luz do estatuto pessoal (artigos 25º e 27º do CC), podendo contudo os direitos serem reconhecidos a título de norma de aplicação necessária e imediata ou por efeito positivo da ordem pública internacional (artigos 16º e 26º do Roma II).

[120] Pode ser por factos ilícitos, objectiva ou pelo sacrifício.

[121] aqui não se trata de *capacidade* em sentido próprio, mas sim de um elemento integrante do regime de responsabilidade, que por isso deve ser regulado por este estatuto, e não p.ex. pela lei pessoal determinada com base no art. 25º).

[122] As presunções de culpa, tal como as encontramos nos arts. 491º, 492º e 493º CC, apesar de serem regras respeitantes à repartição do ónus da prova, materialmente integram o regime da responsabilidade civil extracontratual.

[123] Cfr. Junker, Rom II-VO Anwendungsbereich. 2015., anotação à §40, Rn 26.

DIREITO DA SAÚDE

tra o profissional de saúde que violou o dever de informação. Partindo da regra de que todos os cuidados de saúde pressupõem uma relação de imediação ou presencial, haverá coincidência entre o local do dano e o local onde foi violado o dever de informação. Contudo podem existir situações em que o delito se dispersa espacialmente entre o facto desencadeador do dano (lesão) e o dano *per se*. Serão os casos, por exemplo, de recurso a serviços de telemedicina transfronteiriça, no qual o delito se qualifica como sendo delito à distância[124-125]. Sendo certo que a possibilidade de unificação do estatuto delitual e concretização da proximidade de um lei ao delito através do funcionamento da cláusula de excepção não está aberto ao recurso de critérios de justiça material.

Já poderá ser relevante, a exigibilidade ou previsibilidade do autor do dano contar com a aplicação de um lei distinta que não a do local da con-

---

[124] Sobre o regime da responsabilidade nos casos de telemedicina ver Gerfried Fischer, *Ärztliche Verhaltenspflichten und anzuwendendes Recht bei grenzüberschreitender telemedizinischer Behandlung*, in HUMANIORA MEDIZIN – RECHT – GESCHICHTE. FESTSCHRIFT FÜR ADOLF LAUFS ZUM 70. GEBURTSTAG (Bernd-Rüdiger Kern, et al. eds., 2006). e CHRISTOPH WENDELSTEIN, KOLLISIONSRECHTLICHE PROBLEME DER TELEMEDIZIN: ZUGLEICH EIN BEITRAG ZUR KOORDINATION VON VERTRAG UND DELIKT AUF DER EBENE DES EUROPÄISCHEN (Mohr Siebeck GmbH & Co. K. 2012).

[125] Um caso interessante discutido pelo BGH em 2008 a respeito da violação do dever de informação refere-se aos riscos de um medicamento receitado na Suíça, tendo o paciente tomado o mesmo no país da sua residência, a Alemanha, aí se verificando o dano para a saúde e integridade física. Isto apesar da discussão se ter centrado na determinação da competência internacional à luz do artigo 5º, nº 3 da Convenção de Lugano. Contudo este caso traz consigo algumas dificuldades em termos de qualificação. Isto porque a relevância jurídica do facto, seja ilícito ou não, será determinado à luz do local onde ocorreu o dano, o que significa que o enquadramento de facto pode revelar-se diferente. Por exemplo, no direito italiano a violação do consentimento informado diz respeito à tutela dos interesses vida e integridade física, por oposição à concepção portuguesa. O mesmo sucede com o direito alemão, onde no caso acima citado o BGH concluiu que a violação do dever de esclarecimento se qualifica como uma lesão da integridade física ou da saúde. No entanto a relevância jurídica dos factos dependerá sempre da esfera de competência determinada pela *lex causae* e com respeito à adequação da conexão eleita. O que significa que as considerações a respeito da fixação da competência jurisdicional serão autónomas à da lei competente para regular a substância da situação, estando as primeiras dependentes muito mais das alegações produzidas pelas partes. Sobre o caso discutido pelo BGH ver LEMMERZ, Die Patientenverfügung: Autonomie und Anknüpfungsgerechtigkeit. 2014, p. 161. Sobre o acórdão de 27.5.2008 do BGH ver *NJW*, pp. 2344-2345.

O CUIDADO MÉDICO TRANSFRONTEIRIÇO E O CONSENTIMENTO INFORMADO ...

duta[126]. Podem por isso valer as considerações sobre a condição de previsibilidade feitas a respeito da aplicação da lei do dano, artigo 45º, nº 2 CC, contudo aqui quanto ao local da conduta. No fundo estar-se-ia, em sede de correcção do funcionamento dos nºs 1 e 2 do artigo 4º Roma II, com vista a obter um concordância prática de interesses entre a previsibilidade da lei aplicável e a tutela do lesado, fazendo daquela uma "condição material da competência da lei deste país", CASTELLO-BRANCO BASTOS[127] em sede de justiça formal do DIP[128]. No fundo seria estabelecer uma ligação entre a responsabilidade e as regras de conduta com o autor deve pautar o seu comportamento. Assegurando-se desta forma uma unidade entre regras de conduta e regras de decisão[129] ou entre *conduct-regulating rules e loss-distribution rules*[130]. Aliás a escolha da conexão adequada pressupõe a existência de proximidade com a lei aplicável e não mera ocasionalidade, o que muitas vezes pode suceder ao se considerar exclusivamente a lei do local da conduta[131].

No entanto o próprio Regulamento abre excepções à lei do local do dano. Quer por base numa ligação mais estreita assente na residência habitual comum do autor do facto e lesado à data do facto (artigo 4º, nº 2 Roma II), quer, por funcionamento de uma cláusula de excepção (artigo 4º, nº 3 Roma II) por aplicação de um lei com uma conexão mais estreita, que existirá quando entre autor e lesado exista uma relação jurídica

---

[126] Cfr. Nuno Manuel Castello-Branco Bastos, *Das Obrigações nas regras de conflitos do Código Civil, in* COMEMORAÇÕES DOS 35 ANOS DO CÓDIGO CIVIL E DOS 25 ANOS DA REFORMA DE 1977: A PARTE GERAL DO CÓDIGO E A TEORIA GERAL DO DIREITO CIVIL (2006), p. 671 e pp. 676-677.

[127] Cfr. Id. at., pp. 676-677. Ainda a este respeito Moura Vicente fala da ideia de proximidade da lei ao autor do dano, defendendo que se deve evitar a aplicação à responsabilidade do agente "de uma lei com que esse sujeito não podia razoavelmente contar" (cfr. DÁRIO MOURA VICENTE, DA RESPONSABILIDADE PRÉ-CONTRATUAL EM DIREITO INTERNACIONAL PRIVADO (Almedina. 2011), pp. 491-492).

[128] Cfr. Pinheiro, RIVISTA DI DIRITTO INTERNAZIONALE PRIVATO E PROCESSUALE, (2008), p. 20 e Hein, RABELSZ, (2009), p. 485.

[129] Cfr. BRAINERD CURRIE, SELECTED ESSAYS ON THE CONFLICT OF LAWS (Duke University. 1963), p. 69.

[130] Cfr. Symeonides, AMERICAN JOURNAL OF COMPARATIVE LAW, (2008), p. 190.

[131] Cfr. Erwin Deustch, *Das Internationale Privatrecht der Arzthaftung, in* KONFLIKT UND ORDNUNG: FESTSCHRIFT FÜR MURAD FERID ZUM 70. GEBURTSTAG (M. Ferid, et al. eds., 1978), p. 124.

DIREITO DA SAÚDE

prévia, p.ex. um contrato[132]. Pode-se por exemplo associar à lei que regula o contrato médico, nos casos em que o angariador ou promotor se encontra no país da residência do lesado, onde é concluído o contrato.

B. LEX CAUSAE DO CONSENTIMENTO INFORMADO

1. Consentimento

Uma vez apresentada a solução para a delimitação material entre o Roma II e as regras do Código Civil, temos outro problema: a relevância das causas de justificação, em particular o consentimento. Tradicionalmente, quer à luz do artigo 45º CC quer à luz do Roma II, integram-se no conceito-quadro os pressupostos e as consequências da obrigação de indemnizar, fundada na culpa, no risco ou em facto lícito. Significa que o consentimento, em princípio, será regulado pela mesma lei que regula o estatuto delitual. Estatuto que inclui, *inter alia*, a definição dos direitos e interesses tutelados e das formas de violação contra as quais são tutelado formas de violação contra as quais eles são tutelados, e as causas justificativas do facto, imputabilidade, culpa, nexo de causalidade entre facto e dano, modalidades de indemnização, titularidade, transmissibilidade e prescrição do direito de indemnização, etc. Contudo a existência de um direito deverá ser aferida previamente à luz da lei que o regula, e não do estatuto da responsabilidade delitual.

O consentimento, enquanto manifestação o direito de autodeterminação, seria regulado pelo estatuto delitual e não pessoal, apesar de se tratar de uma manifestação da autodeterminação do titular de interesses juridicamente tutelados à luz do seu estatuto pessoal (artigos 25º e 27º CC). Esta inclusão, apesar da ausência de uma menção expressa do artigo 15º Roma II, decorre como natural e *óbvia* do ponto de vista da Comissão Europeia[133]). Esta apenas se preocupou em concretizar a alínea *b)* do artigo 15º Roma II como englobando as causas de exclusão da responsabilidade respeitantes a *"elementos extrínsecos da responsabilidade"*[134].

---

[132] Cfr. Hein, RABELSZ, (2009), pp. 483 e pp. 484-485 a respeito da interpretação da cláusula de excepção.

[133] Aliás, há quem defenda que a Comissão Europeia na sua proposta partiu do princípio que as causas de justificação estariam integradas no estatuto delitual e desta forma reguladas pelo Roma II (COM 2003 427 final pp. 25-26).

[134] Cfr. Proposta de Regulamento do Parlamento Europeu e do Conselho sobre a Lei Aplicável às Obrigações Extracontratuais ("Roma II"), COM(2003) 427 final, p. 25.

O CUIDADO MÉDICO TRANSFRONTEIRIÇO E O CONSENTIMENTO INFORMADO ...

Daí se darem como exemplos as causas de exclusão da responsabildiade *força maior, o estado de necessidade, a intervenção de terceiros e a culpa da vítima ou até mesmo situações de exclusão de responsabilidade em relações especiais, como é o caso dos cônjuges*[135].

Ora, o conceito de "causas de exclusão da responsabilidade" terá que ser interpretado autonomamente. A *intentio* é determinar não a fonte da responsabilidade, seja ilicitude ou licitude, por culpa ou pelo risco, mas a lei que regula e tutela o interesse jurídico susceptível de ser violado. À *lex causae* do consentimento cabe determinar a tutela de interesses e consequente disponibilidade ou limitação voluntária do mesmo. O que torna relevante ainda mais a escolha da lei competente, pois a autodeterminação sobre a esfera pessoal e patrimonial do titular do direito afectado pela lesão pressupõe que na genése da conduta do lesante este obtenha o prévio consentimento informado. Daqui resulta um dever de informação e um dever de obter um consentimento actual, livre e pessoal, e que, por se prender com a pessoa, poderia estar ligado ao estatuto pessoal. Contudo, não é indiferente o local onde o lesante actua. Será neste que se afere, desde logo, dos limites do consentimento, por ser à luz da concepção de valores do país de atuação que se constrói a licitude ou ilicitude da actuação. Aliás esta conexão será tanto mais pertinente porquanto há um risco de um mesmo comportamento ser simultâneamente licito e ilícito colocando em causa o princípio da harmonia interna se à mesma situação se aplicassem leis distintas quanto à concretização da licitude da conduta. Tal opção tem a vantagem de prevenir potenciais conflitos de qualificação decorrentes da aplicação simultânea de duas leis destinas e que colocam em causa a harmonia interna ao se prever a justificação e a ilicitude simultaneamente[136].

Cabe, em princípio, ao estatuto delitual regular o objecto do consentimento, dever de esclarecimento e respectivo regime: eficácia e revogabi-

---

[135] Cfr. Dickinson, The Roma II Regulation. The Law Applicable to Non-Contractual Obligations. 2013, p. 572 e Caravaca & González, Las obligaciones extracontractuales en derecho internacional privado: el reglamento "Roma II". 2008, p. 133.

[136] No entanto a garantia de unidade em sede de direito privado pode ser posta em causa pela aplicação do direito penal. Sobre este problema ver Andreas Spickhoff, *Die Einheit des Rechtswidrigkeitsurteils im Zusammenspiel von Internationalem Privat– und Strafrecht, in* Medizin und Haftung. Festschrift für Erwin Deutsch zum 80. Geburtstag (Hans-Jürgen Ahrens, et al. eds., 2009).

DIREITO DA SAÚDE

lidade. A razão que se aventa prende-se com a inter-relação congénita da ilicitude no local onde o facto lesivo ocorre, mais do que na continuação e imanência dos interesses pessoais do lesado. Caberá, em princípio, à *lex delictae* que determina o grau de (i)licitude e consequente forma e responsabilidade[137].

Já quanto à capacidade para consentir, é discutível se se deve atribuir ao estatuto delitual a sua regulamentação ou antes autonomizá-la face a este, integrando-a nas matérias de estatuto pessoal[138]. Tendo em contas as qualidades legais exigíveis ao sujeito para limitar ou dispor da sua esfera pessoal de interesses, é indiscutível que o conceito de capacidade diz respeito à formação de uma capacidade natural, integrando por isso, enquanto idoneidade para actuar juridicamente, a esfera pessoal. Daí que a doutrina portuguesa, no estudo do artigo 45º CC integre as questões das causas de justificação e definição dos direitos e interesses tutelados bem como as formas de violação no seu conceito-quadro, mas já não a existência de um direito ou interesse juridicamente protegido, o que parece pressupôr a determinação da capacidade para dispor ou limitar aquele. O desmembramento da relação jurídica implica a resolução de uma questão prévia decisiva: a existência ou não de um direito ou interesse juridicamente tutelado que deverá ser aferida à luz da lei que o regula.

---

[137] Cfr. Markus Nagel, Organtransplantation und Internationales Privatrecht (Springer. 2009), pp. 101-102. Andreas Spickhoff afasta também a aplicação da lei pessoal, mesmo para as situações em que em causa esteja um consentimento prospectivo, dando conta das antinomias que resultariam a aplicação de uma lei estranha ao local onde o facto era realizado, apenas admitindo de forma muita restrita a aplicação da lei pessoal e do equivalente ao nosso artigo 28º CC para os testamentos vitais. Sobre isto falaremos com mais acuidade a respeito dos testamentos vitais (cfr. Spickhoff, Die Einheit des Rechtswidrigkeitsurteils im Zusammenspiel von Internationalem Privat– und Strafrecht. 2009, pp. 918-919). Ver ainda Angela Könning-Feil, Das Internationale Arzthaftungsrecht. Eine kollisionsrechtliche Darstellung auf sachrechtsvergleichender Grundlage § 27 (Peter Lang. 1992), p. 297, Elisabeth Nitzinger, Das Betreuungsrecht im internationalen Privatrecht (Lang. 1998), p. 77 e Lemmerz, Die Patientenverfügung: Autonomie und Anknüpfungsgerechtigkeit. 2014, pp. 162-163.

[138] A favor, no que aos testamentos vitais diz respeito, da conexão ao estatuto pessoal das questões de capacidade se pronunciou Helmut Ofner, *Patientenverfügung und Internationales Privatrecht, in* Das österreichische Patientenverfügungsgesetz (Ulrich H.J. Körtner, et al. eds., 2007), p. 190 ss. Esta questão será abordada *infra*.

Como vimos, no ordenamento jurídico português, o conceito de estatuto pessoal encontra-se definido de forma ampla no artigo 25º CC, que o define pela enunciação do âmbito das matérias que são regidas pela lei pessoal, sejam elas atinentes ao estado individual ou à esfera relacional da pessoa. O mesmo abrange, assim, as questões de "estado dos indivíduos, capacidade das pessoas, as relações de família e as sucessões por morte". Contudo, esta norma é praticamente esvaziada pela tendência para a especialização (desmembramento), isto é pela profusão de regras de conflitos específicas para matérias de estatuto pessoal particular. Isto implica que tal regra de conflitos do artigo 25º CC apenas tenha mais-valia autónoma nas questões atinentes à capacidade jurídica não coberta por normas específicas (ou em hipóteses em que tenha de se assumir como norma de aplicação residual) e, quanto ao conceito de estado, aos títulos honoríficos e nobiliárquicos que não configuram direitos de personalidade, não podendo, por isso, ser sujeitos ao disposto no artigo 27º CC[139]. Todavia, não parece que se possa desvincular do estatuto pessoal a capacidade para consentir, por dizer mais respeito ao titular do interesse tutelado do que ao valor ou desvalor do consentimento para efeitos de apreciação da licitude e culpa do autor do dano. Isto sem prejuízo de um eventual alargamento, por analogia, do artigo 28º CC (excepção de interesse nacional) com vista a proteger o destinatário do consentimento: o profissional de saúde[140].

2. O testamentos vitais

a) *Convenção da Haia de 2000 sobre a protecção de adultos*
Os actos respeitantes à realização de cuidados saúde per se não são considerado uma medida de protecção, para efeitos da Convenção da Haia de 2000, como nos diz o artigo 4º, nº 1 alínea f). Aliás, este foi um dos assuntos mais polémicos e de acesa discussão, tendo havido propostas

---

[139] Sobre o desmembramento e riscos para a frustração da harmonia jurídica internacional e estabilidade de relações jurídicas ver Nuno Ascensão Silva, *Do estatuto pessoal – unidade e dispersão (Algumas notas a propósito da comemoração dos 35 anos do Código Civil)*, in Comemorações dos 35 anos do Código Civil e dos 25 anos da Reforma de 1977: A Parte Geral do Código e a Teoria Geral do Direito Civil (2006).

[140] Cfr. Spickhoff, Die Einheit des Rechtswidrigkeitsurteils im Zusammenspiel von Internationalem Privat– und Strafrecht. 2009, pp. 918-919. Voltaremos ao problema da aplicação analógica do artigo 28º *infra*.

DIREITO DA SAÚDE

de alguns representantes na Comissão para que se excluíssem as questões médicas da Convenção, limitando esta à regulamentação de questões meramente patrimoniais[141]. Havia enorme receio que a inclusão de regras de jurisdição quanto a estes actos fossem demasiado restritivas, o que poderia tornar extremamente difícil e demorada a prestação dos necessários cuidados de saúde[142].

A Convenção assumiu, na redacção final, uma posição descomprometida, não estipulando uma jurisdição específica, mas também não afastando total, ou mesmo parcialmente, estas questões. Determina, pois, a Convenção que os cuidados médicos praticados por profissionais de saúde, no uso das suas *legis artis*, com intenção terapêutica e sob indicação médica, não caem no âmbito desta, uma vez que não são uma medida de protecção enquanto tal, tratando-se de questões do domínio da ciência médica[143].

Já a realização de cuidados de saúde em que se torne necessário a manifestação da vontade do adulto incapaz de prestar o consentimento justifica a adopção de uma medida de protecção para efeitos da Convenção no que toca aos poderes de representação. Assim como se incluem todas aquelas situações em que é necessário obter uma qualquer autorização por parte de uma autoridade jurisdicional, como por exemplo, para finalidades de experimentação terapêutica, interrupção voluntária da gravidez, esterilização, ou cessação de determinado tratamento[144]. No fundo, o problema reside em determinar quando é que o cuidado

---

[141] Cfr. PAUL LAGARDE, EXPLANATORY REPORT -CONVENTION AND RECOMMENDATION ADOPTED BY THE SPECIAL COMMISSION OF A DIPLOMATIC CHARACTER (www.hcch.net. 2003).p. 35, ver igualmente TILL GUTTENBERGER, DAS HAAGER ÜBEREINKOMMEN ÜBER DEN INTERNATIONALEN SCHUTZ VON ERWACHSENEN (Gieseking. 2004), pp. 74-75.

[142] Paul Lagarde ainda menciona que alguns países tinham receio da possibilidade de reconhecimento ou execução de decisões individuais, de natureza médica, que violassem os seus valores essenciais, como seriam as situações de aborto ou de esterilização de incapazes adultos (Cfr. LAGARDE, Explanatory Report -Convention and Recommendation adopted by the Special Commission of a diplomatic character. 2003, p. 35).

[143] Cfr. Id. at., p. 35.

[144] Cfr. Id. at., p. 35, e Paul Lagarde, *La Convention de La Haye du 13 janvier 2000 sur la protection internationale des adultes*, REVUE CRITIQUE DE DROIT INTERNATIONAL PRIVÉ (2000), p. 171. Ver ainda Andreas Bucher, *La Convention de La Haye sur la Protection Internationale des Adultes*, REVUE SUISSE DE DROIT INTERNATIONAL ET DE DROIT EUROPÉEN (2000), p. 44 e GUTTENBERGER, DAS HAAGER ÜBEREINKOMMEN ÜBER DEN INTERNATIONALEN SCHUTZ VON ERWACHSENEN. 2004, pp. 75-76.

médico não é uma decisão técnica, mas sim uma manifestação da autonomia do paciente, ainda que a decisão final seja da responsabilidade do grupo clínico.

Teremos por isso que distinguir entre testamentos vitais e directivas antecipadas em sentido amplo, onde se inclui a representação. A Convenção de 2000 avança como conceito autónomo face aos direitos internos dos Estados Contratantes e procede a uma descrição própria dos institutos jurídicos abrangidos pelos artigos 15º e 16º da Convenção: "uma procuração de representação atribuída por um adulto através de um acordo ou negocio unilateral que deva ser exercida quando este adulto não for mais capaz de proteger os seus interesses". Posto isto, podemos concluir que não se integram no conceito-quadro da convenção os testamentos vitais isolados[145]. Estes dizem respeito a directrizes indicativas ou vinculativas para suprimento do consentimento presencial, pelo que integram o cuidado médico e, como tal, não são medidas de protecção para efeitos da Convenção de 2000. Contudo se para ser reconhecida a sua eficácia é necessário a mediação de uma autoridade jurisdicional, por exemplo para autorizar o cumprimento da vontade do outorgante, como sucede no caso alemão da §1901a BGB e seguintes (em especial o §1904 BGB), já se aplica a Convenção de 2000[146]. Assim, como a existência de uma tal directiva antecipada pode ser relevante para a determinação da lei aplicável à organização de cuidado, por funcionamento da cláusula de excepção do artigo 13º, nº 2 da Convenção de 2000[147], ou pode cumular-

---

[145] Cfr. Ballarino, Yearbook of Private International Law, (2006), p. 20.

[146] Cfr. Anne Röthel, *Teil III. Private Vorsorge im internationalem Rechtsverkehr*, in Handbuch der Vorsorgeverfügungen. Vorsorgevollmacht – Patientenverfügung – Betreuungsverfügung (2009), pp. 456-457 e Erik Jayme, *Die Patientenverfügung: Erwachsenenschutz und Internationales Privatrecht*, in Festschrift für Ulrich Spellenberg (Jörn Bernreuther, et al. eds., 2010), pp. 206-207. Aliás como nota este autor o direito alemão regulamenta o testamento vital, não de forma autónoma, mas integrando no instituto do cuidado (*Betreuung*) ou de uma procuração.

[147] O artigo 13º, no seu nº 2, consagra uma cláusula de excepção que visa acautelar os interesses do adulto – relativos à pessoa e/ou aos seus bens – podendo por isso justificar ou até mesmo impor, a aplicação de lei diferente da do foro, permitindo, deste modo, a flexibilização da regra estatuída no nº 1. Pode ainda ser possível defender-se, ao abrigo do artigo 13º, nº 2 da Convenção, a afirmação de um competência jurisdicional extraordinária por recurso ao mecanismo de *forum conveniens* e *forum non conveniens* dos artigo 7º e 8º da Convenção. Estamos perante uma cláusula de excepção fundada, não só, em critérios localizadores, mas, essencialmente, por interesses materiais (cfr. Lagarde, Explanatory Report -Convention

DIREITO DA SAÚDE

se a atribuição de poderes de representação com a outorga de uma directiva antecipada[148].

Não se pode é subsumir o testamento vital isolado ao artigo 15º da Convenção de 2000 porquanto deste (assim como de instrumentos de autotutela) não resulta a atribuição de quaisquer poderes de representação a um decisor substituto, mas a extensão de uma decisão pessoal e livre[149].

A validade e eficácia de tais instrumentos estarão por isso dependentes de um outro estatuto. No caso da autotutela dependerá do artigo 13º da Convenção de 2000, já o testamento vital veremos o possível enquadramento jurídico a dar em termos de solução conflitual.

Diferente são as situações de representação tal como são definidas no artigo 15º da Convenção de 2000, em que os poderes conferidos visam exclusivamente a representação para cuidados de saúde. Nestes casos estamos a falar de um meio de suprimento da incapacidade, resultante da organização do cuidado privado pelo próprio outorgante que pressupõe a designação de um decisor substituto e, por isso, estão a coberto das regras dos artigos 15º e 16º da Convenção de 2000[150]. Nestas situações é ainda possível associar aos poderes de representação um testamento vital. Ainda assim, para estes casos, ressalvada a possibilidade da autono-

and Recommendation adopted by the Special Commission of a diplomatic character. 2003, pp. 52-53). A conexão com outro ordenamento, para além do foro, é essencialmente preordenada à obtenção do resultado material da protecção dos interesses do incapaz, ao qual não poderão ser alheios interesses espaciais, se bem que não determinantes. Esta conexão de natureza substancial funciona sob a égide do princípio do tratamento mais favorável do adulto. Neste sentido GUTTENBERGER, Das Haager Übereinkommen über den internationalen Schutz von Erwachsenen. 2004, p. 142 e LEMMERZ, Die Patientenverfügung: Autonomie und Anknüpfungsgerechtigkeit. 2014, p. 142.

[148] Pelo que aqui corrigimos a posição por nós defendida que dava a entender ser possível subsumir um testamento vital isolado ao artigo 15º da Convenção de 2000. Porquanto, isoladamente, um testamento vital, por não atribuir poderes de representação, não cumpre uma função análoga ou equivalente a uma procuração para efeitos do artigo 15º. Todavia, a liberdade conferida pelo artigo 15º, permite a determinação e união de um mesmo instrumento as duas valências, e desta forma regendo-se pela Convenção da Haia de 2000. Cfr. Ribeiro, REVISTA DO MINISTÉRIO PÚBLICO, (2011)., p. 55, n. 97.

[149] Cfr. Aimee R. Fagan, *An Analysis of the Convention on the International Protection of Adults*, 10 THE ELDER LAW JOURNAL 329-359(2002)., p. 349., Tobias Helms, *Reform des internationalen Betreuungsrechts durch das Haager Erwachseneschutzabkommen*, 55 FAMRZ (2008); Fagan, THE ELDER LAW JOURNAL, (2002), p. 1999.

[150] Cfr. Bucher, REVUE SUISSE DE DROIT INTERNATIONAL ET DE DROIT EUROPÉEN, (2000), pp. 53-54.

O CUIDADO MÉDICO TRANSFRONTEIRIÇO E O CONSENTIMENTO INFORMADO ...

mia conflitual servir para subsumir ambos os instrumento de vontade a uma única lei, a verdade é que a natureza e função do testamento vital, ainda que associada à procuração, conserva a sua autonomia, quer para efeitos de determinação da sua existência e validade (apresentando-se, assim nos parece, como uma questão prévia), quer para efeitos da sua eficácia.

Esta questão torna-se relevante quando nos confrontamos com a determinação da vontade do outorgante e limites dos poderes de representação. O artigo 13º, nº 2 da Lei nº 25/2012, pela sua função e conteúdo prende-se com a determinação (e consequente delimitação) dos poderes do representante voluntário ao mandar atender à vontade vertida no testamento vital. Resulta desta norma, pelo seu enquadramento sistemático e finalidades dos dois institutos, que é o testamento vital aquele que representa a vontade real (ou presumida) do outorgante e não o decisor substituto, o procurador. É portanto aquela figura – o testamento vital – que fixa os limites de actuação deste solucionado o possível conflito que daí resulte será regulado.

Assim, quando se verifique um confronto entre a eficácia dos poderes do representante e o testamento vital, há quem entenda que a necessidade de uma intervenção de uma autoridade submeta à lei de execução das medidas. O problema da lei aplicável seria resolvido por recurso ao artigo 14º ou 15º, nº 3 da Convenção de 2000, caso se trata do exercício de poderes de representação legal ou voluntária, ou seja à lei de execução dos poderes de representação legais ou voluntário, aqui se incluindo, por exemplo, os casos em que o outorgante simultaneamente realize um testamento vital e em causa esteja a sua execução. Reconhecer um poder vinculativo da decisão nos termos do artigo 13º, nº 1 Lei nº 25/2012 ou a necessidade de autorização judicial (§1904 BGB) dependeria, por isso, para alguns autores, da lei de execução e não da lei que regula a substância[151].

Outras opiniões vão no sentido de que o testamento vital conserva a sua autonomia e portanto os limites e eficácia são enquadrados no quadro de uma questão prévia resolvida por uma conexão autónoma. Como argumento, temos a eventual possibilidade de o representante procurar

---

[151] Cfr. Helms, FAMRZ, (2008)., p. 1999 e Frauke Wedemann, *Vorsorgevollmachten im internationalen Rechtsverkehr*, 57 see id. at (2010), p. 786.

um país onde o exercício desses poderes não seja limitado, quer judicialmente, quer pela força vinculativa do testamento vital. Devendo, por isso,
manter-se as exigências legais do Estado que aplicou a medida (artigo 13º
da Convenção), sendo esta que determina a necessidade ou não de autorização judicial[152]. Neste sentido, a autorização seria a própria medida de
protecção, pelo que só uma autoridade competente à luz do artigo 5º e
seguintes da Convenção de Haia, é que teria competência para decidir.
A autorização quando constitutiva, e não mera condição de eficácia, é
uma medida de protecção, vinculada às regras de competência e à lei
aplicável, nos termos do artigo 13º da Convenção de 2000. Nas palavras
de Paul Lagarde as condições de aplicação devem ser entendidas num
sentido amplo, abrangendo não só a medida de protecção em si, mas
igualmente todos os requisitos necessários para efectivar a execução da
mesma. Contudo ficam excluídas todas as questões que digam respeito
à natureza substantiva da medida de protecção, pois, quanto a estas,
aplica-se o artigo 13º da Convenção. É, por isso, essencial, que da aplicação da lei do local de execução não resulte a desfiguração do regime
material da medida de protecção[153]. Diremos até que, pela natureza da
situação a licitude da actuação do representante dependerá sempre o
exercício dos poderes em conformidade com a *lex causae* da relação de

---

[152] Cfr. LEMMERZ, Die Patientenverfügung: Autonomie und Anknüpfungsgerechtigkeit. 2014,
pp. 142-143. Esta autora dá como exemplo um cidadão alemão que é levado para a Suíça por
decisão do seu *Betreuer* e lá pretende autorizar a realização da eutanásia. A medida decretada
pelo Tribunal alemão não conferiu legitimidade para o *Betreuer* actuar sozinho.

[153] Cf. LAGARDE, EXPLANATORY REPORT -CONVENTION AND RECOMMENDATION ADOPTED
BY THE SPECIAL COMMISSION OF A DIPLOMATIC CHARACTER. 2003, p. 53, nº 94, e Lagarde,
REVUE CRITIQUE DE DROIT INTERNATIONAL PRIVÉ, (2000), p. 173. Este autor realça,
porém, que a necessidade de autorização poderá ser muita mais do que uma mera condição
de implementação da medida, podendo fazer parte dos poderes de representação. Nestes
casos já não será a lei do local da execução, nos termos do artigo 14º, mas sim a do artigo
13º (cf. LAGARDE, Explanatory Report -Convention and Recommendation adopted by
the Special Commission of a diplomatic character. 2003, pp. 52-53, nota 95). Por sua vez,
entende Andreas Bucher que ter-se-á que proceder a um esforço adaptativo da medida
à lei do local da sua implementação, não podendo o mesmo implicar uma modificação
sensível da medida de protecção na sua substância (cfr. Bucher, REVUE SUISSE DE DROIT
INTERNATIONAL ET DE DROIT EUROPÉEN, (2000), p. 50). Segundo Erik Jayme a referência à lei
do Estado de implementação ou execução seria a forma de assegurar o respeito pela sua «data
moralia», sem que contudo fosse afastada a *lex causae* (cfr. Jayme, Die Patientenverfügung:
Erwachsenenschutz und Internationales Privatrecht. 2010, p. 210).

cuidado e portanto ao abrigo do artigo 13º e 15º da Convenção de 2000, porquanto é esta que condiciona a licitude ou ilicitude da sua actuação em sede de responsabilidade extra-contratual[154].

Mas chegados aqui, qual deverá ser a lei que regula os testamentos vitais?

Os problemas que, a este propósito, se colocam referem-se às seguintes questões: a possibilidade de um paciente deslocado internacional outorgar um testamento vital de acordo com o local onde se encontra presente, a validade formal dos testamentos vitais outorgados a partir da lei de outro Estado; a conexão mais adequada a regular o conflito entre a lei que reconhece o testamento vital e a lei que atribui poderes de representação e/ou decisão em benefício do paciente incapaz e, por último, a implementação do testamento vital[155].

b) A regulação dos «testamentos vitais» transfronteiriços

Como vimos o consentimento, ao integrar a categoria de causas de justificação e atenta a sua natureza e função, faz parte, por regra, do estatuto delitual. Todavia esta consideração não nos permite dizer que o testamento vital se encontra igual e necessariamente integrado em tal estatuto. Em primeiro porque em alguns país, como é o caso da Alemanha, o testamento vital (*Patientenverfügung*) é regulado em conjunto com a organização de cuidado dos adultos (§1901a e seguintes BGB)[156], noutros não é reconhecido como é o caso de Itália[157]. Existindo ainda outros países que, à semelhança do nosso (como é o caso da Áustria), autonomizam a figura e o integram como verdadeiro negócio jurídico ou simples acto

---

[154] No entanto iguais efeitos poderiam ser alcançados se em vez da resolução questão prévia pela *lex causae*, se determinasse a aplicação da lei que regulação a relação de cuidado como estatuto delitual (artigo 4º, nº 3 Roma II) ou por ordem do residência habitual comum (artigo 4º, nº 2 Roma II). Sobre o funcionamento da cláusula de excepção com fundamento numa relação pré-existente ver Symeonides, AMERICAN JOURNAL OF COMPARATIVE LAW, (2008), pp. 203-204. No entanto esta solução seria difícil de equacionar se o médico ou outro responsável pelos cuidados de saúde fosse considerado como autor ou co-autor do dano.

[155] Cfr. Ballarino, YEARBOOK OF PRIVATE INTERNATIONAL LAW, (2006), p. 19.

[156] Cfr. Röthel, Teil III. Private Vorsorge im internationalem Rechtsverkehr. 2009.

[157] Cfr. Stefano Rossi & Massimo Foglia, *Testamento biologico (II)*, *in* DIGESTO DELLE DISCIPLINE PRIVATISTICHE SEZIONE CIVILE (Rodolfo Sacco ed. 2014).

DIREITO DA SAÚDE

jurídico[158] sendo o seu conteúdo vinculativo. Por último, há ainda países que reconhecem o testamento vital mas apenas lhe atribuem um carácter indiciário (França). A isto acresce o facto de nos países que reconhecem a figura haver diferentes exigências a respeito da forma: para uns exige-se a forma autêntica como é os casos da Áustria e Portugal e para outros, a Alemanha, não se exige qualquer forma especial. O enquadramento jurídico em termos de direito material é por isso variado cabendo ao Direito Internacional Privado a missão de coordenação e comunicação dos diversos valores, interesses e regras dos ordenamentos jurídicos em confronto com a situação jurídica plurilocalizada. Por isso, o seu carácter instrumental exige à ordem jurídica do *foro* a capacidade de enquadrar e respeitar o âmbito de competência de uma lei estrangeira.

(1) Estatuto sucessório (analogia?)

Um dos possíveis enquadramentos seria avançar para a regulação conflitual através do recurso das disposições respeitantes ao direito sucessório. Contudo, pela natureza e função do estatuto da sucessão voluntária, independentemente do critério da qualificação adoptado, tal solução depende de uma consagração legal expressa, na medida em que os testamentos são declarações de vontade que têm como especificidade estarem dependentes do facto integrante e central da *factti-species* sucessória: a morte do autor da sucessão, e não a sua incapacidade. A morte não integra qualquer cláusula acessória típica de uma condição, antes "significa que cada uma das disposições contidas no testamento forma, até à morte do testador, um facto jurídico incompleto, destituído de valor jurídico autónomo"[159]. A possibilidade de aproveitar as soluções conflituais da sucessão voluntária apenas podem servir como modelo de referência em sede *de lege ferenda*. No entanto, como bem nota ERIK JAYME a consideração da lei da residência (quer a título de estatuto hipotético, artigo 26º nº 5 EGBGB, quer a título de conexão principal, ou ainda através da escolha do testador, na solução dos artigos 21º, nº 1 e 22º Regulamento

---

[158] Ver sobre a Áustria Ofner, Patientenverfügung und Internationales Privatrecht. 2007. e sobre Portugal o nosso Geraldo Rocha Ribeiro, *Direito à autodeterminação e Directivas Antecipadas: o caso Português*, 10 LEX MEDICINAE (2013).

[159] Cfr. MACHADO, Lições de Direito Internacional Privado. 2002., p. 439.

650/2012/UE[160]) permite assegurar o direito à autodeterminação manifestado prospectivamente, ao cristalizar a lei competente que regula e torna eficaz o testamento vital através da aplicação luz da lei da residência ou do Estado por ele escolhido[161]. No caso português tal relevância seria assegurada pelo artigo 63º CC, cabendo a competência à lei da nacionalidade (artigo 31º, nº 1 CC).

O objecto do testamento vital prende-se por isso com as questões que mais dizem respeito à pessoa e que por isso deveriam acompanhar esta onde quer esteja. Desta feita existe um forte interesse na estabilidade da conexão e da previsibilidade da lei aplicável. Em jeito de analogia, a relevância e eficácia do testamento vital depende da incapacidade da pessoa para autodeterminar os seus interesses actuais, equiparando-se aquela a uma espécie de *morte civil*[162]. Contudo, e como já foi referido, esta opção não é viável, nem sequer por recurso à analogia, porquanto as regras de conflitos visam os efeitos sucessórios *post mortem*, não sendo o testamento vital a expressão da última vontade do sujeito, mas de uma vontade de quem não é capaz de decidir.

(2) Estatuto pessoal

No entanto, apesar de afastada a possibilidade do recurso às regras da sucessão voluntária, a natureza e função do testamento vital não deixa de ter profundos reflexos na esfera pessoal do outorgante e que este espera que o acompanhe onde quer que se encontre. As exigências de estabilidade e previsibilidade são por isso coincidentes com aquelas que justificam a unidade do estatuto pessoal. É indiscutível que, enquanto manifestação de tal direito de autodeterminação, os interesses do titular de tal direito devem prevalecer e vingar desta forma através de uma lei próxima que seja a sua e que só pode ser a sua lei pessoal[163]. Atendendo

---

[160] Regulamento relativo à competência, à lei aplicável, ao reconhecimento e execução das decisões, e à aceitação e execução dos atos autênticos em matéria de sucessões e à criação de um Certificado Sucessório Europeu.

[161] Cfr. Jayme, Die Patientenverfügung: Erwachsenenschutz und Internationales Privatrecht. 2010., p. 206.

[162] Cfr. Lemmerz, Die Patientenverfügung: Autonomie und Anknüpfungsgerechtigkeit. 2014, p. 232.

[163] Ainda assim tal não significa que se possam ter que considerar outras leis para regular específicas dimensões da esfera pessoal. Cfr. Albert Ehrenzweig, *Specific Principles of Private Transnational Law, in* Recueil des Cours (1969), pp. 350-351.

à manifestação de uma vontade prospectiva enquanto exercício da auto-determinação do outorgante, a mesma deve ter uma pretensão extraterritorial nos seus efeitos, acompanhando o outorgante. A isto acresce o facto de ser a lei pessoal aquela que o outorgante conhece, ou está em condições de conhecer, e sob a qual elabora o testamento vital com vista a assegurar a sua validade e eficácia.

HELMUT OFNER propôs, atendendo à qualificação do testamento vital como negócio jurídico pelo ordenamento austríaco, que a lei adequada seria a lei pessoal. Na perspectiva do outorgante não seria previsível o quando e o onde o testamento vital poderá vir a ser necessário, por isso a única forma de acautelar os interesses do outorgante será cristalizar a lei aplicável a uma conexão próxima do outorgante relevante à data da outorga. Em especial porque a possibilidade de deslocação espacial e a imprevisibilidade da sua necessidade tornam impossível ao outorgante prever os requisitos de validade e eficácia do testamento vital, quando este seja necessário num país diferente do Estado da nacionalidade ou da residência habitual do outorgante[164].

Numa perspectiva comparada, atendendo à natureza, função e requisitos do testamento vital austríaco previsto na *Patientenverfügungsgesetz* de 8 de Maio de 2006, existem pontos em comum com o regime português. Um deles, assim nos parece, é a natureza de acto jurídico voluntário, que para nós, atendendo ao artigo 295º CC será a de um quase-negócio jurídico, mas sem que ponha em causa a natureza voluntária do acto e que implica a sua autonomização face ao consentimento *per se*[165]. Tanto mais que a vontade prospectiva não pode ser desligada do acto jurídico voluntário que a corporiza. Se é verdade que o testamento vital é um meio de suprimento da incapacidade para prestar um consentimento *actual*, não menos certo é que, enquanto instrumento para a prestação de um consentimento prospectivo, não se pode desligar do acto jurídico que exterioriza a vontade. É por isso uma declaração de vontade que se autonomiza à capacidade para consentir e que acompanha o outorgante.

---

[164] Cfr. Ofner, Patientenverfügung und Internationales Privatrecht. 2007., pp. 190-194, Mario J. A. Oyarzábal, *A Private International Law Perspective: Conflict Rules in Advance Directives and Euthanasia Legislation*, *in* SELF-DETERMINATION, DIGNITY AND END-OF-LIFE CARE. REGULATING ADVANCE DIRECTIVES IN INTERNATIONAL AND COMPARATIVE PERSPECTIVE (Stefania Negri ed. 2011), pp. 132-133.

[165] Sobre a qualificação das directivas antecipadas ver Ribeiro, LEX MEDICINAE, (2013), pp. 108-109.

(3) Capacidade

Por isso, ainda que possa haver tamanha tentação, não parece que possamos integrar o testamento vital na questão de capacidade, conforme os artigos 25º e 28º CC. A capacidade pressupõe, no seu conceito-quadro, a qualidade ou idoneidade para ser titular de relações jurídicas, ou seja titular de direitos e deveres, bem como a aptidão para agir juridicamente, quer da sua esfera pessoal, quer patrimonial (capacidade de exercícios de direitos). Tal significa que, independentemente da noção material de capacidade jurídica e de exercício, o instituto da capacidade para efeitos do direito internacional privado prende-se com as qualidades da pessoa, aqui cabendo a capacidade jurídica negocial ou de agir, quer para actos patrimoniais, quer para actos pessoais[166]. A capacidade jurídica deve ser regulada pela lei pessoal, por decorrência da definição do âmbito da lei pessoal no artigo 25º. Por esta lei deve ser regulado não só as condições de aquisição, como também os efeitos gerais da capacidade ou incapacidade sobre a validade dos actos jurídicos[167]. Nela se incluem assim a maioridade, a emancipação e capacidade de discernimento enquanto incapacidades gerais.

O que significa que a capacidade jurídica é um *aliud* relativamente ao testamento vital, uma vez que não se confunde com acto voluntário e respectivos pressupostos, ainda que seja um elemento essencial à sua perfeição e eficácia[168]. O testamento vital prende-se antes com a exteriorização de uma vontade antecipada e não com as qualidades do outorgante da mesma, pelo que o artigo 25º CC[169] releva quanto ao elemento

---

[166] Sobre o instituto da capacidade de agir e as esferas pessoais e patrimoniais ver o nosso GERALDO ROCHA RIBEIRO, A PROTECÇÃO DO INCAPAZ ADULTO NO DIREITO PORTUGUÊS (Coimbra. 2011).

[167] Cfr. ANDREAS BUCHER, DROIT INTERNATIONAL PRIVÉ SUISSE § II – Personnes, Famille, Successions (1992), p. 78.

[168] Cfr. LEMMERZ, Die Patientenverfügung: Autonomie und Anknüpfungsgerechtigkeit. 2014, p. 250.

[169] Pode-se discutir ainda a possibilidade de aplicação do artigo 28º CC (*excepção de interesse nacional*) a respeito da capacidade do outorgante. No entanto, as directivas antecipadas são actos jurídicos fora do *tráfico corrente de bens e serviços*, pelo que não existe um interesse do comércio jurídico e de terceiro que justifique a tutela da aparência. Daí a doutrina excluir a sua aplicação a negócios pessoais (cfr. CORREIA, Direito Internacional Privado – Alguns problemas. 1985, pp. 50-51 e MACHADO, Lições de Direito Internacional Privado. 2002, pp. 342-343), pelo que só seria de admitir uma aplicação analógica em casos especiais em

DIREITO DA SAÚDE

capacidade diz respeito, através da *dépeçage*, mas não se estende na regulamentação para os pressupostos do acto jurídico, testamento vital[170]. O testamento vital ao ter a sua eficácia condicionada à verificação de um incapacidade jurídica ou de facto estará, em princípio, subordinado ao domínio da lei pessoal, contudo os seus pressupostos de validade tenderão a se autonomizar, desde logo no que à forma diz respeito (artigo 36º CC). Mas não fica afastada a possibilidade de consideramos, como sucede, por meio da *dépeçage*, apreciar a capacidade como integrando o estatuto que rege a substância da situação jurídica ou a favor de um conexão autónoma ao estatuto pessoal e substantivo. É o que sucede com a capacidade para celebrar negócios jurídicos nos casos de protecção de terceiros (artigo 13º Roma I e artigo 28º CC), capacidade delitual (artigo 15º Roma II e Considerando 12), capacidade para constituir ou dispor de direitos reais (artigo 47º CC), a capacidade activa e passiva para a constituição de uma relação de filiação (artigo 56º CC), capacidade matrimonial (artigo 49º CC) e a capacidade sucessória (artigo 63º CC e artigos 21º e 22º *ex vi* artigo 26º, nº 1 *al.* a) Regulamento (UE) nº 650/2012). Parece-nos que caberá ao estatuto pessoal a regulação da personalidade e capacidade jurídicas em geral, enquanto integrando no seu conceito-quadro as normas de competência. A estas cabe a determinação da idoneidade jurídica de uma pessoa para que surja como titular de direitos e obrigações. Pelo que a capacidade geral será regulada pelo estatuto pessoal enquanto lei que define, de forma duradoura, o *status jurídico* da pessoa acompanhando-o além fronteiras. Contudo não será de descartar a possibilidade de relevar o estatuto delitual, ou a intervenção de normas de aplicação necessária e

que o destinatário do consentimento confiança na aplicação da lei do local de actuação do outorgante para determinar a capacidade para consentir. Contudo, tendo em conta a necessidade e relevância do consentimento o interesse do destinatário deste pode justificar a aplicação analógica por respeito ao princípio da confiança. Sobre a possibilidade de aplicação do estatuto pessoal e da excepção de interesse nacional, ainda que respeitante aos artigos 7º e 12º EGBGB Spickhoff, Die Einheit des Rechtswidrigkeitsurteils im Zusammenspiel von Internationalem Privat– und Strafrecht. 2009, pp. 918-919.

[170] Neste sentido Anna-Luisa Lemmerz, que acrescenta que não deve integrar o conceito-quadro de capacidade o testamento vital por causa da dificuldade que representa para os interessados o conhecimento da lei aplicável, em especial para o caso dos países que adoptam a conexão nacionalidade, como é o caso de Portugal e Alemanha (artigo 7. EGBGB) (cfr. Lemmerz, Die Patientenverfügung: Autonomie und Anknüpfungsgerechtigkeit. 2014, p. 250).

imediata, ou mesmo a ordem pública internacional para considerar como competente para regular a capacidade especial para consentir uma outra lei que não a do estatuto pessoal.

(4) Reconhecimento: doutrina de direitos adquiridos e o princípio geral de direito da União (mútuo reconhecimento)

Outra possibilidade seria enquadrar o problema em sede do reconhecimento de direitos adquiridos, quer em sede do método conflitual[171], quer por invocação das liberdades comunitárias no seio do mercado interno europeu[172]. Outra possibilidade seria enquadrar o problema em sede de reconhecimento de direitos adquiridos, quer em termos de método conflitual, quer por invocação das liberdades comunitárias. Atenta a natureza e função do testamento vital, enquanto acto jurídico voluntário que visa exteriorizar um vontade correspondente à autodeterminação de interesses pessoais do outorgante, poderíamos ser tentados a autonomizar este instituto face às matérias que integram o estatuto pessoal. Este enquadramento justificaria que a lei aplicável ao testamento vital fosse determinada através de uma conexão autónoma favorável à sua outorga e reconhecimento, como será o caso da *lex loci actus*.[173].

O impacto de um testamento vital na vida do seu outorgante justifica que se atribua àquele uma vocação extraterritorial, mesmo quando não era expectável a sua utilização transfronteiriça. Desta feita, caberia à *lex loci actus* regular os pressupostos de validade e eficácia do testamento vital, restando à lei que regula o estatuto delitual determinar as condições

---

[171] A discussão passaria pelas soluções avançadas pelos sistemas unilateralistas (ver *inter alia* Pierre Gothot, *Le renouveau de la tendance unilatéraliste en droit international privé*, 60 Revue Critique de Droit International Privé (1971), pp. 415-450 e, numa abordagem geral, mais recente, Gian Paolo Romano, L'Unilateralismo nel Diritto Internazionale Privato Moderno (Schulthess. 2014)) e bilateralistas (correspondente ao nosso, a cujas demandas o artigo 31º nº 2 CC pretende responder).

[172] O direito material e/ou direito internacional privado não pode servir de entrave ou obstáculo à liberdade circulação, salvo justificação proporcional, como veio a decidir o TJUE no Acórdão *Cassis-Dijon* Cfr. Dário Moura Vicente, *Liberdades comunitárias e direito internacional privado*, 1 Cuadernos de Derecho Transnacional (2009), p. 180. Sobre a descrição das vantagens do princípio do mútuo reconhecimento ver María Dolores Ortiz Vidal, *Espacio Judicial Europeo y Tratado de Lisboa: hacia un nuevo derecho internatcional privado*, 2 see id. at (2010), p. 395.

[173] Cfr. Ballarino, Yearbook of Private International Law, (2006), pp. 23-24.

DIREITO DA SAÚDE

para a execução ou implementação daquele (que em regra corresponderá ao local onde é prestado o cuidado médico). Este entendimento asseguraria uma liberdade quase total do outorgante na realização de um testamento vital[174] e, simultaneamente, assegurando a previsibilidade no que à lei aplicável diz respeito[175].

Em termos de lei aplicável, a existência de uma cisão entre o estatuto regulador da forma e substância face ao estatuto de implementação do testamento vital justifica-se por causa da dispersão espacial e temporal que existe entre o momento da outorga e o momento em que o testamento vital é necessário enquanto meio de suprimento da incapacidade para consentir. Desta feita, mais do que falar na utilização de regras de conflitos bilaterais, estaria em causa o reconhecimento de acordo com a *lex fori* (aqui entendida como lei do local do tratamento) de uma situação (no caso o testamento vital) outorgada e reconhecida no estrangeiro (em princípio a lei da residência habitual por ser nesta que com maior probabilidade o outorgante realizará o seu testamento vital). Transpondo para a nossa ordem jurídica, o reconhecimento de testamentos vitais outorgados no país da residência seriam reconhecidos, mesmo para nacionais portugueses, à luz do artigo 31º, nº 2 CC[176]. Contudo, ainda que se prescinda, por esta via do controlo sobre a lei aplicável, o reconhecimento ficaria dependente de uma conexão estreita com a situação (no caso, falhando a nacionalidade, valeria a residência habitual, ressalvando as possibilidades de reenvio, artigos 16º, 17º, 18º e 19º CC).

No âmbito do direito da união invoca-se o princípio de reconhecimento mútuo como meio de reconhecimento dos actos públicos[177], ou

---

[174] Cfr. Id. at., p. 24.

[175] Cfr. ROMANO, L'Unilateralismo nel Diritto Internazionale Privato Moderno. 2014. Numa perspectiva crítica e global ver Jan von Hein, *Anotação ao artigo 3º EGBGB, in* MÜNCHENER KOMMENTAR ZUM BÜRGERLICHEN GESETZBUCH (2015). Rn 122 e 131-138.

[176] Sobre a interpretação do artigo 31º, nº2 e a doutrina dos direitos adquiridos ver ANTÓNIO ARRUDA FERRER CORREIA, LIÇÕES DE DIREITO INTERNACIONAL PRIVADO (Almedina. 2000).p. 362-398, MACHADO, Lições de Direito Internacional Privado. 2002., pp. 170-178, Rui Manuel Moura Ramos, *Dos direitos adquiridos em direito internacional privado*, 50 BOLETIM DA FACULDADE DE DIREITO DA UNIVERSIDADE DE COIMBRA (1974).

[177] Sobre a noção de acto público ver, entre outros, CHARALAMBOS PAMBOUKIS, L'ACTE PUBLIC ÉTRANGER EN DROIT INTERNATIONAL PRIVÉ (LGDJ. 1993). Sobre a proposta da Comissão Europeia de reconhecimento de actos autênticos em matéria de estado civil ver Paul Lagarde, *The movement of civil-status records in Europe, and the European Commission's Proposal of 24 April*

até mesmos actos particulares de outros Estados-membros[178]. O reconhecimento é um instrumento de concretização do mercado interno e garantia das liberdades comunitárias (*comunitarização indirecta*[179]) estendendo-se por isso a áreas que não são directamente integradas pelo princípio da competência da UE[180]. Assim aconteceu no âmbito do direito ao nome, em especial por via do acórdão Grunkin-Paul[181]. Todavia as directivas antecipadas, em especial o testamento vital, ainda que reconhecidos no quadro de valores de referência fornecidos pelas normas-narrativas, como é o caso do artigo 9º CEDHB e Recomendações R(99)4, R(2004)10, R(2012) 1993 e Resolução 1859 (2012)[182] e inferidas do direito à autodeterminação e consentimento informado (artigos 2º e 8º CEDH e artigo 3º, nº 2 *al.* a) CDF), não resultam sequer de um acto

---

2013, XV Yearbook of Private International Law (2013/2014). Como nota Christian Kohler os vínculos quase-federais que interligam os Estados-Membros requerem que um estatuto validamente constituído num Estado-membro seja reconhecido nos demais (cfr. Christian Kohler, *Towards the Recognition of Civil Status in the European Union*, see id. at., p. 27). Princípio esse que está consagrado no artigo 12º proposta de regulamento da lei aplicável ao nome de pessoas formulado pelo *Wissenschaftlicher Beirat des Bundesverbands der Deutschen Standesbeamtinnen und Standesbeamten* (cfr. Working Group of the Federal Association of German Civil Status Registrars, *One Name throughout Europe – Draft for a European Regulation onde the Law Applicable to names*, see id. at.).

[178] Cfr. Giulia Rossolillo, Mutuo Riconoscimento e Tecniche Conflittuali § 102 (CEDAM. 2002), p. 171 e ss, pp. 229-235Heinz-Peter Mansel, *Anerkennung als Grundprinzip des Europäischen Rechtsraums: Zur Herausbildung eines europäischen Anerkennungs-Kollisionsrechts: Anerkennung staat Verweisung als neues Strukturprinzip des Europäischen internationalen Privatrechts?*, 70 RabelsZ (2006);Paul Lagarde, *Développements futurs du droit international privé dans une Europe en voie d'unification: quelques conjectures*, 68 see id. at (2004), p. 651 e ss, em especial p. 687 e ss. e Dagmar Coester-Waltjen, *Anerkennung im Internationalen Personen-, Familien– und Erbrecht und das Europäische Kollisionsrecht*, 26 IPrax (2006).

[179] Cfr. Vicente, Cuadernos de Derecho Transnacional, (2009).

[180] Cfr. Jayme, Die Patientenverfügung: Erwachsenenschutz und Internationales Privatrecht. 2010, p. 209.

[181] Cfr. C-353/06.

[182] A Recomendação de 1999 é relativa à protecção dos incapazes adultos, 2004 a respeito da protecção dos direitos humanos e dignidade dos doentes mentais, 2012, quer a recomendação, quer a resolução, dizem respeito à protecção de direitos humanos e dignidade através da tomada em consideração de vontades e desejos expressamente manifestados. Sobre o papel do Conselho da Europa ver Roberto Andorno, *Regulating Advance Directives at the Council of Europe, in* Self-Determination, Dignity and End-of-Life Care. Regulating Advance Directives in International and Comparative Perspective (Stefania Negri ed. 2011).

DIREITO DA SAÚDE

público (como sucedia no caso do Grunkin Paul), nem, muitas vezes, da intervenção de uma autoridade pública (nem todos os ordenamentos exigem a forma autêntica ou particular autenticada).

A directiva antecipada resulta do exercício de um direito de personalidade típico de uma relação jurídica privada, enquadrando-se no âmbito de soberania de cada Estado o seu reconhecimento, regime e eficácia, pelo que o seu não reconhecimento não afronta as liberdades comunitárias. Isto é, a liberdade de circulação de um cidadão europeu não é, em princípio, posta em causa pelo não reconhecimento do testamento vital, porquanto se reserva aos Estados-membros a soberania quanto à definição das suas *moral data*, não sendo esta contrário ao quadro de valores europeus.

No entanto o estatuto da cidadania europeia associado aos direitos à autodeterminação nos cuidados de saúde – desde que respeitados os limites da ordem pública de cada Estado-Membro – são susceptíveis de deslocar o problema do testamento vital para uma situação de reconhecimento de um acto jurídico que incorpora no seu objecto uma manifestação de autodeterminação e que, por ser reconhecido à luz da *lex loci actus*, deveria ser reconhecido no país de implementação[183]. A favor deste entendimento poderiam não só invocar-se as liberdades comunitárias cujo efeito directo é reconhecido, como o próprio artigo 365º, nº 1 CC: "Os documentos autênticos ou particulares passados em país estrangeiro, na conformidade da respectiva lei, fazem prova como o fariam os documentos da mesma natureza exarados em Portugal". Tanto mais que o que releva nos testamentos vitais é a expressão de uma vontade autêntica do seu outorgante, servindo o documento para comprovar tal vontade[184],

---

[183] O reconhecimento decorreria assim da teoria de *local data,* da autoria de Albert Ehrenzweig (cfr. EHRENZWEIG, Private International Law. 1967., p. 169).

[184] O que significa que, adoptando uma qualificação funcional, o testamento vital elaborado através de documento autêntico não o tornaria uma acto público em sentido estrito porquanto a autoridade pública ou a esta equiparada se limita a atestar a vontade manifestada e desta forma o testamento vital quanto formal é um mero acto público receptivo. Tanto mais que, dentro do quadro de valores fundamentais, uma vontade manifestada é essencial para suprir a incapacidade do paciente sendo sempre relevante, pelo menos para efeitos do artigo 9º CEDHB e artigos 2º e 8º CEDH atendendo aos casos *Pretty* e *Lambert*. O notário ou o funcionário do RENTV à luz da Lei nº 25/2012, limita-se a receber formalmente uma vontade e comprovar a legalidade formal da mesma, contudo o direito e seu exercício é da soberania exclusiva do outorgante (cfr. Charalambos Pamboukis, *L'acte quasi public en droit*

cabendo ao direito do local do cuidado médico atribuir-lhe a sua eficácia. De certa forma o equilíbrio, entre a previsibilidade e estabilidade conducentes à protecção da confiança do outorgante e a conformidade dos seus efeitos com a lei do local do cuidado médico, permitiria assegurar a relevância da lei pessoal (quer fosse a lei da nacionalidade, residência habitual ou de uma lei igualmente próxima escolhida pelo outorgante) e acautelar os limites dessa vontade conforme os *moral data* do país de implementação da vontade[185].

Este entendimento teria como consequência a deslocação do problema da validade e eficácia do testamento vital da lei aplicável para o reconhecimento da situação jurídica. Isto pressupõe a mudança de paradigma quanto ao método de Direito Internacional Privado e de certa forma o regresso ao unilateralismo e a uma ideia de *comitas*. Mais do que determinar a lei competente, seria o reconhecimento da situação jurídica constituída de acordo com o Estado de origem[186]. Todavia, tal não assegura a plena eficácia do testamento vital, nem tão pouco a consideração do seu regime jurídico.

Parece-nos, expostas as possibilidades de enquadramento do testamento vital, que a cisão entre outorga e eficácia deve assentar na distin-

international privé, 82 Revue Critique de Droit International Privé (1993), p. 571). O valor declarativo seria ainda atribuído aos actos de registo Rolf Wagner, *Anerkennung von Personenstandsurkunden in Europa*, 1 Neue Zeitschrift für Familienrecht (2014), salvo nos casos em que o registo seja obrigatório e condição eficácia (como sucede para os factos identificados no artigo 2º Código de Registo Civil português, mas cujo regime legal não se aplica ao testamento vital). Nestes casos poder-se-ia submeter a regulação do testamento vital à *lex loci registrationis*.

[185] Seria a tentativa de resolver as exigências de segurança e previsibilidade conferidas pelo método conflitual inerentes a um determinado estatuto que por definição pressupõe um carácter ilimitado ou duradouro em contraste com a produção de efeitos transfronteiriços e seu reconhecimento, mesmo que temporário. Sobre a utilidade do método do reconhecimento e método conflitual e suas dificuldades fala Paul Lagarde da questão dos efeitos e da proximidade da conexão à regulação de questões de estatuto, em especial pessoal, e o problema do institutos desconhecidos (cfr. Lagarde, RabelsZ, (2004), pp. 232-235). No entanto, nos casos em que o documento seja particular será mais difícil transpor esta teoria Hein, Anotação ao artigo 3º EGBGB. 2015. Rn132. Ver ainda .

[186] Cfr. Erik Jayme & Christian Kohler, *Europäisches Kollisionsrecht 2001: Anerkennungsprinzip statt IPR?*, IPrax (2001)., p. 502 e Erik Jayme, *Il Diritto internazionale privato nel sistema comunitario e i suoi recenti sviluppi normativi nei rapporti con stati terzi*, 42 Rivista di diritto internazionale privato e processuale (2006).p. 355. Para uma perspectiva crítica ver Vicente, Cuadernos de Derecho Transnacional, (2009)., pp. 217-218.

ção entre normas de estrutura ou secundárias e normas de conduta ou primárias, proposta por Baptista Machado[187]. O outorgante de um testamento vital é titular de um legitima expectativa de que a sua vontade previamente manifestada, independentemente do carácter plurilocalizado da situação, seja relevante num processo de decisão quanto a um determinado cuidado saúde. Trata-se de uma manifestação da dignidade e autodeterminação do outorgante que obrigatoriamente se repercute no seu estatuto pessoal, e com isso, terá que ganhar foros de extra-territorialidade quanto à sua relevância jurídica. Tem que ser tomado em consideração e garantido o mínimo de relevância dentro da concepção de meta-ordem pública assente, desde logo no artigo 3º, nº 2 *al.* a) CDF, artigo 8º CEDH e artigo 9º CEDHB. Sem contudo ignorar que a eficácia e vinculatividade do testamento vital está sujeita à não violação da ordem pública internacional do Estado de implementação e, decisivo, da actuação do destinatário do testamento vital, o médico, cujo comportamento depende da prévia determinação de regras de conduta concretizadoras da relação jurídica médico-paciente.

Daí que o testamento vital esteja, quanto às condições de eficácia e implementação, dependente do estatuto delitual, mas já não quanto à sua perfeição, forma e validade. Ao estatuto delitual apenas cabe determinar a existência da causa de justificação e não apreciar a validade ou invalidade do testamento vital, na medida em que não lhe compete regular tal figura por não cair no seu âmbito de competência. Há por isso uma cisão entre lei que regula os efeitos e lei que regula a constituição dos testamentos vitais, na medida em que cabe ao estatuto delitual somente determinar as normas de conduta ou primárias e desta feita os limites de eficácia do testamento vital.

Posto isto, porque a validade e perfeição do testamento vital são determinadas por normas de estrutura ou secundárias, cabe à lei pessoal lei regular aquele. Estamos perante uma verdadeira questão prévia sujeita a uma conexão autónoma circunscrita ao tempo e espaço da sua outorga, quer na substância, quer na forma (artigos 25º, 27º e 36º CC). Assim, um cidadão austríaco com 17 anos, poderá outorgar um testamento vital em Portugal porquanto a sua lei pessoal reconhece capacidade para tal (arti-

---

[187] Cfr. Machado, Âmbito de Eficácia e Âmbito de Competência das Leis (Limites das Leis e Conflitos de Leis). 1998., pp. 131-134.

gos 25º e 31º, nº 1 CC), apesar do nosso artigo 4º *al.* a) da Lei nº 25/2012 não permitir[188]. Ou será reconhecida validade do testamento vital outorgado por um português, residente na Áustria, de acordo com os preceitos desta (artigo 31º, nº 2 CC).

A forma já estará ao abrigo do artigo 36º CC e respectivas conexões nele prescritas. Neste é prevista uma alternatividade de princípio, na mira da consecução da validade formal da declaração entre a lei da substância do negócio, a lei do local da declaração e a lei do Estado para que remeta a lei local. Esta relação de alternatividade só será de aplicar caso as formalidades exigidas pela lei aplicável à substância do negócio não o sejam *ad substantiam*, isto é que gerem a sua invalidade ou ineficácia mesmo relativamente a negócios celebrados no estrangeiro. Sendo-o, será a lei do negócio imperativamente a aplicável, o que equivale a, antecipando um eventual conflito de qualificações, fazer prevalecer a qualificação substância sobre a qualificação forma. Para estes efeitos, lugar da declaração será aquele em que ela é efectivamente emitida ou completada, sendo que se for transmitida através de um núncio ao seu destinatário, será relevante o lugar em que a parte comunica a declaração ao núncio, mas se se tratar de um representante na vontade, será relevante o local em que este emite a declaração[189].

Reportando-nos à nossa lei, é de realçar que a exigência de forma autêntica, ainda que interpretada como verdadeira formalidade *ad substantiam*, é-o para efeitos da norma de protecção que a Lei nº 25/2012 encerra, em especial o dever que dela resulta no artigo 6º, nº 1 e que torna a vontade prospectiva vinculativa[190]. Logo, o testamento vital para ser vinculativo nos termos do artigo 6º, nº 1 terá que respeitar a forma de documento autêntico ou particular autenticado, mesmo que no local da sua outorga haja liberdade de forma (como é o caso na Alemanha). Todavia, fora do quadro legal e atendendo ao artigo 340º, nº 3 do Código Civil o testamento vital com forma menos solene à exigida não deixará de ser considerado, se for admitida à luz de algumas das leis competentes previstas no artigo 36º CC.

---

[188] Cfr. Dirk Olzen, *Die gesetzliche Neuregelung der Patientenverfügung*, JURISTISCHE RUNDSCHAU (2009), p. 360. Sobre o problema de quem decide pelos menores ver Guilherme de Oliveira, *O acesso dos menores aos cuidados de saúde*, in TEMAS DE DIREITO DA MEDICINA (2005).

[189] Cfr. MACHADO, Lições de Direito Internacional Privado. 2002. p. 353.

[190] Cfr. Ribeiro, LEX MEDICINAE, (2013), pp. 118-119.

Parece por isso que o estatuto da constituição do testamento é aquele que corresponde ao direito de autodeterminação e interesse do outorgante, na medida em que assim se promove, na maior extensão possível, a sua validade. A eficácia, contudo, do mesmo dependerá do local de *implementação*, não como pressuposto positivo, mas como pressuposto negativo de tal eficácia. O testamento vital só não produzirá os seus plenos efeitos de acordo com o direito de origem se a tal se opuser os *moral data* do país da conduta, da prestação do cuidado médico. Desta feita é assegurada a unidade valorativa entre estatuto da constituição e estatuto da eficácia, quando estes dois países sejam diferentes[191].

Até porque a eficácia do testamento vital está intimamente ligada à verificação de uma vontade relevante para determinado cuidado médico. Há, assim, um duplo requisito de actualidade do testamento vital quer quanto à validação da vontade prospectiva junto da vontade presumida, quer em termos do grau de informação e esclarecimento face à evolução da ciência médica, que dependerão sempre da consideração das regras jurídicas em vigor no local de tratamento. No momento em que a directiva releva, os seus efeitos resultam da lei e não exclusivamente da vontade. O outorgante apenas manifesta a vontade em aderir ou não a uma determinada terapêutica para estritos efeitos de manifestação do consentimento ou dissentimento necessário para a realização de uma intervenção nos interesses jurídicos vida e integridade pessoal.

3. Normas de Aplicação Necessária e Imediata

Uma das válvulas de escape perante a *rigidez* da consequência da regras de conflitos e salvaguarda de interesses públicos relevantes, em especial do Estado do foro, são as normas de aplicação necessária e imediata, cuja menção é feita no artigo 16º Roma II. Como dá conta Moura Ramos

---

[191] A dificuldade de conhecimento da lei estrangeira, em especial para profissionais de saúde, não relevam autonomamente, nem podem condicionar a lei competente. Ao conhecimento do direito estrangeiro valem as regras gerais previstas no artigo 23º e 348º CC. Cfr. Correia, Lições de Direito Internacional Privado. 2000, p. 427 e ss, em especial pp. 427- -428 e Machado, Lições de Direito Internacional Privado. 2002, pp. 246-250 e Luís de Lima Pinheiro, Direito Internacional Privado § I – Introdução e Direito de Conflitos – Parte Geral (Almedina 3ª edição refundida ed. 2014), pp. 648-656. Numa perspectiva de direito comparado ver a obra AA.VV., Application of Foreign Law (Carlos Esplugues, et al. eds., Sellier – European Law Publishers Kindle ed. 2011).

estamos perante "normas materiais do foro que exigem ser aplicadas a dado círculo de relação, para além e independentemente do domínio das regras de conflito atribuam à ordem jurídica onde se integram"[192]. Retira-se da norma material, quer por via expressa, quer por via implícita, a conexão unilateral *ad hoc* que permite a sua delimitação espacial. Destarte é por força dos interesses especiais previstos nas normas materiais que se estabelece uma conexão autónoma face à prevista na regra de conflitos bilateral[193].

A formulação adoptada no artigo 16º Roma II consagra a relevância e autonomia na aplicação das normas de aplicação necessária e imediata, concedendo a estas normas o poder de afasta a *lex causae*. Todavia, o artigo 16º Roma II, quando confrontado com o artigo 9º do Roma I, não espelha a evolução que neste Regulamento ocorreu, mantendo-se a versão correspondente à do artigo 7º, nº 2 da Convenção de Roma sobre a lei aplicável às obrigações contratuais.

Não poderá, no entanto, deixar de ser tida em consideração a evolução normativa e doutrinal sobre a natureza e função deste tipo de normas, bem como deve ser tido em conta igualmente a formulação do artigo 9º Roma I, ressalvando as devidas adaptações à natureza e fonte das obrigações contratuais e não contratuais. Isto porque, tendo as obrigação não contratuais uma fonte *ex lege*, as normas de aplicação necessária e imediata assumem-se, pelo seu carácter eminentemente territorial, como regras de conduta e normas de protecção de interesses jurídicos do local onde a conduta é realizada e do local onde se produz o dano. Será este o caso das normas *substantivas ou primárias* que estabelecem, atendendo aos interesses predominantemente públicos, como deve (ou o que se espera) um cidadão actuar, resultando a sua violação na aplicação das normas sancio-

---

[192] Cfr. Rui Manuel Moura Ramos, *Aspectos recentes do direito internacional privado português, in* Das Relações Privadas Internacionais. Estudos de Direito Internacional Privado (1995), pp. 97-98. Para mais desenvolvimentos ver António Arruda Ferrer Correia, *Considerações sobre o Método do Direito Internacional Privado, in* Estudos em Homenagem ao Prof. Doutor J.J. Teixeira Ribeiro (1983), pp. 77-80, Machado, Âmbito de eficácia e âmbito de competências das leis. 1998, pp. 277-280. Ver ainda António Novais Marques dos Santos, As Normas de Aplicação Imediata no Direito Internacional Privado – Esboço de uma Teoria Geral § I (Almedina. 1991). e id. at, § II.

[193] Cfr. Wendelstein, Kollisionsrechtliche Probleme der Telemedizin: zugleich ein Beitrag zur Koordination von Vertrag und Delikt auf der Ebene des europäischen 2012., p. 281.

DIREITO DA SAÚDE

natórias ou secundárias[194]. Quando se trate de normas do primeiro grupo que não se apliquem a título de lei do foro ou de lex causae, as normas de aplicação necessária e imediata terão necessariamente que ser tidas em consideração quando o facto danoso integrar o âmbito da sua competência e este tiver ocorrido no local da actuação do lesante ou no local da verificação do dano, desde que exista uma ligação próxima e previsível com os interessados (que não seja meramente ocasional). A relevância destas normas decorre da necessidade de verificação da ilicitude, da culpa ou do risco, enquanto pressupostos constitutivos de um obrigação *ex lege*, na medida em que o local onde actua o profissional de saúde não pode ser irrelevante para a formulação de um juízo de censura à sua conduta. Argumentos a favor da toma em consideração da norma de um terceiro Estado são desde logo os princípios da igualdade e da confiança a respeito da tutela das expectativas e, desta forma, a previsibilidade, quanto ao comportamento a adoptar e a exigir entre o lesado e o lesante, bem como o próprio princípio da proximidade associado à adequação da conexão relevante a regular a situação jurídica.

A aplicação de normas portuguesas desta natureza não depende do reconhecimento da competência do sistema [português] em que se inserem, mas antes da vontade de aplicação a determinadas situações traduzida numa particular "norma de aplicação" do nosso sistema jurídico[195]. O seu âmbito de aplicação é assim determinado, de forma unilateral, por referência aos interesses do sistema onde se inserem[196].

Um dos exemplos que nos parece integrar a categoria de normas de aplicação necessária e imediata diz respeito ao regime da responsabilidade do Estado e entes públicos aprovado pela Lei nº 67/2007[197]. Este regime jurídico, na sua *ratio* e natureza, visa regular a responsabi-

---

[194] Cfr. ALF ROSS, DIRECTIVES AND NORMS (Ted Honderich ed., Routledge & Kegan Paul. 1968), pp. 114-115.

[195] Cfr. Ramos, Linhas Gerais da evolução do Direito Internacional Privado Português posteriormente ao Código Civil de 1966. 2006, p. 537.

[196] Cfr. CORREIA, Direito Internacional Privado – Alguns problemas. 1985., p. 60.

[197] A natureza de direito público atribuído a este diploma não afasta, *ab initio* a susceptibilidade de ser subsumido e chamado à liça por regras de conflito. A questão do direito público e as regras de conflitos ver RUI MANUEL MOURA RAMOS, DIREITO INTERNACIONAL PRIVADO E CONSTITUIÇÃO. INTRODUÇÃO A UMA ANÁLISE DAS SUAS RELAÇÕES (Coimbra Editora. 1994), pp. 123-130.

lidade por actos ou omissões praticados no exercício de funções públicas, aqui entendidas como o exercício de prerrogativas de poder público ou reguladas por disposições ou princípios de direito administrativo[198]. A estes actos opõe-se os actos praticados no exercício de actividades de gestão privada e que estão sujeitos às regras de responsabilidade civil (artigo 501º CC[199]). Isto coloca algumas dificuldades na qualificação do regime jurídico quando os cuidados médicos sejam prestados por Unidades Hospitalares integrantes do Serviço Nacional de Saúde português e cujo regime de responsabilidade é regulado pelo diploma de 2007. Cremos que este regime se deve qualificar como uma norma de aplicação necessária e imediata para efeitos do artigo 16º Roma II, quer por força da sua natureza imperativa decorrente do interesse público subjacente à regulação da responsabilidade dos entes públicos, como pela delimitação unilateral do seu âmbito de aplicação espacial em função da qualidade do sujeito responsável pelo facto danoso, artigo 1º, da Lei nº 67/2007. A lei portuguesa é competente sempre que o facto danoso seja realizado pelo Estado português e demais entes investidos de poderes públicos e na prossecução de um interesse público decisivo para a conservação e manutenção da organização política e social do Estado português conforme a Base XII da Lei nº 48/90, (última alteração Lei nº 27/2002, de 8 de Novembro)[200]. Tal significa que os cuidados médicos prestados no âmbito do serviço nacional de saúde e da relação jurídica dele emergente nos termos da Lei nº 67/2007 estão sujeitos ao artigo 16º Roma II.

---

[198] Cfr. MARIA DA GLÓRIA FERREIRA PINTO DIAS GARCIA, A Responsabilidade Civil do Estado e demais Pessoas Colectivas Públicas. (1997). pp. 30-32.

[199] Com a lei de 2007 deixou de se falar em actos de gestão pública, contudo mantém-se pertinente a distinção entre actos de gestão privada e pública, desde logo porque se mantém em vigor o artigo 501º CC e com isso os dois regimes de responsabilidade. A nova lei se aplica apenas a *acções e omissões adoptadas no exercício de prerrogativas de poder público ou reguladas por disposições ou princípios de direito administrativo*. Dúvidas não existem quanto a este ponto: é precisamente por isso que o artigo 501º do Código Civil não foi revogado pelo novo diploma legal. Significando que a realização de cuidados médicos fora do quadro da prestação de um serviço público sujeita as entidades públicas hospitalares ao regime fixado pelo artigo 4º Roma II.

200 É aliás esta a teoria aceite comummente pela doutrina como o critério de distinção entre o direito privado e o direito público RAMOS, Direito Internacional Privado e Constituição. Introdução a uma Análise das suas Relações. 1994.pp. 123-130.

DIREITO DA SAÚDE

Não deixam de se colocar ainda questões relativas ao *continuum* da tutela das expectativas particulares, um dos fins do direito internacional privado, em especial perante a ausência de unidade *internacional* da ilicitude. Os nossos artigos 3º e 4º do Código Penal (CP) determinam, de forma unilateral, a tutela penal conferida a bens jurídicos reconhecidos pela ordem jurídica portuguesa. Determinar a ilicitude acaba por ser uma tarefa confiada, em regra, ao Estado onde ocorre a conduta ou a lesão dos bens jurídicos. No entanto, pode ser relevante considerar outra lei para apurar ou não a disponibilidade de um determinado bem jurídico e sua ofensa. Muitas vezes a resposta a esta questão constitui uma questão prévia, verdadeira situação jurídica condicionante, que influi no juízo de ilicitude ou culpa[201].

Da aplicação de mais do que uma lei competente, mesmo no âmbito da direito penal, podem resultar antinomias materiais para as quais a excepção de ordem pública internacional, prevista no artigo 22º CC, poderá funcionar como uma instrumento de resolução de tais conflitos normativos, ao permitir a definição unilateral dos interesses juridicamente protegidos e inderrogáveis, mesmo no caso das situações plurilocalizadas. Associar-se-ia o artigo 22º CC aos artigos 4º, 5º, 6º e 7º do CP como exemplo do limite da soberania dos Estados, nomeadamente, no exercício das funções punitivas circunscritas ao seu território, temperado pelo princípio do tratamento mais favorável do arguido por referência às leis em contacto com a situação penalmente relevante[202].

No entanto, podemos igualmente considerar que as normas penais se qualificam como normas de aplicação necessária e imediata, verdadeira ordem pública internacional de funcionamento apriorístico. Posto isto, considerando os artigos 149º, 150º, 156º e 157º CP, em conjugação com os artigos 3º e 7º CP, como normas de aplicação necessária e imediata, estas irão se aplicar sempre que sejam os tribunais portugueses competentes (artigo 5º, nº 3 Bruxelas I) e tenham os cuidados médicos sido

---

[201] Como nota Andreas Spinckhoff o problema da questão prévia não é um coutada do DIP (cfr. Spickhoff, Die Einheit des Rechtswidrigkeitsurteils im Zusammenspiel von Internationalem Privat– und Strafrecht. 2009, p. 920). Entre nós, sobre a questão prévia em DIP e em Direito Penal ver Inês Ferreira Leite, O Conflito de Leis Penais. Natureza e Função do Direito Penal Internacional (Coimbra Editora. 2008), pp. 463-471.
[202] Cfr. Adolf Schönke & Horst Schröder, Sommentar zum Strafgesetzbuch: StGB (C. H. Beck 29., neu bearbeitete Auflage ed. 2014)., §3.

prestados em território nacional ou, não sendo os tribunais portugueses competentes, exista uma conexão relevante com Portugal, por exemplo, o domicílio profissional do médico ser em Portugal ou encontrar-se inscrito na ordem profissional portuguesa[203]. Isto porque, como vimos *supra*, a interpretação do artigo 16º Roma II admite a tomada em consideração de normas de aplicação necessária e imediata de Estados terceiros[204]. Através do funcionamento destas normas limita-se a aplicação da *lex causae* estrangeira, em especial nas situações em que funcione a cláusula de excepção do nº 3 do artigo 4º Roma II, por força da prévia existência de um relação contratual entre lesante e lesado. Parece, pois, que o problema do desvalor da conduta e consequente responsabilidade justifica a tomada em consideração de normas de aplicação necessária e imediata de Estados terceiros que tenham com a situação um contacto relevante[205].

---

[203] Erwin Deutsch e Andreas Spickhoff falam da possibilidade de aplicação do direito do local de tratamento ou a sede da prestação de cuidados de saúde por parte do médico, em especial nos casos de delito à distância (seriam as situações de telemedicina), se as normas destes Estados prescreverem um *standard* mais elevado do cuidado médico do que aquele no local do dano (em regra será o local do tratamento) (cfr. DEUTSCH & SPICKHOFF, Medizinrecht – Arztrecht, Arzneimittelrecht, Medizinprodukterecht und Transfusionsrecht. 2008, pp. 512-513). Veremos contudo que estes standards terão maior relevância em sede de regras de segurança e conduta prescritas no artigo 17º Roma II.

[204] Cfr. Hein, RABELSZ, (2009)., p. 506. Sobre as possíveis interpretações do artigo 16º ver Junker, Rom II-VO Anwendungsbereich. 2015.anotação ao art. 16º Rn 23-28. Como nota este autor, atendendo à formulação do artigo 16º este terá um enquadramento autónomo ao consagrado no artigo 8º Roma I (cfr. *ob. cit.* Rn. 28), bem como, assim parece, não se deverá reproduzir as considerações formuladas a respeito do artigo 7º, nº 2 da Convenção para o artigo 16º Roma I desde logo pela discrepância Wagner, IPRAX, (2008), p. 15 e Helmut Ofner, *Die Rom II-Verordnung – Neues Internationales Privatrecht für außervertragliche Schuldverhältnisse in der Europäischen Union*, 49 ZEITSCHRIFT FÜR EUROPARECHT, INTERNATIONALES PRIVATRECHT UND RECHTSVERGLEICHUNG (2008).p. 23. Mas fundamentalmente pelas considerações autónomas que devem ter sobre os pressupostos e regime das obrigações não contratuais, pois, ao contrário do que sucede nas relações obrigacionais contratuais, a fonte das obrigações reguladas pelo Roma II é *ex lege* e, neste sentido, a relevância das normas de aplicação necessária e imediata terão forçosamente outra relevância e consideração, em especial quando a *lex causae* pode ser uma lei que não a do local da conduta ou do dano (artigo 4º, nº 2 e 3).

[205] Cfr. Acórdão *Arblade*, C-369/96, §30: "leis de polícia e de segurança, cabe entender esta expressão como visando as disposições nacionais cuja observância foi considerada crucial para a salvaguarda da organização política, social ou económica do Estado-Membro em causa, a ponto de impor o seu respeito a qualquer pessoa que se encontre no território nacional

DIREITO DA SAÚDE

Igual natureza terão as normas respeitantes ao consentimento informado no âmbito da colheita e transplante de órgãos e tecidos de origem humana (artigos 2º e 8º da Lei nº 12/93, última alteração Lei nº 36/2013), ensaios clínicos (artigo 28º e seguintes Regulamento nº 536/2014/UE) e investigação clínica (Lei nº 21/2014, de 16 de Agosto, última alteração Lei nº 73/2015). Para estes instrumentos normativos, as exigências de informação e regras sobre consentimento são verdadeiras normas de aplicação necessária e imediata que se aplicam a todos os cuidados médicos realizados sobre o seu manto de competência. Para os demais casos, como será o regime de consentimento informado, o interesse estadual não impõe um âmbito de aplicação espacial fixado de forma unilateral. Apenas seria cogitável quando se falasse de delitos à distância, eventualmente no âmbito da actividade de telemedicina[206].

Chegados aqui cabe ainda referir que existem ainda dúvidas a respeito da relevância e natureza da Lei nº 25/2012, a lei que regula as directivas antecipadas em Portugal. Parece-nos que não se pode qualificar como norma de aplicação necessária e imediata, porquanto o interesse público nela patente advém da protecção de interesses individuais – o direito à autodeterminação do outorgante – não limitando a sua aplicação, nem ela se impondo, ao território português. Bem como a Lei nº 25/2012 não consagra o princípio da taxatividade a respeito das direcitivas antecipadas, continuando a ser relevante, para efeitos do artigo 340º, nº 3 CC e 39º CP, todas as manifestações prospectivas, quer por documento particular, oral ou mesmo as caducadas. No entanto é discutível que não se possa, ainda na sequência do Acórdão *Arblade*, integrar o interesse privado do outorgante e o interesse público da prestação dos cuidados de saúde como uma questão de protecção da parte mais fraca (interesse outorgante) e como forma de organização do cuidado de saúde, em especial, a segurança para o profissional de saúde quanto à eficácia e vinculativadade do testamento vital.

Assim como o seu carácter não é pessoal, nem obedece à ordem de interesses integrantes da nacionalidade, porquanto representa, assim o

---

desse Estado-Membro ou a qualquer relação jurídica neste localizada" e Junker, Rom II-VO Anwendungsbereich. 2015. Anotação ao artigo 16º, Rn 20.

[206] Sobre esta questão ver Spickhoff, Die Einheit des Rechtswidrigkeitsurteils im Zusammenspiel von Internationalem Privat– und Strafrecht. 2009. , pp. 915-916.

entendemos, uma norma de protecção tendente a regular e a proteger o direito à autodeterminação do outorgante. Para isso impõe deveres e ónus jurídicos *especiais* a cargo dos responsáveis pelos cuidados de saúde no âmbito do processo de obtenção do consentimento informado necessário ao cuidado de saúde. Mas não esgota a relevância das directivas antecipadas, mesmo aquelas que não cumpram os requisitos formais e objecto previstos, ou até mesmo para aqueles que tenham caducado por decurso do prazo de 5 anos. A regulamentação do direito à autodeterminação prospectiva não elimina o direito à autodeterminação reconhecido e tutelado como direitos, liberdades e garantias no artigo 27º, nº 1 da Constituição e como direito de personalidade no artigo 70º, nº 1 CC. Daqui decorre que um testamento vital outorgado no estrangeiro, segundo a lei desse Estado, não deixará de ser considerado relevante se válido de acordo com essa lei, apenas dependendo, quanto à eficácia, do respeito pela ordem pública internacional portuguesa e que se encontra concretizado no artigo 5º da Lei nº 25/2012.

Dito isto, se um médico for confrontado com um testamento vital outorgado na Bélgica onde se permite a manifestação de uma vontade tendente à realização de um processo activo de morte, aquele não poderá deixar de apreciar o testamento vital válido à luz da *lex causae* (artigo 25º ou artigo 31º, nº 2 do Código Civil). Apenas não está vinculado à vontade por aquela ser contrária à ordem pública internacional portuguesa tal como resulta do artigo 7º CP e artigo 5º da Lei nº 25/2012. Não se trata por isso de uma questão de validade ou invalidade, mas somente eficácia da vontade prospectiva, logo oponibilidade em relação ao responsável pelos cuidados de saúde, afastando-se as disposições que choquem contra a excepção de ordem pública internacional portuguesa.

4. Regras de segurança e de conduta
Das regras de conflitos consagradas em geral pelo Roma II já pudemos constatar que nem sempre a lei do local do dano directo corresponde à lei do local da conduta. Assim, como pode a lei competente ser outra mais próxima dos interessados, face ao carácter ocasional do contacto com o local onde se produziu o dano. Serão os casos da aplicação da lei residência habitual comum (artigo 4º, nº 2 Roma II), ou da aplicação de uma lei com uma conexão mais estreita (p.ex., a conexão acessória ligada a um contrato de prestação de cuidados médicos regulada pelos artigos

DIREITO DA SAÚDE

3º, 4º e 6 Roma I). Uma vez que é possível existir uma dissonância entre lei do local da conduta e a lei do local do dano (delito à distância), ou entre lei do local da conduta-dano e *lex causae*, há o risco de ocorrer um desfasamento entre o princípio territorial que pauta as regras de conduta (as ditas normas primárias ou substantivas) e a lei que regula o estatuto delitual. Trata-se portanto de normas que, pela sua natureza e função, são consideradas na concretização do *Tatbestand* da responsabilidade à luz da *lex causae* relativa à questão delitual (artigo 17º Roma II). Mais do que falar de uma conexão autónoma, estaríamos considerar as regras de conduta que o autor deve respeitar, isto independentemente da *lex causae* não ser a do local da conduta e/ou do dano. O artigo 17º Roma II, ao ordenar a tomada em consideração das regras de segurança e de conduta, estipula a relevância do local dos factos concretos para a averiguação da responsabilidade, traduzindo por isso uma ideia de localização e não de remissão para o âmbito de competência da lei do local da conduta[207].

Os deveres de esclarecimento estariam assim integrados por esta norma impondo, se necessário, uma adaptação entre a *lex causae* e a lei do local da conduta quando estas não coincidissem. Neste sentido andou ERWIN DEUTSCH ao defender que as regras de consentimento informado, em especial as relativas às exigências do dever de esclarecimento, seriam reguladas pelo local da conduta do médico, isto independentemente do estatuto delitual[208].

Contudo, GERFRIED FISCHER opõe-se a esta qualificação afirmando que as regras sobre o dever de esclarecimento ao visarem essencialmente interesses próprios da relação médico-paciente não seriam análogas às regras de trânsito, e por isso afastadas do artigo 17º Roma II[209]. Segundo este autor, a existência de deveres gerais de cuidado atinentes ao interesse jurídico pessoal (integridade física e saúde) não se autonomizam

---

[207] Na concretização das ideias mestras do Direito Internacional Privado enquanto direito de conflitos, esclarece Baptista Machado que "a ideia de «localização» reporta-se directamente aos factos concretos, ao passo que a ideia de «âmbito de competência» se refere, antes, a questões ou matérias jurídicas." (cfr. MACHADO, Âmbito de Eficácia e Âmbito de Competência das Leis (Limites das Leis e Conflitos de Leis). 1998, p. 317).

[208] Cfr. Deustch, Das Internationale Privatrecht der Arzthaftung. 1978, p. 123.

[209] Cfr. Fischer, Ärztliche Verhaltenspflichten und anzuwendendes Recht bei grenzüberschreitender telemedizinischer Behandlung. 2006., pp. 784 e 787 e ss. Assim também defende Spickhoff, Die Einheit des Rechtswidrigkeitsurteils im Zusammenspiel von Internationalem Privat– und Strafrecht. 2009, pp. 917-918.

do estatuto delitual ou contratual. Este autor, partindo do pressuposto que toda a relação médico-paciente assenta num contrato de prestação de serviços, afirma que o dever de esclarecimento integra os deveres gerais de conduta a que o médico se encontra vinculado. Isto porque o interesse é exclusivamente privado e parte integrante da relação individual especial entre médico e paciente[210]. Daí que nas situações em que se qualifique a situação como integrante do âmbito de aplicação do Regulamento Roma II, se preveja a possibilidade de aplicar o estatuto contratual nos termos do artigo 4º, nº 3 Roma II, admitindo assim a aplicação de um estatuto cujo dever de esclarecimento seja de menor intensidade. A protecção máxima a conferir seria sempre em função aos interesses vida, integridade física e saúde e não ao consentimento informado. Contudo, como vimos acima, podem existir situações em que estejamos perante normas de aplicação necessária e imediata e desta forma se imponha, autonomamente à *lex causae*, um dever especial de esclarecimento e regime de consentimento informado.

Na verdade o artigo 17º Roma II, no que concerne ao seu elemento histórico, inspirou-se no artigo 7º da Convenção da Haia de 1971 sobre a lei aplicável em matéria de acidentes de circulação rodoviária e no artigo 9º da Convenção da Haia de 1973 sobre a lei aplicável à responsabilidade de produto[211]. Estando por isso alinhada com o nosso artigo 45º, nº 3 do Código Civil. Segundo o considerando 34 do Roma II o artigo 17º diz respeito a regras relacionadas com a segurança e a conduta, pressupondo, não a evicção da *lex causae*, mas a sua consideração com vista a concretizar a matéria de facto a subsumir às normas materiais do *Tatbestand* da *lex causae*[212]. Não é portanto uma regra de conflitos, antes servindo de elemento de integração das consequências jurídicas resultantes da aplicação, desde logo, do artigo 4º, tratando-se para alguns autores de *normas*

---

[210] Cfr. Fischer, Ärztliche Verhaltenspflichten und anzuwendendes Recht bei grenzüberschreitender telemedizinischer Behandlung. 2006, p. 787.

[211] Sobre o sentido destas normas ver DICKINSON, The Roma II Regulation. The Law Applicable to Non-Contractual Obligations. 2013, pp. 638-640.

[212] Transcrevendo o considerando: "Para atingir um equilíbrio razoável entre as partes, é necessário ter em conta, na medida do possível, normas de segurança e de conduta em vigor no país em que o acto danoso foi praticado, mesmo quando a obrigação extracontratual seja regulada pela lei de outro país. Os termos «regras de segurança e de conduta» deverão ser interpretados como referindo-se a todas as regras relacionadas com a segurança e a conduta, incluindo, por exemplo, as relativas à segurança rodoviária em caso de acidente".

DIREITO DA SAÚDE

auxiliares[213]. Daí que o elemento literal "tomadas em conta" não seja despiciendo, pois se circunscrevem à situação de facto e não de direito[214].

A este tipo de normas cabe determinar o *padrão mínimo de cuidado* exigível à actuação no local do dano (coincidindo, em princípio, com o local da conduta), sendo que tal poderá servir para fins de exclusão da responsabilidade, como para fundar a responsabilidade do prestador de cuidados médicos[215]. São fontes destas regras de segurança e de conduta normas em vigor no local de actuação, sejam elas de direito público ou privado, ou normas legais, administrativas ou consuetudinárias ou mesmo jurisprudenciais. Isto não descarta a possibilidade da sobreposição de outras normas, nomeadamente normas de aplicação necessária e imediata de natureza penal, o que impõe um esforço de adaptação das disposições materiais em ordem da unidade de ilícito construído ao abrigo do princípio da harmonia interna ou material[216].

Tendo em consideração o paralelo entre o artigo 17º Roma II e o nosso artigo 45º, nº 3 CC, é relevante vermos o que entende a doutrina portuguesa a este respeito. Segundo BAPTISTA MACHADO a referência do nº 3 parte final dizia respeito a normas *de protecção preventiva ou de segurança*, normas que, como p. ex. as regras de trânsito e outros regulamentos técnicos de segurança, se impõem a todas as pessoas como normas de ordem e interesse público, e que nem sequer integram o instituto da responsabilidade civil, mas não podem deixar de ser atendidas, pelo menos no

---

[213] Cfr. Junker, Rom II-VO Anwendungsbereich. 2015, artigo 17º Roma II, Rn. 2.

[214] Cfr. Andreas Spickhoff, *Anotação ao artigo 17º, in* BECK'SCHER ONLINE-KOMMENTAR BGB (2013), Rn. 5.

[215] O artigo 17º, apesar de referir na sua letra "o comportamento da pessoa cuja responsabilidade é invocada" não visa estabelecer um princípio de tratamento de favor do autor, antes, determinar a relevância da lei do local da conduta como ponto de contacto que estabelece o padrão de cuidado, sem contudo, e ao contrário do artigo 16º, derrogar a *lex causae*. Isto significa que tanto poderá relevar como regras de conduta mais ou menos exigentes e não como privilégio a favor do autor (cfr. DICKINSON, The Roma II Regulation. The Law Applicable to Non-Contractual Obligations. 2013., p. 641e). Não procedem assim as críticas de Symeonides, AMERICAN JOURNAL OF COMPARATIVE LAW, (2008), p. 213. Tanto mais que as questões respeitantes à, entre nós conhecida, culpa do lesado não integrarem o âmbito do artigo 17º, mas sim o estatuto delitual conforme o artigo 15º *al.* b) (Junker, Rom II-VO Anwendungsbereich. 2015.anotação ao artigo 17º, Rn. 25).

[216] Cfr. Spickhoff, Die Einheit des Rechtswidrigkeitsurteils im Zusammenspiel von Internationalem Privat– und Strafrecht. 2009., pp. 915-920.

O CUIDADO MÉDICO TRANSFRONTEIRIÇO E O CONSENTIMENTO INFORMADO ...

que toca à determinação da ilicitude da conduta perigosa[217]. Por sua vez MOURA RAMOS pugna por um entendimento de que este nº 3 se refere "leis de aplicação necessária e imediata", uma vez que exigem ser aplicadas independentemente do carácter internacional de uma determinada relação[218]. Já MOURA VICENTE, entende que são regras "apenas tomadas em consideração como um pressuposto dos efeitos jurídicos estatuídos pela regra de conflitos nacional – *hoc sensu* com um elemento da hipótese de facto nela contida"[219].

Efectivamente não nos parece que possamos alocar o nº 3 do artigo 45º CC exclusivamente às normas de aplicação necessária imediata, tanto mais que a sua relevância apenas podia ser entendida quando dissesse respeito a uma lei de um Estado terceiro, ou seja, não era a lei do foro, nem a *lex causae*. Todavia, a *ratio* desta norma é atender às regras de conduta fixadas no local de actuação do autor do dano (a lei do país da conduta). Neste sentido, serão relevantes as normas, independentemente da sua natureza necessária e imediata, que apresentarem como conexão unilateral o local da conduta do autor, não tendo por este facto necessariamente uma vocação derrogatória da *lex causae*. Contudo não é afastada a possibilidade das normas serem de natureza necessária e imediata e relevarem pelo artigo 17º Roma II, para os casos em que se entenda – o que não foi a posição por nós assumida – que para o artigo 16º Roma II apenas remete para as normas de aplicação imediata do Estado do foro[220]. Há aliás, em nosso entender, a necessidade de assegurar o princípio da igualdade, quer numa perspectiva de paridade de tratamento das ordens jurídicas, quer na própria relação jurídica extracontratual emergente do facto lesivo. A apreciação do desvalor jurídico da conduta e da culpa resulta da apreciação das regras de conduta existentes no local do facto lesivo, porquanto seriam sempre à luz destas que se pode partir para a aferição do grau de cuidado e de omissão para com os interesses jurídicos violados. A enorme discricionariedade conferida ao foro, que se estende

---

[217] Cfr. MACHADO, Lições de Direito Internacional Privado. 2002., pp. 373-374.

[218] Cfr. VICENTE, Da Responsabilidade Pré-Contratual em Direito Internacional Privado. 2011, pp. 677-678, n. 642.

[219] Cfr. Id. at., p. 496.

[220] Cfr. Dominique Jakob & Peter Picht, *Anotação ao artigo 17º*, in EUROPÄISCHES ZIVILPROZESS-UND KOLLISIONSRECHT. EuZPR/EuIPR KOMMENTAR. BEARBEITUNG 2011. ROM I-VO – ROM II-VO (Thomas Rauscher ed. 2011)., p. 975.

DIREITO DA SAÚDE

ao *como* e ao *se* da relevância das regras de segurança e de conduta, não pode deixar de vincular o tribunal na consideração efectiva do contacto das partes com a situção que irá determinar a relevância e exigibilidade de uma conduta conforme essas regras[221]. O artigo 17º Roma II seria assim o reflexo da consagração do conceito de *local data* de BRAINERD CURRIE e ALBERT EHRENZWEIG[222-223]. Como decorre da letra do artigo 17º estas regras *são tidas em conta e na medida em que for apropriado enquanto elementos de facto*. De realçar que, apesar da relevância em sede de matéria de facto, em virtude da natureza normativa dessas regras não deixarão aquelas de ser tratadas como verdadeiras questões de direito, pelo que se lhes aplica o artigo 348º, nº 2 CC[224].

Da posição daqueles autores resulta ainda que a competência do estatuto delitual é conservada, pelo que não é o artigo 17º uma norma de conflitos, como se prende somente com a apreciação da conduta e a sua conformidade com as regras vinculativas no local de actuação do autor do dano[225]. Isto significa que a relevância das regras de segurança ou de conduta do local da conduta terão que se justificar pela existência de um comando proibitivo ou preceptivo vinculativo da conduta do autor do dano e que estabeleça uma conexão especial entre o autor e local da conduta, desligada das regras que integram o estatuto delitual. Todavia,

---

[221] Cfr. Id. at., p. 975.

[222] Cfr. CURRIE, Selected Essays on the Conflict of Laws. 1963. pp. 67-71 e 178 e Albert Ehrenzweig, *Local and Moral Data in the Conflict of Laws: Terra Incognita*, 16 BUFFALO LAW REVIEW (1966-1967), p. 55. Em certo sentido a consideração da identidade cultural do interessado e das regras de conduta vigentes no páis em contacto com a situação delitual pressupõem um relevância inexorável e que não pode ser ignorada pela aplicação da *lex causae*. Neste sentido valem as considerações da *Zweitstuffestheorie* (cfr. Erik Jayme, *Identité Culturelle et Intégration: Le Droit International Privé Postmoderne*, *in* RECUEIL DES COURS (1996), p. 167 e ss. e 251 e ss, entre nós ver NUNO ASCENSÃO SILVA, A CONSTITUIÇÃO DA ADOPÇÃO DE MENORES NAS RELAÇÕES PRIVADAS INTERNACIONAIS: ALGUNS ASPECTOS. § 49 (Boletim da Faculdade de Direito da Universidade de Coimbra. 2000). pp. 262-263).

[223] Cfr. Horatia Muir Watt, *Rome II et les «Intérêts Gouvernementaux»: pour une Lecture Fonctionnaliste du Nouveau règlement du Conflit de Lois en Matière Délictuelle*, *in* LE RÈGLEMENT COMMUNAUTAIRE «ROMA II» SUR LA LOI APPLICABLE AUX OBLIGATIONS NON CONTRACTUELLES (Sabine Corneloup & Natalie Joubert eds., 2008), 139.

[224] Neste sentido Junker, Rom II-VO Anwendungsbereich. 2015. Anotação ao artigo 17º, Rn 32. M; Cfr. Ansgar Staudinger, *Internationale Verkehrsunfälle und die geplante "Rom II"-Verordnung*, 12 STRASSENVERKEHRSRECHT (2005), p. 444.

[225] Cfr. Junker, Rom II-VO Anwendungsbereich. 2015., anotação ao artigo 17º, Rn. 23.

por se manter intocável a *lex causae*, ao prenderem-se estas normas com os elementos de factos concretizadores dos pressupostos da responsabilidade extra-contratual, não falamos aqui de uma verdadeira questão prévia[226]. A violação de regras de segurança ou de conduta, ainda que condicionante da questão da responsabilidade e consequente obrigação de indemnização (situação condicionada) refere-se a um dado de facto integrado na hipótese legal e não a um problema de interpretação[227]. Pelo que a sua relevância se incorpora no estatuto delitual. Já no caso *Babcock v. Jackson* os juízes do Supremo Tribunal de Nova Iorque ressalvavam, perante a aplicação da lei do foro, a aplicação de «standards of conduct» da *lex loci delicti*, todavia a solução do Roma II afastou a possibilidade de ocorrer a *dépeçage*, ao conceder liberdade ao tribunal na apreciação de tais regras, bem como a considerar no quadro da *lex causae*. Pensemos no caso em que um médico receita por telefone um medicamento a alguém que se encontra noutro país sem que tenha informado das reacções adversas, que acabam por ocorrer com graves danos para a saúde do paciente. Tomando como certa a aplicação da lei do local do dano, a possível violação do dever de esclarecimento à luz do direito da sede do médico, exigido pelas regras deontológicas (aqui consideradas como regras para efeitos do artigo 17º Roma II), pode não ser suficiente para fundar a ilicitude se o país onde ocorreu o dano a conduta do médico for justificada *per se* pela finalidade de beneficiência. As regras deontológicas serão assim verdadeiras *regras de conduta* por oposição às regras de *distribuição do dano*[228]. Todavia já será diferente quando o delito seja à distância, isto porque a relevância destas normas resulta da sua imposição e previsibilidade que molde e oriente a conduta do autor do dano. Não existindo este efeito psicológico, então não podem estas normas ser relevantes[229].

---

[226] Cfr. EHRENZWEIG, Private International Law. 1967, pp. 33-35. Não são por isso consideradas regras de decisão («rule of decison»), antes regras de conduta («rule of conduct») cuja relevância se circunscreve, no que à situação plurilocalizada diz respeito, ao local de actuação do autor (cfr. CURRIE, Selected Essays on the Conflict of Laws. 1963. p. 69).

[227] Cfr. MACHADO, Lições de Direito Internacional Privado. 2002, p. 108.

[228] Cfr. Symeonides, AMERICAN JOURNAL OF COMPARATIVE LAW, (2008), p. 189 e Phaedon John Kozyris, *Rome II: Tort Conflicts on the Right Track – A Postscript to Symeon Symeonides' Missed Opportunity*, see id. at.pp. 477-478.

[229] Cfr. Engel Leible, *Der Vorschlag der EG-Kommission für eine Rom II-Verordnung – Auf dem Weg zu einheitlichen Anknüpfungsregeln für außervertragliche Schuldverhältnisse in Europa*,

DIREITO DA SAÚDE

Ainda outro exemplo: um médico que se desloca a outro país para proceder a uma cirurgia terá que assegurar que a sua actuação é conforme as boas práticas médicas no local, cumprindo as regras deontológicas nela vigentes. Não pode portanto afastar tais regras invocando as do seu país de origem. Todavia, se no país da cirurgia as regras são menos exigentes, tal não significa a exclusão, p.ex. da culpa, se existir uma ligação entre o médico e o paciente ou ainda, para concretizar o elemento culpa, tomar em consideração os protocolos de actuação existentes no país de origem do médico. Apesar de não podemos assacar efeitos extraterritoriais às regras deontológicas previstas num determinado país, elas não deixaram de ser relevantes para efeitos de apreciação dos standards de comportamento exigiveis e a serem apreciados, por exemplo, a título de culpa por via do estatuto delitual. Isto porque continua a ser esta a lei competente que regula a responsabilidade extracontratual e não as regras de segurança e de conduta. Já será diferente, por exemplo o caso de uma prestação de cuidados de saúde à distância através da prescrição de um medicamento em que não seja previsivel para o médico contar com a aplicação de outra lei que não a da sua sede.

Neste ponto, parece-nos ser indiscutível, como veremos no que ao responsável pelos cuidados de saúde diz respeito, em particular o médico, a liberdade de prestação de serviços reconhecida, não afasta a vinculação da sua prestação às normas em vigor no país da prestação do serviço (artigo 5º, nº 3 da Directiva 2005/36/CE alterada pela Directiva 2013/ /55/UE e artigo 3º, nº 2 Lei nº 9/2009). A natureza substantiva destas normas confere-lhes um estatuto especial, ao determinarem como aplicáveis as normas do local onde o cuidado médico é prestado. Integram, assim nos parecer, o âmbito do artigo 17º Roma II. Aqui se deverão incluir as regras que regulam as *legis artis* no local da prestação dos cuidados médicos, bem como as regras sobre o consentimento informado, ainda que conservem o seu carácter autónomo[230]. Podendo, em certos casos, as regras das *legis artis* do Estado de origem do médico acompanhá-lo, funcionando cumulativamente com as regras do local do tratamento. Esta aplicação cumulativa será relevante em áreas de investigação e ensaios clínicos

---

EUROPÄISCHE ZEITSCHRIFT FÜR WIRTSCHAFTSRECHT (2004), p. 16 e Junker, Rom II-VO Anwendungsbereich. 2015, anotação ao artigo 17º, Rn. 27.

[230] Cfr. MARIA JESÚS GERMÁN URDIOLA, TRATAMIENTOS INVOLUNTARIOS Y ENFERMEDAD MENTAL (Thomson Reuters – Aranzadi. 2012). pp. 124-126.

incorporando, por recurso normas-narrativas (inter alia, Declaração de Helsínquia da Associação Médica Mundial, CEDHB e Recomendações do Conselho da Europa), um estatuto deontológico internacional que vincula o médico onde quer que se encontre.

Assim, as exigências respeitantes à validade e eficácia do consentimento informado serão regidas pelo estatuto delitual, sem contudo deixar de ter em consideração que nem sempre a lei será a *lex locci delicti*, bem como a conduta do médico pode ser justificada à luz de uma lei estrangeira por oposição à lei penal do Estado onde o facto ocorreu.

5. Ordem pública internacional e meta-ordem pública europeia

A ordem pública internacional era entendida inicialmente como um meio de defesa do salto do escuro que representa a aplicação do direito estrangeiro, assumindo-se, apesar da designação internacional, como sendo de natureza e origem nacional. Contudo hoje é indiscutível entender que existem valores que se transmutam de uma categoria do ordenamento do foro para se afirmarem como verdadeiros valores transnacionais. Os tratados e convenções, bem como o próprio *ius gentium* concretizam valores e interesses *supra-nacionais*, em especial a partir da Convenção Europeia dos Direitos do Homem e a Carta dos Direitos Fundamentais formando uma *ordem pública europeia ou comunitária*[231] e que integram, enquanto meta-ordem pública, a ordem pública internacional de cada Estado[232].

A excepção de ordem pública internacional consagrada no artigo 22º CC está também prevista nos instrumentos normativos convencionais e comunitários. Já o vimos no artigo 21º da Convenção de 2000 e nos artigos 21º e 26º do Roma I e II, respectivamente. Este mecanismo de salvaguarda dos valores fundamentais do Estado do foro deve censurar somente o resultado da aplicação da norma material estrangeira e não o sistema de onde provém. E mesmo quando tal resultado ocorra, deve

---

[231] Cfr. Jayme, Identité Culturelle et Intégration: Le Droit International Privé Postmoderne. 1996, p. 231.

[232] A favor da integração do instituto de ordem pública internacional ver Pierre Mayer, *La Convention européenne des droits de l'homme et l'application des normes étrangers*, 80 REVUE CRITIQUE DE DROIT INTERNATIONAL PRIVÉ (1991)., pp. 662-664. Ver ainda Susana Chabert, *Ordem Pública Internacional e Direito Comunitário, in* NORMAS DE APLICAÇÃO IMEDIATA, ORDEM PÚBLICA INTERNACIONAL E DIREITO COMUNITÁRIO (2004), pp. 247-275.

DIREITO DA SAÚDE

valer o princípio do mínimo dano, ressalvando ao máximo o âmbito de competência da *lex causae*.

A cláusula de excepção de ordem pública, quando integrada no âmbito de aplicação dos regulamentos de direito internacional privado da UE, continua a ser uma prerrogativa estadual de cada Estado-Membro, todavia o TJUE assume competência para sindicar os limites da sua invocação. Apenas admite o seu recurso a título excepcional e se colidir de modo inaceitável com princípios fundamentais do Estado do foro[233]. Entendimento do TJUE que, ainda que aplicado às regras de reconhecimento, se deve alargar para as regras de conflito[234].

Curioso é verificar que o Parlamento Europeu na sua primeira leitura à proposta de regulamento do Roma II da Comissão indicou que fossem formulados critérios materiais conducentes à concretização do conceito de «ordem pública comunitária» ao se pretender a inclusão como critério materializador a "violação de direitos e liberdades fundamentais tal como são consagrados na Convenção Europeia dos Direitos do Homem, nas normas constitucionais nacionais ou no direito humanitário internacional"[235]. No entanto, apesar desta proposta ter sido rejeitada pelo Conselho, a mesma deve ser considerada na medida em tais direitos não poderão deixar de ser consideradas num conceito em sede de meta--ordem pública, desde logo porque existe uma obrigação do Estado no respeito dos mesmos[236].

Cumpre referir que a integração na ordem jurídica comunitária dos direitos fundamentais ocorre por força do TJUE ao consolidar como valor fundamental da UE o respeito pelos mesmos e ao mesmo tempo evitando a fragmentação que poderia resultar da consideração individual dos *standards* de cada Estado-membro[237]. A integração dos direitos fundamen-

---

[233] O TJUE pronunciou-se no âmbito da Convenção de Bruxelas a respeito do artigo 27º nos Acórdãos *Krombach c. Bamberski*, C-, §37, *Renault SA c. Maxicar SpA*, C-38/98, §30.

[234] Cfr. DICKINSON, The Roma II Regulation. The Law Applicable to Non-Contractual Obligations. 2013., p. 627.

[235] Cfr. Relatório do Parlamento Europeu sobre a proposta de regulamento do Parlamento Europeu e do Conselho relativo à lei aplicável às obrigações extracontratuais ("Roma II"), de 27.06.2005, PE 349.977v04-00, A6-0211/2005, (2003/0168(COD)), p. 35.

[236] Cfr. DICKINSON, The Roma II Regulation. The Law Applicable to Non-Contractual Obligations. 2013, p. 628.

[237] Cfr. ANTHONY ARNULL, THE EUROPEAN UNION AND ITS COURT OF JUSTICE (Oxford University Press. 1999), p. 207.

tais já acontecia, mesmo antes de existir a CDF e a previsão de adesão à CEDH[238]. É indiscutível que os direitos fundamentais fazem parte integrante dos princípios gerais de direito que vinculam do direito da União e que por isso são susceptíveis de ser objecto de fiscalização pelo TJUE[239]. Para a densificação daqueles princípios o TJUE, como que num exercício de direito comparado, vai buscar às tradições constitucionais comuns aos Estados-Membros e nas indicações fornecidas pelos instrumentos internacionais relativos à protecção dos Direitos do Homem, em que os Estados-Membros colaboraram ou a que aderiram. A CEDH reveste, neste contexto, um significado particular tendo as suas normas e a própria jurisprudência do TEDH sido assimilada pelo TJUE[240].

Parece-nos, por isso, que é inevitável falar na existência de uma estatuto de garantias mínimas do paciente, em especial no direito à autodeterminação em cuidados de saúde, que devem acompanhá-lo onde quer que se encontre. Das várias normas invocadas, desde logo os artigos 2º, 8º, 14º da CEDH, o artigo 3º nº 2 *al.* a) da CDF e ainda o próprio artigo 12º, nº 4 da Convenção de pessoas com deficiência respeitante às garantias no processo de decisão de questões relativas a incapazes. A ligação entre estas diferentes disposições e a sua concretização no artigo 3º, nº 2 *al.* a) CDF permite-nos avançar com uma ideia de valores e consequentemente interesses mínimos nas relações transfronteiriças no quadro do mercado interno europeu. Elas serão tanto mais vinculativas e garantísticas conforme o grau de regulação do conteúdo do direito dos pacientes. Assim será o caso dos transplantes de órgãos e tecidos humanos, sangue e, em especial, ensaios clínicos. Deste último verificamos, entre outros que o consentimento pressupõe liberdade de decisão sobre a sua esfera pessoal, informação adequada sobre a intervenção e riscos da mesma e livre revogabilidade. É óbvio que estas notas, quase integrantes do *core* europeu de valores, não afastam as particularidades nacionais de cada

---

[238] Cfr. Maria Luísa Duarte, *O Direito da União Europeia e o Direito Europeu dos Direitos do Homem – uma defesa do "triângulo judicial europeu". in* Estudos de Direito da União e das Comunidades Europeias (2003), p. 197.
[239] A este respeito ver o caso *Schmidberger*, C-112/00. Ver também a síntese de Samuli Miettinen, Criminal law and policy in the European Union § 3 (Routledge. 2013), p. 202 e ss.
[240] Para mais desenvolvimentos Romain Tinière, L'office du juge communautaire des droits fondamentaux (Bruylant. 2008), p. 119 e ss.

DIREITO DA SAÚDE

Estado-Membro. Assim resulta do próprio teor do artigo 3º CDF que impõe um standard mínimo de direitos e garantias a favor do paciente, ainda que com a ressalva dos princípios da competência e da subsidiariedade que regem a União Europeia e a liberdade de circulação, quer do paciente, quer dos profissionais de saúde.

O princípio da igualdade pressupõe, a meu ver, a imposição de regras de cuidado a favor dos interesses do paciente com vista a salvaguardar a sua esfera de integridade, independentemente do local onde os cuidados de saúde sejam prestados. A isto se associa a garantia de autonomia nas situações em que o paciente se encontra incapaz de consentir. Os modelos de organização de cuidado, que se encontram fora da competência directa da UE, mas cuja mediação pela Convenção da Haia de 2000 relativa à protecção de adultos pretende ser assegurada, não deixa de tomar em consideração a autodeterminação conflitual do interessado e com tal reconhecimento a consequente faculdade de planeamento da sua vida e desta feita o reconhecimento da organização de cuidado de acordo com uma lei próxima (artigo 15º, nº 2 da Convenção de 2000).

Isto é tanto mais relevante quando a capacidade para autodeterminação continua, em nosso entender, a ser uma coutada do estatuto pessoal e, como tal, é pressuposta a sua regulação pela lei da nacionalidade ou da residência, consoante a opção de cada Estado. E, desta feita, a ideia de um consentimento informado não pode ser desligada das directivas antecipadas (em especial nos casos do testamento vital) e da aferição da vontade real ou presumida do paciente, independentemente do reconhecimento nacional do direito à autodeterminação de uma vontade actual, prospectiva ou presumida, ainda que o consentimento seja regido pelo estatuto delitual. É óbvio que os limites desta vontade e sua vinculatividade integram a ordem pública nacional, mas o reconhecimento e relevância dessa vontade, em especial se prospectiva, bem como as exigências de um consentimento informado estarão salvaguardas por um quadro de valores comuns e vinculativos dentro do mercado interno.

No entanto porque se trata de uma quadro mínimo de garantias, deve ser respeitada a identidade cultural de cada Estado e a diversidade legal. Ao contrário do que sucede em Portugal e na maioria dos países europeus, existem países na UE que admitem a inclusão no testamento vital disposições referentes à ajuda activa à morte, a eutanásia. É o caso dos

Países Baixos e da Bélgica[241]. Tal possibilidade não pode significar uma imposição de interesses e valores dissonantes com os consagrados no direito português, todavia não poderá ser ignorada a vontade do paciente e respectivas consequências jurídicas, em particular em sede de unidade material do ilícito transfronteiriço. Olhando agora para o testamento vital, este está de tal *forma enraizado no fundamento ético condicionado de cada ordem jurídico que o reconhecimento ilimitado choca com o conceito de ordem pública internacional* (ERIK JAYME)[242]. Resulta daqui, quer da leitura do artigo 22º CC, quer dos artigos 16º e 26º Roma II, quer do próprio abrigo 15º, nº 3 (e ainda o artigo 14º) da Convenção da Haia de 2000[243] que a ajuda activa no resultado morte consubstancia-se num *moral data* da ordem jurídica portuguesa e por isso integra os limites da aplicação da lei estrangeira e, consequentemente, do reconhecimento e produção de efeitos de um testamento vital ou procuração antecipada outorgada no estrangeiro no país de implementação.

Mas não só a ordem pública serve como limite, como pode produzir um efeito positivo tendente a mitigar a concretização da ordem pública internacional ao impor o reconhecimento do consentimento ou dissentimento para recusar um determinado tratamento médico, ainda que cause a morte do paciente. Será o caso de um italiano, residente em Itália, mas internado em Portugal, tendo cá manifestado o seu dissentimento expresso para a alimentação artificial.

Neste sentido, em normas de aplicação necessária e imediata, em particular quanto às disposições do Código Penal, estão em causa os limites da autodeterminação. Trata-se de determinar a concretização dos limites dessa autonomia, definidos unilateralmente por cada Estado. No caso português o artigo 5º da Lei nº 25/2012 é a expressão desse mesmo limite ao reconhecimento e eficácia de um direito à autodeterminação à luz de um direito estrangeiro. A invocação da excepção de ordem pública internacional portuguesa, assente no princípio do mínimo dano, não vai impedir o reconhecimento da manifestação de autonomia prospectiva, apenas irá considerar ineficaz a manifestação de vontade na parte em que o outorgante pretende a ajuda activa à morte.

---

[241] Cfr. Jayme, Die Patientenverfügung: Erwachsenenschutz und Internationales Privatrecht. 2010., p. 204.
[242] Cfr. Id. at., p. 209.
[243] Cfr. Id. at., p. 210.

DIREITO DA SAÚDE

Contudo, a ordem pública também pode funcionar positivamente se a *lex delictae* estrangeira não reconhecer a autodeterminação, nem formas de suprir a incapacidade para um decisão médica respeitadora dos artigos 9º CEDH e artigo 12º da Convenção sobre as pessoas deficientes. Num quadro multinível, o reforço dos valores e princípios do ordenamento português será tanto maior quanto mais disseminada for a sua consagração ao nível do direito internacional público e mais estreita for a conexão da situação com o ordenamento jurídico português. Neste último, será relevante o local de tratamento ter ocorrido em Portugal ou a partir de Portugal (pense-se nos casos de assistência médica à distância através de telemedicina).

A respeito do direito penal internacional (artigos 7º CP) a autonomização entre questões de direito público e direito privado traz a lume a natureza auto-limitada do direito penal ao prever no artigo 7º unilateralmente o âmbito da sua aplicação espacial. No entanto a consagração do princípio da ubiquidade[244] como forma de acautelar um conflito negativo de leis penais pode implicar uma cisão na apreciação do desvalor de uma mesma conduta, daí se consagrar o princípio da dupla incriminação. O alargamento do âmbito de aplicação da lei penal implica o consequente alargamento da tutela penal estadual e desta forma, porque intimamente ligado ao poder punitivo, a competência da lei penal determina a competência jurisdicional.

No entanto o confronto com a lei penal portuguesa de um consentimento prestado à luz de um direito estrangeiro não afasta a possível antinomia, contrariando o princípio da unidade da ilicitude. Ora, é neste campo que se sentem os limites, no que ao consentimento diz respeito, da ordem pública internacional temperada pelo princípio da harmonia material ou interna.

Um exemplo de onde podemos retirar o problema da questão prévia bem pode ser, com adaptação ao caso a uma situação internacional,

---

[244] A doutrina penal fala em *solução mista* ou *plurilateral* (cfr. JORGE DE FIGUEIREDO DIAS, DIREITO PENAL – PARTE GERAL § I – Questões Fundamentais. A Doutrina Geral do Crime (Coimbra Editora 2ª ed. 2007)., p. 211) ou *critério bilateral alternativo* (AMÉRICO TAIPA DE CARVALHO, DIREITO PENAL. PARTE GERAL (QUESTÕES FUNDAMENTAIS. TEORIAL GERAL DO CRIME) (Coimbra Editora 2ª ed. 2008).), p. 213. De uma forma geral ver LEITE, O Conflito de Leis Penais. Natureza e Função do Direito Penal Internacional. 2008., p. 404 e seguintes.

o Acórdão do BGH de 11 de Março de 2015[245]. Neste discutia-se a indignidade sucessória do marido que tinha tirado a sonda gástrica da mulher por respeito à sua vontade presumida. No caso concreto não se deu como provada a existência de um testamento vital, bem como estava em causa a conduta activa do marido e não a cessação de um meio de tratamento médico. Contudo podemos imaginar a decisão do médico que respeita o testamento vital onde se prescreve a recusa de meios de alimentação artificial, ou até mesmo por decisão do representante voluntário. As implicações sobre a eficácia de tais directivas antecipadas serão necessariamente reguladas de acordo com o estatuto delitual, por ser este que determina a licitude ou ilicitude da vontade prospectiva, em último termo, é ele que determina os limites de tal autodeterminação. E isso significa que vale como verdadeira questão prévia para efeitos, p.ex. de indignidade sucessória, ou até mesmo como causa de justificação em sede de responsabilidade penal ou mesmo civil (para os casos em que a lei competente não seja a lei do local da conduta).

C. Conclusão Intermédia

Parece, pelo menos num primeiro momento, que a relação médico-paciente extravasa a mera relação privada cujos interesses, assim com as *legis artis*, em especial as regras deontológicas, tenderão a ter uma efeito espacialmente dilatado, ainda que não abrogante da *lex causae*. As particularidades dos cuidados médicos, pelo menos no que toca às áreas de saúde regulamentadas (médicos, médicos dentistas, farmacêuticos, ...) em princípio não estarão desligadas do local do tratamento e, desta forma, do local do dano. Todavia, quando não seja esta a lei a aplicar, em especial nas situações da conexão acessória ao contrato (artigo 4º, nº 3 Roma II) não é possível isolar a actividade de cuidados de saúde do local onde ela é exercida e, em alguns casos, da própria sede de actuação do profissional de saúde. Ressalvadas as situações de verdadeiros delitos à distância, parece-nos que as regras que regulamentam os cuidados médicos, pelo menos no quadro europeu, são verdadeiras *local data*.

No entanto, tendo em conta a circunscrição de eficácia espacial das normas de aplicação necessária e imediata ao foro competente (e desta forma, em regra, ao artigo 5º, nº 3 Bruxelas I), as regras portuguesas não

---

[245] Cfr. BGH, IV ZR 400/14, disponível no sítio juris.bundesgerichtshof.de.

DIREITO DA SAÚDE

deixarão de ser tomadas em consideração à luz do artigo 17º a respeito da actuação do médico em Portugal ("...o lugar e no momento em que ocorre o facto...") quando os danos directos não se verifiquem em Portugal e desta forma não seja esta a *lex causae* à luz do artigo 4º Roma II.

A respeito do consentimento, já vimos que em regra ele será absorvido ao conceito-quadro do estatuto delitual (artigo 4º e 15º Roma II). Apesar de não ser permitida o funcionamento da cláusula de excepção do nº 3 do artigo 4º a título distributivo, as regras sobre o consentimento poderão descolar-se do estatuto delitual unitário desejado. Tal será o caso da aplicação ou tomada em consideração de normas de aplicação necessária e imediata (artigo 16º Roma II) ou regras qualificadas como *local data* (artigo 17º Roma II).

Por último, quanto às directivas antecipadas, na modalidade da procuração as mesmas serão integradas nos artigos 13º, 14º, 15º e 16º Convenção da Haia, assim que esta entre em vigor. Aqui se incluem também os testamentos vitais quando associados à procuração antecipada. Já quanto aos testamentos vitais isolados caberá às regras de conflito do Código Civil e do Roma II regular. Serão regulados pelo artigo 25º CC (sendo admissível o recurso por analogia ao 28º CC, atenta a posição social relevante do médico) com vista à determinação da capacidade (remetendo paras normas de competência), aplicando-se ainda os artigos 25º e 36º CC a respeito da constituição, forma e validade do testamento vital, ressalvando-se o reconhecimento do mesmo à luz do artigo 31º, nº 2 CC. Todavia os seus efeitos e implementação dependerão da lei de execução, uma vez que o testamento vital, enquanto declaração de vontade prospectiva visa suprir a incapacidade de prestar um consentimento actual e desta feita, submete-se ao estatuto delitual enquanto causa de justificação do ilícito (contudo ressalvando-se as considerações feitas a respeito dos artigos 16º e 17º Roma II e artigo 22º C e do problema da questão prévia. Estamos por isso tentados a enquadrar o problema dos testamentos vitais no âmbito da questão de reconhecimento, quer em termos conflituais (artigo 31º, nº 2 CC), quer em termos do princípio do mútuo reconhecimento no plano da União Europeia.

V. CONCLUSÕES

Como afirmado no início, este artigo é um trabalho exploratório ao problema dos cuidados de saúde transfronteiriços, deixando muitas questões em aberto, desde logo a respeito do próprio método do direito internacional privado. A afirmação da identidade cultural dos Estados e a construção de um quadro de valores comuns tendentes à construção de uma meta-ordem pública europeia traz consigo tentações unilateralistas na resolução das situações plurilocalizadas. Em especial quando as questões dos cuidados de saúde bulem com interesses público e privados cuja tutela é conferida por instrumentos de direito privado e público (em especial o Direito Penal) e que implicam sobreposição espacial de normas materiais que podem chocar com a unidade da ilicitude, em especial quando em causa esteja o funcionamento de causas de justificação previstas e reconhecidas por lei estrangeira que não a lei penal.

Fica esta primeira abordagem do que pensamos vir a revelar-se um longo e difícil caminho a trilhar, com vista à clarificação dos estatutos jurídicos transfronteiriços dos responsáveis pelos cuidados de saúde e dos respectivos pacientes, em especial no que diz respeito à matéria do consentimento informado.

O apelo de Ulisses – o novo regime do procurador de cuidados de saúde na lei portuguesa*

PAULA TÁVORA VÍTOR*

*"Às Sereias chegarás em primeiro lugar, que todos
os homens enfeitiçam que delas se aproximam. (...)
Mas se tu próprio quiseres ouvir o canto,
Deixa que, na nau veloz, te amarrem as mãos e os pés
enquanto estás de pé contra o mastro; e que as cordas sejam
atadas ao mastro, para que te possas deleitar com a voz
das duas Sereias. E se a eles ordenares que te libertem,
então que te amarrem com mais cordas ainda."*
Homero, Odisseia, Canto XII[1]

---

* O presente texto corresponde, com poucas alterações, ao artigo homónimo, objecto de publicação no número especial da Revista "Julgar" dedicado ao consentimento informado, que gentilmente autorizou que fosse novamente publicado neste livro de homenagem. Esta reflexão tinha já servido de base à palestra proferida no dia 1 de Junho de 2013, na acção de formação "Directivas Antecipadas de Vontade", organizada pelo Centro de Direito Biomédico da Faculdade de Direito da Universidade de Coimbra e pela Secção Regional do Centro da Ordem dos Médicos. Não queria deixar de referir que a versão final deste texto beneficiou dos comentários do Senhor Doutor André Dias Pereira, do Senhor Dr. João Maia Rodrigues e da Senhora Drª Sofia Henriques proferidos no debate subsequente à palestra, em particular, relativamente ao problema da forma da procuração de cuidados de saúde.

** Assistente da Faculdade de Direito da Universidade de Coimbra.

[1] Homero, *Odisseia*, tradução de Frederico Lourenço, Livros Cotovia, Lisboa, 2003, p. 200.

1. Introdução

Ulisses foi desta forma aconselhado pela feiticeira Circe a assegurar a sua sobrevivência, assim que perdesse a razão. Na previsão de sucumbir ao encantamento das vozes das Sereias, que o levaria à morte certa, Ulisses, "o dos mil artifícios", socorre-se mais uma vez de um engenhoso mecanismo que lhe permite superar a adversidade – ordena aos seus marinheiros, de ouvidos tapados e, portanto, surdos aos seus rogos e às vozes das Sereias, que o amarrem ao mastro do seu barco e que não obedeçam às suas ordens ensandecidas pelo feitiço do canto. Abdica, enquanto está privado do controlo racional do seu pensamento, do comando do seu barco e da sua pessoa, para o atribuir à sua tripulação. E, deste modo, a epopeia homérica cria uma poderosa imagem do exercício da *autonomia prospectiva*[2], do planeamento para a eventualidade de uma incapacidade futura[3].

O apelo intemporal ao controlo da própria vida, mesmo quando a faculdade de a entender e de nos determinarmos em função desse entendimento já não exista, tem recebido poucas respostas por parte do ordenamento jurídico português. Todavia, a consagração recente, pela Lei nº 25/2012, de 16 de Julho, da figura das directivas antecipadas e, no que aqui nos ocupa, do procurador de cuidados de saúde veio temperar esta afirmação.

A procuração de cuidados de saúde é definida pela lei como o "documento pelo qual se atribui a uma pessoa, voluntariamente e de forma gratuita, poderes representativos em matéria de cuidados de saúde, para que esta os exerça no caso de o outorgante se encontrar incapaz de expressar de forma pessoal e autónoma a sua vontade" (art. 12º, nº 1, da Lei nº 25/2012, de 16 de Julho).

---

[2] O termo foi cunhado por DWORKIN, Ronald em *Life's dominion: an argument about abortion and euthanasia*, London: Harper Collins Publishers, 1993.

[3] Ao recorrermos a esta imagem, não ignoramos, todavia, os ensinamentos de Maria Helena da Rocha Pereira e que, não obstante o reconhecimento de que o herói da Odisseia busca conscientemente a excelência (*arete*) através do seu comportamento, a noção de livre-arbítrio só surgirá posteriormente e, portanto, não integra a concepção do homem nos Poemas Homéricos. V. PEREIRA, Maria Helena da Rocha, *Estudos de História de Cultura Clássica*, vol. I, 6ª edição, Fundação Calouste Gulbenkian, 1987, pp. 114 e 124. Sobre esta imagem, v. STAVIS, P. F., "The Nexum: a modest proposal for self-guardianship by contract: a system of advance directives and surrogate committee-at-large for the intermittently mentally ill." *The Journal of Contemporary Health Law and Policy*, vol. 16, 1999, p. 41.

1.1. A procuração de cuidados de saúde como resposta à incapacidade

Em primeiro lugar, o novo instrumento é apresentado como uma *resposta à incapacidade*, que pensamos ser a pedra de toque do regime e referência incontornável para a sua análise.

Assim, por um lado, o procurador de cuidados de saúde surge como um *elemento perturbador* do arranjo clássico da resposta às incapacidades. Na verdade, estamos perante um mecanismo de representação voluntária, que é tradicionalmente reservada a quem presumivelmente está na plena posse das suas faculdades, a pessoa capaz para o exercício de direitos. Já a incapacidade reclamaria, antes, um representante legal (ou um assistente)[4].[5] Ora, aqui é a própria incapacidade (veremos em que termos) que espoleta o exercício dos poderes representativos por parte do procurador. Por outro lado, simultaneamente, apresenta a *configuração adequada* para responder às actuais exigências no campo da regulação da incapacidade, nomeadamente, a exigências de natureza constitucional.

Na verdade, a figura do procurador de cuidados de saúde pretende encaixar-se no quadro das respostas delineadas pela *doutrina da alternativa menos restritiva*[6] que aponta para a prioridade de uma intervenção mínima

---

[4] Cf., entre outros, PINTO, Carlos Alberto da Mota, *Teoria Geral do Direito Civil*, 4ª Ed., por António Pinto Monteiro e Carlos Mota Pinto, Coimbra: Coimbra Editora, 2005, p. 195, HÖRSTER, H. E., *A Parte Geral do Código Civil Português, Teoria Geral do Direito Civil*, Coimbra: Almedina, 2007, p. 309.

[5] Quanto à admissibilidade da procuração de cuidados de saúde no ordenamento jurídico português, veja-se LOUREIRO, João Carlos, "Metáfora do Vegetal ou Metáfora do Pessoal? – considerações em torno do estado vegetativo crónico", *Cadernos de Bioética*, nº 8, p. 41, e PEREIRA, André Dias, *O Consentimento Informado na Relação Médico Paciente. Estudo de Direito Civil*, Coimbra: Coimbra Editora, 2004, p. 250 ss., VÍTOR, Paula Távora, "Procurador para Cuidados de Saúde – importância de um novo decisor", *Lex Medicinae– Revista Portuguesa de Direito da Saúde*, nº 1, Ano 1, 2005, p. 123-125 e RAPOSO, Vera Lúcia, "Directivas antecipadas de vontade: em busca da lei perdida", *Revista do Ministério Público*, nº 125, Janeiro/Março de 2011, p. 176.

[6] A doutrina da alternativa menos restritiva foi enunciada pelo Supremo Tribunal dos Estados Unidos, em 1960, no caso *Shelton v. Tucker,* que estabeleceu o princípio geral segundo o qual os Estados, na prossecução dos seus objectivos, deveriam escolher os métodos menos lesivos dos direitos fundamentais dos seus cidadãos e foi concretizada no âmbito das incapacidades em *Lake v. Cameron.*
B. T. Shelton et al., Appellants, v. Tuck, Everett, Jr., etc., et al. Max Carr et al., Petitioners, v. Young, R. A. et al. 364 U.S. 479, 81 S.Ct. 247 Nos. 14, 83. Argued Nov. 7, 1960. Decided Dec.

DIREITO DA SAÚDE

no âmbito da restrição de direitos fundamentais e, portanto, também do direito à capacidade civil (art. 26º, nº 1 da Constituição da República Portuguesa). É, aliás, o que nos exige o regime consagrado na Lei Fundamental, que define que as limitações à classe dos direitos, liberdades e garantias se pauta, entre outros, pelo princípio da proibição do excesso ou proporcionalidade em sentido amplo (art. 18º, nº 2, da Constituição da República Portuguesa)[7], segundo o qual qualquer restrição deve ser "adequada (apropriada), necessária (exigível) e proporcional (com justa medida)"[8]. É também para esta orientação que apontam as Recomendações do Conselho da Europa mais relevantes nesta área, nomeadamente a *Recomendação nº R(99)4 do Conselho da Europa, relativa aos Princípios Respeitantes Protecção Jurídica dos Maiores Incapazes*, que consagra os princípios da necessidade e da subsidiariedade (princípio 5)[9], nos termos dos quais uma "medida de protecção" só deve ser adoptada quando necessária e que deve ser adoptado o "mecanismo menos formal", a "reacção perfeitamente adaptada às necessidades da situação", o que, segundo o Princípio 2 (flexibilidade na resposta jurídica), só se justifica defender quando os sistemas jurídicos disponibilizam um largo leque de soluções jurídicas adequadas a diferentes situações[10]. A mais recente *Recomendação nº CM/ /Rec (2009)11 do Conselho da Europa (Principles concerning continuing powers*

12, 1960.Supreme Court of the United States. *Cf.* Leary, Jamie L., "A Review of Two Recently Reformed Guardianship Statutes", *The Virginia Journal of Social Policy and the Law*, vol.5, n.1, Fall 1997, p. 263 ss..

[7] No contexto do Direito alemão, Claus-Wilhelm Canaris desenvolveu idêntica aproximação ao princípio da proibição do excesso no âmbito das incapacidades, ainda face ao anterior regime da *Vormundschaft* e da *Entmündigung*. V. CANARIS, Claus-Wilhelm, "Verstöße gegen das verfassungsrechtliche Übermaßverbot im Recht des Geschäftsfähigkeit und im Schadensersatzrecht", *Juristen Zeitung*, 42. Jahrgang, 21, 6. November, 1987, p. 993-995 e CANARIS, Claus-Wilhelm, "Zur Problematik von Privatrecht und verfassungsrechtlichem Übermaßverbot im Recht des Geschäftsfähigkeit und im Schadensersatzrecht – Ein Schlußwort zu den vorstehend abgedruckten Erwiderungen von *Ramm* und *Wieser*", *Juristen Zeitung*, 42. Jahrgang, 21, 6. November, 1988, p. 495.

[8] CANOTILHO, J. J. Gomes, *Direito Constitucional e Teoria da Constituição*, 7. Ed., Coimbra, Almedina, 2003, p. 457.

[9] Conseil de L'Europe, *Principes Concernant La Protection Juridique des Majeurs Incapables, Recommandation nº R(99)4 adoptée par le Comité des Ministres de Conseil de l'Europe le 23 février 1999 et exposé des motifs*, Strasbourg, Éditions du Conseil de l'Europe, juillet 1999, p. 31.

[10] Conseil de l'Europe (nota 9), p. 27.

of attorney and advance directives for incapacity) ancora-se na sua predecessora de 1999 e recomenda aos Estados-membros que introduzam (ou actualizem) legislação sobre procuradores permanentes (*continuing powers of attorney*) e directivas antecipadas, no sentido de se promoverem também aqueles princípios[11].

Ora, a consagração da procuração de cuidados de saúde representou a introdução verdadeiramente inovadora de um mecanismo[12] *tailorable,* ou seja, moldável em função das circunstâncias pessoais de cada um na área das incapacidades. Por esta via, passa a ser possível também integrar *as exigências de promoção da autonomia* que devem presidir aos regimes jurídicos de resposta à capacidade diminuída, que se podem identificar em *dois níveis distintos*: por um lado, na manutenção de um nível máximo de capacidade adequado à situação concreta, *i.e. incapacitando o mínimo*; por outro lado, na *valorização de manifestações antecipadas de vontade*, que prevêem situações em que a autonomia já não existe.[13]

Ao facultar um instrumento de exercício de autodeterminação, o legislador permite gerir autonomamente a própria esfera de interesses[14], evitar incertezas em relação a quem tem o poder para decidir em questões de saúde, honrando o desejo de atribuir a determinada pessoa o

---

[11] Recommendation CM/Rec(2009)11 of the Committee of Ministers to member states on principles concerning continuing powers of attorney and advance directives for incapacity *(Adopted by the Committee of Ministers on 9 December 2009 at the 1073rd meeting of the Ministers' Deputies).*

[12] A *Recomendação nº R 99(4) sobre princípios respeitantes à protecção jurídicas de maiores incapazes* classifica como "mecanismos de protecção" os instrumentos que são da lavra da própria pessoa protegida ou de terceiros, que não agem no exercício de funções judiciárias ou administrativas e como "medidas de protecção" os que provêm de uma autoridade judiciária ou administrativa. Conseil de l'Europe (nota 9), p. 25

[13] Veja-se o nosso, Vítor, Paula Távora, *A Administração do Património das Pessoas com Capacidade Diminuída*, Coimbra: Coimbra Editora, 2008, p. 15.

[14] Neste sentido, *v*. Joaquim de Sousa Ribeiro, que distingue os conceitos de "autonomia" e "autodeterminação". Para o Autor, a autonomia privada é "um processo de ordenação que faculta a livre constituição e modelação das relações jurídicas pelos sujeitos que nela participam" e a autodeterminação refere-se ao "poder de cada indivíduo gerir livremente a sua esfera de interesses, orientando a sua vida segundo as suas preferências". Ribeiro, Joaquim de Sousa, *O problema do contrato. As cláusulas contratuais gerais e o princípio da liberdade contratual*, Coimbra: Almedina, 1999, p. 21 ss.

DIREITO DA SAÚDE

poder de tomar decisões em vez da pessoa com incapacidade[15]e definindo o padrão de actuação[16].

Além destas considerações inerentes à natureza e ao carácter jurídico do referido expediente, convirá não esquecer que a sua importância vai crescer *pari passu* com o fenómeno do envelhecimento das populações ocidentais e, em particular, do nosso país. Deste modo, o movimento demográfico, mas também a sedimentação e crescimento de uma cultura (também jurídica) ligada ao *empowerment* deste grupo etário, têm a potencialidade de catapultar a relevância social do procurador de cuidados de saúde.

1.2. A procuração de cuidados de saúde como instrumento da área da saúde

A procuração de cuidados de saúde apresenta-se como uma resposta à incapacidade, mas *limitada à área da saúde*[17]. Assim, emerge, em primeira linha (embora não exclusivamente) como um meio de suprimento da vontade para prestar o *consentimento para o acto médico*[18]. É verdade que, no

---

[15] Continua a causar-nos grande perplexidade que o artigo 143º, al. b) do Código Civil possibilite aos pais ou progenitor que exercer as responsabilidades parentais designar o tutor do filho em testamento ou documento autêntico ou autenticado e que o próprio representado, em previsão de uma incapacidade futura, não o possa fazer. A figura do procurador de cuidados de saúde, ainda que numa área limitada, tem o mérito de permitir a designação de um representante.

[16] Sobre estas possibilidades abertas pela procuração de cuidados de saúde, ver o nosso, Vítor, Paula Távora (nota 5), pp. 126 ss.

[17] Espera-se, há muito, do legislador português que reformule o tratamento jurídico das incapacidades e tornando-o mais consentâneo com o actual entendimento dos direitos fundamentais das pessoas com capacidade diminuída e com a compreensão clínica e social dos fundamentos da incapacidade. Esta intervenção global não teve ainda lugar, subsistindo, assim, como resposta primeira do sistema a interdição ou a inabilitação da pessoa com capacidade diminuída. A introdução de um representante voluntário na área das incapacidades representa um passo à frente na actualização do nosso quadro de respostas. Todavia, teria sido também possível abrir o recurso a este tipo de representante também noutras áreas, nomeadamente na área patrimonial. Já tivemos oportunidade de propor que se recorra à figura do "mandato permanente" para este efeito. Veja-se o nosso, Vítor, Paula Távora (nota 13), p.229 ss. e 323-326.

[18] Sobre o consentimento médico no direito português, ver Oliveira, Guilherme de, "A estrutura jurídica do acto médico, consentimento informado e responsabilidade médica", *in Temas de Direito da Medicina*, Coimbra: Coimbra Editora, 1999, p. 59-72, Pereira, André Dias (nota 5), especialmente pp. 95 ss., e Rodrigues, João Vaz, *O Consentimento Informado*

O APELO DE ULISSES ...

esquema clássico da aproximação à capacidade diminuída, enquadrado pela interdição (e, eventualmente, pela inabilitação)[19], ao tutor (e, quando assim é determinado na sentença[20], ao curador) cabem as funções de representação também em matéria de saúde e, tradicionalmente, a pessoa incapacitada deixaria de ter uma palavra a dizer neste âmbito[21]. No entanto, a Convenção Europeia dos Direitos do Homem e da Biomedicina introduziu, em 2001, um novo elemento, dispondo que "[a] pessoa em causa deve, na medida do possível, participar no processo de autorização" (art. 6º, nº 3 da CEDHB). E, deste modo, dá relevância à capacidade de facto da pessoa com capacidade diminuída relativa a este acto específico.

Assim, o destacamento da área da saúde justifica-se. Não é nova a exigência de uma categoria relativa à "capacidade para consentir" (*competence to consent*)[22], que se autonomize da "capacidade de exercício de direitos", pensada para o mundo das transacções patrimoniais e dos interesses de natureza económica. E, se a falta de capacidade (ou melhor, a capacidade diminuída) foi pensada nestes termos, as respostas dadas pelo ordenamento jurídico acompanharam-na[23]. Ora, face à inadequação e rigidez dos esquemas tradicionais, a procuração para cuidados de saúde

---

para o Acto Médico no Ordenamento Jurídico Português (Elementos para o Estudo da Manifestação de Vontade do Paciente), Coimbra: Coimbra Editora, 2001, especialmente pp. 49 ss. Quanto à discussão acerca da natureza jurídica do consentimento, v. RESCH, Reinhard, *Die Fähigkeit zur Einwilligung – zivilrechtliche Fragen, in Einwilligung und Einwilligungsfähigkeit* (hrsg. Christian Kopetzki), Wien, Manzsche Veralgs – und Universitäts buchhandlung, 2002, p. 52. No contexto nacional, André Dias Pereira pronuncia-se pela natureza de quase-negócio jurídico do consentimento, em PEREIRA, André Dias (nota 5), p. 137.

[19] Não ignoramos que possam estar em causa situações de incapacidade de facto, em que não houve incapacitação judicial, no entanto, as respostas do ordenamento jurídico pensam-se em torno da interdição e da inabilitação.

[20] Na verdade, pensamos que no âmbito da inabilitação que pode ser moldado pela sentença, podem atribuir-se poderes ao curador para além da tradicional área patrimonial, inclusivamente, atribuindo-lhe poderes de representação. VÍTOR, Paula Távora (nota 13), p. 42.

[21] Na sua revisão dos requisitos da validade do consentimento, João Vaz Rodrigues apresenta a capacidade como o primeiro elemento a considerar. RODRIGUES, João Vaz (nota 18), pp. 197 ss.

[22] Sobre esta categoria, ver a obra de GRISSO, Thomas; APPELBAUM, Paul, *Assessing competence to consent to treatment: a guide for physicians and other health professionals*, New York; Oxford: Oxford University Press, 1998.

[23] Sobre os limites do poder do tutor relativamente aos actos pessoalíssimos, ver SANTO-SUOSSO, Amedeo, "Trattamenti medici in situazioni critiche: la discussione in Parlamento sulle direttive anticipate", *in Scelte sulle Cure e Incapacità: Dall'Amministrazione di Sostegno di*

DIREITO DA SAÚDE

emerge como um mecanismo concebido, ou, pelo menos, passível de ser pensado, para responder às particularidades do consentimento médico e da protecção das dimensões da personalidade que estão implicadas.

2. A procuração de cuidados de saúde no ordenamento jurídico português

Antes de 2012 (da Lei nº 25/2012, de 16 de Julho), as manifestações antecipadas de vontade na área da saúde (incluindo a procuração para cuidados de saúde) não eram figuras totalmente estranhas à ordem jurídica nacional. De facto, encontravam-se já vozes[24] a defender a atendibilidade de manifestações de vontade anteriores ao advento de uma incapacidade. E, na verdade, tal posição encontrava-se estribada na própria lei. Com efeito, a ratificação, em 2001, da Convenção Europeia dos Direitos do Homem e da Biomedicina, introduziu no ordenamento jurídico nacional as regras aí consagradas, não só o já referido artº 6º, nº 3, mas, também o artº 9º, que dispõe que a *"vontade anteriormente manifestada* no tocante a uma intervenção médica por um paciente que, no momento da intervenção, não se encontre em condições de expressar a sua vontade, *será tomada em conta"* (itálico nosso).

Também o Conselho da Europa, dirigindo-se aos seus Estados-membros, se posicionou claramente a favor da atendibilidade destas manifestações de vontade, particularmente nas já mencionadas Recomendação nº R(99)4, e Recomendação nº CM/Rec(2009)11, que versa especificamente os procuradores para casos de incapacidade e as directivas antecipadas.

Não é de estranhar, portanto, que as normas constantes do Código Deontológico da Ordem dos Médicos consagrem desde 2008 que, no caso de haver "uma *directiva escrita* pelo doente exprimindo a sua vontade, o *médico deve tê-la em conta* quando aplicável à situação em causa" (artº 46, nº 2, do Código Deontológico da Ordem dos Médicos).

Sostegnoalle Direttive Anticipate, a cura di Patrizia Borsellino, Dominique Feola, Lorena Forni, Varese, Insubria University Press, 2007, p. 86 s.

[24] Loureiro, João Carlos (nota 5), p. 41 e "Advance Directives: a Portuguese approach", *Lex Medicinae – Revista Portuguesa de Direito da Saúde*, Ano 5, nº 9, 2008, p. 7, Pereira, André Dias (nota 5), p. 250 e "Declarações Antecipadas de Vontade: Vinculativas ou apenas Indicativas?" *in Estudos de Homenagem ao Prof. Doutor Jorge de Figueiredo Dias*, Vol. IV, Coimbra, Coimbra Editora, 2010, pp. 828, 829.

Este quadro favorável à consideração de manifestações antecipadas de vontade na área da saúde foi reforçado pelo Conselho Nacional de Ética para as Ciências da Vida (CNECV), em particular em dois pareceres que se referem em geral às declarações antecipadas de vontade, incluindo o Procurador de Cuidados de Saúde (Parecer sobre os projectos de lei relativos a declarações antecipadas de vontade do Conselho Nacional de Ética para as Ciências da Vida (59/CNECV/2010)[25] e Parecer sobre o estado vegetativo persistente do Conselho Nacional de Ética para as Ciências da Vida (45/CNECV/2005)[26])[27].

O interesse do legislador nesta matéria é relativamente recente, não obstante assistirmos a iniciativas legislativas desde 2008 no sentido de consagrar um regime das declarações ou directivas antecipadas de vontade, nomeadamente do procurador de cuidados de saúde, que não vieram a desembocar em nenhum diploma legal.[28]

---

[25] Neste parecer, "O CNECV reconhece a conveniência em se regular por via legislativa a forma como os cidadãos, maiores de idade e na plena posse das suas capacidades e direitos, *podem declarar a sua vontade no que se refere a tratamentos e outros procedimentos relacionados com a sua saúde*. Assim, se perderem a sua capacidade em exprimir a sua vontade, esta pode ser conhecida tal como anteriormente a expressaram". Parecer nº 59 do Conselho Nacional de Ética para as Ciências da Vida (59/CNECV/2010) Parecer sobre os Projectos de Lei relativos às Declarações Antecipadas de Vontade (Dezembro de 2010), p. 2, (itálico nosso).

[26] "O CNECV é de parecer que: (...) 3. Toda a decisão sobre o início ou a suspensão de cuidados básicos da pessoa em Estado Vegetativo Persistente deve *respeitar a vontade do próprio*. 4. A vontade pode ser expressa ou presumida ou *manifestada por pessoa de confiança previamente designada* por quem se encontra em Estado Vegetativo Persistente. (...)". Parecer nº 45 do Conselho Nacional de Ética para as Ciências da Vida (45/CNECV/2005) Parecer sobre o Estado Vegetativo Persistente (Fevereiro de 2005), p. 3.

[27] Também no Parecer nº 46 sobre objecção ao uso de sangue e derivados para fins terapêuticos por motivos religiosos do Conselho Nacional de Ética para as Ciências da Vida (46/CNECV/2005) é abordado o tema das declarações antecipadas de vontade, mas a figura do procurador de cuidados de saúde não é autonomamente referida, sendo o parecer orientado em função da consideração do testamento vital. Veja-se o trabalho de André Dias Pereira, sobre o significado das orientações em sentido diverso dos pareceres de 2005 do CNECV, Pereira, André Dias, "Declarações Antecipadas de Vontade: Vinculativas ou apenas Indicativas?", *in Estudos de Homenagem ao Prof. Doutor Jorge de Figueiredo Dias*, Vol. IV, Coimbra, Coimbra Editora, 2010, pp. 823 ss.

[28] Vejam-se nas anteriores legislaturas, o projecto de lei nº 788/X, relativo aos direitos dos doentes à informação e ao consentimento informado, e os projectos de lei nº 413/XI, nº 414/XI, nº 428/XI e nº 429/XI.

3. Regime jurídico da procuração de cuidados de saúde

Ocupemo-nos, agora, de algumas *questões relativas ao regime* da nova procuração de cuidados de saúde, que a lei define como o "documento pelo qual se atribui a uma pessoa, voluntariamente e de forma gratuita, poderes representativos, em matéria de cuidados de saúde, para que esta os exerça no caso de o outorgante se encontrar incapaz de expressar de forma pessoal e autónoma a sua vontade" (art. 12º, nº 1[29]).

A Lei nº 25/2012, de 16 de Julho, dedica-lhe especificamente o capítulo III, quatro artigos de entre os dezoito do diploma, negligenciando a referência expressa a vários aspectos do regime. Dir-se-ia que o termo "directivas antecipadas de vontade" inclui comumente tanto a figura do testamento vital como a do procurador de cuidados de saúde e que, aliás, os projectos que antecederam o diploma analisado assumem a terminologia pacificamente aceite. Tal abriria a porta para aplicar tudo aquilo que está previsto para as "directivas antecipadas de vontade" no capítulo II à procuração de cuidados de saúde. No entanto, o legislador não deixou esta via desimpedida. Preocupou-se em dar uma definição de "directivas antecipadas de vontade" no artigo 2º, nº 1 que não parece querer incluir o procurador de cuidados de saúde, mas apenas definir o que é o testamento vital, separação, aliás, que já encontramos no título do diploma ("Regula directivas antecipadas de vontade, designadamente sob a forma de testamento vital, e a nomeação de procurador de cuidados de saúde e cria o Registo Nacional do Testamento Vital (RENTEV)) (sublinhado nosso)[30]. [31]Não parece assim que o legislador se tenha limitado a

---

[29] Na ausência de referência do diploma a que pertencem, as disposições mencionadas neste artigo referem-se à Lei nº 25/2012, de 16 de Julho.

[30] Veja-se, também, a formulação do artigo 15º, nº 1, relativo ao Registo Nacional de Testamento Vital, em que a formulação do preceito separa novamente as duas figuras: a finalidade do RENTEV é "rececionar, registar, organizar e manter actualizada (...) a informação e documentação relativas ao documento de diretivas antecipadas de vontade e à procuração de cuidados de saúde" e do artigo 16º, nº 1, que nos indica que o "registo no RENTEV tem valor meramente declarativo, sendo as directivas antecipadas de vontade ou a procuração de cuidados de saúde nele não inscritas igualmente eficazes (...)"(sublinhados nossos). Cf. ainda os artigos 16º, nº 2 e 17º, que se referem às "directivas antecipadas de vontade e ou procuração de cuidados de saúde" (*sic*).

[31] O Conselho Nacional de Ética para as Ciências da Vida, no Parecer sobre as Propostas de Portaria que regulamentam o Modelo de Testamento Vital e o Registo Nacional do Testamento Vital (RENTEV) (69/CNECV/2012 (dezembro de 2012), p. 3, também parece assumir esta revisão terminológica feita pela lei, já que refere que "[o] cidadão deve ser avisado, tanto

DIREITO DA SAÚDE

expressar-se de forma imperfeita. Pelo contrário, consistentemente insistiu na demarcação daquilo a que chama "directivas antecipadas de vontade" face ao "procurador de cuidados de saúde". Assim, não parece que o capítulo II tenha sido configurado como o repositório das "disposições gerais" aplicáveis aos dois instrumentos.

Aliás, se adoptássemos uma interpretação generosa de inclusão do procurador de cuidados de saúde nas "directivas antecipadas de vontade" da Lei, demonstrando muito pouco apego à formulação literal escolhida, enfrentaríamos com perplexidade algumas das opções do legislador: o facto de ter entendido como necessária a remissão do artigo 11º, nº 2, para o artigo 4º (que nesse caso seria desnecessária); a remissão para os artigos relativos à procuração no Código Civil, nomeadamente, ao artigo 262º, nº 2, do Código Civil, relativo à forma, que, ou serve para afastar a forma de documento escrito a que se refere o artigo 3º, ou para fazer uma alusão à combinação com o testamento vital (que não tem de existir, como veremos); a determinação da livre revogabilidade pelo outorgante no artigo 13º, que repetiria a norma do artigo 8º, nº 1, que nos diz que o "documento de directivas antecipadas de vontade é revogável ou modificável, no todo ou em parte, em qualquer momento, pelo autor".

De todo o modo, não raro encontraremos os mesmos fundamentos para aplicar ao procurador de cuidados de saúde as regras do testamento vital, pelo que, embora não procedendo directamente à sua aplicação, a analogia pode justificá-la, como oportunamente indicaremos.

3.1. O outorgante

Em termos de regime, em primeiro lugar, há que definir *quem é o outorgante* deste documento, o representado, cuja figura se delineia sob o signo da (in)capacidade. Na verdade, é a falta ou a diminuição de capacidade do representado que justifica e que conforma este instrumento, a vários níveis.

---

na Portaria como no modelo de preenchimento, que pode optar <u>apenas pela</u> designação de um <u>procurador de cuidados de saúde, apenas pela</u> redação da <u>DAV</u> (em modelo proposto ou redação livre), <u>ou por ambos</u>", ao arrepio, aliás da formulação que tinha adoptado em 2010 (Parecer nº 59 do Conselho Nacional de Ética para as Ciências da Vida (59/CNECV/2010) Parecer sobre os Projectos de Lei relativos às Declarações Antecipadas de Vontade (Dezembro de 2010), p. 2 e 4), em que considera que as "declarações antecipadas de vontade" (utilizadas comummente no mesmo sentido de "directivas antecipadas de vontade") encerram duas dimensões: a de "testamento vital" ou disposições escritas e a designação de procurador de cuidados de saúde.

O APELO DE ULISSES ...

A procuração de cuidados de saúde é o documento em que alguém *"voluntariamente"* nomeia um representante para a área dos cuidados de saúde.

Assim, num primeiro momento, há que aferir se a vontade expressa pelo outorgante é regular, nomeadamente, quanto à sua *capacidade* para a formar e exprimir. O artigo 4º (por remissão do artº 11º, nº 2) estabelece tais requisitos de validade: ser maior de idade, não se encontrar interdito ou inabilitado por anomalia psíquica e encontrar-se capaz de dar o seu consentimento consciente, livre e esclarecido.

Deste modo, afastam-se os menores de idade, mas nem todos os "incapazes para o exercício de direitos". Admite-se que quem seja interdito ou inabilitado por outra causa que não anomalia psíquica (ou seja, surdez--mudez, cegueira, ou no caso de inabilitação, prodigalidade ou abuso de bebidas alcoólicas ou estupefacientes) possa ser outorgante de uma procuração de cuidados de saúde. Tal é imediatamente perceptível para a inabilitação, que estabelece um círculo de incapacidade mais delimitado (cujo núcleo intangível abrange apenas os "actos de disposição de bens entre vivos" – art. 153º, nº 1 do Código Civil), mas não para a interdição, que determinaria, à partida, uma incapacidade geral.

Atentemos, então, no terceiro elemento a considerar: é necessário que "[se] encontrem capazes de dar o seu consentimento consciente, livre e esclarecido". Isto implica uma avaliação casuística da *capacidade para consentir*, que adquire aqui relevância autónoma e se destaca de uma incapacitação geral eventualmente determinada, que é assim limitada (e abre necessariamente a porta para um novo representante coexistir com o tutor, que, em princípio, teria poderes de decisão também nesta matéria). Mas, se, por um lado, por esta via se possibilita o recurso à procuração de cuidados de saúde também por adultos incapacitados, por outro lado, é ela também que permite vedar o acesso àqueles que se encontrem numa situação de incapacidade de facto, *i.e.* que não sejam capazes de querer e entender, mas que não tenham sido judicialmente incapacitados (interditos ou inabilitados), se não apresentarem a mencionada capacidade "de dar o seu consentimento consciente, livre e esclarecido".

Mas como se faz a avaliação dessa capacidade? Ou seja, ultrapassando os dois primeiros momentos, de verificação formal do *status*, como se determina a *capacidade para consentir*?

DIREITO DA SAÚDE

Impõe-se enveredar por um modelo funcional[32] da determinação da capacidade, assumindo que esta não é um conceito monolítico, mas que depende também da particular decisão que tem de ser tomada[33]. Ou seja, a capacidade pode ser considerada como um *continuum* que apresenta vários níveis. O respeito pela autodeterminação exige que se faça a determinação da capacidade para cada actividade, para cada decisão específica[34]. Esta postura assume, aliás, particular importância quando lidamos com doenças neurodegenerativas, em que as pessoas podem manter capacidade para tomar determinadas decisões.

Aliás, a avaliação da falta de capacidade ou da capacidade diminuída do outorgante vai ser relevante também num segundo momento – na verdade, o procurador só é nomeado para actuar em vez do outorgante quando este se encontrar "incapaz de expressar de forma pessoal e autónoma a sua vontade".

Assim, no primeiro momento está apenas em causa aferir da possibilidade de formar e exprimir a vontade para outorgar aquele documento, mas, neste segundo momento, está em causa determinar a (in)capaci-

---

[32] Foi este último modelo que mereceu o aval dos conferencistas de *Wingspread* e que tem recebido acolhimento nas mais recentes reformas legislativas dos Estados americanos. Quais os benefícios de uma avaliação funcional? A avaliação funcional define a situação do requerido e permite ao tribunal uma avaliação objectiva da capacidade. O relatório de avaliação poderá conter informações que incluam o grau de incapacidade, um prognóstico e o tratamento recomendado, *vide* TOR, Phillip, "Finding Incompetency in Guardianship, Standardizing The Process", *Arizona Law Review*, vol. 35, n.3, 1993, p. 757. Ao contrário de um juízo clínico que exibe um forte apego a categorias psiquiátricas, tantas vezes não consentâneas com categorias jurídicas ou dificilmente compreensíveis pelos profissionais do foro, a avaliação funcional fornece informação descritiva. Ora, o conhecimento dos comportamentos observados, do ambiente que serviu de pano de fundo à avaliação, das principais características do requerido, entre outros factores, poderá ser de uma importância primordial para efectivamente avaliar as "capacidades" e "incapacidades" em causa. *Idem*, p. 758. A perspectiva canadiana também vai neste sentido, *Cf.* VERMA, Sarita; SILBERFIELD, Michel, "Approaches to Capacity and Competency: the canadian view", *International Journal of Law and Psychiatry*, vol. 20, n. 1, 1997, p. 41.

[33] GLASS, Katherine Cranley, "Refining definitions and Devising instruments: Two decades of assessing mental competence", *International Journal of Law and Psychiatry,* vol. 20, n. 1, 1997, p. 8.

[34] Sobre a avaliação da capacidade para consentir, veja-se obra de SCOTT Y.H., Kim, "Evaluation of capacity to consent to treatment and Research", New York, Oxford University Press, 2010 e em particular sobre a preferência pelo modelo funcional, v. p. 11.

dade para abrir um espaço para que alguém aja "em vez de", ocupando o seu espaço decisório.

Isto não significa que o funcionamento da procuração de cuidados de saúde implique consequências ao nível da capacidade civil do outorgante – a lei nada diz relativamente à possibilidade de continuar a agir no mundo jurídico, o que está em conformidade com a orientação internacional na área[35]. No entanto, de facto, teremos alguém a *agir em nome da pessoa com capacidade diminuída*. Assim, como cremos, podemos ter um procurador de cuidados de saúde que age em vez da pessoa incapacitada (interdita ou cuja inabilitação abrange este tipo de decisões), mas também podemos ter um procurador de cuidados de saúde a representar alguém que não é legalmente incapacitado.

Ora, a simples desconsideração de um processo formal de incapacitação não é de reprovar. Na verdade, a incapacitação legal, tendo em conta a rigidez dos esquemas actuais, não será, muitas vezes, o desfecho desejável. Aliás, este processo exige que os fundamentos de incapacitação revistam determinadas características – nomeadamente a habitualidade – que podem ser alheias às situações que reclamam uma resposta jurídica. Note-se que a ciência psiquiátrica baseia os seus modelos actuais no princípio da reabilitação[36]. Para além disto, a "doença mental" é hoje vista como facto polideterminado e reversível e a reinserção na comunidade como objectivo do tratamento.

Mas falta-nos uma âncora legal para percebemos quem e como se determina esta diminuição de capacidade (ao contrário do que o Conselho da Europa expressamente recomenda[37]) – que, não obstante, não

---

[35] Na verdade, a recente *Recommendation CM/Rec(2009)11 of the Committee of Ministers* to member states on principles concerning continuing powers of attorney and advance directives for incapacity *(Adopted by the Committee of Ministers on 9 December 2009 at the 1073rd meeting of the Ministers' Deputies)*, consagra no seu princípio 9 a regra da preservação da capacidade, determinando que a produção de efeitos da procuração, ou melhor, do mandato permanente *(continuing power of attorney)* – v. princípio 2 – não deve afectar a capacidade jurídica do outorgante.

[36] BELLOMO, Antonello, SUMA, Domenico, "La tutela civile del disabile psichiatrico: attualità e prospettive", *Aspetti dell'agire psichiatrico*, Milano, Giuffrè, 2002, p. 59.

[37] Segundo o princípio 7 da Recomendação CM/Rec(2009)11, os Estados devem regular o modo como as procurações, ou melhor, os mandatos permanentes *(continuing powers of attorney)* entram em vigor, na eventualidade de capacidade do outorgante, nomeadamente como a incapacidade deve ser determinada e a prova requerida. Recommendation CM/

DIREITO DA SAÚDE

resultar de um processo judicial de incapacitação, há que lembrar, é um conceito jurídico e não médico[38].

Parece-nos, aliás, que a *produção dos efeitos da procuração de cuidados de saúde* fica diferida para aquele *momento*[39]. O procurador só pode exercer os seus poderes representativos quando o outorgante "se encontrar incapaz de expressar de forma pessoal e autónoma a sua vontade" (art. 11º, nº 1 e artº 12º, nº 1). Aproxima-se, assim, da figura do anglo-saxão *springing durable power of attorney*, que só produz efeitos após a determinação da incapacidade, ao invés de o fazer na sequência da outorga e sobreviver à incapacitação do representado.[40]

Aliás, tendo em conta o princípio da reabilitação, também seria útil prever o **caminho inverso** – determinar a reaquisição de capacidade, que obste à actuação do procurador de cuidados de saúde, por então o outorgante poder agir pessoal e autonomamente.

/Rec(2009)11 of the Committee of Ministers to member states on principles concerning continuing powers of attorney and advance directives for incapacity *(Adopted by the Committee of Ministers on 9 December 2009 at the 1073rd meeting of the Ministers' Deputies).*

[38] "É tarefa do Tribunal seleccionar, tomar em conta e avaliar os aspectos médicos e não médicos da situação necessários para fazer uma determinação jurídica da capacidade", ver STAVIS, Paul F. (nota 3), p. 5, nota 6 e p. 35. Esta foi também a orientação da decisão judicial Rivers v. Katz, 67 N.Y. 2d. sobre o papel do psiquiatra na "tradução dos conceitos legais" para proceder a uma avaliação, *v.* Kopelman, Loretta, "On the evaluative nature of competency and capacity judgements", *in International Journal of Law and Psychiatry,* vol. 13, 1990, p. 311 e Spar, James E.; Hankin, J. D.; Stodden, Ann B., "Assessing Mental Capacity and Susceptibility to Undue Influence", *Behavioral Sciences and the Law,* vol. 13, n. 3, 1995, p. 395.

[39] O carácter pessoalíssimo dos bens envolvidos obsta à representação enquanto o outorgante se encontre plenamente capaz de decidir. Note-se que a Doutrina tem defendido a intransmissibilidade dos poderes sobre a personalidade física ou moral, não admitindo, por isso, a representação voluntária, pelo que o direito teria de ser exercido sempre pelo seu titular ou por representante legal. CAPELO, Rabbindranath V. A., *O Direito Geral de Personalidade,* Coimbra: Coimbra Editora,1995, p. 403. Sobre estas exigências e a sua compatibilização com a procuração de cuidados de saúde, ver VÍTOR, Paula Távora (nota 5), pp. 124 e 125.

[40] Note-se que, embora a questão não seja isenta de controvérsia, prevalece a posição de que num *health care durable power of attorney,* o *agent* não pode actuar como representante de pessoa *capaz.* SCHMITT, M. N.; HATFIELD, S. A. "The Durable Power of Attorney: Apllications and Limitations", *Military Law Review,* 132, 1991, p. 222.

3.2. O procurador de cuidados de saúde

Tendo já desenhado a silhueta do representado, há que perceber quem é o seu representante, ou seja, *quem é o procurador de cuidados de saúde*.

Na aproximação que faz a esta figura, a lei remete, em primeiro lugar para requisitos de capacidade, que são os mesmos do representado (artº 4º, por remissão do artº 11º, nº 2): ser maior de idade, não se encontrar interdito ou inabilitado por anomalia psíquica e ser capaz de dar o seu consentimento consciente, livre e esclarecido.

Ora, se para o representado – tendo em conta uma ideia de favorecimento da capacidade num sentido lato e de promoção da autonomia – se justifica um entendimento menos rígido do que é *ser capaz*, já há mais dúvidas que estas razões se estendam para o procurador. Na verdade, uma coisa é preservar e valorizar a capacidade residual, outra é admitir que um interdito por uma causa que não seja a anomalia psíquica, ainda que sectorialmente capaz de prestar o seu consentimento, tenha o encargo de suprir a incapacidade de outrem. O caso da inabilitação não levantará tantos problemas – pode implicar, e normalmente só implicará – uma capacidade diminuída no plano patrimonial[41]. Parece-nos, todavia, que a ausência de mecanismos de controlo pensados especificamente para a actuação do procurador de cuidados de saúde, pelo menos se está em causa a interdição, aconselha uma abordagem cautelosa.[42]

Dir-se-á que para o regime geral da procuração, também não se exige que o procurador tenha a capacidade de querer e entender exigida pelo negócio que haja de efectuar (art. 263º do Código Civil). No entanto, lembre-se que, no regime geral, a procuração não é um expediente de suprimento da incapacidade e que esta se encontra vocacionada para a gestão de outro tipo de interesses, mormente patrimoniais.

---

[41] É possível que tenha jogado nesta definição algum desconforto do legislador em lidar com a manutenção determinados fundamentos de incapacitação, que aliás já afastou em matérias como a capacidade de gozo para casar, em que só os interditos ou inabilitados por anomalia psíquica são contemplados (art. 1601º, al b), do Código Civil).

[42] No seu Parecer nº 59 sobre os Projectos de Lei relativos às Declarações Antecipadas de Vontade (Dezembro de 2010) (59/CNECV/2010), o Conselho Nacional de Ética para as Ciências da Vida considerava que podia ser procurador de cuidados de saúde qualquer pessoa "maior de idade e na posse das suas capacidades e direitos", o que, pese embora o coloquialismo da expressão, dificilmente se pode sustentar quanto ao interdito, que continua a ser titular de direitos, em geral, mas perde a capacidade para o seu exercício.

DIREITO DA SAÚDE

A lei foi, noutro plano, mais restritiva, ao afastar determinadas categorias de pessoas do cargo de procurador de cuidados de saúde (v. art. 11º, nº 3, als. a) e b))[43]. Em primeiro lugar, prevenindo eventual suspeição, veda a nomeação aos funcionários do Registo Nacional de Testamento Vital, bem como do cartório notarial que intervenham nos actos em causa. Justifica-se a reserva pelo fácil acesso. Em segundo lugar, os proprietários e os gestores de entidades que administram ou prestam cuidados de saúde também são excluídos, por um lado, pelo perigo de abuso que podem comportar as relações de sujeição que normalmente estão associadas a estas situações, mas também com um fim de prevenção de suspeição. Aliás, os instrumentos internacionais chamam a atenção para a existência de conflitos de interesses entre as pessoas internadas e as instituições que as acolhem[44], nas quais incluímos os seus funcionários, que não são todavia contemplados nesta disposição[45].

A lei abre uma excepção a este último caso (v. art. 11º, nº 4) "para as pessoas que tenham uma relação familiar com o outorgante". Vislumbramos a ideia subjacente a esta excepção, mas não nos esqueçamos do sentido técnico de "relação familiar" – é uma expressão que abrange não só as relações matrimoniais e de filiação (e adopção), mas também afinidade e parentesco em graus mais afastados, com relevância jurídica, na linha colateral, até ao sexto grau (art. 1582º do Código Civil), o que alarga bastante este leque. Nas relações familiares mais próximas, aliás, poderíamos mesmo equacionar que, mais do que a ausência de entraves à assunção deste cargo, a lei (neste caso, o Código Civil) imporá, observadas as circunstâncias do caso, a obrigação de o assumir. Na verdade, tanto o dever de cooperação vincula os cônjuges a prestarem socorro e auxílio mútuos (art. 1674º do Código Civil), como o dever de auxílio entre pais e filhos (art. 1874º, nº 1 do Código Civil) depõe neste sentido. É verdade que se

---

[43] Da Recomendação CM/Rec(2009)11 resulta também a preocupação de estabelecer restrições à nomeação de um *attorney*, quando os Estados o considerem necessário para protecção do outorgante (princípio 4, nº 2). Recommendation CM/Rec(2009)11 of the Committee of Ministers to member states on principles concerning continuing powers of attorney and advance directives for incapacity *(Adopted by the Committee of Ministers on 9 December 2009 at the 1073rd meeting of the Ministers' Deputies)*.

[44] Conseil de l'Europe (nota 9), p. 27.

[45] LEENEN, H.J.J.; GEVERS, J.K.M.; PINET, G., *The Rights of Patients in Europe*, Devener, Boston, Kluwer Law and Taxation Publishers, 1997, p. 109.

O APELO DE ULISSES ...

poderia objectar que tal poderia levar a situações em que um procurador, que estivesse limitado por directivas mais estritas da parte do representado, fosse vinculado a tomar decisões que se opõem aos seus princípios ético-morais – nomeadamente aquelas que justificam o estatuto de objector de consciência aos profissionais de saúde, nos termos do art. 9º. No entanto, o problema não se chega a pôr. A não ser que esteja associada a um instrumento como o mandato[46], a procuração, apesar de atribuir poderes de representação, não vincula o procurador a exercê-los[47]. A procuração é um *negócio jurídico unilateral*, para cuja perfeição basta a declaração de vontade do outorgante[48]. Ao contrário do mandato, esse sim, um negócio jurídico bilateral, não se cria uma obrigação de agir a favor do mandante[49].

O legislador português optou pelo instrumento correspondente ao *durable power of attorney* anglo-saxónico, ao qual, aliás, se aponta como uma das maiores falhas o facto de este mecanismo não criar para o representante a obrigação de agir[50]. Assim, este pode em qualquer altura cessar a sua actuação, deixando a pessoa incapacitada numa situação de desprotecção[51].[52] Mas, em segunda linha, não podemos deixar de referir

---

[46] Note-se que a Recommendation CM/Rec(2009)11 of the Committee of Ministers to member states on principles concerning continuing powers of attorney and advance directives for incapacity *(Adopted by the Committee of Ministers on 9 December 2009at the 1073rd meeting of the Ministers' Deputies)* define o seu "continuing power of attorney" como "mandate".

[47] A este propósito já nos pronunciámos, na área patrimonial, a propósito da figura do mandato permanente. VÍTOR, Paula Távora (nota 13), p. 236-238.

[48] No contexto português, Carvalho Fernandes classifica-a como um negócio "não recipiendo", FERNANDES, Luís A. Carvalho, *Teoria Geral do Direito Civil*, vol. I, Universidade Católica Editora, p. 213, no entanto, H. E. Hörster nota que "[n]ormalmente, aquele acto de atribuição de poderes representativos consta de uma declaração receptícia", Hörster, H. E. (nota 4), p. 484. Para alguma Doutrina estrangeira, a procuração é um negócio *receptício*, dado que o conhecimento, para uns por parte do representante, para outros autores, por parte de terceiros, é condição da sua eficácia, *v.* GOMES, Orlando "O Poder de Representação", *Jurídica*, nº 109, ano XV, Abril-Junho, 1970, p. 39.

[49] BIANCA, C. Massimo, *Diritto Civile– Il Contratto*, vol. III, 2. Ed., Milano, Giuffrè Editore, 2000, p. 87.

[50] Ver por todos, DESSIN, Carolyn, "Acting as an Agent Under a Financial Durable Power of Attorney: An Unscripted Role", *Nebraska Law Review*, 1996, p. 586.

[51] BRISK, William J.; TALLIS, William G., *Legal Planning for the Elderly in Massachusetts*, Lexis Law Publishing, 1997, p. 2-6.

[52] Ora, na eventualidade de uma inacção, o mandatário pode ser responsabilizado pelo incumprimento de deveres contratuais. *Cf.* arts. 790º ss. do Código Civil.

DIREITO DA SAÚDE

a difícil e peculiar situação do procurador que foi investido nesta função sem a sua aceitação e, porventura, sem o seu conhecimento. É certo que se poderá invocar que, não obstante o *como* da sua actuação estar subordinado ao interesse do representado, o *se* e o *quando* se encontra na sua disponibilidade. Ora, apesar de isto se passar, na pureza dos princípios, o procurador nomeado não deixa de poder ser confrontado com a *urgência da decisão*, ainda que não queira assumir tal encargo.

Por fim, lembramos que pode ser nomeado um segundo procurador para o caso de impedimento do indicado (art. 11º, nº 5), cuja substituição segue, com as necessárias adaptações, o disposto no artigo 264º do Código Civil. A lei podia ter ido mais longe, prevendo não só a substituição, mas actuações concertadas ou concorrentes[53], que, todavia, não se encontram excluídas[54].

3.3. Poderes do procurador de cuidados de saúde

O procurador de cuidados de saúde é titular dos *poderes representativos* para decidir *sobre os cuidados de saúde* a receber ou a não receber pelo outorgante.

Assim, em primeiro lugar, o procurador de cuidados de saúde é um "representante voluntário" e que, portanto, decide *em nome* do outorgante da procuração, e neste caso, *no interesse deste*[55], tendo em conta, na medida do possível, os seus *desejos* reconhecíveis[56].

---

[53] Ver princípio 4, nº 1, Recommendation CM/Rec(2009)11 of the Committee of Ministers to member states on principles concerning continuing powers of attorney and advance directives for incapacity *(Adopted by the Committee of Ministers on 9 December 2009at the 1073rd meeting of the Ministers' Deputies).*

[54] Tendo em conta a remissão do artigo 12º, nº 2, para o nº 2 do artigo 264º do Código Civil, parece ser de considerar a regra de que "[a] substituição não envolve exclusão do procurador primitivo, salvo declaração em contrário."

[55] O representante voluntário tem de agir em nome do representado, mas não tem de agir necessariamente no interesse deste, podendo os poderes representativo ser concedidos para servir o interesse próprio do procurador. V. PINTO, C. A. da Mota (nota 4), p. 540. Isto, todavia, não pode acontecer na procuração de cuidados de saúde, em que o interesse do representado tem de ser o único servido.

[56] Veja-se o princípio 10 da Recommendation CM/Rec(2009)11 of the Committee of Ministers to member states on principles concerning continuing powers of attorney and advance directives for incapacity *(Adopted by the Committee of Ministers on 9 December 2009 at the 1073rd meeting of the Ministers' Deputies),* que alude tanto ao interesses quanto aos desejos e sentimentos do outorgante como norteadores da actuação do *attorney.*

As características da figura do procurador de cuidados de saúde que lhe são dadas pelo facto de se tratar de um representante voluntário, tornam-no num mecanismo que consegue superar algumas das mais acesas desvantagens que são apontadas a outros instrumentos que podem funcionar neste âmbito. O carácter *voluntário* desta representação, permite atender à vontade que a pessoa com capacidade diminuída exprimiu não só no sentido de nomear um representante, mas também de estabelecer quais são os seus melhores desejos e elegê-los como padrão de actuação, o que não acontece na representação *legal*. O facto de estarmos perante um instrumento de representação, em que o procurador decide em vez do representado quando confrontado com a questão concreta a decidir (embora tomando como referência o seu quadro de valores e preferências expresso ou presumido), fá-lo superar as críticas de possível falta de actualidade com que sempre se tem debatido o testamento vital.

A matéria que estes poderes representativos abrangem encontra-se delimitada pelos "cuidados de saúde". Ora, isto tanto pode ser entendido de forma mais restrita – limitando-se ao consentimento na área dos cuidados de saúde, como assumir um recorte mais amplo, abrangendo tudo aquilo que esteja implicado, ainda que de forma mais distante, nestes cuidados. Pensamos que a lei permite que o outorgante estenda os poderes do procurador de cuidados de saúde neste sentido. Assim, pode compreender decisões relacionadas com a contratação de profissionais de saúde ou a autorização de ingresso em estabelecimentos de saúde, permitir acesso ou revelação de dados médicos, que, num sentido restrito, não se poderiam classificar como decisões sobre os cuidados de saúde.

Da definição do procurador de cuidados de saúde (art. 11º, nº 1) também resulta que este tanto pode assentir e decidir sobre cuidados de saúde a receber como recusá-los. Para concretizar o âmbito de actuação dos procurador no uso dos seus poderes representativos, justifica-se atentar no artigo 2º, nº 2, bem como nas limitações estabelecidas no artº 5º.

No artigo 2º, nº 2, o legislador entendeu apresentar uma lista de "disposições que expressem a vontade clara e inequívoca do outorgante". A definição do conteúdo destas disposições, nas alíneas a) a e) é bem justificada pelo carácter estático (e pretérito) do testamento vital, o que motivou que o legislador entendesse conceder alguma orientação para a sua precipitação nas disposições deste instrumento[57]. No entanto, no que diz

---

[57] Não obstante a possibilidade de modificação e revogação – ver art. 8º.

respeito à procuração de cuidados de saúde, o processo decisório central é assumido pelo procurador, situado temporalmente no presente e, portanto, realizado no confronto com as realidades a que tem de dar resposta, o que aponta, em princípio, para uma maior rarefacção da vontade expressa pelo outorgante. É certo que o representado pode entender ser mais específico e, para além de nomear o procurador e determinar áreas de actuação, indicar quais as decisões que pretende que este tome. Nesse caso, no entanto, se não restar espaço decisório para o procurador, podemos perguntar-nos se ele não se afastará de um verdadeiro representante para se aproximar da figura do núncio.

De todo o modo, os limites estabelecidos pelo artigo 5º não podem deixar de ser aplicar à procuração de cuidados de saúde. Aliás, mesmo na ausência de uma disposição legal neste sentido, nunca poderia deixar de se ter em conta o facto de ser contrária à lei, à ordem pública ou determinar uma actuação contrária às boas práticas, a circunstância de o seu cumprimento poder provocar deliberadamente a morte não natural e evitável, tal como prevista nos artigos 134º e 135º do Código Penal e extrair consequências de o outorgante não ter expressado, clara e inequivocamente, a sua vontade. No entanto, há que atentar, aqui, que a sanção prevista – a inexistência – não é a que resultaria das regras gerais. Assim, e porque estamos perante um instrumento que serve propósitos análogos aos do testamento vital, justificando-se proteger os mesmos interesses, se pode sustentar que também a procuração de cuidados de saúde padece de inexistência em idênticas circunstâncias.

Por fim, há que equacionar se o procurador de cuidados de saúde, enquanto representante de uma pessoa com capacidade diminuída, está sujeito aos mesmos limites que um representante legal de alguém judicialmente incapacitado no âmbito das decisões de saúde. Na verdade, há específicas decisões em matéria médica em que o legislador entendeu limitar o poder decisório do tutor. Vejam-se, por exemplo, as exigências da Lei nº 21/2014, de 16 de Abril, quanto ao consentimento para a realização de estudos clínicos com maiores incapazes de prestar o consentimento informado. Neste caso, o consentimento tem de ser obtido junto do representante legal e deve reflectir a vontade presumível do participante, mas, para além disso, não pode contornar uma série de outras exigências, nomeadamente que esteja "diretamente relacionado com o quadro de perigo de vida ou de debilidade de que sofra o participante em causa" (art. 8º, nº 2, al. a) e nº 3, al. b) da Lei nº 21/2014, de 16 de Abril).

O APELO DE ULISSES ...

Ou atente-se na Lei nº 12/93, de 22 de Abril, relativa à colheita e transplante de órgãos, tecidos e células de origem humana, que proíbe sempre a dádiva e a colheita de órgãos ou de tecidos não regeneráveis quando estejam em causa incapazes (artigo 6º, nº 4).

Pensamos que em casos como este valem as mesmas razões de protecção do incapaz, tanto no caso de estarmos perante um representante legal, como perante um representante voluntário de um doente com capacidade diminuída que esteja munido deste poderes apenas ao abrigo de uma referência genérica. Só assim não será se o afastamento daquelas exigências estiver previsto pelo outorgante da procuração de cuidados de saúde. Nesse caso, prevalece a expressão da sua autonomia, que entendeu conceder esse poder mais amplo ao procurador. Assim, parece ser de admitir, por exemplo, que o representado, ciente da existência de uma doença familiar, preveja a possibilidade de doar futuramente um órgão a membro da sua família e que queira garantir isto na eventualidade da sua incapacidade. Ou que queira conceder poderes ao procurador para decidir acerca da sua participação em ensaio clínico ainda que os riscos superem os eventuais benefícios para a sua pessoa[58].

Note-se que a definição do conteúdo da procuração de cuidados de saúde, pelo seu carácter predominantemente clínico, deveria envolver o aconselhamento por parte de um médico[59]. O artigo 3º, nº 2, refere-se *ao caso de* haver recurso à colaboração de um médico para elaboração das directivas antecipadas de vontade[60]. Mas limita-se a referir uma possibilidade e não a exigir a sua intervenção, que se imporia tanto no caso do testamento vital, como no da procuração de cuidados de saúde, para

---

[58] No que diz respeito à gratuitidade da actuação do procurador de cuidados de saúde, estabelecida no artº 12º, nº 1, verificamos que o legislador tomou uma opção diferente da que está estabelecida para a representação legal que estabelece a possibilidade de remuneração do tutor (cf. art. 1942º do Código Civil, aplicável a tutela de maiores).

[59] Debruçando-se sobre o "testamento de paciente", em 2010, André Dias Pereira propõe o estabelecimento de um "sistema procedimental de emanação da declaração antecipada de vontade", que, segundo o Autor, envolveria necessariamente um médico que prestaria o seu conselho e garantiria o "esclarecimento e liberdade do paciente". Pereira, André Dias (nota 24), p. 829.

[60] Fá-lo para fazer indicações de natureza formal, como a possibilidade de a identificação e a assinatura do médico constarem do documento, se for essa a opção do outorgante e do médico.

DIREITO DA SAÚDE

garantir o verdadeiro esclarecimento do outorgante relativamente às opções que efectue[61].

3.4. Carácter vinculativo dos poderes

Certo é que o regime jurídico do procurador de cuidados de saúde fixa que as decisões tomadas por este "dentro dos limites dos poderes representativos que lhe competem, devem ser respeitadas pelos profissionais que prestam cuidados de saúde ao outorgante" (art. 13º, nº 1)[62]. Aliás, está previsto que o "médico responsável" (e não outros membros da equipa) se assegure da existência de procuração de cuidados de saúde consultando o RENTEV, devendo a procuração ser anexada ao processo clínico (art. 17º).

Em caso de urgência ou perigo imediato para a vida do paciente, todavia, jogam as mesmas razões para a equipa médica responsável pela prestação de cuidados de saúde não ter de considerar a procuração de cuidados de saúde, à semelhança do testamento vital, no caso de o acesso a esta e a obtenção de uma decisão por parte do procurador "implicar uma demora que agrave, previsivelmente, os riscos para a vida ou a saúde do outorgante" (art. 7º, nº 4). Aliás, tendo em conta que se trata dos bens vida e integridade física, não seria sequer necessária expressa previsão legislativa.

Em casos-limite[63], todavia, como poderão os profissionais de saúde opor-se às decisões de um procurador de cuidados de saúde com poderes de representação regularmente concedidos?

Não foi criada no sistema português uma instância de controlo[64] que permita supervisionar a actuação do procurador de cuidados de saúde,

---

[61] Note-se que no Parecer nº 59 sobre os Projectos de Lei relativos às Declarações Antecipadas de Vontade (Dezembro de 2010) (59/CNECV/2010), p. 3, o Conselho Nacional de Ética para as Ciências da Vida quis deixar claro que "qualquer pessoa capaz pode optar por não querer ser informada, sem que tal afecte a validade da sua decisão".

[62] No caso de desrespeito pelo mandamento desta disposição legal, os prestadores de cuidados de saúde poderão incorrer em responsabilidade civil, preenchidos os requisitos legais, e eventualmente, criminal (cf. art. 156º do Código Penal).

[63] Os casos que a lei define que as "directivas antecipadas" não devem ser respeitadas encontram-se no artigo 6º, nº 2, que se pode equacionar aplicar-se *mutatis mutandis* à procuração de cuidados de saúde que, como vimos, pode apresentar um conteúdo mais ou menos densificado e, portanto, justificar a avaliação da existência de alguma daquelas circunstâncias.

[64] Cf. o nosso, VÍTOR, Paula Távora (nota 55), p. 133.

ao arrepio das recomendações do Conselho da Europa neste sentido[65]. Todavia, há que encontrar um expediente que permita, quando se justifique, controlar se o procurador norteia a sua acção pelos *melhores interesses* do outorgante (quando não segue os *melhores desejos* expressos no documento). Parece-nos que aqui a via adequada será recorrer ao controlo judicial, requerendo as "providências concretamente adequadas a evitar a consumação de qualquer ameaça ilícita e directa à personalidade física ou moral ou a atenuar, ou a fazer cessar, os efeitos de ofensa já cometida", no âmbito de um processo especial de tutela da personalidade, nos termos dos artigos 878º e seguintes do Código de Processo Civil.

3.5. A procuração de cuidados de saúde e o testamento vital

A lei só estabelece de forma directa e explícita limites ao poder decisório do procurador de cuidados de saúde para proteger a vontade do outorgante expressa em *directiva antecipada*, "designadamente sob a forma de testamento vital".

Na verdade, estes mecanismos podem coexistir, subsistindo separadamente, ou confluindo num instrumento de carácter misto, que combine uma faceta de testamento vital com a nomeação de um representante para a área dos cuidados de saúde. Daí que possa surgir conflito entre a vontade expressa na primeira pessoa que conste do testamento vital e as decisões de um "terceiro" (em sentido impróprio), o representante. Não espanta, portanto, a opção de fazer prevalecer o "discurso directo" do outorgante, até porque a actualidade da sua vontade é controlada a vários níveis (v. artº 6º, nº 2, e 7º). Aliás, a preservação e o respeito adequado à vontade reconhecível como actual do representado levam a lei a criar expedientes de informação do procurador de cuidados de saúde relativamente ao "estado" das directivas antecipadas (v. art. 6º, nº 3, art. 7º, nº4, eart. 8º, nº 4).

---

[65] Veja-se o princípio 12, que recomenda aos Estados a introdução de um sistema de supervisão ao abrigo do qual são concedidos poderes de investigação a uma autoridade competente. Cf. Recommendation CM/Rec(2009)11 of the Committee of Ministers to member states on principles concerning continuing powers of attorney and advance directives for incapacity *(Adopted by the Committee of Ministers on 9 December 2009 at the 1073rd meeting of the Ministers' Deputies).*

DIREITO DA SAÚDE

3.6. A procuração de cuidados de saúde e a representação legal

A relação do procurador de cuidados de saúde com outro representante do outorgante foi, no entanto, ignorada. O novo regime não faz referência à concertação das actuações do procurador de cuidados de saúde e de um *representante legal*.

Poder-se-ia dizer que uma das vantagens do procurador de cuidados de saúde é poder evitar a imposição da medida da tutela. E, na verdade, podemos assistir à actuação do procurador quando é necessário decidir em vez do *incapaz de facto*.

Mas resulta também da lei que pode ser um interdito ou inabilitado por outra causa que não a anomalia psíquica a outorgar a procuração. Daqui se retira que é possível a coexistência deste instrumento com as medidas de protecção clássicas do nosso ordenamento jurídico. Na verdade, se assim não fosse, a possibilidade concedida àquelas categorias de incapacitados de recorrerem ao instrumento da procuração de cuidados de saúde perderia todo o seu sentido útil, pelo menos no caso de interdição, que determina incapacidade geral do interdito e o poder do tutor no âmbito pessoal e patrimonial.

A admissibilidade da coexistência destas figuras vale, assim, tanto para os casos de incapacitação anterior, em que um interdito ou inabilitado por outra causa que não a anomalia psíquica a outorga a procuração, como para os casos de outorgante plenamente capaz que vem a ser supervenientemente incapacitado[66].

A existência em simultâneo deste representante voluntário e do representante legal reclama que se estabeleça qual a decisão que prevalece em caso de conflito. A Lei nº 25/2012 não se pronuncia, mas a solução só poderá ser a da prevalência do procurador de cuidados de saúde. O tutor é detentor de poderes gerais relativos também à pessoa do interdito, mas, com o regime da procuração de cuidados de saúde, a lei cria uma excepção a esta competência geral do representante legal, atribuindo competência especial ao procurador na área da saúde. Só desta forma se garante que o respeito pela vontade da pessoa incapacitada seja salvaguardado,

---

[66] E nem se pode invocar que a existência de uma procuração de cuidados de saúde anterior à instauração da tutela ou da curatela deveria ser tomada em conta na fixação da medida de protecção. Ora, se isto pode ser verdade para a inabilitação (e para a curatela), está vedado no campo da interdição (e para a tutela), tendo em conta o carácter monolítico desta medida (artº 139º do Código Civil).

O APELO DE ULISSES ...

pois, caso contrário, a procuração de cuidados de saúde só seria relevante no contexto de uma incapacidade de facto. Deste modo, respeita-se o princípio da subsidiariedade, dando prioridade a um mecanismo de protecção sobre uma medida de protecção[67].

Podemos, no entanto, configurar uma situação em que, existindo procuração de cuidados de saúde e representante legal judicialmente nomeado, o problema do conflito não se venha a pôr, nem em termos abstractos. Parece-nos ser admissível que o outorgante designe o seu procurador de cuidados genericamente como aquele que venha a ser nomeado o seu tutor. Por esta via negocial, poderia introduzir alguma flexibilidade no instituto da tutela, nomeadamente expressando os seus *melhores desejos* que o tutor poderia honrar, não obstante o critério tradicionalmente imposto do exercício dos seus poderes: "com a diligência de um bom pai de família" (art. 1935º do Código Civil).

3.7. Forma

A forma que deve assumir a procuração de cuidados de saúde não resulta clara das disposições da Lei nº 25/2012[68]. No artigo 12º, nº 2 é feita uma remissão para o artigo 262º, nº 2 do Código Civil que, ao invés de elucidar, só causa maiores perplexidades. Este preceito ocupa-se da forma da procuração e determina que "[s]alvo disposição legal em contrário, a procuração revestirá a forma exigida para o negócio que o procurador deva realizar".

Ora, admitindo que o acto que ocupará a mais importante fatia das incumbências do procurador de cuidados de saúde é a prestação do consentimento informado e que para este, por regra, não é exigida forma especial pela lei, prevaleceria o princípio geral da liberdade de forma (art. 219º do Código Civil).

---

[67] Ver princípio 1 *da* Recommendation CM/Rec(2009)11 of the Committee of Ministers to member states on principles concerning continuing powers of attorney and advance directives for incapacity *(Adopted by the Committee of Ministers on 9 December 2009at the 1073rd meeting of the Ministers' Deputies).*

[68] No seu princípio 5, o Conselho da Europa recomenda a forma escrita – Recommendation CM/Rec(2009)11 of the Committee of Ministers to member states on principles concerning continuing powers of attorney and advance directives for incapacity *(Adopted by the Committee of Ministers on 9 December 2009 at the 1073rd meeting of the Ministers' Deputies).*

DIREITO DA SAÚDE

Sabemos, no entanto, que está generalizada a prática hospitalar de o reduzir a escrito o consentimento e que a própria lei veio paulatinamente consagrando uma longa lista de casos em que existe o consentimento escrito[69].

Considerando estes elementos, poderíamos concluir que a procuração de cuidados de saúde viria, então, assumir a forma escrita na maioria dos casos. Esta é, no entanto, uma constatação de natureza circunstancial e não significa que tal aconteça necessariamente. É certo que a lei parece pressupor uma determinada precipitação formal do documento quando se refere aos funcionários de "cartório notarial que intervenham nos actos aqui em causa" ou aos "funcionários do Registo Nacional de Testamento Vital", para excluir do acesso ao cargo de procurador de cuidados de saúde.

Na hipótese de se recorrer a um instrumento híbrido, que combine o testamento vital e a procuração de cuidados de saúde, esta assumirá a forma exigida para o primeiro ("documento escrito, assinado presencialmente perante funcionário devidamente habilitado do Registo Nacional do Testamento Vital ou notário")[70].

Relativamente ao registo, resulta da lei que não é um passo imperativo. Se fosse, garantir-se-ia a redução a escrito por esta via, já que este exige a apresentação ou envio de um documento, com assinatura reconhecida (art. 16º, nº 2). Todavia, a lei sublinha que tem " valor meramente declarativo", pelo que a procuração de cuidados de saúde que não conste dele, continua a ser plenamente eficaz desde que formalizada de acordo

---

[69] A lista de excepções é longa, mas veja-se a título de exemplo os regimes de testes genéticos (Lei nº 12/2005, de 26 de Janeiro), da electroconvulsivoterapia e intervenção psicocirúrgica (Lei nº 36/98, de 24 de Julho), da colheita e transplantes de órgãos e tecidos de origem humana (Lei nº 12/93, de 22 de Abril; Lei nº 22/2007, de 29 de Junho), da dádiva, colheita, análise, processamento, preservação, armazenamento, distribuição e aplicação de tecidos e células de origem humana (Lei nº 12/2009, de 26 de Março) e da procriação medicamente assistida (Lei nº 32/2006, de 26 de Julho).

[70] Deste devem constar: a) A identificação completa do outorgante; b) O lugar, a data e a hora da sua assinatura; c) As situações clínicas em que as diretivas antecipadas de vontade produzem efeitos; d) As opções e instruções relativas a cuidados de saúde que o outorgante deseja ou não receber, no caso de se encontrar em alguma das situações referidas na alínea anterior; e) As declarações de renovação, alteração ou revogação das diretivas antecipadas de vontade, caso existam" (artigo 3º, nº 1).

com a presente lei, designadamente no que diz respeito à *expressão clara e inequívoca da vontade* (art. 16º, nº 1).

Voltamos, então, à questão inicial – que tipo de formalização é exigida "pela presente lei"?

Desde logo, é sublinhada a *expressão clara e inequívoca da vontade* (que, note-se, só nos parece que possa ser *expressa*). Ora, embora não haja uma relação necessária entre a forma escrita e esta inequivocidade temos de reconhecer que é um meio mais seguro do que a expressão oral, com todas as dificuldades de prova que lhe estão associadas.

Parece-nos, aliás, que as razões que estão na base da exigência de um documento escrito, assinado presencialmente perante funcionário do RENTEV ou notário no testamento vital são as mesmas, justificando-se, então, que se aplique, por analogia, à procuração de cuidados de saúde. Na verdade, não se pede menor ponderação e certeza do que naquela directiva antecipada.

A exigência de um momento deste género em que se plasma por escrito a procuração de cuidados de saúde é, aliás, essencial para a determinação da capacidade do outorgante, que tem de ser capaz, no momento em que manifesta a sua vontade. Ora, tal tem de ser feito perante instâncias adequadas para controlar tal capacidade e, à cabeça, temos o notário[71].

3.8. Extinção

Por último, a procuração de cuidados de saúde conhece o seu fim por duas vias.

Diz-nos o artigo 14º, nº 1, que, em primeiro lugar, é *livremente revogável* pelo seu outorgante[72]. Esta livre revogabilidade compreende-se facilmente relativamente a um outorgante que seja plenamente capaz e ainda relativamente àquele que mantém a mesma capacidade que lhe permitiu criar o instrumento. Mas, o que acontece, no caso de uma incapacidade

---

[71] Quanto aos funcionários do RENTEV, mas o seu estatuto depende da regulamentação anunciada pelo artigo 19º.

[72] Cf. artigo 265º, nº 2 do Código Civil. Neste sentido, também o princípio 6 da *Recommendation CM/Rec(2009)11 of the Committee of Ministers to member states on principles concerning continuing powers of attorney and advance directives for incapacity (Adopted by the Committee of Ministers on 9 December 2009at the 1073rd meeting of the Ministers' Deputies).*

superveniente[73] ou de um agravamento da incapacidade? Não nos parece que, face ao quadro de competências que foi traçado e às posições relativas das pessoas em causa, um eventual representante legal possa ter uma actuação relevante neste contexto, substituindo-se ao incapacitado e revogando ele mesmo a procuração. Em casos limite, não nos parece que o problema se resolva pela via da revogação e resta-nos remeter para o que dissemos supra acerca dos casos em que a procuração de cuidados de saúde (de forma claramente excepcional, note-se) não deve ser respeitada pelos profissionais que prestam cuidados de saúde.

A outra via para a extinção da procuração de cuidados de saúde é a renúncia do procurador, que deve informar – e agora a lei di-lo inequivocamente – por escrito, o outorgante (art. 14º, nº 2). Antes, porém, de se operar esta consequência jurídica, pensamos ser necessário averiguar da existência de um "segundo procurador de cuidados de saúde", que é admitido por lei (art. 11º, nº 5), no caso de "impedimento" do indicado. Parece-nos que a referência a "impedimento" deve ser interpretado extensivamente no sentido de abranger também a renúncia.

Por fim, queremos notar que poderia, e deveria, também ter sido feita a articulação da extinção da procuração de cuidados de saúde com outras medidas de protecção, para que esta circunstância não lance para o vazio jurídico principalmente a situação do incapaz de facto[74].

---

[73] Também a lei catalã não fez qualquer reserva. V. artigo 7 do Decret 175/2002, de 25 de Juny.
[74] Veja-se o princípio 13, nº 2, da *Recommendation CM/Rec(2009)11 of the Committee of Ministers to member states on principles concerning continuing powers of attorney and advance directives for incapacity (Adopted by the Committee of Ministers on 9 December 2009 at the 1073rd meeting of the Ministers' Deputies)*, segundo o qual, em caso de cessação, a autoridade competente deve ter em consideração quais as medidas de protecção que devem ser adoptadas.

ÍNDICE

Patients' rights relating to patient safety
JOHAN LEGEMAATE — 7

A natureza de complexidade dos sistemas de saúde – Implicações para a segurança dos doentes e para a responsabilidade médica
JOSÉ I G FRAGATA — 27

Patients' right to access to quality of healthcare throughout the european union: the role of eu legislation
HENRIETTE ROSCAM ABBING — 39

The information rights of the patient in the European Patients' Rights Directive
HERMAN NYS — 67

Notificação de incidentes e eventos adversos: o peso da "culpa" e a não regulamentação em Portugal
PAULA BRUNO — 83

Fines de la pena e inhabilitación profesional: su relevancia para la inhabilitación profesional médica
JAVIER DE VICENTE REMESAL — 95

Estudio de derecho comparado sobre el consentimiento informado en los tratamientos médicos curativos
VIRGILIO RODRÍGUEZ-VÁZQUEZ — 133

DIREITO DA SAÚDE

A consagração do direito ao consentimento informado na jurisprudência
portuguesa recente
ANDRÉ GONÇALO DIAS PEREIRA   161

Do exercício da medicina dos *«médicos escravos para escravos
e (dos) médicos livres para os homens livres.»*
JOÃO VAZ RODRIGUES   181

Informed consent in aesthetic treatments: remarks on a recent
judgment of the Italian Supreme Court
VITULIA IVONE   223

O Cuidado Médico Transfronteiriço e o Consentimento informado:
as suas repercussões em sede de direito internacional privado.
Um primeira abordagem
GERALDO ROCHA RIBEIRO   235

O apelo de Ulisses – o novo regime do procurador de cuidados
de saúde na lei portuguesa
PAULA TÁVORA VÍTOR   321